ENCOUNTER WITH EMANCIPATION

The Jewish Publication Society of America
Philadelphia • 5744 / 1984

ENCOUNTER WITH EMANCIPATION

THE GERMAN JEWS IN THE UNITED STATES 1830–1914

NAOMI W. COHEN

Library of Congress Cataloging in Publication Data
Cohen, Naomi Wiener, 1927–
    Encounter with emancipation.
    Bibliography: p.
    1. Jews, German—United States—History—19th century.
2. Judaism—United States—History—19th century.
3. United States—Ethnic relations. I. Title.
E184.J5C618   1984   973′.04924   83-26781
ISBN 0-8276-0236-7

Designed by Adrianne Onderdonk Dudden

For Gerson,
who taught me the full meaning of
dayah kanitah u-meh hasartah.

CONTENTS

ACKNOWLEDGMENTS

IT is a pleasure to thank publicly those who facilitated my task. For help in making available library and archival resources I am grateful to Menahem Schmelzer and Herman Dicker of the Jewish Theological Seminary, Joseph Weiss of Hunter College, Nathan Kaganoff of the American Jewish Historical Society, Jacob Marcus and Abraham Peck of the American Jewish Archives. Colleagues and friends Naomi Miller, Abraham Ascher, Melvin Urofsky, Morton Leifman, Lifsa Schachter, Rahel Hammer, Elizabeth Weingartner— offered wise counsel and brought out-of-the-way material to my attention. Hector Guzman handled the onerous typing chore with unflagging skill and good cheer, and copy editor Carol Flechner guarded me from careless slips.

I have reworked sections of three of my articles for incorporation into the book. Permission to reproduce that material has been graciously granted by the American Academy for Jewish Research, the Conference on Jewish Social Studies, and Spertus College. Full citations to the original articles appear in the footnotes.

I am especially indebted to two good friends, Francine Klagsbrun and Yosef Yerushalmi. They read the original manuscript with patient care, and their suggestions served to enhance whatever merit the book has. From my editor, Maier Deshell, I have received expert guidance and warm encouragement throughout the process of converting a manuscript into a book.

As always, the emotional support that sustained me through all phases of my work was supplied by my children—Jeremy and Debbie, Judy and Barry—my grandson, Rafi, and, above all, my husband. To him this book is lovingly dedicated.

PREFACE

JEWS of German origin, who after 1840 dominated the American Jewish scene, have received inadequate critical study. Historians have preferred to concentrate on the first Jewish settlers, the Sephardim, or the colorful east European immigrants of the turn of the century. Yet, as it unfolds, the story of the German Jews reveals that it merits far greater attention than it has customarily commanded. Its significance extends beyond any arbitrarily imposed chronological date, for it was the German Jews—not the Sephardic pioneers nor the numerous Russian Jews—who laid the foundations of the modern American Jewish community. They set the institutional framework and the codes of behavior that, with relatively few important qualifications, obtain today.

The American experience of those Jews newly transplanted from central Europe was shaped by the impact of emancipation. Once citizenship and legal rights were attained, Jews labored on to win acceptance and integration within the larger society. With that overriding goal in mind, they hammered out the social values and forms of communal expression compatible with the broader dimensions of freedom.

Simultaneously, the emancipated Jew was forced to wrestle with the problem of Jewish identity. Emancipation had canceled out Jewish corporate status, and legally the Jew had the option to determine how Jewish he wanted to be. New questions forced him to rethink age-old principles and behavior: Was there still a discrete Jewish people to which he belonged? How did a modern Jew affirm his Jewishness?

The quests for both integration and identity were complicated by the cultural baggage that immigrant Jews carried with them to America. Bearers of a tradition both ethnic and religious, most were permanently conditioned by a heritage that for millennia had proclaimed the chosenness and distinctiveness of the Jews. The ties of Judaism that still bound them to a faith and to a people had to be interpreted in ways that would not obstruct their acceptance as Americans. Nevertheless, Jewish pride and historical memory could—and did on occasion—steer them to behavior at variance with American opinion.

Answers to the problems of Jewish integration and identity depended in the main on the interaction between the majority and the minority. Americans had their own views on what a Jew was, how he should behave, and what determined his acceptability. Despite democratic constitutions and a relatively fluid social structure, prejudice nurtured through long centuries held its ground. Accustomed to their premodern status as a rejected, if not despised, group within Christendom, American Jews were ever alert to Jew hatred. At times the effect was lulling, restraining them from higher aspirations or even paralyzing them into passivity. More often it generated a dynamic of its own, dictating the choice of institutions and forms adopted by a group desperately seeking security. The Jew walked an emotional tightrope, attempting to strike a viable balance between his dream of full integration, his religious-ethnic heritage, and the demands, rational or otherwise, of his gentile compatriots.

This book examines in depth certain challenges confronting American Jews of the nineteenth and early twentieth centuries who sought to live as free men and as Jews. That dual-faceted aim dictated the stand they took on matters as diverse as freedom of religion, politics, missionary crusades, public schools, anti-Semitism, Zionism, as well as Jewish philanthropy, theology, and manners. It determined how Jews structured their priorities, built their institutions, and chose their spokesmen. It explained their relationship with fellow Jews at home and abroad and with non-Jewish fellow Americans.

Among other findings, the history of the German Jews in America, told according to the theme of an encounter with emancipation, discloses differences between the Jewish experience and that of other minorities in the United States. It also underscores the inadequacies of theories that interpret ethnicity as a function of economics. With respect to American anti-Semitism, it explains how post–World War II analyses, differentiating between ideological hatred of the Jew and overt clashes resulting from conflict-of-interest situations, cannot be applied to the pre-1914 experience. Finally, it suggests that in their legacy to future generations of American Jews the German Jews bequeathed ambivalences and dilemmas as well as institutions and values.

Periodization of American Jewish history has serious pitfalls. Unqualified labeling of the colonial period up until the 1830s or 1840s as the Sephardic era, the 1830s to 1881 as the German era, and 1881 and beyond as the east European or Russian era is both overly simplistic and misleading. German Jews immigrated to the United States before 1830, and east European Jews arrived prior to 1881. By the same token, neither the Sephardim nor the German Jews automatically disappeared upon the advent of new waves of immigrants. The German/east European confrontation, to be discussed at greater length, requires no further elaboration here. The earlier transfer of hegemony—i.e., from the Sephardim to the Germans—was less a conscious battle than a virtually automatic process.

Before the numbers of German immigrants assumed significant proportions, the central Europeans often affiliated with the Sephardim. Isaac Leeser, for example, a leading figure in this book, was a German Jew who became hazzan, or minister, of Mikveh Israel, the prestigious Sephardic congregation of Philadelphia. Other Germans established their separate organizations, but overall, in terms of status and influence, the latter ranked below those of their predecessors until the mid nineteenth century. The influx of numerous Germans after 1830 plus the concomitant fact that the Sephardic constituency received no reinforcement in manpower from Europe meant that the Sephardim could not hold back German domination for long. Geographical settlement and rapid economic mobility, in addition to numbers, quickly overwhelmed the static Sephardic group. Not only did the Germans found most of the Jewish settlements within the nation's heartland, but in the major port cities, where the new immigrants encountered their predecessors, Germans who were excluded from or dissatisfied with the Sephardic agencies erected a panoply of organizations that soon overshadowed the original synagogues or charities with which they competed. Sephardic institutional life survived, but confined primarily within a handful of independent congregations, it gradually ossified. At the same time, the absence of an automatic amalgamation between the strata—although on an individual basis there was intermarriage as well as cooperative public service—freed the Germans to create new institutional patterns which in a relatively short time spoke for the American Jewish community at large.

A synthesis of both published and unpublished material, the book makes no claim to all-inclusiveness. To capture better the essential flavor of the multiple facets of the emancipation experience, it employs generally a thematic rather than a chronological approach. The problems and processes discussed herein—from religious equality to the Americanization of Judaism—have, to my knowledge, never been dealt with in this fashion before. Interpretation of themes illuminated by detailed analyses of pertinent episodes more effectively points up their persistence to this very day.

Since the primary focus is on the German Jews who identified with the Jewish community, the frequently used terms "the Jews" and "the Jewish view" are shorthand references to them; those who converted, "passed," or in no way affiliated with or impressed themselves upon the larger group are beyond the scope of this study. Even within the circle of committed Jews, not all Germans abandoned traditional Judaism for Reform, nor did every individual agree with the group's public posture on matters like free immigration or political Zionism. In such instances "the Jewish view" represented a more circumscribed element but still one that articulated the dominant opinion of American Jewry from the first half of the nineteenth century until World War I.

ENCOUNTER WITH EMANCIPATION

1

HORIZONS OF FREEDOM

GABRIEL RIESSER drew a warm welcome from fellow Jews during his visit to the United States in 1856. The man who had courageously fought for German Jewish emancipation in the post-Napoleonic period symbolized the aspirations of an entire generation. Rabbi Isaac Mayer Wise, editor of the weekly *Israelite*, published in Cincinnati, paid tribute to "the man of the people, the advocate of justice, the friend of humanity and the pleader of German Israel." Wise's deep admiration for the German Jewish jurist was revealed more fully in the rabbi's memoirs. There he wrote of the influence that Riesser had on him during his boyhood days in Bohemia. Teaching that Jews, like all human beings, had inborn rights, Riesser lifted his listeners "to a new sphere of right and freedom then unknown to the masses of our coreligionists. . . . Riesser made us feel free."

There was much about Riesser that inspired young Jews who shared his passion for freedom. They could understand the pain and frustration of the university graduate with a degree in law who had been barred from an academic post and a legal career because he was Jewish. They could respect his rejection of conversion as the "admission ticket to European civilization" in a period when others followed the lead of Ludwig Börne and Heinrich Heine to the baptismal font. In full accord with his denial of a separate Jewish nationality and his love of German culture, they could applaud his determination to equate Jewish emancipation with universal rights and to merge their cause with the larger goal of a unified Germany under a constitutional government. Riesser became their liberator while he fought for liberalism and nationalism in Germany. He instructed Jews in the duties of citizenship, that equal rights meant equal obligations, that they, like all citizens, had to give military service. "There is only one baptism that can consecrate a man to a nationality: that is the baptism of blood shed in a common battle for freedom and fatherland." He also taught that church and state had to be kept separate. A free country was one where the individual enjoyed the right to believe or not to believe as he saw fit, where the concept of a Christian state had no validity. Riesser earned the esteem of Jews and gentiles alike, and he took an active part in the Frankfurt Assembly, the climax of the German revolutionary movement of 1848, where he spoke out for the rights of citizens of all faiths.

The grandson of a former chief rabbi of Hamburg, Riesser retained an attachment to Judaism and refused to mask his Jewishness even after he broke with Orthodoxy. In writings directed to his fellow Jews he sought to instill similar convictions. Since emancipation was their due, he urged Jews to agitate actively and collectively for their rights. He scorned Jewish apologetics and efforts to tailor behavior or religious beliefs out of a desire to please non-Jews. The yearning for freedom demanded neither self-abasement nor the renunciation of group pride. Even if he were not fully emancipated, the proud Jew never forgot that morally and mentally he was the equal of those who controlled his political fortunes. In 1856 the *Israelite* reprinted a passage that Riesser had written fourteen years earlier:

We . . . the Jews . . . suffer no longer of your haughtiness, though we suffer of your oppression. We may be civilly oppressed, but we can not be morally chastized. We claim political equality but mental equality we have laboriously achieved. We know the despicable and the low of your . . . prejudices . . . and, therefore, we . . . struggle against it.[1]

Riesser never made his home in the United States, but his vision continued to inspire fellow Jews who sought their freedom in the New World. The principles he espoused, more American than German, echoed in the immigrants' vocabulary and became part of their living experience. In many ways their ideological mentor, Riesser takes on a special importance in the understanding of the German Jewish story, a story that began in western Europe at the end of the eighteenth century.

Forces for Emigration

Although the term *emancipation* was not used in connection with Jews until 1828, the idea had taken hold in German Jewish circles a generation before Riesser. After 1750, as Professor Jacob

Katz has explained, the long-standing European system of two societies, one Jewish and one Christian, came under increasing attack. The spread of the Enlightenment's teachings among the Jews and the growing communion between enlightened Jews and non-Jews signaled the way for the breakdown of the barriers between the two communities. Imbued with the ideas of universal natural rights and rationalism, the enlightened questioned both the restrictions imposed by the state on the Jew's political status, residence, and occupation, as well as the relevance of an autonomous ghetto which rigidly structured Jewish internal life. Moses Mendelssohn and the circle gathered about him, and similar gentile reformers who followed the lead of Christian Dohm, Prussian official and political writer, influenced Jews and non-Jews to conceive of a future where Jews would enjoy equal civil rights and be accepted without qualifications into the body politic. That desired end, they thought, would come about not merely through the enlightened beneficence of a secular state but as a result of an expected transformation of the Jew himself. Both friends and foes of emancipation agreed that the ghetto Jew, unsavory to most and sinister to some, was unfit to enter society, but those supporting the extension of rights were optimistic. In good Enlightenment fashion, Jewish and Christian reformers believed that the proper secular education could reshape the Jew. He would shed the garb of the ghetto—his Yiddish jargon, his "addiction" to trade, his separatist culture and irrational religious beliefs. Schooled in the culture of the majority, he would lose alien and distasteful ways and his unproductive economic habits. The emergent Jew thus seasoned would prove an asset to the state and acceptable, if not desirable, to society at large.

Infected by the passion for change through education, enlightened Jews worked intensively to disseminate the ideas of the Age of Reason through books and periodicals. They also founded new schools for their communities that broke with the age-old Jewish educational and cultural goals. "The Jews were seized with a hunger for the new education. To belong to the educated classes became for the German Jews especially the watchword of life, which sometimes threatened almost to take the place of religion." Concomitant with experiments in education, some Jews took the first steps in what would ultimately flower into Reform Judaism. In the first flush of enthusiasm for the glorious results to be derived, most Jews refused to worry about the weakening of their faith or communal bonds, or about the Christian expectation that emancipated Jews would shortly find their way to Christianity. To make themselves more like their neighbors was what they themselves wanted, and they would not permit traditional Jewish practices to stand in the way of their liberation.[2]

The ideology underlying emancipation arose first in Germany but was translated into practical measures by the French Revolution. After the French Jews received the rights of citizens, the French armies spread the ideas of reform by their conquest of western Europe. Progress toward full emancipation was uneven, but by the end of the Napoleonic period most western Jews on the Continent had been affected in some fashion. In certain places special taxes were lifted; in others laws were enacted compelling Jews to attend state schools, serve in the army, and diversify their economy. Overall, the civic and religious equality of the Jews was still circumscribed, but a radical step had been taken. "The common feature of all legislation . . . was that it acknowledged Jews as part of the population, perhaps in need of improvement and correction, but still not aliens who could be expelled at will."[3]

The Congress of Vienna that convened in 1814–15 to restore Europe to its pre–French Revolutionary order marked regression for the cause of Jewish freedom. The congress discussed the subject of emancipation in Germany, but most German states blocked the recognition of Jewish civil rights. German patriotism unleashed after the departure of the French found a handy target in the Jews, the beneficiaries of the French invasion and the culprits who allegedly financed the operations of the French occupation. Former legal grants were rescinded, and special disabilities were reinstated or newly imposed. Reactionary politics drew support from the post-Enlightenment mood of Romanticism, which substituted national ardor for universal justice and emphasized the concept of a German Christian state. A spurt of "Teutomania" again marked the Jews as aliens. As long as such beliefs persisted, there would be no room for Jews within the larger community. To underscore the bleak prospects that the future held out for German Jews, anti-Jewish agitation arose in the universities in 1819; in the streets cries of "Hep! Hep!" and "Jude verrecke" accompanied physical assaults on Jews and their property.[4]

Nevertheless, Jews could not pick up their life at the mid-eighteenth-century mark just because Metternich and the Holy Alliance had so ordained. Over a period of sixty years they had taken step after step along the path of freedom, demonstrating their eagerness to partake of the majority culture and, as good patriots, to be of service to the state. They had been quick to take advantage of secular education and ready to modify their religion. Halted just as the promised land was in sight, they felt the bitter pangs of frustration and despair. Even if they had so desired, they could not go back to the self-contained Jewish life of the early eighteenth century. Not only had the communities been badly weakened by the ideological onslaught of the Age of Enlightenment,[5] but the educated and enlightened among the Jews also had burned their bridges. Their appetites had been whetted and their horizons broadened by the ideas they had imbibed and the progress they had made. They disdained the ghetto, which in their eyes stood for primitivism, intellectual stultification, and social deprivation.

Political regression caused pain but not paralysis. The new education had engendered greater self-awareness within the Jewish ranks, which in turn bred a determination not to revert to a state of servility. Responses varied, but, as Selma Stern-Taeubler has concluded, the "watchword of political and civil emancipation" united all factions, "the Orthodox and the Reformers, the conservatives and the liberals, the irresolute and the faithful, the indifferent and the baptized." At the extremes were the few who considered suicide and the scores who turned to baptism—negative but nonetheless active statements of despair. Most Jews like Riesser continued to look for redemption through political emancipation. Many cast their lot with the German liberal cause and actively supported the revolutions of 1830 and 1848 for improvements in both the German and Jewish conditions. Despite a resurgence of popular animosity, Jews drew up petitions for their rights, especially in Bavaria, where the taxes and restrictions on domicile were particularly onerous. Other Jews stressed the need to demonstrate the worthiness of Jews and Judaism for emancipation or, like the Reformers, the desirability of recasting Judaism into a modern mold. Still others opted for emigration. The youth in particular chafed under repressive measures that strictly regulated their numbers and choice of vocations. More secularized and sophisticated than their forebears of the eighteenth century, they preferred uprooting themselves to the prospect of a hopeless future of "hatred and shame."[6]

For a while the vision of America stirred the hopes of a group of young intellectuals who had banded together in 1819 to form the *Verein für Cultur und Wissenschaft der Juden.* Their purpose was to foster economic and religious reform among their fellow Jews in Germany and to stem the alarming rate of conversions to Christianity. Twenty-one-year-old Eduard Gans, later a distinguished professor of law, served as president, and twenty-eight-year-old Leopold Zunz, who subsequently earned the title of father of modern Jewish scholarship, was vice-president. The poet Heinrich Heine, who like Gans ultimately succumbed and abandoned Judaism for Christianity, joined the *Verein* in 1822. The group's mounting personal despair over conditions in Germany prompted their interest in Mordecai Manuel Noah's plan to colonize European Jews on Grand Island, off the city of Buffalo. They wrote a flattering letter to Noah in New York, informing him that he had been appointed honorary member of their society and expressing their deep interest:

Amidst the general distress and public calamity under which a great part of the European Jews laboured, some years ago, and still are seen to labour, it was, indeed, no small consolation . . . to hear the noble voice of a most excellent partaker of our faith, animating the abject spirits of the members of an oppressed creed, by *summoning them* from an ungrateful and unjust country, to that part of the globe which they style the *new* world, but would yet, with greater reason, name the better one. . . . Since that time, *the better part of the European Jews are looking with the eager countenance of hope to the United States of North America, happy once again to exchange the miseries of their native soil for public freedom.*

They asked Noah for practical suggestions for "transplanting a vast portion of European Jews to the United States, who would prefer leaving their country to escape endless slavery and oppression." Several months later, when the order came down disqualifying Jews from academic teaching posts, the emigration project exerted a more personal appeal over the German society. Since his scheme was more chimera than substance, Noah did not respond until 1825, and by then the original *Verein* had been dissolved.[7] Nevertheless, another link joining the cause of Jewish freedom with emigration to America had been forged.

The focus on freedom, or the lack of it, sharpened in the revolutionary movement of 1848. Since emancipation rode on the coattails of liberalism, many Jews allied themselves actively with the revolutionaries—on the barricades, in revolutionary parliaments, as student agitators, or as radical journalists. Their activity attested to the inroads made by the progress of enlightened thought among Jews. Products of a secular education, some were freethinkers or agnostics who had abandoned Judaism and considered all religious systems the handmaids of reaction. Culturally and nationally they were Germans (or Austrians or Hungarians) first and Jews second, if at all. Different from the pre-1780 Jews, the mid-nineteenth-century generation also worried about the image they projected to the gentiles. For example, how would it look if the Jew did not participate in revolutions? "He would have been judged to be the cowardly and insensitive slave."[8]

The failure of the 1848 revolutions unleashed a new round of repression, frustration, and emigration. Political refugees fleeing the avenging arm of the state for their personal involvement in the wars turned to the United States. Low in number but disproportionately high in talent, the group included a large percentage of physicians, journalists, and rabbis. Several achieved distinction in their new American careers—doctors Abraham Jacobi and Ernest Krackowizer, physician and chemist Joseph Goldmark, editor and journalist Michael Heilprin, Rabbi Benjamin Szold. Still loyal to German culture and to the principle of liberalism, many became involved in the German American community and participated actively in American reform causes. Those engaged in Jewish affairs appeared to have been more concerned with philanthropic and associative ventures than with religion. The rabbis among them had also broken with Orthodox Judaism; all were moderate Reformers or Conservatives.[9]

Like their counterparts among the Christian German emigrants, the Jewish Forty Eighters have customarily been regarded as an elite group, one whose talents infused the community already established in America with intellectual strength and leadership.[10] The wars affected thousands of other Jews in central Europe who although not active revolutionaries were of comparable talents. To them the wars meant increased privation or the final attempt to gain freedom in Europe. They, too, looked for a land where "the man comes first, then religion and the state and all else." The emigration thus stimulated accounted for a dramatic jump in the number of American Jews—from 15,000 in 1840 to 50,000 in 1850 to 150,000 in 1860. Immigration from central Europe became insignificant only around 1870, when Jews finally won their rights in Germany and Austria-Hungary.[11]

Many did not wait until the 1848 revolutions were crushed. In cities in Germany, German Poland, and Austria-Hungary Jews learned firsthand that rebels, and even so-called liberals, did not necessarily make Judeophiles. In Prague, where the opening salvos of the revolutionary agitation marched hand in hand with anti-Jewish riots, Leopold Kompert struck a responsive chord when he called for an organized "On to America" movement. The Jewish poet argued passionately and persuasively that Jews concentrate exclusively on the goal of freedom. He stressed immediacy. Neither questions of finance nor choice of occupation constituted valid objections for delay. "To become free at once, without any delay, without parliamentary pros and cons, without sympathies and anti-pathies, right there and then on the spot, as soon as the ship drops its anchor and the ocean strikes its partition walls." Yes, it was possible to exist solely on freedom, Kompert said. Moreover:

A person who is capable of becoming free commits the greatest wrong when he does not; one liberated person is a gain that can be distributed over . . . a thousand persons. . . . Whoever seizes the initiative in becoming free serves and carries the torch for thousands of other Jews!

Within a very short time emigration committees with plans on how prospective emigrants should prepare themselves sprang up in various communities. Jews of all classes responded enthusiastically, and the exodus began. One sympathetic newspaper correspondent reported from Prague in August 1848:

The list of those persons who in the last few days have left Prague forever, as well as of those who will do likewise in the days to follow, in order to find for themselves a new and better home in North America, could fill an entire page. There are among them entire families, people from all walks of life— among them two compositors, one soap-boiler, several jewelry workers, and doctors. Some of them are well off, others are scarcely in possession of their traveling expenses. One may term them cowardly, another foolish. But he who judges intelligently will completely justify their actions; and he who knows North America will consider them wise and happy.

The emigration wave thus encouraged by Kompert lasted well into 1849.[12]

The image of America facilitated the decision to emigrate. Ever since the colonies declared their independence, Europeans closely watched the unfolding of the American experiment. The enlightened took heart from the founding of the new nation which signified the climax to the Age of Reason. It became the model for political reform, translating into practice the doctrines of natural rights and social contract. Enthusiasts called the infant republic the hope of humanity and the asylum of liberty. Discussions about America were not confined to intellectual circles. In Germany, as R. R. Palmer has written, most ardent admirers of the United States were the "unknown and obscure" people.[13] To freedom-hungry Europeans, America by its sheer existence lent substance and reality to dreams of liberty. It also held out the reassurance that if oppression in Europe became unbearable, a refuge was available across the Atlantic.

Understandably, Jews fell under the American spell. Just as the Declaration of Independence and Constitution circulated in German liberal circles before the revolution of 1848, enlightened Jews since Mendelssohn had drawn inspiration from American political principles. Foes of emancipation also recognized the logical attraction that America exerted upon Jews. In the era of the Congress of Vienna, taunts that Jews should leave for America emanated from Jew baiters in the Bavarian Diet. Even earlier, a document of 1783, purporting to be a letter from German Jews to the Continental Congress petitioning for the right to found colonies, circulated in Germany. Apparently written by a non-Jew and never submitted to the American government, its aim was to warn Germans that Jews had a way out of oppression, that they would emigrate unless fully emancipated. As for the Jewish emigrant, once he despaired of freedom in Germany, he severed his political loyalties forever. A Bavarian Jew was asked on the eve of his departure in 1845 whether he planned to return to his homeland if he achieved economic success in the United States. His answer: "[N]ot until America becomes Bavarian." Charles Mailert, a Jewish teacher in the Electorate of Hesse who was prevented by family responsibilities from leaving his native Germany, believed that liberty had died in Europe, that its only hope lay in America. "Whatever you and many others may say about America, you do not know European slavery, German oppression, and Hessian taxes," he wrote to his brother, who had settled in the United States. "There is only one land of liberty which is ruled according to natural, reasonable laws, and that is the Union."

Mailert and others went further in their idealization of America. For them the United States was not merely a new land but a spiritual dimension. One who felt that way, even if he lived in Germany, could, therefore, be an American at least spiritually. Thus Mailert stated:

America still keeps me going somewhat. If this thought, too, proves deceptive; if one may not or cannot be a human being there, either, then my life would be unbearable.

Rabbi Isaac Mayer Wise held similar beliefs. He wrote that Gabriel Riesser was American in spirit. As for himself, "I was already an American in Bohemia."[14]

The Jewish image of America persisted even after the immigrants landed on these shores. It became their measuring rod for judging the behavior of both the government and its citizens. On numerous occasions Jewish leaders assumed the role of stern guardian, reminding the nation of the duties and obligations imposed by its original creed. The image of America also influenced American Jewish theology. During the nineteenth century, spokesmen for Reform in particular used the concept "America is liberty" to breathe religious fervor into patriotism and to find a spiritual nexus between Judaism and Americanism.

Of the 10 million immigrants to America between 1830 and 1880 probably fewer than 200,000 were German Jews, a far cry from the 2.7 million Irish, 950,000 English, 3 million Germans, and 400,000 Scandinavians. To be sure, German Jews—and German is used here to include those from central Europe and Poland who spoke German or looked to Germany for intellectual and cultural leadership—had lived in the United States long before 1830. In fact, by the middle of the eighteenth century they had constituted a majority of American Jewry. Nevertheless, the tone of the Jewish community of colonial and early national days had been set by the Sephardim (Jews of Iberian ancestry who prayed according to the Spanish rite), the very first Jewish settlers and the founders of the five earliest congregations along the eastern seaboard. Well into the nineteenth century the Germans accepted Sephardic direction, and only after 1840, in the wake of the stepped-up immigration from central Europe, did they become predominant. The Germans reigned over the American Jewish community until World War I. They in turn yielded to the east European wave of immigrants, who between 1880 and 1914 boosted the American Jewish population from 250,000 to about 2.5 million.[15]

Like all immigrant groups, the German Jews suffered the trauma of uprooting and confronted the physical and psychological problems of adapting to a new country. They, too, were beset by the antithetical forces that buffeted alien groups—forces leading to assimilation on the one hand and to ethnic insularity on the other.[16] But from the outset several distinct factors added up to a German Jewish experience in America that was different from that of the others. To begin with, ever since their dispersion from Judea in ancient times, Jews had constituted a minority both religiously and ethnically in all countries in which they had lived. They carried that twofold distinction with them to America along with a history scarred by persecution. Second, as a legally recognized group that had enjoyed religious and civil autonomy through most of its history, Jews were experienced in maintaining separate communities which translated ethnic ties and needs into everyday reality. Third, the nineteenth-century Jewish immigrants were the bearers of two cultural traditions, the Jewish—of which religion was only one component—and the German. Long before Americans talked about cultural pluralism, Jews were acting out that concept in their personal experience. Fourth, the German Jews had stood on the brink of emancipation in Europe but had seen their hopes thwarted. Newcomers in America to freedom and equality, they retained the zeal of the neophyte in defending the Enlightenment's doctrines for themselves and for others.

The hunger for the fruits of freedom took on paramount importance in the very decision to emigrate. To be sure, Jewish emigration paralleled and was stimulated by the exodus of large numbers of non-Jews from the southern and western regions of Germany. That exodus resulted principally from economic causes. Although Jews, too, suffered from the generally depressed state of the economy, their migration owed much to their peculiar straits as Jews, or what one contemporary called "a special Jewish pressure" within the general German pressure. With deep feeling Ludwig Börne explained that "special Jewish pressure": "[B]ecause I was born a bondsman, I therefore love liberty more than you. Yes, because I have known slavery, I understand freedom more than you. Yes, because I was born without a fatherland my desire for a fatherland is more passionate than yours."[17] In the case of the Jews the "push" from Germany and the "pull" from America coincided, lack of freedom drove them out of their homeland, and the prospect of freedom directed them to the New World.

For the Jew freedom promised more than economic opportunities and political rights. It meant the liberation of the individual from restrictions imposed by his own community as well as by the outside world. In a free society each person would enjoy the right to fashion his own way of life, culturally and religiously as much as politically and economically. The choices would be his—the job he took, the party he voted for, the day on which he rested, the clubs he joined. If the American Dream came true in full, the individual Jew would be judged solely according to his merit and not by any group affiliation. He might even be able to escape the hatred that the Jews collectively had so long endured.

Commitment to the ideology of individual freedom was one of the elements that distinguished the German Jewish migration to America from that of the Sephardim. By 1830 the Sephardim were the urbane and sophisticated established Jews who looked down on the immigrant *tedescos*, the German boors. Initially, however, the Sephardic outlook had been far more circumscribed than the German. The Sephardim had come to the New World in quest of a corporate freedom, or the right to exist as a religious community without special disabilities and on a par with their Christian neighbors. Pre-Enlightenment people, they lacked the historical conditioning of the Germans, who had experienced the changes that accompanied the destruction of the *ancien régime*. Before their arrival in America the Sephardim had neither wrestled with the challenge of reshaping the Jewish tradition and communal structure nor forged a blueprint of one integrated society which they hoped to join.[18]

The yearning for freedom similarly distinguished the nineteenth-century Jewish immigration from that of the non-Jewish Germans. According to Mack Walker, the German "Auswanderung" of 1830–1845 was primarily one of the lower middle class—farmers, independent shopkeepers, artisans—who felt squeezed out by the growth of population in Germany and the signs of industrialization. Fearful of losing status and falling into the ranks of the proletariat, they turned to the United States, where they hoped less to build something new than to reconstruct and preserve the old.[19] Unemancipated Jews, however, did not enjoy the luxury of status anxiety. Intoxicated by the ideology of freedom, they consciously prepared for a different experience. It was the drive to break with the old, to realize the political, economic, and social aspirations gone sour in Europe, that attracted prosperous and well-educated Jews along with the more numerous poor and untutored to the United States.[20]

From 1830 to 1880 the official American reaction to immigration was one of welcome. In 1841 President John Tyler said in a message to Congress:

We hold out to the people of other countries an invitation to come and settle among us as members of our rapidly growing family, and for the blessings which we offer them we require of them to look upon our country as their country and to unite with us in the great task of preserving our institutions and thereby perpetuating our liberties.[21]

Sympathy usually flared for revolutionaries in Europe and for those suffering under despotic governments, and Americans held on proudly to Tom Paine's teaching about the United States, the asylum for the oppressed. To be sure, the antithetical strand of nativism had been woven into the American fabric since colonial days. The En-

glish settlers had brought with them to the New World fixed stereotypes and suspicions of the French and Spanish, Catholics and Jews,
as well as of other deviant religious and ethnic groups. Early on,
colonists worried about the burdens that destitute and sick immigrants would foist upon them, a fear that soon widened into the
commonplace that immigrants were responsible for numerous social ills. Even cosmopolitans like Benjamin Franklin and Thomas
Jefferson saw danger in the influx of alien groups who without the
purifying experience of an American education could turn America
into "a heterogeneous, incoherent, distracted mass." Before 1880
nativism erupted in local disturbances (notably the anti-Chinese
campaign in California) and, most significantly, in the political activities of the Know-Nothing movement that peaked after 1848.
Nevertheless, the government still supported open immigration,
and white aliens of good character were able to acquire citizenship
after five years of residence.[22]

Most Americans remained confident of their powers to absorb
the immigrants. The onset of the heavy stream from Europe coincided with the Jacksonian era, when optimism and national cocki-
ness rode high. Americans extended the benefits of democracy, at
least to white males, pioneered in a wave of humanitarian reforms
for the less fortunate, and experimented in a rash of utopian settlements for the purpose of shaping a more perfect universe. Shielded
by the Atlantic from the conflicts that rumbled through Europe,
Americans believed that they, a superior nation because they practiced democracy, had been chosen by God to conquer the continent
and spread the blessings of liberty.[23]

Although the Civil War left unhealed wounds, it helped integrate the immigrants into the mainstream of American life. Heightened patriotism generated by the conflict, military service, and
economic prosperity during the war years removed many points of
difference between immigrants and native-born. In the immediate
postwar era, American intellectuals again boasted of the country's
ability to assimilate aliens and forge a new, diversified collectivity.
Only in the last decade of the nineteenth century, when a mood of
doubt replaced national self-confidence, did Americans grow more
fearful of the physiological and cultural menace embodied in
immigration.

Economic needs both before and after the Civil War dovetailed
with ideology and mood. The rapidly expanding economy caused a
hunger for population. America needed manpower to expand its
system of production—to develop the still unsettled land, to build
the railroads, to work the foundries and factories, to forge new links

in the system of distribution—and to buy up what was produced. In their eagerness for labor and for consumers, railroad companies and states, particularly in the West and South, sent agents abroad to entice prospective immigrants with special inducements. By 1860 the ratio of foreign-born to the general population had risen to its peak of almost 1 to 7, a level that held constant until 1920.[24]

While ambivalent currents of thought enveloped the immigration question, a veritable hodgepodge of beliefs characterized popular attitudes toward the Jews. In the first place, beliefs frequently were based on what had been absorbed in the European Christian milieu or learned in books, rather than on actual dealings with Jews. The famous story was told of Joseph Jonas, the first known Jew who came to Ohio. When Jonas arrived from England in 1817 an old Quaker woman came to see him.

She asked: "Art thou a Jew? Thou art one of God's chosen people. Wilt thou let me examine thee?" She turned him around and finally said . . . "Well, thou art no different to other people."

Second, Bible-oriented Protestants distinguished between the ancient Israelites and their modern descendants. The former, the architects of the original city on a hill, were admired role models. The New Englanders had used the Old Testament for their early law codes and for the names they gave their children and their settlements. (In Litchfield County, Connecticut, alone, there were a Bethlehem, Canaan, North Canaan, Goshen, and Sharon.) Some ministers and men of affairs had likened the struggle of the colonies against George III to the Israelite experience under Pharaoh. The favorable image of the pre-Christian Israelites persisted, but so did the image of their successors, the stubborn and accursed people who had not only refused to accept the divinity of Jesus but had crucified the messiah. New England's clergy may have been well versed in Hebrew, and the language may originally have been required at Harvard and Yale, but the Jew Judah Monis was not permitted to teach it at Harvard until he embraced Christianity. Zealous American Christians as far back as Increase and Cotton Mather prayed for the conversion of the Jews, and many of their descendants labored to that same end.[25]

Besides religious antipathy, other negative myths and attitudes were brought over from Europe—the Shylock figure, the exotic but eternally alien Jew, the socially contemptible and power-hungry race. At the same time, a countertradition of acceptance grew up in the colonies. The Jew in theory might be evil, but in the flesh he looked very much like the other settlers. Small numbers made him even more inconspicuous. The principles of toleration dictated acceptance of the Jews, and, more important, so did reasons of economic benefits. Informal associations and reciprocal gestures of friendship, philanthropy, and intermarriage multiplied; Jews and Christians found common meeting grounds in politics, civic affairs, and organizations, like the Masonic order.[26]

Some of the contradictory opinions about Jews were aired in the 1820s during the debates on Jewish officeholding in Maryland, where the pro-Jewish position finally won out. In other states Jews gained their political and civil rights almost automatically. On the eve of the migration from Germany only two states, North Carolina and New Hampshire, still barred Jews from political office. Conflicting attitudes toward the Jews persisted throughout the German period of American Jewish history. Now, however, the images and stories that made their way into American literature and folklore fused impressions of the *real* Jew with earlier stereotypes of the mysterious, romantic stranger or the malevolent Christ killer.[27] Negative myths gained ascendancy in the last quarter of the nineteenth century, when the "Jewish question" made its way from Europe to the United States.

Economic Pursuits

America, the "common man's utopia," was well advertised. Books by travelers to the New World, guidebooks circulated by shippers, American consuls stationed abroad, and above all personal letters from relatives and friends about their migration experiences fed the "emigration fever" that swept Europe in the second quarter of the nineteenth century. In village reading clubs, homes, and other meeting places the information was debated and weighed. Usually it strengthened the resolve to emigrate. The prospective emigrants took heart from reports about America's economic advantages. Gold did not line the streets, but the country was blessed with natural abundance. There was work for all, and industrious labor reaped tangible and rapid rewards. Free from repressive taxation, a man had the right to enjoy what his labors produced. Perhaps even more attractive than prosperity was the promise of mobility and of equal economic opportunity. Neither government nor guild, nor social standing nor origins, determined the immigrant's geographical destination, his choice of vocation, or the limits to his success. "Amerika du hast es besser," Goethe wrote, and those who dreamed of economic freedom agreed.[28]

Jews studied and pondered the same advertisements. Villagers who had emigrated earlier and returned to visit their families spread accounts of the fabled land. A prosperous New Orleans cotton broker recalled in later years that he had been enticed to leave his native village in the Rhineland by just such an account. Jews also had their own reading clubs, where they eagerly discussed the advantages enjoyed by Jews in America. In the German Jewish press—the *Allgemeine Zeitung des Judenthums,* for example— steady reportage of American conditions began in 1837.[29]

For most Jews it was difficult to disentangle the economic from the political motives that spurred their emigration. Since they suffered both kinds of restrictions, economic considerations fused with political ones. In the urgent pleas of the "On to America" movement, the essence of emancipation—to live and breathe as free men—could not but include economic liberty:

Become farmers, merchants or artisans, peddlers or members of Congress . . . , exchange-brokers or vice-presidents of the Free States of North America, become cotton-planters or sugar-refiners, that concerns you not us. In your new fatherland . . . no one will interrogate you about it, for there an individual passes for what he is and he is what he represents. . . . [Y]ou . . . possess the virtues and qualities—circumspection, sobriety, thriftiness, discipline and tenacity—to build up prosperity and welfare over there.[30]

During the course of the nineteenth century, German Jewish immigrants to the United States became everything that Kompert had mentioned and more. They worked as lowly laborers, skilled artisans, small shopkeepers, and wealthy operators and owners. They were found in all branches of the economy—trade and commerce, agriculture and related industries, mining, manufacturing, real estate, and banking. There were Jews who earned their living as servants, as professionals, at white-collar jobs, and in the arts and entertainment world. They were, however, not evenly distributed among the various fields, nor did their distribution correspond to that of the general population. Whereas most Americans were farmers, laborers, and craftsmen, the overwhelming majority of Jews concentrated in urban-based and consumer-oriented fields.

In the search for economic freedom, trade and commerce held out the greatest attraction for German Jews. Some who in Europe had worked as skilled craftsmen or had been compelled by the state to learn a specific craft discarded their training and opted for trade. In their historical experience, guild restrictions, if not outright proscription, beset the path of the Jewish artisan. Gabriel Riesser offered another explanation. Since handicrafts required closer interpersonal relations between Jew and Christian, the latter would tolerate only the minimal connection demanded by commerce.[31]

Agriculture was an even more unlikely pursuit, since customary legal barriers to land ownership during the Middle Ages had long since stripped the average Jew of a taste or aptitude for agrarian life. To be sure, the American scene presented no a priori impediments, but a vivid historical memory influenced the minority to shun entry into those sectors of the economy where they had frequently encountered anti-Semitism. "Naturally, there is never any talk about . . . agriculture, landed estates, etc.," a German newspaper reported in connection with the Jewish emigration from Bavaria. One writer has suggested that the Seligman family's initial reluctance to own the very stores and homes they occupied stemmed from Jewish experience with previous restraints and even expulsion. That would explain the fear of tying up assets in immovable property.

The limited role of the Jew in the economy of the premodern Christian state sharpened his talents for trade and other urban, middle-class occupations. At the same time, the Jew brought to those areas the virtues of which Kompert spoke—industry, prudence, sobriety, and thrift—the markedly middle-class characteristics so eminently suited to entrepreneurial ventures. Patterns of familial behavior reinforced the tendencies bred of historical conditioning. Rudolf Glanz has pointed out the significance of what he calls the rationally planned Jewish emigration, an emigration of siblings rather than families, and the above-average number of Jewish fraternal business firms that took root in America. The ties of kinship, often strengthened by marriages among business associates, minimized the risks faced by the solitary entrepreneur while they maximized the growth potential of the enterprise. Kinship also increased the chances of Jewish businesses and their profits to remain independently within Jewish hands.[32]

The average Jewish immigrant arrived in the United States with a small amount of capital. On his own, or with a bit of assistance from friends and relatives, he garnered sufficient funds to begin on the bottom rung of the economic ladder. He became a peddler. The advantages he saw in peddling far outweighed its menial quality. Most important, peddling appeared to be only a temporary phase. The Jew grasped what Barry Supple has called "a central proposition of entrepreneurship," and to him peddling afforded the opportunity for the accumulation of capital that would lead in turn to the establishment of retail and wholesale stores. It therefore attracted ambitious young men of various backgrounds and education. There were even religious functionaries whose jobs in Europe had evaporated with the depletion of village populations in the ranks of the peddlers. The appeal of peddling was ubiquitous in the cities as well as in the countryside. Outside the larger and established cities the peddler was especially visible. For example, in Easton, Pennsylvania, a town located in the heart of an agricultural district, more than 60 percent of the gainfully occupied Jews in 1855 were peddlers. That same year in New York, less than 10 percent of the Jews, but hundreds more in actual numbers, engaged in peddling.[33]

Equally important, peddling appealed to the Jewish desire for independence. "The Jew likes to be 'his own boss,'" economist John Commons once noted. No matter how small the venture, the peddler worked for himself, and his private business enabled him to invite family participation. An independent businessman could also decide more easily for himself how much of his religious tradition he desired to preserve. True, the very fact that a peddler undertook to invade the hinterland revealed that his Orthodoxy had cooled and his dependence upon a Jewish community was far less than that of the earlier American Jews. Parental strictures on living an Orthodox life were frequently ignored, for in practical terms it was well nigh impossible for the solitary individual on the road to observe the Sabbath and holidays or to adhere to dietary laws. Abraham Kohn, a New England peddler in the 1840s, bitterly indicted peddling for separating a man from his religion:

[L]eading such a life, none of us is able to observe the smallest commandment. . . . Thousands of peddlers . . . forget completely their Creator. They no longer put on the phylacteries; they pray neither on working day nor on the Sabbath. In truth, they have given up their religion for the pack which is on their backs.

Nevertheless, as in the oft-cited story of Meyer Guggenheim, who returned home every Friday to mark the Sabbath, the underlying choice was still his.[34]

The saga of the Jewish peddler was woven into the drama of the burgeoning American economy. After 1815 the United States changed its economic focus from East to West. By 1860 it had been transformed from a colonial economy dependent upon Europe to one geared to new domestic markets. Indicators like population distribution, growth of the urban centers, internal improvements, investments in factories, and per-capita income revealed how rapidly the economy was expanding in direct relationship to the physical conquest of the continent.[35] In the early stages of that conquest and until the day of the railroads, the Jewish peddler played a significant role. Serving the outlying agricultural and mining areas, he linked producer and consumer. His activities freed the farmer from enforced self-sufficiency. No longer totally dependent on home industry, he could increase his concentration on agricultural concerns and still obtain small manufactured goods and luxuries from the peddler's traveling general store. The excitement and fascination that the ware of the itinerant merchant occasioned in the wilderness were described many times by contemporaries and later authorities. Somehow the bolts of cloth or the combs, ribbons, and jewelry took on a special luster when displayed on the farmer's rough kitchen table or the peddler's own collapsible table. Along with his treasures and finery the peddler brought news to his customers in their isolated cabins. On many levels he was their link to civilization.

A pioneer in expanding the nation's arteries of distribution and communication, the peddler advanced the wholesale and retail operations of his suppliers. Although some peddlers worked from older cities like New York and Philadelphia, their contributions to opening up the more sparsely settled regions were especially dramatic. At the typical crossroads or village where the peddler had his base or eventually settled down (sometimes an unintentional location—"the horse died"), his business often stimulated the growth of new towns.[36] By the same process he pioneered in the establishment of new Jewish communities. Unlike the prerevolutionary Sephardic Jews who clustered in five urban centers along the Atlantic seaboard, the immigrant peddlers dispersed, carrying the seeds of Jewish institutional life into most states and territories of continental America.

On the eve of the Civil War most of the more than 16,000 peddlers in the United States were Jews. They walked in the footsteps of the Yankees, who by then had moved up the economic ladder.[37] Through the major entry ports of New York, Philadelphia, Baltimore, and New Orleans and through midwestern distribution centers like St. Louis and Milwaukee, the traveling Jewish storekeepers, singly or in partnership, followed the roads and rivers into most regions of the country. Unlike the petty retailer who catered to the peculiar tastes of his fellow villagers from the Old World, the Jews sought better opportunities than those that could be provided in the few communities of their coreligionists. Many chose to stay close to the new German settlement concentrated around the Cincinnati–Milwaukee–St. Louis triangle, where they enjoyed the security of a common language and origin. A significant number went farther afield. The news of the gold rush spurred some to California to become the provisioners for the mining camps. Others, usually after army service in the Mexican War and Civil War or various Indian campaigns, were even attracted to the southwestern frontier.

Endurance and optimism were basic requirements, for the peddler faced innumerable hardships. Extremes of weather, loneliness, heavy physical burdens, language barriers, high license fees, muggers, anti-Semites, and vicious dogs—all tested his courage and adaptability. One Jewish peddler, captured in Indian country by the Apaches and traded by them to the Comanches, rode the warpath with the Indians until his release two years later. Those who endured received a rich education. Peddling forced them to learn English and, in the Southwest, Spanish and various Indian dialects. It opened up new vistas about the country and its inhabitants. Dependent upon strangers for his bed and board while on the road, the peddler was taught to suffer snubs or slurs and to reciprocate cordiality and warmth. His daily work also gave the peddler lessons in business deportment—whom to trust, how to reward favors—that would serve him well when he reached the rung of storekeeper.[38]

Of all the regions of the country, the South with its closed slave economy and rigidly stratified society appeared least inviting on the surface. Eli Evans has drawn a sensitive picture of the stark contradictions suggested in the meeting of the foreign Jewish peddler with the primitive poor white southerner:

The Jew, back-bent and bone-weary, trudging the dusty back roads, stumbling past the yelping hound dogs and the chickens, to be met at the porch of the patched-up shack by the blue-eyed Aryan ["the 'crackers' and the 'dirt eaters,' brawling, lanky, raw-boned clod busters out of the red clay and smelly swamps"] with a rifle across his chest . . .

Nevertheless, that region, too, offered a compensatory feature. The slaves—and the Jew traded with the blacks as he did with the plantation owners and the poor whites—constituted a buffer for the peddler. The latter could be a Jew and a foreigner, but he was still white. Isidor Straus of Macy's, whose successful mercantile career had its roots in his father's peddling venture in Georgia, wrote that the southern peddler "was treated by the owners of the plantations . . . with a spirit of equality. . . . [Slavery] drew a line of demarcation between the white and black race and was largely instrumental in giving every white man a sort of status of equality which probably did not prevail in sections where slavery did not exist." The same advantage obtained in the Southwest, where bigotry was deflected to the Indian or Mexican.[39]

Not all peddlers climbed to higher rungs. In 1836 Shanarai Chasset Congregation of New Orleans buried a poor itinerant merchant who died in their midst. The list made of his effects was brief: "a trunk of gold clothing . . . ; a basket containing four glasses, one pair of glass fruit dishes, four flower pots, nineteen glass and china cups, and seven wine glasses; and one 'lot' of gilt jewelry, consisting of earrings, finger rings, breast pins and beads." Doubtless many reached similar impecunious ends. However, those who witnessed such hardship cases still believed that the gamble was worthwhile. One Jewish inhabitant of New Orleans wrote around the same time that the city, despite its fever and cholera, offered opportunities that Europe could not equal: "[A] man inclined to labour can gain a livelihood, not only for himself but also for his children"; in Europe "an honest man . . . , despised and trodden-under-foot as he already is by religious prejudice, is still not allowed to enjoy in quiet the fruits of his own limited industry."[40] The right to labor freely, to reap the benefits of one's labor, and to improve one's status summed up the Jewish immigrant's view of economic freedom.

For Jews and non-Jews peddling continued to be a sure method of economic advancement. It, too, had its own hierarchy—basket peddler, trunk carrier, pack carrier, wagon baron, and jewelry count. At the top of the ladder was the store prince, the man who had graduated to a permanent establishment. That traditional account, based on the colorful reminiscences of Rabbi Isaac Mayer Wise, did not exhaust the ways in which the lowly peddler advanced. For example, some became wholesale peddlers and supplied the retailers instead of the consumers. In an extremely fluid system of distribution, there were those, like the Seligmans, who established a store and with the help of a seemingly endless supply of brothers continued to peddle from that base. The successful storekeepers eventually upgraded their peddling adjuncts—the latter became traveling salesmen. Of course, not every storekeeper had to begin at the very lowest rung. With the proper combination of assets, luck, and timing some bypassed peddling entirely. The retail store in turn supplied the next wave of peddlers. It also contributed to the eventual displacement of the peddler, because it offered a larger stock, as well as credit and the possibility of barter, to customers who knew the sedentary retailer far better than the traveling peddler.[41]

The owner of a small general store who worked from dawn well into the night occupied an important place in the community. As a merchant he brought manufactured goods to his customers, and he introduced them to new products. He bartered goods for crops, furs, and bales of cotton and relieved the farmer of the need to market his produce. As merchant-cum-banker, he dealt in agricultural crops, extended credit, and held money deposits. His store was a social center for the town, a place to share personal problems and gossip, or to discuss politics and civic affairs. If his store prospered and grew, so did his influence on the economic development of the town. In sum, the merchant ranked with the trapper, soldier, and settler as a pioneer on the frontier. Small shopkeepers, however, took little pride in their merchandising and were not content to wait for accolades from future historians. Ready to shift to banking and other commercial enterprises, they preferred to look upon the store as another step on the ladder of mobility. Within Jewish circles, just as rank was determined by how early one left peddling to open a store, banking was considered a "higher calling" than storekeeping, even when the establishment in question was a successful department store.[42]

Like their non-Jewish counterparts, Jewish shopkeepers succeeded by dint of hard work and the ability to swim with the tide of fluctuating economic conditions. The career of William Filene, who built up a small shop in Salem, opened a wholesale business in New York, was wiped out by the market collapse in 1868, and succeeded again after a second start in a small store, can doubtless be repeated for many of his contemporaries. The Jewish retailer, however, bore an extra burden in the penalties imposed by credit-rating firms for being "an Hebrew." Character and moral references were always important in determining credit risks. It was Lazarus Straus's sterling character, so the story goes, that enabled him to switch from peddling to storekeeping in Georgia. Immediately after the Civil War, Straus's determination to pay off his debts to northern wholesalers earned him the lasting goodwill of creditors, facilitating his move to open a crockery firm in New York as well as his sons' later purchase of Abraham & Straus. In Isidor Straus's understated account, one creditor "saw in my father a demonstration of the keen sense of integrity which . . . was the reverse of what his . . . prejudice had led him to expect, for . . . in considering a merchant of the south, as to his worthiness for credit, the Jew or the new comer, which were interchangeable terms, was always viewed with that suspicion which did not attach to the native-born."[43]

Specialized firms like the Mercantile Agency, forerunner of Dun & Company and later Dun & Bradstreet, continued to supply wholesalers with assessments of retailers' moral worth. Reporters for Dun & Company carefully noted which retailers were Jewish. Recent studies of Jewish economic mobility show that unless the investigator included the phrase "white Jew" or "an Israelite of the better classes," the subject of his report was usually assigned a poor credit rating. Sometimes, no doubt, a positive reference from a Dun investigator who knew the retailer personally canceled out the flaw of Jewishness. An entry of Dun's for Louisville, Kentucky, from 1857 contains information on a Julius Sues, who dealt in baby carriages and notions. The investigator reported enthusiastically:

His wife is a very handy woman and makes money by sewing. Julius, after his day's work was over, would ply the sewing machine for his wife until 11 or 12 o'clock at night, and up in the Morning at 4 o'clock and at it again until it was time to go to the store. I believe him an honest a man as the Sun ever Shone on.

Those who did not pass muster needed to budget their own savings more carefully or to borrow from a Jewish "credit network" of relatives or associates in America and Europe.[44]

A similar hardship to the small trader was the refusal of insurance companies to take on "Jew risks." As early as 1852 the instructions of various companies to their agents contained caveats against insuring itinerant peddlers, small merchants, strangers, and Jews. While "Jew" seemed at first to be a generic term interchangeable with any of the other categories that signified instability, an insurance executive later charged that Jews as a class constituted the worst swindlers. The specific indictment that had grown up since the 1850s was that Jews committed arson and defrauded the companies for the losses that they had purposely incurred.

Discrimination came to a head in 1866 when firms in New York and Connecticut, with business in southern and western states, openly refused to insure Jews and canceled some existing policies. According to New York's leading Anglo-Jewish newspaper, the *Jewish Messenger*, the companies had suffered severe financial losses and attempted to justify themselves to their shareholders by providing a scapegoat. The Board of Delegates of American Israelites, the first and newly formed Jewish defense agency, added "religious fanaticism," "ignorance," and "envy" to the motives.

Two elements in the situation stunned the Jewish community. First, denial of insurance lowered the standing of local Jewish merchants. Like the practices of the credit-rating agencies, the hardships foisted upon the small retailer could also injure the business of the larger eastern suppliers. More serious, and again parallel to the credit-rating policies, the stigma of dishonesty was put upon the entire group. In some places "respectable" (i.e., wealthier and better established) Jews were exempted from the restrictionist policies, but all Jews bore the humiliation when the word "Jew" was used to connote "rogue" and "swindler." The issue reverberated throughout the community. From Connecticut to Virginia, from Pennsylvania to Missouri, local Jews staged protest meetings and passed angry resolutions. The favorite response was to advise a boycott of the discriminating companies and of the agents who represented them, a weapon that Rabbi Isaac Leeser of Philadelphia had recommended as early as 1857. The *Jewish Messenger* published blacklists of the offending firms, and there was even talk of founding a Jewish insurance company, one that would deal fairly with Christians, too. The non-Jewish world joined in the discussions. In New York City one actor delivered an extemporaneous speech on stage in which he attacked a discriminating fire insurance company. Surprisingly, the general press was divided on the rectitude of the companies' policies, and a significant number upheld the firms.

The *Jewish Messenger* continued to sputter indignantly. It called upon the wealthy Jews of New York to use their power and influence on behalf of their poorer fellow Jews. "These men (if they be men), will not submit tamely to the insult to which impertinent Insurance officials have subjected them, as well as their poor brethren more immediately concerned." The paper did not come up with any practical advice beyond the call for a strict boycott, but the editor, Rabbi Samuel Isaacs, insisted on a proper show of self-respect. If, for example, all Jewish merchants observed the Sabbath and indicated that they were jealous of their honor, not only would they gain respect but "prejudice or *rishus* [Hebrew for evil] . . . will be wholly dispelled." At the same time, however, Isaacs chided his readers on the need for self-improvement. If Jews "encouraged and sustained a spirit of enlightened zeal in promoting the cause of education, they would effectually overcome the reproach that they are actuated solely by aspirations for wealth." His timidity was shared by a group of New York Jews who banded together to handle the issue. Their first step was to ask the companies whether they approved of the restrictive practices, and they were only too happy to accept denials at face value. They called for a boycott only of those that failed to give the proper answers. The Board of Delegates also shrank back, declining to pursue the matter. The pervasive desire to avoid confrontation reflected the insecurity of a minority who had witnessed ugly flare-ups of anti-Semitism during the Civil

War. The callous insults of the insurance companies and their sympathizers among the press revealed, too, that in the larger society anti-Semitism was far from unrespectable. No wonder, since the agitation reached its peak during the month of the Jewish holiday of Purim, the *Jewish Messenger* yearned for an American Mordecai to combat the "Hamanic" spirit and bring about true equality for the Jews.[45]

Storekeeping, like peddling, enabled the fortunate ones to branch out into various fields of higher economic achievements. For some, retail trade led to wholesaling; for others, to the modern department store. A few of the department-store owners or "merchant princes" who "arrived" via the peddling–small store route were the Strauses (Macy's, Abraham & Straus), Filenes, Gimbels, Rosenwalds (Sears, Roebuck), and Riches. Peddling and storekeeping also resulted, as in the cases of the Seligmans, Lehmans, and Marcus Goldman (Goldman, Sachs) in banking and finance. In those instances the Civil War brought prosperity, and the financial world of New York attracted the men with "agile minds and the requisite capital."[46]

Peddling and shopkeeping flowed into another stream of American commerce that has been known ever since as a Jewish field—the production and distribution of ready-made clothing. Well into the nineteenth century, ready-made clothing was unheard of to most Americans. The rich ordered custom-made garments from their tailors, the ordinary people sewed their own, and the very poor bought the discarded clothes of the wealthy in secondhand shops. The first steps that eventually led to the ready-to-wear industry were taken in the 1830s in Massachusetts and New York, where clothes were turned out for the southern poor and slaves, sailors, miners, and frontiersmen. As consumer demand began to soar, German Jews entered the industry. In the 1840s Haiman Spitz, a Posen-born Jew who came to New York via England, manufactured clothing for the southern market. He himself would accompany his shipments from New York to his distribution center in New Orleans. Shortly before the Mexican War, he filled an army order for 1500 summer uniforms at the price of $6 each. The appearance of the sewing machine in 1846 gave further impetus to the new industry. In the next decade Levi Strauss came up with copper-riveted canvas trousers for the laborer, a creation allegedly inspired by the miner who complained that he tore his pockets and seams. The Civil War opened a new period in the expansion of the clothing industry. The

government demand for uniforms sent additional capital and labor
into clothing manufacturing. In Milwaukee one Jewish firm held a
government contract for 12,000 uniforms; in Cleveland another
turned out 500 officers' uniforms in one month. The Seligmans'
experience was probably unmatched, for the government ran up a
bill for $1 million with that firm alone for uniforms produced. After
the war, popular demand for ready-made clothes of a finer quality
soared, and the permanency of the garment industry was
guaranteed.[47]

The Jews entered the clothing industry through several doors.
As peddlers and small shopkeepers they included ready-to-wear
garments in their stock. Their success with those goods encouraged
many to shift from a general trade to specialty clothing firms. Increased retail sales in turn advanced the suppliers, usually back
East, to the rung of wholesaler and manufacturer. By the 1880s, in
the Midwest and on the western coast, scores of former peddlers
and general-store owners operated retail clothing businesses.
Pioneers in a new industry, Jews quickly learned to harness advertising to merchandising skills. The verses of one clothier in mid-
century Cleveland anticipated Madison Avenue's later efforts:

> I have only one objection,
>   Said a maiden to her lover;
> I have only one objection
>   To the matters you propose;
> I would no longer tarry,
>   I am ready now to marry;
> But I cannot wed a lover
>   In those unwelcome clothes. . . .
> He went back unto his charmer,
>   With a suit of Isaacs' latest,
> And the maiden filled with rapture
>   In his open arms did fall. . . .[48]

Others who rose to clothing merchants came from the ranks of
dealers in old clothes. The Jew had been an "old clo'" man in Europe, and many entered the same business in America. In New York,
where Chatham Street was their center, old-clothes stores were a
Jewish business; eighteen out of twenty firms advertising in the *New
York Herald* for May 1863 were owned by Jews. Some who started
out as peddlers or as artisans and helpers in the needle trade—
again a field that they knew from Europe—saved enough money to
open their own old-clothes shops. That transition represented for
the tailor or apprentice a step up on the economic ladder. The

image of the "old clo'" Jew of Chatham Street lived on in American folklore long after the "old clo'" man had disappeared. It bore the overtones of dingy surroundings, low status, and shrewdness and cunning of the confidence man—an unpleasant footnote to the Shylock image.[49]

Preceded by native Americans as well as English, Irish, and German immigrants, the Jews alone came to dominate the clothing industry. According to one analyst, part of their success stemmed from new methods they introduced: smaller profits, lower prices, direct selling, and the use of specialized clothing stores. Statistics of all sorts reveal the extent of Jewish participation in the field and the success of the participants. A tabulation of American Jewish business firms in 1880 showed that 50 percent were engaged in clothing and allied occupations. At that time 80 percent of all retail and 90 percent of all wholesale clothing firms in New York City were owned by Jews. An account published in 1888 claimed that 234 of the 241 clothing manufacturers in that city were Jews, doing an annual business of $55 million. Led by firms like Hart Schaffner & Marx in Chicago, 75 percent of the clothing companies outside New York were also Jewish. Smaller cities showed impressive percentages, too. In Columbus, Ohio, by 1872 every retail clothing store was owned by a German Jew. To non-Jewish observers it appeared to be a Jewish monopoly. In later years the fact that fellow Jews were the owners and operators accounted in some measure for the swarms of east Europeans who sought employment in the needle trades.[50]

From the happy union of America's economic needs and the industry and attributes of the Jewish peddler and shopkeeper came numerous success stories. To be sure, the usual qualifications that the failures went unrecorded and that most successes were hardly of the Guggenheim, Lehman, or Straus type still apply. Nevertheless, the rapid upward mobility of the group, as noted by observers who commented on the lull in business activity on Jewish holidays,[51] was impressive. "Rags to riches" is too extreme a description. Not all Jews were destitute when they began, nor did the combined fortunes amassed, including those of the highest echelon, match the wealth and economic power of the American tycoons who controlled the heavy industry and directed the flow of investment capital. But in a sense Jews more than others lived the Horatio Alger legend. William Miller's study of the top American business executives in the first decade of the twentieth century challenged the myth long purveyed in history books about the humble immigrant origins of American business leaders. In his sample, admittedly of a slightly later period, the overwhelming number came from native-born fathers, from middle- and upper-class families, and with a high-school education or better. On the other hand, the outstanding Jewish successes went in one generation from immigrant, lower-class, and untutored (at least in American schools) origins to affluence.[52]

Social scientists have long been intrigued by the extraordinary mobility displayed by American Jews. Commenting on their educational and occupational achievements, sociologist Nathan Glazer has written that "the rise in the social and economic position of the Jews has been extremely rapid, far surpassing that which can be shown for any other immigrant group." Historian John Higham specifically addressed himself to the phenomenon of German Jewish affluence by the 1870s: "Proportionately speaking, in no other immigrant group have so many men ever risen so rapidly." Indicators like numbers of Jewish firms listed in city directories, or assessed value of synagogue property, or philanthropic donations, or the flourishing network of Jewish social clubs confirmed the upward path of Jews before 1880. Much of the extant data still needs to be refined; but where analyzed, it bears out impressionistic accounts. In 1889 the Bureau of the Census studied 18,000 Jews, of whom four-fifths were German immigrants or their descendants. Allowances for the possible unrepresentative character of the sample do not cancel out the undeniable level of prosperity that many Jews had reached. Among other things the survey disclosed that about 50 percent of the men were wholesale or retail merchants; 20 percent were accountants, bookkeepers, and clerks; 2 percent were bankers, brokers, and company officials; 5 percent were professionals; and less than 1 percent were peddlers. Occupational mobility was reflected in the German Jewish standard of living. Of the 10,000 families, 40 percent had one servant, 20 percent had two, and 10 percent had at least three.[53]

More sophisticated recent studies by urban historians have dealt with ethnic mobility in selected time periods during the nineteenth century. In various accounts of working Jews in Boston, Poughkeepsie, Atlanta, Los Angeles, San Francisco, and Columbus, the same conclusion was reached—Jews surpassed non-Jews in occupational and social mobility. That the similar patterns emerged in cities of different sizes, regions, and histories suggests that much of the explanation lies in the very condition of Jewishness.[54] Simon Kuznets has written:

[S]ince the immigrant minority tends to occupy the lower rungs of the economic ladder within these sectors [with greater growth potential], it has a greater opportunity to rise; especially if, because of a long history of adjustments, it possesses equipment which it can use to advantage.[55]

Versatility sharpened by a "long history of adjustments," the middle-class traits so long a part of the Jewish cultural baggage, and the ties of kinship which enabled the Jew to withstand economic discrimination (as in the matter of credit) gave Jews an advantage in a growing economy that rewarded new entrepreneurial ventures.

Ascent up the economic ladder vindicated the faith of the German Jews in America and the rectitude of their decision to immigrate. Their successes were recounted by contemporaries in Europe and the United States, and those reports influenced others to try their luck in the New World. As early as 1847 the German *Allgemeine Zeitung des Judenthums* reported on the phenomenal rise of Jewish storekeepers who began six years earlier as pack peddlers and advanced to own shops worth more than $100,000. Rabbi I. J. Benjamin, the Jewish world traveler of the day, wrote admiringly about his coreligionists' achievements that he witnessed throughout the land. According to Rabbi Isaac Mayer Wise of Cincinnati, "The large and numerous mercantile establishments" of formerly poor and friendless immigrants were telling proof of "Hebrew talent and genius." Dr. Sigismund Waterman, himself an immigrant and, incidentally, one who would have preferred to see Jews in agriculture rather than trade, referred in 1855 to the monotonous metamorphosis from peddler to merchant. "Have the history of one of these men," he said, "[and] you have the history of them all."[56]

Mobility was not necessarily a mark of successful integration within the general American business framework. As the matters of credit and insurance showed, the Jews on their way up encountered obstacles imposed by gentile prejudice. For their part the Jews contributed to a condition of separateness by their penchant for independent entrepreneurship. Furthermore, the preference of Jewish firms for family members or at least Jewish associates above gentiles, and the concentration of Jewish white-collar and manual workers in Jewish businesses, added up to what the historian of Atlanta's Jews has called "an economy within the economy." Christian patterns of employment reinforced that dichotomy, and men excluded because of their Jewishness from gentile firms found opportunities within their ethnic group. In William Miller's list of business leaders at the turn of the century there were six Jews, approximately three times the percentage of Jews in the population. All of the six, five of German and one of Swiss origin, came from Jewish firms started by their fathers or other relatives.[57]

Separateness became more glaring when mobility and even affluence failed to ensure automatic social acceptance of the Jewish businessman by his Christian neighbors. The Jews may have been economic pioneers whose businesses and taxes contributed significantly to the growth of cities. They may even have won praise for their economic virtues and law-abiding character. But they were still a class apart. Successful Jews were barred for the most part from militia and fire companies dominated by native Protestants and from private social clubs.

Rapid mobility on the part of the Jews may actually have contributed to the hardening of the barriers. Jewish achievements aroused hostility, Isaac Leeser, owner and editor of the prestigious *Occident,* bitterly observed in 1865:

[W]ith the great increase of Hebrew residents in America, their general prosperity has also augmented in the same ratio. . . . Now, if nothing else would cause prejudice, this circumstance will. . . . While we are poor and unsightly, we may be tolerated; but let us only look up, and become the social equals of our neighbors, and their ire will be at once roused.

According to John Higham, that resentment in turn prompted the competitors of the Jews to seize upon noneconomic trappings, like clubs, as their exclusive perquisites and to bar entry to the Jews. The scramble for status and prestige intensified in the fourth quarter of the century and resulted in pervasive patterns of social discrimination. San Francisco's Elite Directory for 1879, which included a Christian "Calling and Address List" and a parallel "Jewish List" of successful businessmen, was just one example among many.[58]

After the 1840s, when the German Jews became more visible in the economy, the Jewish peddler, merchant, and even banker were the targets of slurs and caricatures. The hook-nosed and frequently unkempt trader was less important in the picture of the despised Jew than the cunning and devious businessman who bested the Christian in economic dealings. Cartoons, fiction, and juvenile reading material, too, embellished the stereotype of the unscrupulous, usurious, and undesirable Jew long before the *nouveaux riches* awoke to the fact that positions of status were limited. By the

1840s "Jew" was used as a verb in popular parlance—"to jew" meant to strike a sharp bargain, to employ questionable ethics in business dealings. Whether or not Americans were acting out their own frustrations or ambivalences—i.e., the admiration of hard-nosed behavior in the equally admirable pursuit of material gains as opposed to moral qualms about unbridled anti-Christian behavior in the capitalistic race—is immaterial. The Jew was the target, and not just because his mobility patently illustrated the road of the self-made man in an economy that rapidly broke with the American agrarian past.

Nor was anti-Jewishness merely an aspect of the intolerance that in varying degrees hit all ethnic groups. Prejudice against Jews found a ready-made base in America; it updated the age-old myths about a group that had always stood apart from Christendom. "Rich as a Jew," "eternal alien," "Shylock" were myths that had originated in Europe long before the birth of America and had come to the New World in the cultural baggage of the earliest settlers. Doubtless the heavy concentration of the Jews in trade abetted the popularization of the refurbished images of the conniving and cheating Jewish peddler and merchant ("Shylock") who worshiped the golden calf ("rich as a Jew") and who, according to some, refused to take root in the land but merely skimmed off its bounty ("eternal alien").[59] No matter what his occupation, it is unlikely that the Jew would have shrugged off his unsavory reputation. The fact, for example, that the historical base for Shakespeare's Shylock was a Christian, a point that the Jewish press belabored,[60] failed to erase the alleged characteristics that were by mid-nineteenth century accepted as endemic to the Jewish character. In 1859, when American Jews bemoaned the forced conversion and abduction of little Edgar Mortara of Bologna, Italy, and pressed for international remonstrance against the papal authorities, the *New York Herald* contemptuously dismissed the episode. It mattered little, the paper wrote, if all the Jews were formally baptized at one fell swoop: "Whether the old clo' men would drive easier bargains, or the brokers give easier shaves on first rate paper, in consequence of their properly becoming Christians, is a matter of some dubitation."[61] Americans may have been entertained by such and less offensive caricatures of the different ethnic groups that continued to appear in print and on the stage in the latter part of the century, but those who were the butt of the jokes, like the Irish and the Jews, were not amused.[62] Somehow the focus of the caricature shifted too easily from physical or linguistic peculiarities to what were purportedly innate characterological traits.

Just as the alleged Jewish business characteristics evoked deroga-
tory remarks, so did Jewish concentration in trade. The Jew did not
work the fields, an Ohio newspaper taunted in 1841, and similar
criticisms of nonproductivity or parasitic behavior continued to
crop up long before the east European masses settled in American
urban ghettos. The English-language periodicals, the most important defense agencies of the nineteenth-century community, usually retorted with praise for the Jewish merchant and his
contributions to the country or with explanations of the reasons that
had kept the premodern Jews off the land. We are proud of the
Jewish record in commerce, the *Israelite* affirmed in 1854. For the
country, commerce ranked as important as agriculture, and the
charge that Jews neglected agriculture was probably circulated in
the first place by their non-Jewish commercial competitors. At the
same time, however, the paper claimed that more Jews were farmers than was generally acknowledged. By its attempt to cover all
bases, the *Israelite* revealed its own ambivalence. It could not justify unreservedly the preference of Jews to stay clear of
agriculture.[63]

Ever since the debates on emancipation, modern Jews had not
been entirely at ease with their overdeveloped commercial proclivities and their corresponding underrepresentation in agriculture. From friends and foes alike they had heard the argument that
their economic pursuits accounted for their moral deficiencies and
made them unfit to enter the new nation-states as equal citizens.
Economic regeneration of the Jews through farming and manual
labor became a popular goal among intellectuals and statesmen in
the late eighteenth and early nineteenth centuries. Several European rulers attempted to divert Jews by force from their traditional
occupations, but their efforts had little effect. The prospect of succeeding in agriculture or crafts in Europe were not sufficiently real
to induce Jews willingly to abandon areas in which they had developed recognized skills. Furthermore, hadn't Moses Mendelssohn, the eminent philosopher and father of German Jewish
emancipation, defended the importance of commercial activity?[64]
Neverthless, since the physiocratic concept of virtue continued to
pervade Western thought, and in America it underlay the myth of
the noble yeoman, it could not fail to rub off on the Jews. In the
United States most applied themselves to trade, but the dream of
Jews in agriculture, a fantasy that promised to uplift the individual
as well as to enhance the desirability of the entire group, continued
to haunt them. Some Jews turned defensive about their commercial
achievements. Others touted the same line that had been preached

at them to the succeeding waves of Jewish immigrants who landed on American shores.

The Brandeis and Wehle families of Austria were different, for unlike most they were inspired by the prospect of self-renewal through a back-to-the-soil movement. Their prosperous textile firms had suffered financial setbacks in the rapidly changing social conditions that swept Europe alongside the political upheavals of 1830 and 1848. Lured by the natural bounty with which America overflowed and the dream of fulfilling themselves spiritually as well as materially, they sent Adolf Brandeis, a young man of twenty-six and later the father of the first Jewish Supreme Court justice, to spy out the land and find a favorable location for their experiment. In his travels and his work as a farm hand in the Midwest, Brandeis learned a good deal. Indeed, he found much that lent credence to romantic notions of the glorified yeoman and the virtues of farm living. His letters also touched upon the special concern of liberal Jews—the right of the individual to control his own destiny. Brandeis wrote admiringly that the farmer "is a man completely his own master, able to make his own decisions, to take his own risks, with none to say him nay. [He] . . . can 'take endless satisfaction in his extraordinary, indeed unrivalled independence.'" However, despite the positive side, Brandeis recommended that the families stay away from farming. They lacked the necessary capital required for investment, and as city-bred people they were unaccustomed to the physical burdens, the heat, and the tedium that agrarian life entailed.[65]

From 1815 to 1860 the idea of colonizing immigrant groups mustered support from various quarters. Social reformers dismayed by urban blight saw a way out if those who inhabited the squalid slums and taxed the philanthropic resources of the municipalities were removed to settled lands in the West. Philanthropists concerned about the demoralizing effect of the city on new arrivals and land speculators eager to realize large profits on their holdings also approved of the idea. Ethnic separatists welcomed the opportunity to preserve cultural distinctiveness through geographical isolation, even though the American government refused to assist the creation of separate foreign settlements. In the case of the Jews, missionaries of the American Society for Meliorating the Condition of the Jews favored the establishment of a colony—an "asylum of safety"—of those converted to Christianity in Europe who had still not been accepted by older Christians. Into that web of motives the thread of agricultural virtue was also woven. William Davis Robinson, a Christian merchant who wrote a "Plan for Establishing a

Jewish Settlement in the United States" in 1819, emphasized the financial advantages that would accrue to Jewish sponsors who undertook to transport Jews from Europe and settle them in an agricultural colony in the upper Mississippi territory. The settlers in turn would reap moral as well as political benefits. Mordecai Manuel Noah's better-known but equally unsuccessful scheme to settle European Jews on Grand Island, New York, preparatory to their return to Palestine also underscored the importance of agriculture in a diversified economic distribution. Agriculture, Noah said in 1818, "is the natural and noble pursuit of man."[66]

The diary of twenty-three-year-old Abraham Kohn, a well-educated Bavarian who arrived in the United States in 1842, revealed how accustomed prospective immigrants had become to talk of colonization schemes. Kohn started out by peddling in New England, but he bemoaned the "inherent instinct for trade" among Jews that sent them into so unhappy an occupation. His thoughts turned to the advantages of an agricultural colony:

Could not each of us, instead of carrying a burden on his back, cultivate the soil . . . ? Would not such labor be more profitable? Why would it not be possible to form a society, based on the good will of its members, which would purchase a large tract of land for tillage and for the foundation of a Jewish colony? . . . Here thousands and thousands of people could enjoy in happiness the profits of the soil they tilled themselves.[67]

If farming failed to attract large numbers of Jews on an individual basis, it proved even less alluring as a group enterprise. Unlike many of their fellow Germans who colonized in various types of experimental communitarian settlements, the Jews neither followed charismatic leaders nor established utopias. One could deduce that the desire for freedom from Jewish communal restraints, a goal that accompanied the agitation for emancipation in Europe, made the Jew uninterested in group settlements. The very pattern of German Jewish immigration—more single males and fewer family units than the other Germans—also militated against putting down roots in predetermined groups.[68]

Whereas Robinson and Noah had sought settlers directly from Europe, an enterprise aimed at immigrants already in the United States was undertaken in New York City in 1837. Known by the piquant Hebrew name Zeire Hazon ("Tender Sheep"), it adapted the concept of mutual aid long familiar to the Jewish experience into a form of cooperative agricultural settlement. The founders drew up elaborate plans for the purchase and cultivation of a colony in the West. They spelled out the duties of each member to the group, and they provided for the government of the community. However, because of the economic panic of 1837 and the lack of interest shown by the two oldest synagogues of New York City, the experiment did not get off the drawing board. Nevertheless, it perpetuated the notion that the only options available to many urban immigrants were of a "triffling [sic] character, which tend to lessen their own respectability, and that of the society of which they are members." An agricultural undertaking promised, however, "to add so much lustre to the Jewish character."[69]

The swell of immigration in the 1840s and 1850s kept alive the talk of agricultural settlement. Now more than before, ideas were propagated by Jews who were already established and who, with no thought of removing themselves from the cities, urged colonizations for the succeeding waves of new arrivals. Like Rabbi Isaac Leeser, they worried lest the increasing numbers of Jews who followed peddling and retailing injure the reputation of the community. Leeser argued that petty trading had "a debasing influence on the mind." The Philadelphia rabbi also advanced practical considerations. Since commerce would not remain an inexhaustible supply of wealth, Jews would be forced to other occupations. Agricultural colonies also offered religious advantages. "A farming population could keep the Sabbath. . . . [T]he settlers . . . should be supplied with a Hazan and Shochet, with proper books and Synagogue furniture; and a teacher for their children should accompany them in their first settling down in their new homes."[70]

At first Leeser thought that it was too late to channel the German Jews into agriculture, since they lacked the necessary expertise. He suggested that agricultural colonies in America might be the solution for the suffering Jews in Russia and Poland. Nevertheless, he reverted to the possibilities of settling Germans on the land when he fell under the influence of one Simon Berman. The latter had propagandized in different cities to gain support for such a group, and in New York his ideas prompted a B'nai B'rith lodge under the leadership of Dr. Waterman to push for agricultural colonization. The New York men agreed with Leeser that the economic distribution of the Jews was unsound and injurious to the Jewish image. Their appeal to the community at large for support revealed that they, too, had adopted Christian criteria for judging the desirability and loyalty of the Jews:

The almost exclusive pursuit of commerce . . . by our people is often used as a reproach, and it must be confessed with some good show of reason. The mechanical arts have found few representatives among us in this country [but the] agriculturist . . . is entirely wanting. It is on this account that we are looked upon as transitory inhabitants having neither the desire nor the capacity of settling as permanent citizens. This view, erroneous in itself, is nevertheless justified by the predominating pursuit of commerce, which permits the accumulation of wealth without the requirement of permanent interest in the soil of the land which, more than anything else, enhances the title to citizenship and the full enjoyment of freedom and independence.

To stimulate an interest in farming and to ameliorate the problem of the unemployed who relied on philanthropy, they worked out a plan for establishing an agricultural colony that would include a school for teaching agricultural skills. The entire project was short-lived. It had been stimulated to some degree by the antiforeign agitation which peaked with the political successes of the Know-Nothing movement in the 1850s. When that agitation began to subside, the urgency to remove foreign Jews to the land may have paled.[71]

The discussions on colonization raised other questions that had troubled Jews since their emancipation. If Jews settled in separate enclaves, would the process of acculturation be retarded? Worse, would bigots who faulted Jews for their clannishness find justification in such settlements to feed their own discriminatory behavior and impede Jewish acceptance into society? Furthermore, how Jewish should a Jewish settlement be? Traditionalists like Leeser and the founders of the 1837 Zeire Hazon group saw the projected colonies as bastions of Orthodoxy, where religiously observant settlers would have the means by which they could keep the Sabbath and holidays, observe dietary laws, and give their children a Jewish education.[72] Their feelings were not shared by all American Jews, particularly after the rise of Reform Judaism.

These problems persisted into the twentieth century, but by then the focus of attention had shifted. In the 1870s, in response to the ever-rising number of immigrants who arrived annually from Romania and Russia, a new round of concerted efforts at colonization began. Since anti-Semitism was simultaneously on the rise, agricultural settlement of the Jewish immigrants took on particular urgency. It promised to decrease the visibility of those who headed for the overcrowded urban ghettos, thereby protecting the image of the established Jews while blunting the efforts of immigration restrictionists. It also fit the popular agrarian myth that hard-pressed American farmers were trumpeting more loudly as their financial problems mounted. From 1875 until World War I the Anglo-Jewish press and leaders of the B'nai B'rith, the Union of American Hebrew Congregations, and the Baron de Hirsch Fund reiterated arguments about the advantages of colonization both to the Jews and to the nation. Numerous agricultural settlements were founded, but like their predecessors most failed.[73] Notwithstanding, the Anglo-Jewish establishment was loath to repudiate its faith in the panacealike attributes of agricultural life. As the *Jewish Messenger* reminded its readers, "Paradise was a garden, not a city."[74]

The failure of agricultural colonization also meant the failure to rectify the so-called abnormal economic distribution of American Jews. Although that consideration continued to rankle at least into the 1930s, recent analysts have judged differently. Simon Kuznets wrote that it was pointless to discuss the abnormality of a minority's economic pattern if normality was measured by the economic structure of the total population. A minority could not be expected to reproduce the full range of activity of a much larger society nor to retain its cohesion if it approximated the normal structure. The desire for cohesion, Kuznets said, "is naturally translated into a desire for proximity and close links at many levels. The minority, rather than be dispersed, tends to be concentrated in selected industries, selective occupations, and selected classes of economic status." To do otherwise (i.e., to be "normal") spelled extinction for the minority. Nathan Glazer pointed out that the "abnormality" was rapidly shrinking. The uneven economic distribution of the Jews actually anticipated the natural upward movement of Americans as a whole from farming and manual labor to business and the professions. Thus, if Jews sought a greater spread in order to mirror the American pattern, they would be working not only against their own inclinations but against the direction of the country's development.[75]

Religious and Secular Organization

The geographic distribution of the 200,000 German Jews who arrived in the United States between 1830 and 1880 differed radically from that of their predecessors, the Sephardim, and their successors, the east Europeans. The latter two groups, for different reasons, clustered mostly along the Atlantic seaboard, but the Germans spread out through the length and breadth of the nation. The dramatic rise in Jewish population, from fewer than 3,000 in 1820 to around 250,000 in 1880, was accompanied by an equally dramatic increase in Jewish congregations. Eight in 1820, the number rose to 19 by 1840 and 77 by 1850. Ten years later the Board of Delegates of American Israelites put the figure at 160. In 1877 an exhaustive survey undertaken by two Jewish agencies counted 277 Jewish congregations in 37 of the 38 states of the Union and the District of Columbia. New York City and Philadelphia together accounted for a disproportionate number—72,000 Jews in 28 congregations. But as significant as the fact that 72,000 represented more than one-third of synagogue-attending Jews is the statistic for congregations. The two cities housed only one-tenth of the established Jewish organizations. Ninety percent were scattered, many far removed from the eastern port cities. There were 53 congregations in the old Northwest, 13 in Louisiana, 12 in California, and numerous single outposts in less familiar places like Keokuk (Iowa), Port Gibson (Mississippi), Eureka (Nevada), and Waco (Texas).[76] The mid-nineteenth-century Jews rooted Judaism in all corners of the United States, and their pioneering ventures set the broad geographical contours of the present-day community. Distribution in turn significantly influenced the evolution of American Jewish history, bearing as it did on problems of assimilation and community cohesiveness.

The pattern of settlement among all groups of immigrants resulted from many variables. The newcomer generally looked for family, friends, or native villagers who had immigrated earlier for easing his adjustment to the strange environment. Advice from those he trusted could also direct him to a specific destination. Often the immigrant stopped his journey at the port of debarkation, if the long and unpleasant journey had dampened his enthusiasm for even farther horizons or if he had no ready cash to continue inland. Most important, he sought a place where he could use his skills profitably for earning a living.[77]

In the case of the Jews, those same factors operated. An urban-oriented group with entrepreneurial talents, they flocked to the cities, the hubs of the rapidly industrializing society. Their path was not unique; the cities also drew native Americans as well as other immigrant groups, notably the Irish. Jews preferred but did not limit themselves to the established cities of the East. The 1877 survey listed 20 congregations for New York, 13 for Baltimore, 10 for Boston, and 8 for Philadelphia—less than one-fifth of the total number tabulated. Many Jews had the means and the desire to fan out from the gate cities of New York, Philadelphia, and New Orleans to points farther west. Large numbers identified with the non-Jewish German immigrants and followed the latter's lead into the Mississippi and Ohio valleys.[78] Since the old Northwest experienced more rapid and diversified economic growth before the Civil War than New England or the southern slave states, it shared with the mid-Atlantic states a special attraction for the immigrants. Thus, for economic and cultural reasons Cincinnati became an important and vibrant Jewish center early on. The "Queen City of the West," where both industry and German culture flourished, Cincinnati boasted a Jewish population of 6,000 in 1858. According to a contemporary report, most Jews were wholesale and retail merchants who dominated the clothing industry of the West and Southwest and thereby provided employment for thousands of others. Besides their participation in the local—i.e., mainly German—social and cultural organizations, Cincinnati's Jews maintained five synagogues, two schools, one Jewish hospital, six charitable organizations, four literary and social organizations, and four fraternal lodges. When the first Jewish congregation was established there in the 1820s, the *Occident* recalled, 100 pounds of matzoth sufficed; 25 years later, it appeared as if 20,000 pounds baked by machine would be too little. By then Cincinnati's Jews may have already become the suppliers of matzoth for congregations in Indiana, Illinois, Tennessee, Kentucky, and Missouri. Rabbi Isaac Mayer Wise, who published two Jewish periodicals in Cincinnati, one in English and one in German, unabashedly called his city "the Jewish metropolis, from which must emanate all that is great and excellent."[79]

As a rule, though, the pattern of Jewish distribution did not replicate the German. Whereas more than one-half of the Germans settled in the Ohio and Mississippi valleys, only one fifth of the Jews did. In the Far West the percentage of Germans fell below the ratio of Germans to the general population. The Jews, however, who in 1880 constituted roughly one-half of 1 percent of the American population, accounted for 1.5 percent of the combined population of California, Oregon, and Washington. In all the geographic regions, Jews were almost exclusively urban, while the Germans were heavily represented in agriculture.[80]

German example and economic opportunity alone failed to explain the outstanding feature of the Jewish distribution. Even when not compelled by law to live in ghettos, Jews had clung together for reasons of self-protection and religious fulfillment. For tens of thousands to bypass the established cities and existing congregations and to strike out on their own was a novel turn in Jewish history. It bespoke a greater optimism about Jewish security than ever before. Besides, the established American Jews were far from cordial. Two Sephardic congregations purposely tightened their membership requirements in order to keep the newcomers out. Isaac Leeser of Philadelphia advised immigrants to settle in smaller cities, where economic opportunity was greater, and William Renau of New York organized a Jewish Colonization Society to remove them from the seaboard to the Chicago area. Moreover, since the German wave of immigrants included those from Austria, Hungary, Bohemia, and Poland—and even from England and Holland—different languages, customs, and rites of worship separated them from the old-timers and from each other. Only new congregations made up of those from similar backgrounds could properly satisfy their religious and ethnic wants.

A good part of the answer lay, however, in yet another circumstance, the "seasoning" for emancipation which German Jews had undergone prior to emigration. For many of them, unlike the Sephardim or the shtetl Jews of eastern Europe, the bonds of Jewish community had already been weakened. The goal of emancipation connoted freedom within the Jewish group as well as within the nation at large. The inroads of secular education had caused a reaction against the closed, "unenlightened" communal structure, its all-embracing discipline and autocratic leadership. Within Germany those who had abandoned religion and converted or moved to larger villages and cities contributed to the erosion of communal solidarity and authority. The very act of emigration to America further indicated a readiness to break the hold of a rigid community which one did not choose but was born into. Emigration meant exchanging a traditional Jewish setting which met all religious needs, from prayer and education to circumcision and burial, for the unknown cultural deprivations of an alien environment. More important, it signified a reshuffling of priorities, which put individual freedom above control by the group or even above group survival.

The Jews may not have realized it yet, but emigration foreshadowed a secularization of their faith. Their idyllic America could fast become the promised land, the kingdom of God on earth. Most immigrants to the United States still wanted institutions to service their religious needs, but having taken the first steps out of the old community, they preferred to establish their own new ones. The "independence of thought, liberty and self-assertiveness of the immigrants," Max J. Kohler stated, "impelled each little body or clique to form a separate and distinct congregation for itself, in which their own shades of beliefs and dogma might find expression, instead of coalescing . . . into a few large congregations or organizations." In a land that did not mandate religious affiliation and where, Joseph Blau has cogently reasoned, protestantism and pluralism were accepted norms in religious behavior, those Jewish proclivities were reinforced.[81]

The evolution of individual congregations usually followed a customary road. First came a burial society, then a synagogue, and only later a school. Such was the case in Fort Wayne, Indiana, where Congregation Achduth Vesholom was organized in 1848. Shortly thereafter it established a school to supplement education received by its children and instruct them in religion and Hebrew. Twelve years after its founding, the congregation reported a membership of "108 males" and "77 females"; 34 pupils were enrolled in the Hebrew school, where they received 15 hours of instruction weekly.[82] Some congregations went no further than a synagogue. Rabbi Isaac Mayer Wise reported contemptuously on the vapid quality of congregational life in mid-century Pittsburgh. In a city of fifty Jewish families, thirty belonged to congregations, one German and one Polish, but they had neither school not spiritual content within their synagogues. "They meet every Sabbath to read a set of prayers, eat *kosher* meat, and quarrel. That's all." Nor did the existence of congregational schools necessarily reflect a higher level of observance. Isaac Leeser visited Cleveland in 1857 and liked the educational system he saw there. As in all western cities, he said— and Cleveland was actually better than most—the falling off of observance particularly with respect to the Sabbath was deplorable. Not a trained sociologist, Leeser was learning empirically about the inroads of assimilation, especially in outlying regions and areas of less dense Jewish settlement. He blamed religious laxity and apathy at least in part on the influence from the outside—anti-Jewish prejudice, the materialistic spirit of the country, the example of gentiles who neglected their religion, the desire to be "fashionable" in matters of religion.[83] Leeser was also learning the difficulties that emancipation and the Jewish struggle for acceptance put in the way of traditional Judaism. How to be part of a free society and yet retain the integrity of a separate religio-cultural body troubled him and all future generations of American Jewish leaders.

Leeser counted 118 American Jewish congregations in 1856, but he argued that numerical growth alone was not enough. The Philadelphia rabbi, who usually fretted more about preserving traditional Judaism than how Judaism would appear to outsiders, insisted in this instance that Americans awaited substantive growth and creativity from its Jews. "[T]he very active spirit of enterprise which distinguishes the American people will pronounce our condemnation, if, with the progress of our growth, we remain . . . standing still on the spot where we were placed through the paucity of our early numbers, and the insignificance of the means then at our command."[84] Thus, emancipation introduced the new factor of group image into the internal development of the community. Indeed, so long as Jews labored to integrate themselves into society, no area of their endeavor could remain hidden.

Few American Jews agreed with Leeser's plan for unifying educational and philanthropic resources. Unmoved by the advantages that unity held out, they proceeded to construct a maze of separate, single institutions—synagogues, schools, charitable agencies, fraternal lodges, cultural societies, and social clubs. A sense of pride, if not taste, dictated the construction of lavish buildings for their favorite institutions. "[W]hy should not . . . gorgeous temples and grand edifices devoted to charity tell of the prosperity and gratitude of the Jew?" Kaufmann Kohler asked. Indeed, Jews benefited twice by this. Proving both their affluence and the proper use of their wealth, they lived up to the American standards of worthy citizenship. In 1868 New York was properly awed by Temple Emanu-El's new building and by the sale of pews to members which netted $200,000 above the actual cost of $650,000. According to the government census of 1890, the value of synagogue property in the United States—including buildings "with their sites, their furniture, organs, bells, etc. owned and used for worship"—amounted to more than $9 million. Close to $7 million worth was held by only 217 congregations with an overall membership of roughly 73,000. Donations to Jewish institutions also proved that neither economic integration nor mobility automatically doomed the continued existence of a minority group.[85]

While the large Romanesque and neo-Gothic buildings multiplied, the German Jews were constricting the role of the synagogue. No longer was the religious congregation the community as it had been in the colonial and early national periods. Then, the all-inclusive congregation (or kahal) stood at the center of Jewish group life. More than a house of worship, the synagogue was "a place for prayer, education, charity, meetings, and gossip." Signs of specialization and secularization had appeared as early as 1801 with the founding of a Jewish orphan asylum in Charleston, but after 1840 the trend gained rapid momentum. Organized recreational and social activities, like social clubs, had always existed outside the synagogue, but now new independent agencies arose to meet the philanthropic and cultural needs of the community. Their increased numbers shifted the balance of communal power from the religious institutions to the secular.[86]

The mid-century communal superstructure, a mosaic of voluntary, autonomous, and unconnected units, reflected the changed character of American Jewry. The rise in the Jewish population demanded a corresponding increase in charities, schools, and other forms of association. Differences among the immigrants in language and cultural background often motivated each subgroup to found its own societies. Larger numbers also meant new kinds of needs— e.g., hospitals, defense agencies—that the smaller and less visible Sephardic community rarely felt. The newly established synagogues were powerless to fill those needs, particularly when issues transcended the confines of a limited geographic neighborhood. Intercongregational divisiveness usually obstructed attempts to initiate cooperative ventures. In theory at least, a specialized organization could cut across congregational lines and effectively harness communal energies for a particular project.

More often than not, specialization made for greater fragmentation. Duplication and overlapping abounded. Petty bickering and personal rivalries precluded effective cooperation, let alone overall unity. Clubs and fraternal orders jealously guarded their territory, and barriers against fellow Jews who differed in cultural background or economic status were common. Even charities divided according to land of origin, and each subgroup was expected to care for its own without turning for help to other Jews. Frequently the ethnic origin of a pauper determined which group was morally obligated to handle his funeral and which synagogue to provide a cemetery plot.[87] Pluralism connoted democracy in the marketplace of ideas, but pluralism and voluntarism running wild took a toll in communal strength.

The secular communal institutions were largely the work of the German Jews. In America, the proverbial land of voluntary associations, such activities were eminently respectable. Some immigrants doubtless knew of the voluntary, extrasynagogal, mutual-benefit organizations that had existed in the larger German cities since the end of the eighteenth century. As a group, according to Max J. Kohler, they also brought with them to the United States "an extreme love for liberty . . . with a genius for organization, order and systematization."[88] While they went about establishing organizations, they indulged their freedom to choose their communal priorities. The same independence of spirit that predisposed them to question the rigidity of the premodern community propelled them to experiment with different expressions of group behavior. The smorgasbord they concocted reflected the whims of small cliques as much as the objective needs of the group. The results, however, eased the path of the unsynagogued, the Jews who rejected religious affiliation but still considered themselves part of the Jewish collectivity. Such Jews could, and still can, satisfy their ethnic urge by identifying with a secular Jewish institution. Ironically, the followers of Reform Judaism, the faith that in theory stripped Judaism of its ethnic properties, contributed disproportionately in manpower and money to the secularized but still ethnic communal forms.

Despite a more impressive exterior, the synagogue's control over its members steadily waned. Shorn of many roles—in the field of education it yielded inevitably to the public school—it was reduced primarily to cultic functions. Not until the twentieth century did the centrifugal force abate and the synagogue again resume its character as a community center. In terms of power, however, the individual synagogue lost out permanently. From the beginnings set by the German Jews before 1850, the burgeoning philanthropic institutions in particular came to dominate the community and ultimately, by their allocation of funds, to determine its evolution.

Secularization and fragmentation compounded the problem of communal leadership. The weakened synagogue and the fact that no ordained rabbi arrived in the United States until the 1840s prevented most rabbis from assuming undisputed control over their congregations, let alone over a wider geographic area. Erudition, personality, and charisma or activity within the larger society determined the rabbi's power over his laity and the weight accorded his opinions on intercongregational affairs. Without a strong union of congregations, there was none among the laity who by virtue of institutional affiliation automatically became the national spokesman. The Board of Delegates of American Israelites, founded in 1859, represented only a fraction of the congregations, and, therefore, its voice carried little authority. In practical terms the first national leaders were the independent editors, usually rabbis, of the Anglo-Jewish periodicals who, until the establishment of the twentieth-century defense agencies (American Jewish Committee, Anti-Defamation League), were the self-appointed guardians of Jewish rights in the United States and abroad. They were also responsible for establishing a network of ongoing communication among the Jews of different cities as well as between American and foreign Jewries.

Since the communal institutions were directed by volunteers rather than paid professionals, national recognition accrued later in the century to those at the helm of the entrenched fraternal orders (e.g., B'nai B'rith), the notable philanthropies (United Hebrew Charities of New York and, later, the National Conference of Jewish

Charities), and the organizations of Reform rabbis and congregations (Central Conference of American Rabbis, Union of
American Hebrew Congregations). Alongside them stood the communal stewards, prominent individuals without a base in an organization or journal, who quietly used their personal wealth and influence to gain the ear of government authorities and American
opinion molders on matters of Jewish interest. For the entire period
under discussion (1830–1914) leadership was undemocratic. Men
earned the respect and loyalty of the community at large for their
wealth or status and for their proven commitment to their fellow
Jews. Leaders asked little of the community, and the latter gladly
permitted them to assume the onerous and generally unrewarding
tasks of raising funds, defending Jewish rights, or mediating Jewish
interests to the government and Christian America.

The resultant pattern of leadership was often one of uneven
talent, lack of coordination, and personal and organizational rivalries. Nevertheless, two major factors operated to bring order into
what otherwise could have been total disarray. First, by the acceptance of an accommodationist posture, leaders adhered to a common definition of their duties. Like spokesmen of other ethnic
bodies, they worked to defend group interests and preserve ethnic
identity and, simultaneously, to advance the participation of the
group in American society. Second, the great "homogenizer"
within the Jewish community—overshadowing similarities in religious, vocational, or political behavior—was the acceptance by
Jews, irrespective of economic class or national origins, that at bottom they were eternally and indissolubly bound to all other Jews.[89]
That consciousness, the Jewish imperative, shaped the roles of communal leaders just as it preserved ethnic cohesion.

Structuring a community on the principle of voluntary association
and divorcing its multiple functions from the confines of the synagogue indicated both the effect of emancipation and the eagerness
of the newly emancipated to accommodate their ethnic heritage to
American surroundings. To have refrained from establishing Jewish
institutions altogether was unthinkable. Not only did all immigrant
groups need the emotional support derived from the association
with fellow group members, but also the bulk of the Jews were
unprepared to cast off the ethnic dimension of a three-thousand-
year-old heritage. Even if they had been, Protestant America maintained its own barriers, most pronounced in social and cultural
areas, against their total integration. Like other accommodationist

minorities, Jews Americanized the shape of their community. In so doing they grappled with the basic dilemma inherent in emancipation: how to define the boundary lines between cultural assimilation and Jewish identity.

Although most of the voluntary associations were Jewish in membership if not in content, their forms and activities drew inspiration from the organizations within Christian America. From the regalia of fraternal lodges to the lavish annual balls of charitable societies, Jews absorbed American practices which they blended with Jewish traditional values.[90] In the areas of recreation and amusement, the external influences weighed more heavily. The pre-emancipation Jews, as Salo W. Baron has written, had only "the realm of ideas" in which to find compensation for the lack of recreation.[91] When the legal walls between the Jewish and Christian worlds crumbled, the Jews copied the structured leisure pastimes of their urban middle-class countrymen—social clubs, fraternal lodges, dramatic circles, and literary societies.

The founding of one of the earliest German organizations, the B'nai B'rith, was a direct reponse to both American influences and Jewish ethnic impulses.[92] Although individual Jews participated in American secret orders, some were apparently barred around 1840 from lodges of the Odd Fellows. A handful of New York Jews who met informally from time to time at Isaac Rosenberg's place of business at 450 Grand Street discussed the problem. Instead of organizing an all-Jewish branch of the Odd Fellows, they would build a Jewish fraternity from scratch. The first formal session of B'nai B'rith (Son of the Covenant), a name suggested by the highly esteemed Rabbi Leo Merzbacher, was held in October 1843. Like American societies, it provided for local lodges coordinated by district and national bodies. It, too, had a secret ritual, vestments, handshakes, and degrees, but it used Hebrew terms for its panoply of titled officers. Its ritual lessons employed illustrations from Jewish history, thus providing members with a rudimentary knowledge of their ethnic heritage. German was the language used by most lodges and by the national council until the next generation took over. But the fact that the original tongue was German, and not Hebrew or Yiddish, showed how far the central Europeans had progressed on the road to cultural assimilation. In content, too, B'nai B'rith provided its members with typical lodge benefits: it · gave loans to the needy, assisted the sick, buried the dead, aided the widows and orphans. Taking its cue from other social organizations, the order labored to make membership a symbol of status. It looked for "best elements" among Jews and even disbanded a local lodge where quarrelsome or "lower" types disrupted smooth operations. East Europeans were excluded by some lodges for many years. (One American newspaper took the Chicago lodge to task on that score for thus abetting the anti-Semitic crusade that raged in Germany in 1881.[93]) The order also insisted that its lodge meetings counteract the "prevailing tendency for coarse and corrupting pastimes" with "elevating social entertainments." "It is a sad commentary upon 'the spirit of the age,'" the editor of the order's periodical piously wrote, "that so many of our young men . . . indulge in the demoralizing habit of 'playing at cards,' a frivolous pursuit at best, a great loss of time and money, and worse still, a degeneration of manhood."[94]

According to the first chronicler of the order's history, the founders aimed primarily at restoring a semblance of unity to the fragmented community. Julius Bien, who served as president of B'nai B'rith for thirty-five years, arrived in the United States when the organization was six years old, but he was apparently appalled by the dissension within Jewish ranks that pitted individual against individual and group against group. In his history he praised the order's curative effect. Members imbibed the spirit of harmony that B'nai B'rith preached and applied it to their personal dealings with other Jews. Quarrels that racked congregations simmered down; contestants who originally brought their petty claims to the courts settled their differences within the privacy of the lodges. To head off serious divisions that could endanger its effectiveness, the order purposely remained neutral on theological matters and took no official stand on the rifts that increasingly separated traditionalist from Reform.[95] Localism did not automatically disappear. At the beginning, different lodges put forth different ideas for projects that the order should undertake on a national scale, and they vied with each other on the location for national institutions. The governing council purposely delayed its decision on the first national project, and when it did make a decision it wisely chose a project that could antagonize none—a home for widows and orphans. But like other American religious and social bodies of a national character, B'nai B'rith suffered the impact of the Civil War. Lodges divided according to their sectional loyalties, and the order's work was temporarily impaired.[96]

The founders of the order also emphasized what they called "elevating" the cultural level of American Jews. One reason why some upheld the order's decision to exclude non-Jews stemmed from their educational goal. We are here to give Jews a degree of education and civilization that the world had closed off, a committee in the early 1850s reported; if the doors of the order were open to all, that specific need would be overlooked. In 1850 B'nai B'rith started the Maimonides Library Association in New York, followed shortly thereafter by the Mendelssohn Library in Cincinnati, where members and others could use a circulating library and be entertained by social evenings and lectures. The report of the association for 1855 pointed to the "high order" of the lectures and to the heavy circulation of classical books as opposed to light literature. At this time, the peak of the public lecture in America, Jews, like other audiences, listened to talks on a wide range of topics—mnemonics, temperance, American politics, Lessing. The influence of the intellectuals—some reformers, some freethinkers—who arrived in greater numbers after 1848 enriched the cultural content of the library associations.[97]

As B'nai B'rith's cultural work showed, representatives of the newly emancipated Jews worried about the image outsiders entertained of the Jewish group. Bien's account conveys the impression that the original founders were quite aware of the intellectual shortcomings of the Jews and did not fault the other lodges for excluding them. The year the library was founded, one member wrote that a purpose of the organization was "to obtain such moral and intellectual culture as would place them on an equal plane with their fellowmen." That self-consciousness, a virtual obsession about being constantly judged, was a legacy of emancipation. It dictated an unending concern over what made Jews respectable and acceptable to their Christian countrymen. Secondarily, it constituted the measuring rod against which the order weighed its own goals and activities. The principal aim of unity was prompted in large measure by the belief that the intercongregational animosity demeaned the Jews in Christian opinion. B'nai B'rith's support of agricultural colonization for the immigrants similarly emphasized the beneficent effect on the Jewish image through a move out of commerce. Members of the order who founded the Cultus Verein out of which the Reform congregation Temple Emanu-El emerged were also prompted by image considerations when they called for religious forms that would gain them Christian respect. Christian favor helped determine as well what the order did not do. For example, B'nai B'rith's interest in education could not be translated into secular schools for Jews, for the outside would call it Jewish separatism. Although secrecy and regalia constituted the stock in trade of non-Jewish lodges, some B'nai B'rith members worried about whether a Jewish secret order would evoke the charge that Jews were abusing their social freedom and equality.

The order expanded rapidly in succeeding years. Its specialized services on behalf of American Jews—including the organization in 1913 of the Anti-Defamation League—were matched by a concomitant interest in the problems of foreign Jewry and the establishment of a network of lodges abroad. B'nai B'rith also inspired the organization of other Jewish fraternal orders in the United States. For them and for itself it continued to emphasize the idea of Jewish self-improvement. Whatever improved the Jew and elevated the group, Simon Wolf said, neutralized the strength of the anti-Semites.[98]

An organization new to the Jewish experience, and one that evoked sharp criticism within the community, was the nineteenth-century social club. First, the very idea of a club dedicated to proving superior social status and defending the propriety of self-indulgence was alien to Jewish traditional values. Second, Jewish clubs arose in answer to the exclusionary patterns of the gentiles, who saw a contradiction between "clubbable" and Jewish. At bottom, therefore, status and recognition in the larger society according to the fashion of that society, and not a desire for Jewish content or association, underlay the establishment of the clubs. In the colonial era individual Jews had joined Christian social clubs and Masonic lodges, but even then, when smaller numbers facilitated assimilation, gentile rejection may have activated the Jews to organize an all-Jewish Masonic lodge and an exclusively Jewish club in Newport. The rise of an affluent Jewish business class in the mid-nineteenth century with the financial means and leisure time to seek out the respect and status that club membership afforded scarcely dented the set exclusionary patterns. Clubs accepted gentiles of similar economic standing but bypassed Jews; the occasional Jew who was admitted could not, as other Americans did, pass on his membership to his son. The barriers became more rigid in the last quarter of the nineteenth century, when gentiles, even liberals, unashamedly defended discrimination. To some extent the Jewish craving was met by participation in German clubs, but there, too, Jews lagged behind Christian Germans in acceptance and in achieving positions of leadership. A better solution lay in the establishment of Jewish clubs, where the Jews could copy gentile habits more directly and prove their readiness to enter gentile society.

By the 1860s, according to Rudolf Glanz, German Jews enjoyed a "lively" Jewish club life in New York. (The most prestigious one that endured from those years was the Harmonie, organized in 1847.) The pattern repeated itself in other cities, and clubs like the

Harmonie or the Standard of Chicago or the Phoenix of Cincinnati gained the attention of the public through reports in periodicals that underscored (again) their impressive buildings and lavish facilities. Within those handsome quarters Jews aped the gentiles and constructed their own tight codes for membership. Here, too, the motive was outer-directed: "It was not sufficient merely for club society to consider itself an elite; it also had to be fully recognized as such by the outside world." Although club members proved their affluence—and there is no evidence of insolvency for any Jewish club—Jewish club activities evoked strong disapproval in some Jewish quarters. Unfamiliar with the sports emphasized in gentile clubs, Jews drew from the models of the German clubs—dramatics, music, carnivals, and card playing. The last was blamed for its immoral and corrupting influence, particularly on the young men who frequented the clubs. One account admitted the clubs kept the young adult with his friends and "away from damaging society," but it added that expensive clubs were "often too much so for young men of limited means, to whom they become ruinous." Other critics worried lest the influence of the home be undermined; Jewish women, like their gentile counterparts, resented the club for luring their husbands out and for occupying eligible bachelors who otherwise could be introduced to marriageable daughters. The *Jewish Messenger*, which thought that the gentile clubs far surpassed the Jewish because of the intellectual and civic stimulation they offered, injected a consideration that was to reverberate thereafter in American Jewish circles. It claimed that self-segregation or clannishness might have suited the Middle Ages but had no place in the "enlightened age" of emancipation. That criticism could be disputed, but few could challenge the fact, also noted shortly after the Civil War, that clubs diverted time and money away from serious communal enterprises.[99]

The *Jewish Messenger* and serious-minded Jews found a measure of comfort in the establishment of the Young Men's Hebrew Association (YMHA). If club habitués who concentrated on the self-indulgent pursuit of pleasure were to be deplored, how much more so were the unaffiliated youth, dropouts from the Jewish community who spurned even nominally Jewish recreational associations. Both lay and rabbinic leaders lashed out repeatedly against the evils of secularism and materialism that ensnared the young. The indictment leveled by Joseph Blumenthal, at that time a member of New York's legislature, was typical:

But while the mind has been improved, have the social, moral and religious traits been so developed by practice and by example as to enable us to point with pride or even satisfaction at the sayings and doings of the young men and women of our race as seen in our daily experience? What is the response that they make to the higher claims and duties of Jewish manhood and womanhood? What interest do they take in the religious and communal work of our synagogues, our Sunday-schools and our charitable and philanthropic institutions? Especially for many of our young men, the club, the race-track, the billiard and drinking saloon, or even more pernicious attractions, have not only great but almost entire sway over their hours not devoted to the necessary calls of business.[100]

The YMHA served as a weapon for preserving religious community in the secular city. More specifically than the club, it worked to capture the vulnerable group of young adults. Initially, the YMHA stressed intellectual leisure activities for the average middle-class college graduate and recreation that "improved the mind"—lecture courses, literary and musical programs, classes in French, German, and English literature. The favorite pastimes of the clubs and the sinister city—gambling, cards, drinking—were forbidden.

The direct progenitors of the Young Men's Hebrew Association were local Jewish literary societies that sprang up after 1840 and offered lectures, debates, library facilities, and social activities. The YMHA's name suggests that it owed its inception to the Christian organization, brought over from England in 1851, but a literary club as early as 1850 called itself the Young Men's Hebrew Literary Association. Nevertheless, the immediate popularity of the Christian association also influenced the founding of new YMHAs. Not only were the Jews inspired to establish their own organizations—which increased to sixty by 1880—but actual forms, e.g., an employment bureau or a gymnasium, were appropriated from the Christian model. Doubtless the latter also colored the outreach program of the YMHA. Like the Christian association, which transcended the divisions among the Protestant churches, the YMHA saw its mission as city-wide, with a single platform that could embrace all shades of belief within the Jewish community. By providing young men with respectable forms of fraternization, the YMHA, again like the Christian association, took on a social-service task that the impersonal churches and synagogues ignored. Since there was not enough in contemporary Judaism to inspire youth, the *Jewish Messenger* candidly admitted, they could easily be "lost to the church." Different from the early literary club, which was usually Jewish in name only, the YMHA articulated a positive interest in Judaism and Jewish affairs in which to envelop its membership.

On the question of religion, however, the Jewish and Christian organizations were poles apart. The Christians were out to watch over the souls of the newcomers who flocked to the cities from rural areas or from abroad. They joined Bible study and prayer meetings to the physical amenities provided for members. Their religious fervor spilled over to missionary work on the city streets, antivice crusades, and revivalist campaigns. The YMHA, on the other hand, watered down traditional religion in order to substitute unity for factionalism and to appeal to the areligious and antireligious youth. They spoke about positive Judaism and Jewish fellowship, about a pride in being Jewish, and about "the protection of Jewish interests," but at best they could hope to inculcate a broad, humanistic ethical code, a smattering of knowledge about Jewish literature and history, and some sense of Jewish identity. Even though rabbis were among its most ardent supporters and guest lecturers, the YMHA's deliberate fuzziness about religious issues, as in the case of B'nai B'rith, permitted the ethnic dimension of Judaism to win out by default.[101]

In the period immediately following the Civil War, Jewish opinions on the purpose of the Young Men's Hebrew Association varied. Oscar Straus, one of the young founders of New York's YMHA in 1874, saw it as an avenue for personal recreation and intellectual stimulation. Rabbis Isaac Mayer Wise and Max Lilienthal hoped that Cincinnati's association would be an adjunct to Reform Judaism's mission "to promulgate the sublime and eternal principles of Judaism to the world." Assemblyman Joseph Blumenthal longed for ways to teach young men refinement and simultaneously to guard them against "fashionable" agnosticism. Here, too, image considerations surfaced. Only if the Jew respected himself as a Jew would he gain Christian support. Until Jews showed a proper veneration for Judaism, "we will always be looked upon as . . . making money our God." The *Jewish Messenger* preferred an organization that in addition to its intellectual and moral pursuits would unite Jewish young men of all classes and, like the YMCA, give comfort to the lonely and homeless.[102]

Until the community leaders felt the presence of their brethren from eastern Europe, the YMHA remained an institution primarily dedicated to the educational interests of the middle-class German Jewish youth. The advent of the east Europeans shifted the focus from intellectual self-improvement to the service and Americanization of the new immigrants. Now resembling their Christian counterparts more closely, the Young Men's Hebrew Associations turned to what contemporaries called constructive "missionary" work.

That usually meant classes in religion, sewing, and civics, as well as libraries and kindergartens for the newcomers. By establishing neighborhood centers and pioneering in the American settlement-house movement, the YMHA labored with other Jewish organizations to raze the newly erected Jewish ghettos.[103]

Jewish and German Identification

In wrestling with the antithetical forces of assimilation and ethnic solidarity, German Jews charted an independent course. The example of the Sephardim had little practical relevance. Small in number and quick to carve out successful careers in commerce and merchandising, that group also had assimilated automatically. Its rapid adoption of the country's language and social manners made members generally acceptable to their Christian contemporaries. Affluence and acceptance went along with a steady erosion of Jewish culture. Without trained clergy, teachers, or prayer books, their knowledge of Hebrew and Judaism fell to a shockingly low level. Since the immigration of Sephardic Jews had long petered out, they did not receive the reinforcement that successive waves of newer arrivals, better grounded in their cultural heritage, brought from Europe. By the middle of the nineteenth century the native-born Jews of Sephardic congregations were still Orthodox in synagogal customs and worship, but their social acclimatization was more pronounced than their Jewishness. Rabbi Isaac Mayer Wise, who thought that the Sephardim took on the coloring of the high-status churches of their cities, wrote that "it is characteristic of the peculiar aristocratic turn of the Portuguese orthodoxy of this country [to be] Quakerish in Philadelphia, Episcopalian in New York and Huguenot in Charleston."[104]

The aristocratic pretensions of the Sephardim, who would not permit the masses of the "boorish" Germans to ride on their coattails, antedated their American experience. When Jews from Spain and Portugal established themselves economically and socially in cities like Amsterdam, London, and Hamburg in the seventeenth and eighteenth centuries, they developed the theory of their superiority to the later Ashkenazic (those who worshiped according to the German rite) arrivals. The Iberian Jews of cultivated manners, noble lineage, and worldly education despised the uncouth, provincial Germans. The latter's industry and drive disconcerted the aristocrats, who, as one of their group wrote, "looked upon their pushing . . . German brethren . . . very much in the same way . . . as a marquis of ancient descent regards from his paternal acres the ambitious and self-asserting manufacturer." Prejudice persisted even after the Germans had risen to higher economic ranks. "Many old-fashion Portuguese . . . held themselves socially aloof from their Ashkenazi brethren, and would no more have given to one of the latter their daughter in marriage than a Brahmin would have affianced a dusky child of his to a Sudrah." Similar prejudices carried over to the United States, where in fact they were reinforced by the Germans. The latter, familiar with the more rigid patterns that obtained in Europe, spoke of the "hauteur" but also "nobility" of the Sephardim. By the twentieth century, Christian racist writers in the United States had also adopted the myth of Sephardic superiority.[105]

The American Jewish community remained Sephardic in style until the large influx of German Jews in the nineteenth century. True, the Germans had outnumbered the Sephardim by the time of the Revolution, but trickling in slowly, they were accepted by the original congregations and easily shaped to fit the Sephardic mold. (In the process some Ashkenazic words connected with matters of ritual were adopted by the congregations.) The Germans intermarried with the Sephardim, and many rose to positions of importance within the community. Giving up their own cultural distinctiveness, they bowed to the supremacy of the Sephardic rite and synagogal discipline. At no time before the nineteenth century did they pose a threat to the communal structure of the Sephardic founding fathers. By functioning as an open elite the Sephardim prospered. They gained manpower, enriched their synagogues by mixing, as one writer—himself a hybrid—put it, Sephardic values with German strength and enterprise, and averted serious competition. For their part the Germans gained, too. The cultural and religious variations among the newcomers precluded as yet the establishment of enduring congregations of their own. The Sephardim controlled a viable apparatus that could cater to basic religious needs. To exchange certain customs and prayers for Sephardic counterparts might seem alien but in no way signified a break with the content of traditional Judaism. Despite their snobbishness or peculiarities, the Sephardim were still Jews who provided an anchor in an alien society which preferred men to affiliate with any church rather than with none. In the minds of some Germans "Sephardization" also symbolized a way of achieving social status.[106]

Sephardic congregations became more castelike after 1825. Confidence in assimilation gave way to feelings of exclusiveness and jealous resentment. At the same time that the Sephardim fulfilled their charitable obligations to the needy German immigrants, they worked to keep them out of their synagogues. They also kept aloof from German charitable ventures. When community-wide discussions were being held in New York on the need to establish a Jewish hospital, a member of the Spanish-Portuguese Congregation bypassed all but native and English Jews to found Jews' Hospital, the forerunner of Mount Sinai. The old Jewish elite reinvigorated social barriers against the *tedescos*. Their reactions stemmed less from a distaste of the socioeconomic status or cultural behavior of the newcomers than from a dread of being inundated by the vast numbers. Not only did they stand to lose their authority, but the entire community also might disintegrate. They were alerted to those possibilities when, in 1825, B'nai Jeshurun broke away from the Spanish-Portuguese Congregation Shearith Israel. On the heels of that rift came new secessions from established synagogues and the mushrooming of extrasynagogal voluntary associations. The Sephardim doubtless knew that even with the help of the Jews from England, who on occasion allied themselves with the native-born and acculturated Jews, they could not stem the tide of fragmentation. Refusing to surrender or compromise their power, they preferred isolation to cooperation. Shearith Israel did not even join the community's protest of the Damascus libel of 1840. Until the Civil War its fear of being outvoted by the Germans dictated its opposition to efforts at unifying American Jewry. Between 1830 and 1860 the Sephardic Jews of New York at the "top of the Jewish social ladder" constituted an exclusive and isolated group. Only the labors of some individual Sephardic Jews who devoted themselves to community-wide enterprises kept the Sephardic presence felt in the evolution of American Jewry.[107]

The Germans stood at the receiving end of Sephardic snobbishness, but they were not free of similar prejudices. Critical of what they called religious laxity and the lack of a true charitable spirit on the part of the Sephardim, they soon boasted of the superiority of their religious leaders, men trained in German universities. Kaufmann Kohler described the Sephardim as Oriental in outlook and the bearers of a separatist and retrogressive Judaism; the Germans, however, were inspired by Western thought and hence were freedom-oriented and universalistic. Germans, too, accepted a social pecking order and as early as the 1840s looked down upon those Jews who had come from Prussia-dominated Poland and places farther east. Farther east, as in the Sephardic-German case, presupposed a less cultured stratum. Despite the strictures from the press on the ill-advised divisiveness, distinctions persisted. In Los Angeles, for example, Polish-Prussian Jews tried to identify as Germans in order to be acceptable to the German Jewish elite of that city.[108] When the heavy immigration from Russia began in the 1880s, the now-established German Jews had the advantage of economic affluence, ethnic origin, and prior arrival. Nevertheless, since their status and hegemony were threatened by the vast numbers, a violent antipathy emerged toward the newcomers. And so the pattern repeated itself. The earlier immigrants became status symbols to succeeding waves. Those who had climbed the economic ladder displayed both their contempt for those who followed and a deep fear of being displaced.

The German Jewish immigrants, unlike the Sephardim or east European Jews and, for that matter, other immigrant groups to the United States, consciously acted out a dual ethnicity. They were both Jews and Germans. Because of that duality some later historians of the German experience in America could not agree on how to treat them: to ignore them completely or to set them apart, either as a non-German group whose arrival happened to coincide in time with that of the Germans, or as a discrete subgroup within the larger German parameters.[109] The duality takes on a more significant meaning when analyzed in the context of the inner community built by the German Jews. On the one hand, Jewish participation in German social and cultural activities weakened the focus on Jewish institutions. On the other hand, identification with the Germans enabled the Jews to broaden their geographical settlement and to adopt forms and ideas for the enrichment of their own community.

Most immigrant Jews proudly[110] accepted the label "German" with which ordinary Americans stamped them. In fact, their Enlightenment-bred goal of acceptance and integration into German society was achieved thereby, albeit on alien shores. The Jew, the legendary man without a country, was endowed with a modern homeland and put on a par with all other immigrants from western Europe. Since America accorded him the same recognition extended to those who had enjoyed full political freedom in Germany, it thereby upgraded his status.

German Jews maintained their German connection in their internal Jewish world. They spoke German at home and sought teachers to instruct their children in German. When Cincinnati's Hebrew school advertised for teachers, it specified that instruction had to conform "to the modern German method." Applicants for teaching posts in Hebrew, German, and French were required to have graduated from German schools and to have taught in Germany. In their congregations Jews listened to German sermons, kept their records in German, and, especially with the onset of Reform Judaism, prayed in German. They started a German-Jewish press (reality forced the English periodicals to add German supplements), and German was the official language of their social, cultural, and service societies and orders. Many of the single young men went back to Germany to choose their wives. Those who could afford to sent their sons to German universities.[111]

More than nostalgia accounted for the use of the German language or ties with the Old World. Jews shared the German immigrants' pride in the culture of the fatherland, which they and many native Americans ranked superior to the American. The searing message of the Enlightenment had impressed Jews in particular with the belief that freedom was endemic to German thought. Gabriel Riesser, for example, maintained that the language and poetry of the country "kindled the sacred flame of freedom in our bosoms." One German Jew in San Francisco proudly announced that neither he nor his children would forget the language in which "our Mendelssohn" wrote. Dr. Kaufmann Kohler, prominent theologian of Reform Judaism, added: "What France and America have done towards liberating men, German thought did towards emancipating the human mind." Jews who continued the work of men like Mendelssohn, Riesser, and Kompert, the reasoning implied, participated in the process of universal emancipation.

By divorcing German thought from the action of its government, the unemancipated Jews overlooked political restrictions and honestly proclaimed their love of Germany. Similarly, the emigrants to America found a way to retain cultural bonds with the Germans without compromising their new political nationality. "The German and the Jew have so many traits in common," Kohler stated, "the same idealism, the same craving for the . . . universal truth, the same desire of recognizing the good and the true in every one."[112]

Like the Christian Germans, many Jews believed that the language of prayer also took on a sacred cast. Perhaps the fact that early Hebrew schools in Cincinnati and Cleveland insisted on teaching Bible and religion in German owed as much to the veneration of German as to practical expediency. Rabbi David Einhorn, a pioneer of Reform theology, equated freedom in religion with Reform; and unless Reform stayed grounded in the German matrix, he said, it would wither away. Jews endowed German thought with ethical properties, too. When explaining the goals of B'nai B'rith for elevating the intellectual and moral level of its members, President Bien called the program "a German conception in the best meaning of the term."[113]

German identification propelled immigrant Jews into close contacts with other Germans, who shared their language, their memories of the homeland, and even the experience of the Atlantic crossing. The German immigrants, the largest group of non-English-speaking people to enter the United States in the nineteenth century, provided ample opportunities to the newcomers in the way of social and cultural outlets. Sooner than the Sephardim, the Germans answered the immigrants' calls for companionship and conviviality. If Jews knew of a German presence in regions removed from the eastern port cities, their fear of settling in those remote areas away from a developed Jewish community was lessened. For many, the Germans functioned as an emotional anchor. Jewish secularists and freethinkers had the means to sever all ties with fellow Jews and, through affiliation with German *Vereine,* still to hold on to the familiar in an alien land. As long as the Germans accepted Jews, identification with that larger group came easily. Jews shared the German's taste in amusements, many of his political ideas (notably a resistance to Protestant reform movements like temperance and Sabbatarianism), and they desired his friendship. On the other hand, they were not interested in the purist cultural crusades of the ultra–"soul Germans," as Frederick C. Luebke has dubbed them, or those eager to build a cultural "little Germany" on American soil. Their Jewish heritage held in check their ideological commitment to German group causes and kept them independent of the vicissitudes accompanying the evolution of a German American community. Less deeply committed to a separate culture, they assimilated more rapidly than the Germans.[114]

Jews actively and visibly took part in the German organizational structure. They contributed to German charities, supported German secular schools, and joined German lodges, glee clubs, songfests, and gymnastic societies *(Turnvereine).* German newspapers needed Jews as readers and advertisers. Without Jewish audiences and patrons the German theater in America would not have flourished. Dependent upon Jewish contributions, Germans resented those who turned their attention from German cultural activities to Jewish institutions. Jews, too, took credit for their enrichment of German American life and through it American life generally. *Die Deborah* of Cincinnati stated:

The Queen City is unsurpassed by any other city in the Union in social life.

If puritanic stiffness and coldness has anywhere given way to the cheerful German disposition, this is certainly the case here. Our Israelites have greatly contributed to this happy victory.[115]

Degrees of intermingling varied. There were some Jews, notably among the Forty-Eighters, who behaved ethnically only as Germans; at the other extreme were doubtless Jews who stayed rigidly within the confines of their own community. Most, however, maintained some sort of presence in both the Jewish and German worlds. As for the Germans, the tightly knit, separatist Catholic and Protestant groups resisted fraternization. Conservative on political as well as religious issues, the "church Germans" lived in rural areas and small towns. They used the German language and culture to further their religious goals, and each group supported its own superstructure of schools, periodicals, and societies. Their opposites, the "club Germans," were the city dwellers who came into contact with the Jews. More liberal in politics and religion, they preferred secular ethnic organizations and used German cultural institutions as ends in themselves. It is probable, then, that the German circles in which they moved contributed to the secularist and Reform tendencies of the Jews.

The cultural connections between the two groups were especially pronounced in the German triangle of the Midwest. In Milwaukee, the German "Athens," the Jewish community's identity as a part of the city's "Germandom" lasted through most of the nineteenth century. Aside from their bonds with German societies and schools, Jews indulged enthusiastically in the German taste for music and theater. Many of the city's Jews followed the lead of fellow Germans into free-thought circles and liberal politics. During the Civil War, Jews joined units of German volunteers to fight on the side of the Union. Milwaukee Jews saw some of the benefits that they as Jews reaped through German associations. "We have here a strong German Jewry," the *Zeitgeist* wrote in 1880, "which has certainly contributed a great deal to the spiritual revival of our people. By the medium of the German language, that kind of noble Jewish spirit can be preserved that was first conceived by our immortal Moses Mendelssohn." The influence was not all one-sided. German leaders commented, sometimes with envy, on the achievements and intellectual qualities of the Jews. Some held Jews up as role models, and others noted admiringly how carefully Jews preserved their culture throughout history.[116]

Within the Jewish community, the champions of rapid Americanization, usually the ones most at home in English, criticized the Germanic loyalties of the immigrants. The *Occident* urged early on that rabbis preach in English. Since Reform thinkers stressed the inextricable connection between religion and the use of German, traditionalists of Leeser's kind had another reason to dislike the German influence. In their corner, however, the German speakers had the eminent Carl Schurz, who ably countered the charge that the use of German was un-American.[117]

After 1870 the German Jewish nexus dissolved rapidly. In both the Jewish and non-Jewish communities the inexorable force of Americanization weakened foreign customs and loyalties. In addition, the Germans who immigrated after 1870 were more politically nationalistic than the previous generation. Their heightened sympathies with the newly unified Reich disenchanted the Jews, smarting from the eruption of anti-Semitism in Bismarck's Germany. More important, Jews came to believe that German bigotry inspired the shocking onslaught of anti-Semitism unleashed in Russia after 1881. When the mass immigration of east Europeans to the United States began, "the Jew" became more visible to Americans and racist tracts highlighted the differences between the lowly Jews and the desirable Aryans.[118] In their own minds and in the eyes of their countrymen the American German and Jewish communities were pulled poles apart.

World War I revealed how far removed the two groups were. True, Jews of German origin did not entirely escape the anti-German hysteria and harassment that swept the country. Although some Jewish spokesmen loudly championed the Allied cause even before America entered the war, German agents dispatched to the United States were directed to make a special effort for Jewish group support. By that time, however, American Jews were responding to different motives. Those Jews who sympathized with the Central Powers chose sides more out of a hatred of Russia than a love of Germany. When the czarist regime was overthrown in March 1917, the way was clear to support wholeheartedly America's entry into the war. The Allied victory also redounded to the advancement of Jewish interests. Not only had Britain in the Balfour Declaration recognized the right of the Jews to a homeland in Palestine, but the Paris Peace Conference also held out the chance to secure Jewish rights in eastern Europe according to the Wilsonian principle of self-determination.[119]

The devastating impact of the war on German cultural institutions in America and on German ethnic pride did not seriously affect the Jewish group. The latter's own communal structure was intact and even gaining greater strength with the contributions of the east Europeans. Identification with the German world had enriched the nineteenth-century American Jew culturally, but only in rare cases had it eclipsed his Jewish loyalties. Now fully Americanized, with an established Jewish community behind him, and sensitized to the barriers that Western society still maintained against his integration, the German Jew was less dependent on, or infatuated with, his German heritage. Dual ethnicity among the American Jews had finally evaporated. It is hard to imagine a twentieth-century Jew trisecting his identity the way German-born Rabbi Bernhard Felsenthal did in 1901: "Racially I am a Jew. . . . Politically I am an American. . . . Spiritually I am a German."[120]

2

"ALIKE WITH ALL OTHER PERSUASIONS"

ON the eve of the American Revolution, by a circuitous route that had led him from his native Germany to London, Charleston, Albany, and New York, Jonas Phillips settled in Philadelphia. There he prospered as a dry-goods merchant and became a prominent figure in the city's synagogue. Like other members of Mikveh Israel, Phillips resented the religious test oath of Pennsylvania's new state constitution of 1776 barring Jews from office in the state legislature. If for no other reason, Philadelphia's Jews believed that the service they rendered to the revolutionary cause entitled them to equal political rights. The Pennsylvania Council of Censors took no action on a petition drawn up by the Jews, and in 1787 Phillips addressed the same grievance to the delegates assembled at the Constitutional Convention. He asked that the convention "alter" the oath in order that "the Israelites will think themselves happy to live under a government where all Religious societies are on an Equal footing." Whether Phillips hoped for a federal constitution under which Pennsylvania's test oath would be invalidated is unclear. It is not unreasonable to think that he did, for throughout their history Jews characteristically turned to the central authorities for protection against local oppressors. Whatever his motives, Phillips's letter had no effect. The convention had resolved two weeks earlier that no religious test would be required for *federal* offices.[1]

That clause (Article 6, Section 3), followed shortly thereafter by the First Amendment of the Bill of Rights, constituted the essence of Jewish emancipation in the United States. It had been an undramatic, even anticlimactic, process. Different from the series of events that accompanied the revolutionary turmoil in France, the question of Jewish enfranchisement had not generated controversy or debate. (The only one at the Constitutional Convention who openly questioned the need to outlaw religious tests was Roger Sherman of Connecticut, who thought that such a provision was superfluous in the liberal climate of America.)[2] Nor were the Jews asked to pay a price for their rights—to swear fealty to the state or to disclaim any ties to their fellow Jews or to promise to conduct themselves in any special way. True, Jewish rights were still at the mercy of the states, but Jews had won the more important assurances that Congress could not violate freedom of conscience or establish a national church, and that the federal government was blind to religious distinctions among its citizens. Since within the contours of the modern state there was no room for discrete subnational or corporate groups, the Jews could be no more than members of a church or faith. Religious liberty, therefore, was particularly significant. The foundation for all privileges and immunities that the Jew as Jew enjoyed under law, it was the key to social equality and integration.

During the succeeding generations Jews labored to preserve and widen the federal guarantees of religious freedom as well as to break down the state barriers against it. With or without Jewish prodding, most of those barriers quickly crumbled. Maryland permitted Jews to hold office in 1826; the church in Massachusetts was finally disestablished in 1833. Scattered limitations on the rights of Jews to bear witness or to serve on juries persisted (usually in the form of religious oaths), but by the time the serious influx of German Jews began, only New Hampshire and North Carolina still kept them out of certain elective offices.

Ironically, during the same period that state constitutions were becoming more democratic, the second Great Awakening was reaching its peak. American Protestantism, experiencing a new upsurge in evangelicalism, devoted itself, according to Sidney E. Ahlstrom, to "moral renewal, missionary advance, and humanitarian reform. . . . [P]rimarily it hoped to make America the world's great example of a truly Protestant republic." Its aggressive campaigns to combat irreligion and infidelity, to win the West for Protestantism, and to fight a myriad of social problems from dueling to slavery wove Protestantism ever more inextricably into the fabric of Americanism. European visitors to American shores—Alexis de Tocqueville, Harriet Martineau, Frances Trollope—noted the seeming paradox: the absence of state support weakened neither popular religious fervor nor the influence (and even tyranny) that Protestantism wielded over American behavior.[3]

For American Jews in the twenty years before the Civil War, Protestant crusades were generally suspect. Two of those crusades—rigorous Sunday laws and structuring public education as Protestant education—directly challenged the Jews' equality.[4] Besides, the more zealous Americans became about their faith, the less likely they were to countenance nonconformists or those whose presence negated the underlying sameness of a Protestant people. The Know-Nothing movement may have been directed at Catholics, but its implications were clear to any non-Protestant minority. As in the anti-Catholic agitation, Jews saw that public opinion could easily lead to discriminatory legislation. Not long removed from a continent where rights were often rescinded, they feared that their freedoms might be curtailed by affirmative Christian legislation or by Christian interpretations of existing law. Thus, after 1840 the Jewish fight to widen freedom of religion took a more serious turn as a counterreaction to the advances of Protestantism.

Missionary Challenges

The "Equal footing" desired by Phillips applied not only to Jews but also to Judaism. At a time when organized movements to convert the Jews abounded, and respectable Americans as well as missionaries talked of the need to save the Jews from their erring ways, Judaism by definition was less than legitimate. Conversionist efforts stemmed from both specific churches as well as nondenominational agencies. The oldest and most important single missionary organization was the American Society for Meliorating the Condition of the Jews (ASMCJ). Founded in 1820, it boasted a distinguished roster of directors, which for a time included John Quincy Adams. Around 1840 it shifted its focus from European to American Jews. Abandoning its original plan of colonizing new Christians, it concentrated on the recently arrived and poor Jewish immigrants of the cities and towns.[5]

Like other ideological currents that influenced American popular thought about Jews in the nineteenth and twentieth centuries, missionary activity echoed revived efforts at conversion in Europe. Missionary literature, most notably sermons, were imported and reprinted in the United States. One series, entitled *A Course of Lectures on the Jews by Ministers of the Established Church in Glasgow*, was reprinted in Philadelphia in 1840 by the Presbyterian publication board. Reflecting a resurgence of interest in millennialism, it urged commitment to organized programs of proselytism. The Scottish ministers indicated an awareness of Jewish development in the postemancipation period, but that turn of events had lessened neither the need of Jews for Christianity nor that of Christians to bring the blessings of their faith to the still degraded people.[6]

The religious leaders of the young Jewish community were very much alert to the evangelical fervor that characterized important segments of Protestant activity before the Civil War. Isaac Mayer Wise, whose first rabbinical post was in Albany, experienced the "conversionist craze" that he described as more acute than in England or Germany. On one occasion he attended a church meeting called to consider the formation of a missionary organization to work among the Jews. Before the visiting missionary could deliver the address of the evening, Wise rose from his seat, forcefully denounced conversionary tactics, and with the cooperation of the Unitarian minister succeded in having the meeting adjourned.[7]

So strong was the missionary presence that Wise and others saw a would-be proselytizer in every pious church attender. Isaac Leeser said that all Christian sects thought alike on the need "to withdraw the Israelites from their religion, or, where this is impracticable, to weaken their attachment to its behests." He cautioned the readers of the *Occident* to beware especially of snares set for Jewish children by Christian teachers in both public and private schools. A sermon delivered in Charleston in 1841 also warned of gentiles who called Jews their brothers but who, by persuading them in the name of friendship to forsake the Sabbath and dietary laws or to marry non-Jews, made a mockery of Judaism.[8]

The picture of Judaism and the Jews disseminated by the missionaries and by conversionist literature was condescending, humiliating, or downright abusive. Judaism was a dead religion, long superseded by a loving and benevolent Christianity, and no longer relevant to civilization. Those who continued to practice it proved their moral backwardness and their proverbial stiff-neckedness. When a prominent Philadelphian, Warder Cresson, converted to Judaism in the 1840s, his very sanity was challenged in a court trial. Proselytizers agree that Jews must not be converted by force, but conversion was for their own spiritual elevation. For some Christians conversion of the Jews signified a proper atonement for the crime of deicide, for others the fulfillment of a precondition to the Second Coming of the Messiah. Still others were attracted by the social function of conversionary activity which, by offering material aid to the deprived, linked social misfortune with religious errors. The agents of the conversionist societies, often apostate Jews who aggressively took their cause into hospitals, homes, and synagogues, frequently packaged the promise of salvation with gifts or money.[9]

Antebellum Jews could not laugh off conversionist activity even though, as they claimed, the very few captured by the missionaries scarcely justified the budgets of those societies. Since the government never restricted the occupations of non-Christians, Jews did not fear a significant loss of numbers through formal conversion. Rather, the issue was in part one of pride. Jews required no social rehabilitation or outside support, least of all from missionaries. Wise asserted at the Albany meeting: "[W]e ourselves provide for our poor, our widows, and orphans, etc., and rear our children. There are no rowdies, streetwalkers and gamblers among us. We need no help and accept none."[10]

At bottom, however, Jews believed that missionaries menaced their claim to equality. Often the only sources of information about the Jew, missionaries who canvassed outlying settlements around the country for financial support kept alive the anti-Jewish stereotypes. Conversionist arguments implied that emancipation had been a gift by Christians in order to bring about mass conversion rather than a right of the Jews. By misrepresenting and denigrating Judaism, missionaries encouraged intolerance of Jewish beliefs and of Jews. In the latter's opinion, even freedom of speech failed to make *organized* efforts at seducing Jews to Christianity quite fair; Americans ought to recognize, some said, that combinations attempting to interfere with matters of conscience were contrary to the spirit of the country. Such considerations troubled one critic of the ASMCJ, who wrote:

No one will deny that the Jews have as just a claim to protection as the Christians; but if laws are passed authorizing the latter to combine as a body politic to deprive the others of their religion; if there exists a union of men, honourable from their high standing, whose very formation as a society gives countenance to the prevailing calumnies; if such a combination continues to disseminate its pernicious principles: it is impossible that this persecuted people can ever obtain that standing in the community to which their equality in the eyes of the law and their moral worth justly entitle them.[11]

An apt illustration of the easy transference of missionary rhetoric to specific situations involving the equal recognition of Jews was furnished in 1855 by an Episcopal journal, the *Churchman*. At a banquet celebrating the visit to New York City by members of the state legislature, one of the numerous toasts was to "The Clergy—To them we look for sincerity, truth, and admonition." As was the custom, a participant at the banquet responded to each toast, and in this case, to the horror of the *Churchman*, a rabbi was chosen. How was it possible that in "a professedly Christian assembly, in an avowedly Christian city, a Jew — a disbeliever in, a reviler of Christianity" was the respondent? The honor rightfully intended for a Christian clergyman was appropriated by a rabbi "to his own defiant, infidel system." The rabbi, who called for religious fellowship, was secretly mocking Christianity; from the days when Jews persecuted the first Christians, the former never looked upon gentiles as their brethren. But, after all, one could not expect the truth from those who believed that Christianity was a lie.[12]

More ominous in the light of the anti-Semitic charges that would sweep western Europe after 1870 was a report that appeared in a London missionary journal in 1846 and was reprinted in the *Occident*. It talked in fanciful terms of the incredible amount of power grasped by European Jews since their emancipation and the insidious influence they wielded over gentile minds. Armed with extraordinary mental abilities, the Jews strove for education, and, once educated, they worked their way into the control of the European press, their weapon for destroying political foes. Aside from personal aggrandizement, their motives were distinctly anti-Christian; "Judaism is at present walking abroad in Europe . . . propagating Deism." Still worse, the emancipated Jew had neither lost his alien habits nor his prime loyalty to the perpetuation of a Jewish national existence:

We must not, however, imagine that modern Jews are no longer Jews, because they are clamorous after present honours: they do not thereby shake off the sharp lines which distinguish them from other nations, neither can they so easily rid themselves of habits of thought which have been hardened by time, and which seem to be engraven on the Jewish mind. The different sections of Judaism will be found willing, we believe, upon any great national crisis, to unite and cooperate for the advancement of any great political interest; and we see that in spite of the repeated declarations to the contrary, they take the deepest interest in the present state and future prospects of the land of their ancient and traditional glories.[13]

Thus, decades before the rantings of an Edouard Drumont or an Adolf Stoecker, missionaries raised the specter of the powerful, unassimilable Jew who menaced Western society. By cloaking their cause in secularist, political garb, Christian religious figures helped pave the way for the virulent new anti-Semitism.

American Jewish antimissionary literature began in 1820 with a brochure entitled "Israel Vindicated," a series of letters against the newly organized ASMCJ. The latter also sparked the appearance of *The Jew*, the first Jewish periodical in the United States, which combined attacks on the society with a defense of Judaism. When *The*

Jew ceased publication after two years, its successor, Leeser's *Occident,* picked up the antimissionary cudgels.[14]

Years earlier, Leeser had begun an antimissionary campaign in a series of letters to the *Philadelphia Gazette* entitled "The Claims of the Jews to an Equality of Rights." There he defended the moral teachings of Judaism, the trunk of Christianity, and the religious steadfastness of the Jews. He pointed to the virtuous and law-abiding Jewish citizens who could not prove more useful to the state were they to be converted. Don't deprive us of our equality for which we paid the same price as you, he asked of the Christians. Since you have no right over our consciences, "do not attach any odium to the name of Israel." He added:

Liberty precludes the idea of *toleration,* and the majority, no matter how large, have no right to claim any merit . . . for leaving the minority undisturbed in the enjoyment of equal rights; and surely there exists no equitable rule to render odious the opinions and to restrain the actions of an individual or of a body of men, unless their opinions and conduct might become injurious to the public weal. . . . This being the case, we utterly deny the right of our Christian neighbors to bring up our people and our religion as a constant topic of discussion; and what is more, to raise funds to bring about a defection of our members.[15]

In the pages of his journal, Leeser kept a record of conversionist societies in Europe and Palestine as well as in the United States, and he conducted spirited exchanges with the *Jewish Chronicle,* the publication of the ASMCJ. He sought to expose the missionaries on several levels—the theological inaccuracies of their teachings; the "shameless" tactics used with children, poor, and hospital patients; and their unfounded reports of success.[16]

Isaac Mayer Wise, who fought with Leeser over theology, employed the same tactics against the missionaries. The first issue of his weekly, the *Israelite,* launched in 1854, opened with a fictional story (by Wise) entitled "The Convert." The five-part serial, about a young German who had embraced Catholicism in order to advance his professional career, indicted both the anti-Jewish disabilities in Europe and the stagnant religion of the Jewish community. At the end, however, after having ripped apart his family, the convert recognized the shameful politics of religion and admitted the error of his ways. He emigrated to America, where, to the reader's delight, he helped found a synagogue in the Far West.

Having softened his audience to the problems of conversion, Wise plunged almost frenziedly into a running tirade against the "hypocrisy" and "immorality" of missionaries in the United States.

Isaac Mayer Wise
Courtesy of The American
Jewish Historical Society
and The American Jewish Archives

Sigismund Waterman
Courtesy of The American
Jewish Historical Society

Isaac Leeser
Courtesy of The American
Jewish Historical Society

Judah P. Benjamin
Courtesy of The Library of Congress
and The American Jewish
Historical Society

Abe Ruef
Courtesy of The American
Jewish Historical Society

Oscar S. Straus
**Courtesy of The American
Jewish Historical Society**

Max Lilienthal
**Courtesy of The American
Jewish Historical Society**

Alexander Kohut
**Courtesy of The American
Jewish Historical Society**

Rebecca Gratz
Courtesy of The Philadelphia
Jewish Archives Center
and The American Jewish
Historical Society

Emil G. Hirsch
Courtesy of The American
Jewish Historical Society

Jacob Henry Schiff
Courtesy of The American
Jewish Historical Society

He ran a nineteen-part series called "A Peep into the Missionary Efforts," and almost weekly he and other writers reviled the apostates who worked for those societies. Charging them with the misuse of funds and attempts to bribe and ensnare the helpless, the writers urged Americans to recognize the "humbug" of conversionist activity and direct their contributions to worthy charities. The paper's favorite target was the ASMCJ—which it dubbed a "perversion" and "diversion"—and when the latter disbanded in 1855 (temporarily, as it turned out), Wise took credit, albeit misplaced, for its demise.

Wise's attacks drew countercharges from missionary organs, usually repetitions of the old stereotypes of the mercenary, bigoted Jews responsible for the crucifixion of Jesus. Christians also accused Jews of persecuting their coreligionists who inquired into the merits of other religions.[17] For the Jews, the most frustrating aspect of the situation was Christian refusal to acknowledge that "different" could still be "equally legitimate." Tolerate our opinions as you tolerate our bodies, Leeser had cried in 1841. As long as that goal went unrealized, defenders like Leeser and Wise had to resort to apologetics about Jewish moral behavior and to claims about the equal if not superior moral code of Judaism.

Throughout the nineteenth century, communal leaders emphasized the importance of Jewish education as the most effective means of checking the missionaries. The Hebrew Free Schools movement, for example, was begun in 1864 to keep poor Jewish children out of mission schools and within their own religion. Various attempts to establish a Jewish publication society also cited the need to build up Jewish knowledge and thereby shield the ignorant from missionary propaganda.[18]

Even earlier, the establishment of the first Jewish Sunday school in 1838 stemmed in part from antimissionary sentiment. By 1830, its Christian progenitor had assumed an evangelical role; the American Sunday School Union stood alongside the Bible and tract societies actively working to spread a vibrant Protestantism throughout the expanding nation. Leeser, who with Rebecca Gratz planted the seeds of the Jewish school, seized upon that device for countering both the missionaries as well as religious apathy within his community.

No secondary account of the Jewish Sunday school movement alludes to the antimissionary motive, but Leeser's own words attest to its importance. In an article of 1840 he wrote that Jews converted to Christianity for materialistic purposes or out of ignorance. He added:

It is certainly not the interest of Christianity to bribe the interested to an outward profession which their soul does not feel; and as to the ignorant, we pray fervently to the Lord to give them light and knowledge, and there are always among us those whose study it will ever be to diffuse the truth which they have received. In accordance with this plan we have established Sunday-schools within the last two years, for the gratuitous instruction in religion in New York, Philadelphia, and Charleston, and similar ones are proposed for Richmond and St. Thomas.

At the second annual examination of the Philadelphia Sunday school, Leeser closed the ceremony with the following blessing for the "daughters of Israel" who served as the school's unpaid teachers: "[M]ay their reward be a multitude of disciples, . . . armed with the knowledge of truth, that they may be able to withstand the attacks of those who love not Israel, and who would gladly wean them away from the observance of thy precepts." In Leeser's opinion a better answer was the day school, but at least the availability of Jewish classes kept some Jewish children out of Christian Sunday schools and further removed from the zealous missionaries.[19]

Although missionary activity among Jews never ceased, it climbed to new heights with the arrival after 1880 of the large numbers of Russian Jews. The dense urban ghettos attracted church and nondenominational groups as well as free-lancers. They swooped down upon the poverty-stricken and preached salvation from street corners, rented storefronts, and hastily erected schools. In terms of their propaganda and tactics, as well as Jewish defense, the picture replicated that of Leeser's and Wise's generation. Above all, the stigma of inequality continued to rankle within the Jewish community. As the *American Hebrew* explained, to be "singled out for conversion is in itself galling," and for Christians to treat "a whole class of people . . . as if . . . they were total outcasts" only excited prejudice.[20]

Barriers to Religious Equality

Louis Lewisson operated the Clothing Bazaar at 21 South Main Street in Providence, Rhode Island. In 1852 he issued a personal Thanksgiving "Proclamation to the People." On the Wednesday before Thanksgiving he promised holiday gifts for all those who had ever worked for him, and on Thanksgiving morning he would dispense to needy widows the necessaries for a holiday dinner.

"Whoso giveth to the poor, tendeth to the Lord," the proclamation piously affirmed. Lewisson's action—he gave out 1,200 pounds of bread and 500 pounds of meat—was the merchant's way of rebuking the governor of Rhode Island, who had couched his Thanksgiving proclamation in Christological terms. The *Asmonean*, an Anglo-Jewish weekly of New York, applauded Lewisson for his fitting response to "the Pharisee" (i.e., Governor Phillip Allen) for the latter's sectarian message.[21]

Allen was not the only state official before the Civil War whose messages proclaiming Thanksgiving or special days of prayer were pitched to the worshipers of Jesus. In 1841, President John Tyler also appealed to the "Christian people" when he set aside a day to commemorate the death of his predecessor, William Henry Harrison.[22] On the surface only trivial ceremonials, those occasions took on a particualr significance for American Jews. They had participated in Thanksgiving celebrations with their Christian compatriots since the eighteenth century; some synagogues had put together special prayers for marking the holiday.[23] To be excluded from national fasts or feasts involved no tangible economic or political hardship. Rather, it signified that Jews were a class apart from Christians, not yet entitled to celebrate or mourn with the rest of the nation.

Ever sensitive to the odium imposed by those sectarian proclamations, Jewish leaders would note each Thanksgiving those governors who offended them. Frequently, when the matter was raised, the offender apologized for the slight. On several occasions, the Jews of New York "boycotted" Thanksgiving and kept their synagogues closed. The editor of the *Asmonean* taunted the New York governor, who looked for the Jewish vote but forgot his Jewish constituents after election day.[24] In 1856, Rabbi Isaac Mayer Wise, intrepid publisher of Cincinnati's *Israelite*, tongue-lashed Governor Salmon P. Chase of Ohio, a man "who associates in politics with deists, infidels, and even atheists," for a piously worded Christian message that sounded like a papal bull. While any designation of an official Thanksgiving was tantamount to the exercise of an "ecclesiastical prerogative," Wise demanded that in this instance, where the design was sectarian and offensive, it be withdrawn by a second official proclamation. Wise's colleague, Isaac Leeser, speaking for the Jews of Pennsylvania, summed up what Jews throughout the United States believed:

We contend that we are a part of the commonwealth; as much citizens as all others; equal in the eye of the law, being so by the spirit *and* letter of the constitution. We contribute by our taxes and military service to the protection of the State, and hence there can exist no reason *why we should be forgotten* whenever the people of the commonwealth are called on for any service. We ask for no exemptions of the burdens because we are Jews; we recognise not in the Christians the prerogative to support and defend the republic; nor do we recognise in them the right of appropriating to themselves the whole protection of the laws, all the offices, all the immunities of freemen, much less the right of being alone regarded as religious and God-fearing men.[25]

The repeated episodes in the 1840s and 1850s with respect to Thanksgiving indicate how increasingly defensive the Jews had grown in response to the Protestant crusade and to the growing popularity of the concept of a Christian nation. The following case in South Carolina provides a graphic illustration.

Among Jews, South Carolina had an enviable history of liberalism. Although John Locke's constitution for the colony guaranteeing freedom of religion to all inhabitants had not been adopted, four Jews had been naturalized there as early as 1697. Before the Revolution Jews voted in some elections, and one Jew, Francis Salvador, was elected to serve in the provincial congress of 1774. Close relations obtained between Jew and non-Jew, and Charleston sympathized when its Jews protested the infamous Damascus libel in 1840. A year later, at the dedication of the Beth Elohim synagogue, Rabbi Gustav Poznanski may have indulged in hyperbole, but Charleston's Jews would probably have said amen to his oft-quoted statement: "This synagogue is our *temple*, this city our *Jerusalem*, this happy land our *Palestine*."[26]

No wonder, then, that in 1844, when Governor James Hammond called on South Carolinians of all denominations to observe Thanksgiving by uniting in special prayers "to God their Creator, and his Son Jesus Christ, the Redeemer of the world," the blow was particularly odious. Since Hammond ignored private and public letters challenging the injustice, the two Jewish synagogues of Charleston joined in passive resistance. Thanksgiving came and went unobserved by the Jewish community.

Subsequently, one hundred Jews of Charleston dispatched a lengthy letter to the governor in which they stressed their fealty to their "ancient and holy religion" and challenged his proclamation on the grounds that it was "offensive," "arbitrary," and in conflict with the guarantee of religious freedom in South Carolina's constitution. Hammond's reply was worse than his original declaration. He had not intended to insult anybody, he said, but he had no apology to offer. "I know that the civilization of the age is derived from Christianity, that the institutions of this country are instinct with the same spirit, and that it pervades the laws of the State as it does the manners and I trust the hearts of our people." Hammond turned the attack upon the Jews, who, "inheriting the same scorn for Jesus Christ which instigated their ancestors to crucify him, . . . would have felt themselves degraded and disgraced in obeying my exhortation." The Jews would only have been satisfied if he, Hammond, had struck out "the cornerstone of the Christian creed" and called upon "a Christian People to worship after the manner of the Jews." The Jews published a report on the governor's letter in the newspapers of Charleston and Columbia. Deploring Hammond's reference to the crucifixion of Jesus as an attempt to incite anti-Jewish prejudice, they asked their fellow citizens to remember the aid lent by Jews to the churches. They also warned that if principles like Hammond's were permitted to flourish, no group was ever safe from possible discrimination.[27]

Only a very broad interpretation of religious freedom could serve to protect Jewish equality. Narrowly defined, liberty of conscience, the right of the individual to believe or not believe as he saw fit, was inadequate even for Jewish religious needs. A Jew who wanted to practice his Judaism depended on a group, which in turn depended on the right to organize a congregation, conduct public services, purchase burial grounds. Thus, an early law of Washington, D.C., that permitted the incorporation only of Christian religious societies constrained the religious rights of the Jewish group,[28] but technically it did not deny freedom of conscience to Jews as individuals in the nation's capital.

Nor did state or federal constitutional guarantees respecting liberty of conscience preclude the imposition of disabilities or hardships upon Jews. Some early state constitutions, like that of Pennsylvania which irritated Jonas Phillips and his circle, upheld the inviolability of religious freedom at the same time that they limited certain political privileges to professing Christians.[29] Restrictions on officeholding and Sunday laws may have narrowed Jewish political and economic opportunities, but, like the recognition of Christianity in executive proclamations or in treaties negotiated by the United States with foreign powers, they did not compel the Jew to alter his private mode of worship. Indeed, what one's actual beliefs were mattered little. For example, nonobservant Jews were barred along with their more devout brethren from holding office, if the state constitution limited that right to Christians. The real issue was Christian versus non-Christian. If Christians were singled out in proclamations, or if only Christians were appointed to the chaplaincy, or if Christianity were taught in the classroom, one had to be Christian, at least nominally, to enjoy the benefits. Those who practiced another or no religion were equally slighted.

To offset Christianity's advantages under law, nineteenth-century Jews invoked the concept of freedom of religion but gave it a broader meaning. What they were really talking about was religious *equality;* what they worked desperately to ward off was the stigma of second-class citizenship. Jews wanted recognition of their rootedness in the United States and of their right to share equally in the favors extended by law. They sought an atmosphere conducive to their survival as a group, where individuals would not to be tempted to drop out because of legal hardships or official rebuffs. In an era when the term *Christian state*, then popular in Europe, reverberated in the message of an aggressive American Protestantism, their efforts were uphill at best.

The struggle to lift the barriers against officeholding in North Carolina illustrated the almost automatic fusion of religious liberty with equality by Jewish defenders. The state's constitution of 1776 forbade civil office to all persons "who shall deny the being of God or the truth of the Protestant religion or the Divine Authority, either of the Old or New Testament, or who shall hold religious principles incompatible with the freedom and safety of the State." Colonial Dissenters who had successfully fought the Anglican establishment thus entrenched their own prejudices in fundamental law.

Despite the constitutional provision, Catholics and Jews were elected to the legislature, but in 1809 an enemy of Jacob Henry, a Jewish member of the lower house, demanded that Henry vacate his seat. Henry, whose family had been in the state since the eighteenth century, formally responded in an address to the legislature. Building his case on the provision in North Carolina's Declaration of Rights that guaranteed "that all men have a natural and inalienable right to worship Almighty God according to the dictates of their own consciences," Henry contended that no subsequent constitutional provision or state law could undo that fundamental right. He thereby equated discrimination on officeholding with the abridgment of religious liberty. His lengthy defense of religious freedom impressed his audience as well as men outside the state; his arguments were later invoked in the Maryland debates on the very same issue. Although Henry was permitted to retain his seat, the objectionable constitutional clause remained.

When the state constitution was revised in 1835, liberals, with the Jews in mind, tried to amend the clause, but their labors resulted only in the full emancipation of Catholics. At that time, a North Carolina newspaper picked up Henry's argument that the "odious" restriction impinged on liberty of conscience. Jewish spokesmen pursued the same idea as the fight dragged on. In 1859 the *Occident* wrote that *"perfect freedom and equality are inherent to every man"* and that "no one has any claim to investigate, as a test for office, what any man thinks." A committee of the legislature agreed that religious liberty was at stake but opposed legislative amendment of the state constitution. Seven years later the Board of Delegates of American Israelites addressed a memorial to "the friends of Religious Liberty in the State of North Carolina" in which it called the restriction against Jews a denial of religious liberty and civil equality.

Both the *Occident* and the board insisted that they were arguing not for political office but for the principle involved. The fact that so few Jews lived in North Carolina doubtless weakened their efforts. A handful in Wilmington petitioned the legislature for a redress of grievances, and a small group in Charlotte pointedly asked candidates before the 1860 election whether they would support a constitutional change. Not until the state constitutional convention of 1868, however, was the right to hold office granted to the Jews.[30]

The Jewish pioneers for religious equality generally asked for government neutrality on matters of religion—a stand that grew out of European emancipationist thought but that fell short of the twentieth-century purist interpretation of the separation between church and state. Although they spouted the rhetoric of separationism, and even cited Jefferson's famous letter on the wall of separation, Jews usually meant a neutral-to-all-religions rather than a divorced-from-religion state. Indeed, the latter concept, which in the climate of the nineteenth century was tantamount to an antireligion stance, was as abhorrent to Jews as it was to most Americans. Rabbis, long the most influential leaders of the community, taught that religion was a vital component of the good life and, like Christian clergymen, inveighed against the inroads of secularization. Louis Marshall, the national spokesman of American Jews on the eve of World War I, found nothing intrinsically offensive about Bible reading in the public schools, so long as it did not become sectarian.[31] Prudence also dictated an accommodationist position to the rules of the American game, for any efforts on behalf of complete separationism might have evoked a severe backlash.

A neutral government in matters of religion was considered the most satisfactory alternative. Asking for positive recognition of Judaism—e.g., the right of Jewish schools to share in state appropriations for religious education—was tried but was unrealistic so long as Jews constituted so small a fraction of the population. Another possibility was to secure exemptions for Jews from religious requirements—just as Parliament in 1740 had waived the requirement of a Christian oath for Jews in the colonies who applied for naturalization. Exemption technically condoned both the government's right to translate Christian forms into law as well as to distinguish between Christian and non-Christian. Nevertheless, in the case of Sunday laws, Jews generally refrained from opposition once exemption for Sabbath observers was secured.[32]

Early Jewish spokesmen who argued on behalf of religious equality elaborated on the natural-rights philosophy that suffused the ideals of the Constitution and the Founding Fathers. "It matters not . . . ," Rabbi Isaac Leeser wrote, "whether the majority be Christian or Jewish; the constitution knows nothing of either; and . . . in the fundamental charter of the United States, neither Christianity nor Judaism is mentioned by name. Consequently, neither can be said to govern the land. . . . [B]oth Jews and Christians . . . were placed upon such an equality that a preference was given to neither. . . . Let no one believe that such men as Franklin and Madison were ignorant of what they were doing."[33] However, when the Jews dealt with disabilities imposed by states or municipalities, such pleas were irrelevant. The First Amendment of the Bill of Rights only prohibited *Congress* from tampering with religious freedom or from establishing religion. Indeed, the establishment clause was inserted at the insistence of the states eager to insulate their own established churches from congressional interference. In 1845, the Supreme Court ruled that the Constitution left the protection of religious liberties exclusively to the states and imposed no "inhibition" on state conduct respecting religion. Supreme Court Justice Joseph Story even doubted whether the spirit of religious equality underlay the Constitution: "Probably at the time of the adoption of the Constitution, . . . the general if not the universal sentiment in America was, that Christianity ought to receive encouragement from the state so far as was not incompatible with the private rights of conscience." [34]

Nineteenth-century Jews built up their case on other grounds as well. Freqently they argued the respectability of Judaism, a religion which, they reminded their compatriots, was the trunk of Christianity. Their point was that Judaism was neither outlandish nor menacing, but rather a faith suited in values and temperament to the mood of America. If their religion warranted equal treatment on its own merits, how much more so were they, loyal patriots, entitled to religious equality? By their military service in particular—antebellum Jews mentioned the Revolution, the War of 1812 and the Mexican War, and the next generation added the Civil and Spanish-American wars—the Jews had sealed a compact with the United States with their blood. In Riesser's words, they had been "consecrated" as American nationals, and the country owed them no less than equal status.

Like their successors in the twentieth century, workers in the cause of Jewish equality generally favored publicity as their most effective weapon. In the decades before national agencies like the American Jewish Committee and the Anti-Defamation League, the Anglo-Jewish periodicals served as the forum for communal defense. Their editorials reflected the concerns of the Jewish readers, who in turn were urged by the editors to circulate the periodicals among their Christian neighbors. Particularly gratified by unsolicited support, the journals also publicized writings or speeches by Christians that dovetailed with their own arguments. Education of the out-group was the aim—education about the meaning of Judaism and the character and the interests of the Jews. They believed in the efficacy of rational arguments, and they hoped that an appeal to reason, combined with what they liked to call the inherent goodwill of Americans, would bring about the desired results.[35]

With refinements in emphasis as well as in sophistication and polish, the rationalist accommodationist approach of nineteenth-century American Jewry charted the behavior for generations to follow. Perhaps in no other area has American Jewry been so consistently alert to its needs. Eternal vigilance as the price of liberty—an admittedly tired and overworked phrase—truly applied here. No episode touching on religion under law was too trivial to be ignored, and vigilance in turn made the Jewish minority both active conservators of American ideals and innovators in widening the benefits of religious freedom.

The Jews of South Carolina and Governor Hammond had alluded to the Sunday-law question in their interchange over the governor's Thanksgiving proclamation. Both correctly recognized the two issues as symptoms of the wider movement to gain official recognition of Christianity in American law. Antebellum Jews especially feared the potency of the "entering wedge." If any legal mark or favor, no matter how innocuous in itself, were bestowed on Christianity or any Christian sect, further inroads in the name of religion—compulsory church attendance or even involuntary baptism—might follow. Such measures in turn would utterly destroy the basic liberty of Jews or even of less favored, weaker Christian sects.[36]

Fortunately for the numerically small and divided Jewish community, a sufficient number of American Protestants out of a distaste for clericalism, a fear of one established church, or a fealty to the principles of liberty and equality resisted the extremist manifestations of religious zealotry. Jews found encouragement in statements like that of Congressman Richard Johnson, who reported in 1830 to the House of Representatives against petitions to halt the transportation of mail on Sundays. Agreeing with the Jews who defined democracy as more than majoritarianism, Johnson stated: "The constitution regards the conscience of the Jew as sacred as that of the Christian, and gives no more authority to adopt a measure affecting the conscience of a solitary individual than that of a whole community."[37]

Less well known but equally in tune with the Jewish cause was the work of William S. Plumer, a Presbyterian minister in Virginia. In 1846 Plumer wrote a pamphlet entitled "The Substance of an Argument Against the Indiscriminate Incorporation of Churches and Religious Societies." Responding to a petition introduced into the Virginia House of Delegates for legislative aid to Christian sects, Plumer attempted to show the dangers of the proposed aid. Even if it could be tackled practically, state aid to all Christian sects—and Plumer calculated about twenty of them in Virginia—still discriminated against the Jews, atheists, and "the great mass of men indifferent to all forms of religion." Certainly aid to merely a few denominations would breed divisiveness among the citizens and would favor the strong sects over the weak. Plumer did not believe that all religions were equal; nor did he sound particularly enamored of the Jews, whom he numbered outside the stream of Christendom along with Fourierites, infidels, atheists, and "Nothingarians." But "[h]owever evil the practice and corrupt the doctrines of many in the state, they are yet citizens, . . . entitled to every blessing or privilege which legislation can confer, in common with the most orthodox and pious."

For the *Occident*, which reprinted part of the pamphlet, Plumer's views were perfectly adequate. A greater show of respect for Judaism would have been more gratifying, but the immediate

need was to prevent a legally recognized Christian state. With freedom and equality at stake, Jews had no choice but to resist the
multiple forms that the religious crusade took. "We are slaves,"
exclaimed Rabbi Wise, "if we . . . allow priest-ridden demagogues to
deprive us of our rights as citizens and free men."[38] Jewish spokesmen like Wise criticized the fanaticism of other social causes in
which Protestant clerics actively participated. But whereas Jews
had the option to stay out of abolition and temperance movements,
they could not escape the actual workings of the Sunday laws.[39]

Legislation compelling the observance of Sunday as the day of
rest had existed in the United States since colonial times. In the
nineteenth century, Protestant reformers generated a revival of municipal and state attempts to clamp down on commerce and labor
performed on the first day of the week. "The moralists," one historian of religion has written, "felt that American virtue depended
upon observance of the Lord's Day not merely as a day of rest but as
a day of worship, on which work and amusements should be prohibited." Between 1845 and 1855 more court cases dealt with the
impact of Sunday laws upon Sabbatarians than in any ten-year
period before the Civil War.[40] As litigants or concerned spectators,
American Jews made opposition to Sunday laws a prime and lasting
interest to their community.

In 1845 the Jews of Richmond, a community made up largely of
merchants and shopkeepers, petitioned for the repeal of a municipal ordinance that increased the penalties imposed by state law on
violators of the Christian Sabbath. Although the purpose of the
ordinance was to inhibit the movement of slaves and free Negroes,
the restrictions fell on those who kept their shops open and traf-
ficked with the blacks. The Jews, however, treated the issue in
broader terms. They denied that the forced observance of Sunday,
unlike "compulsory honesty" or "the abstinence from homicide and
incest," could be justified on the grounds of public morality or
peace. The swelling tide for stricter Sunday observance was solely a
religious manifestation—hadn't the Christians appropriated the
very term *Sabbath* in an attempt to prove that Sunday was the
biblically ordained day of rest?—and the civil authorities, therefore, had no right to become involved. To compel the keeping of
Sunday, the Jews warned, would constitute a precedent that could
lead to more onerous religious requirements.

As for themselves, the Jews said, the ordinance violated their
constitutional rights as citizens of Virginia, their right to the pursuit
of happiness, and, most of all, the principle of equality under the
law. They insisted that numbers should make no difference—if Jews

and Seventh-Day Baptists ever constituted a majority of the community, their imposition of their own day of rest would be just as wrong. Discounting the importance of economic interests in prompting their action, the petitioners emphasized their concern about the threat of sectarianism, which was undermining America's image as the haven of the oppressed:

Your petitioners see with sorrow the manifestation of the sectarian spirit, which deems it paramount to bring every one to its own mode of thinking. The American United States are the bulwark of liberty, whither the oppressed of all parties have for many years been enabled to come, to be secure against the wiles and tyranny of political and religious oppression. They see, however, with deep regret, that a new spirit is abroad: that the rulers of Churches, and their adherents, are not satisfied with the equal portion of liberty which is theirs in common with all other citizens, but must invoke the aid of civil power to enable them to propagate their doctrines and practices. They feel that this is but the beginning of a revolution backwards, to abridge the rights of individuals, which have been opened as wide as the gates of mercy, by the sages of the Revolution.

The petition devoted several paragraphs to extolling the civic virtues, noble character, and steadfast loyalty of Richmond's Jews—qualities derived, it said, from the Jewish religion. Invoking the contract between the United States and its faithful Jews, the petition recalled that when the *Chesapeake* was attacked by a British warship in 1807, the Jews of Richmond hastened to take up arms: "They felt themselves blessed that their limbs were free and their hands unshackled to serve the country which looked upon them as children, dear alike with all other persuasions."

The Richmond episode directed the attention of the Anglo-Jewish journal, the *Occident,* to the Sunday-law issue. The *Occident's* editor, Rabbi Isaac Leeser of Philadelphia, had lived in Richmond for four years after his arrival in the United States from Germany. Between 1843, when he began publication of the *Occident,* and 1849 Leeser's monthly was the only Anglo-Jewish periodical in existence, the one voice that could speak for the far-flung Jewish communities. Leeser believed that it was the duty of an independent press to remonstrate against injustice, and even after his first serious competitors appeared, the *Asmonean* in 1849 and the *Israelite* in 1854, he continued to use the *Occident* in defense of American Jewish interests. In the Richmond matter this first national spokesman of American Jews agreed with the petitioners that the Sunday ordinance violated freedom of conscience and "the spirit of the original federal compact, and the state constitutions which declare universal equality." He, too, asserted that Sunday laws could not be justified by calling them police regulations; if the purpose was other than to underscore the religious sanctity of the day, why not Wednesday as the day of rest? Leeser blamed the Sunday movement on clergymen of different denominations who were able to influence an otherwise passive or indifferent majority.[41]

The Richmond ordinance was shortly repealed,[42] but while the matter was pending, a Jew in Charleston, Solomon Benjamin, was charged with having violated an ordinance of that city by selling a pair of gloves on Sunday. The heart of Benjamin's defense was that the ordinance conflicted with South Carolina's constitution, which provided for the "free exercise and enjoyment of religious profession and worship, without discrimination or preference." The city magistrate who first heard the case decided for Benjamin, but the state court on appeal reversed the magistrate's decision.

It was Judge John O'Neale's reasoning more than the verdict that troubled the Jews. He posited that the Christian religion was part of the common law of South Carolina just as Christianity, and not Judaism, was the source of all morality. In fact, the very clause in South Carolina's constitution safeguarding freedom of religion was the product of Christian love. According to O'Neale, that clause guaranteed freedom of worship to all believers and non-believers without distinction, but the no-preference phrase applied only to matters of individual conscience. Since a Sunday law did not compel a Jew to desecrate his own Sabbath, it did not impinge upon his freedom of conscience. To argue, as Benjamin's counsel had, that the Bible enjoined the Jew to work six days and that two days of abstinence from labor violated his religious principles was an unwarranted interpretation of the biblical commandment.[43] O'Neale, who openly divorced himself from Jeffersonian principles, secured his opinion on nonreligious grounds, too. A Sunday law, he said, was a police regulation and nothing more. It compelled the Jew like all others to desist from business; that his religion made him observe another day was the consequence of that religion and not the law.

When the *Occident* printed O'Neale's decision, it evoked a protest from readers who denounced the judge's narrow interpretation of the religious-freedom clause and his view that Christianity was part of the common law. Especially galling was his condescension to Jews—his implication that their religion was tolerated by favor and not by right, and his rejection of Judaism as the source of morality. One angry letter stated:

I call upon Judge O'Neal [sic] to point out one moral precept in the Christian's New Testament, which is not found in the Bible of the Jew. Take from the Christian *our* moral law, *our* standard of morals, and he will, indeed, be enveloped in thick darkness.

Another reader commented that O'Neale's decision indicated how far the spirit of toleration had regressed since the revolutionary period.

Although the judge later disclaimed any intention of snubbing the Old Testament, his opinion prompted a "J. V." of South Carolina to write a series of articles denying that Christianity was the true source of morality. Only the newspaper owned and edited by a Jew, Mordecai Manuel Noah, the politician-editor-dramatist who was very much involved in Jewish affairs, accepted the verdict more calmly. Agreeing that the Sunday law was a police regulation, an editorial stated that Jews would behave the same way if they had their own state.[44]

The *Benjamin* decision further beclouded the question of whether the Sunday laws were valid because they reflected accepted Christian usage or because they were legitimate expressions of the police power. From the Jewish point of view the laws were more vulnerable if they were openly recognized as laws imposing religious norms. To challenge their constitutionality on the grounds that they violated the principles of freedom of religion and civil dissociation from religious matters was a stronger position than to contest the legitimacy of police powers regulating personal behavior in the interest of public welfare. If courts could be brought to admit that Sunday laws prompted by religious motives were invalid, Jewish claims to religious equality would win out. Thus, Jews emphasized the issue of religious freedom and made short shrift of the police-power argument. Nevertheless, that posture, too, had its pitfalls, for it placed the Jews in opposition to the legitimate powers of the states and municipalities as well as to those interests which might benefit from a specific police regulation. Leeser, for example, did not want to create the impression that he, a prominent rabbi and spokesman for the Jews, opposed a compulsory day of rest for labor. He argued rather that it be left to the laborer to choose which day he desired or whether he desired any prescribed rest at all. Civil power, he said, could treat Sunday no differently from political holidays, when labor was suspended but no penalties were imposed for nonobservance.[45]

Barely had the flurry aroused by the O'Neale decision subsided when the issue blazed forth again in the Pennsylvania case of *Specht v. Commonwealth*. Specht was a Seventh-Day Baptist, but since the issues were the same and since the court referred to Jews in its decision, the *Occident* gave the case its close attention. Like the South Carolina decision, the court defined Pennsylvania's guarantee of religious freedom in narrow terms. It meant freedom of conscience to all persons, even infidels, but no more. "[B]eyond this, conscientious doctrines and practices can claim no immunity from the operation of general laws made by the government . . . to promote the welfare of the whole people." The state's Sunday law may have stemmed from religious belief, and indeed Pennsylvanians were a Christian people, but the law was in fact a civil (or police) regulation. It never commanded the performance of certain religious rites nor demanded that Jews or other Sabbatarians desecrate their own Sabbath. Abstinence from labor was not a restraint of conscience; as for the state constitutional clause that stipulated "no preference," the law did not confer a superior religious status on observers.

Again, since Sunday laws were thus justified by both Christian usage and police power, Jews lost out on both levels. Not only were Jews subjected to pecuniary loss and inconvenience if they kept their own Sabbath, but as non-Christians their claim to equality was weakened. In two editorials entitled "Political Inequality," Leeser lashed out against the *Specht* decision. He reiterated his earlier assertion that a Sunday law was not a proper use of police power. More important, the law was actually intended to be a religious regulation—the very words "Lord's day" and "profaning" which appeared in the text proved that the legislators meant to enforce their own religious practices and preferences on the community. Dissidents lost their inalienable right to labor and, if punished for nonobservance, were stigmatized in the public's eye. Thus, the law was both an offense to their religious conscience and an invasion of their constitutional rights. Since, Leeser continued, constitutional rights rested on the equality of all members of the community, freedom of religion was not achieved without equality of religions.

Like the Richmond petitioners of 1845, Leeser assumed a virtual contract between America and the Jews guaranteeing the latter's equality. Jews had fought for America's independence, and thereby they had "purchased the *right* of being equal and free." Moreover, when the Constitutional Convention of 1787 had adopted the clause forbidding religious tests for officeholding, "religious equality was at once established as the fundamental law of the land."[46] Leeser's claim was exaggerated, but like Jonas Phillips before him, his point reflected another characteristic of American Jewish behavior. Jews tended early on to invoke the spirit, if not the authority, of the federal government in their struggles with the state governments. Years later but in a similar manner Jews would defend federally imposed standards on civil rights.

An inviolable and unqualified equality continued to be Leeser's main goal in the decade immediately preceding the Civil War. Although like other Jews he had minimized economic interests before the need to erase laws that stigmatized Jews as inferior, he claimed that Sunday laws also denied Jews their equal economic opportunity. "If it requires the labor of all other citizens during six days to maintain their families respectably, why should [Jews] be restricted to do it in *five*?" He mentioned still another facet of equality, the right of Jews to equal protection in their own Sabbath observance. Two earlier court decisions had ruled that the Jewish Sabbath could neither excuse a witness from testifying nor prevent a trial from taking place. But if equality were consistent, Jews could demand such "Saturday" laws. "Why claim that [a Christian] conscience should be more guarded than ours? . . . Who protects our faith and its practices?" In point of fact Leeser was less concerned about the recognition of Judaism than the need to limit the recognition of Christianity. Since Sunday observance was protected by public opinion, a potent force that caused Jews to violate their own Sabbath rather than risk ill will by working on Sunday, Sunday laws were really superfluous.[47]

Reality forced Jews like Leeser to compromise their goals. They urged the repeal of Sunday laws but appeared ready to settle for removal of the penalties on Sabbath observers. When the Virginia legislature in 1849 amended the state Sunday law and provided for such exemptions, the *Occident* hailed the "enlightened" legislation. Ignoring the fact that exemption breached the desired wall between church and state, it also reported enthusiastically about an Ohio court opinion that freed Jews from Sunday-law penalties. The prime issue was to compel the admission that Jews were equal to Christians and not liable to legal disabilities because they were Jews. "To our mind," wrote the *Occident*, "it would be perfectly in spirit with a republican equality either to repeal the penalties which operate against Sabbatarians, or for the courts to rule their unconstitutionality."[48]

A Sunday case of 1858 pushed the *Occident* into interpreting in broader terms the separation of church and state. Even though Ohio law exempted those who observed the Sabbath, a Jewish ice dealer in Cincinnati was fined for working on Sunday because his sons carried on his business on Saturday. We don't need civil judges to vindicate our religion, averred the *Occident*. Much as we cherish

Sabbath observance, we cannot permit any outside party, ignorant of Jewish law, to decide what constitutes an infraction of the Sabbath. Shifting its ground, the *Occident* now stated:

[W]e maintain that it is no one's business, in a political point of view, whether we Israelites keep Sabbath or not; for the enforcement of Sunday laws is an infringement on natural right, and could only have been engrafted on the statutes out of a non-comprehension of the business of a republican government, which should abstain from interfering, in every possible manner, with the religious obligations of the people subject to its rule.[49]

The exemptions for conscientious Sabbath observers provided by some Sunday laws would ultimately be outdated by the ever-swelling number of nonobservant Jews. Even before the Civil War, the *Asmonean* wrote that it could not honestly support exemptions, since Jews violated their own day of rest. The *Occident* on the other hand charged the Sunday laws with encouraging Jewish nonobservance. While it scolded Jews who blamed their laxity on Sunday laws, it called the laws a bribe to get Jews to forgo their religion. It is interesting that only the Reform journal the *Israelite* refused to admit, at least for the purposes of the argument, that American Jews were guilty of transgressing their Sabbath.[50]

The Sunday-law issue before the Civil War was one on which most Jews put limits to accommodation. Like the Jews of Richmond, they would be willing to labor "unobtrusively and within doors" and to respect the right of their Christian employees to abstain from work,[51] but most refused to accept passively the less-than-equal status that Sunday laws foisted upon them. Their community was too young and inexperienced to mount a defense campaign of more than newspaper articles and editorials. But even those pioneer efforts showed that the Jews were building their case on strong grounds. They, the minority, were living up to their contract with the United States. Their opponents—those who supported religious legislation like Sunday laws—were trampling upon civil and human rights and hence were false to the spirit and faith of the nation.

The numerous denominations and sects making up Christian America in 1850 included groups, like the Jews, that opposed different facets of the Protestant crusade. Quakers and Seventh-Day Baptists, for example, attacked the Sunday laws. Catholics, with 1,112 churches at mid-century, were particularly vocal in resisting Protestantization of the public schools. Some of the denominations could also look back on a stormy history of persecution in colonial America. Protestant dissenters and Catholics had often faced special economic burdens, disenfranchisement, or banishment. Jacob Lumbrozo, the Jewish physician in seventeenth-century Maryland who escaped death on the charge of blasphemy (lodged despite the colony's so-called Toleration Act), was luckier than the Quakers who were executed around the same time in Massachusetts Bay.[52] It would seem, therefore, that Jews could find willing allies in the fight for religious equality among churched as well as unchurched Americans.

In the matter of Sunday laws Jews noted the opposition of Quakers and Seventh-Day Baptists. As has been pointed out, Jews carefully followed the *Specht* case even though it involved them only peripherally. However, they never entertained the idea of creating a common front with fellow settlers or sympathizers. Inexperience with defense tactics was the obvious explanation. But even if they had considered it, they may have calculated that those dissenting on the Sunday issue were still Christians, concerned about the specific legislation but less likely to be troubled about the laws as symbols of a Christian state.

Outside the pale of Christendom, Jews were frequently stigmatized for the unsavory company with which they were classified. Governor Hammond had linked them in the Thanksgiving episode with atheists, deists, Mormons, and Mohammedans (an updated version of the old Anglican formula of Jews, Turks, heretics, and infidels). Judge O'Neale's Sunday-law opinion had contrasted Christianity with pagan morality. The judge had also recalled an earlier case in which Jew and atheist were codefendants, and by implication he equated Jew with infidel.[53] In that climate of opinion Jews may well have believed that an alliance with unpopular minorities could be counterproductive, or that no self-respecting Christian would willingly find common cause with "the seed of Abraham." For their part, Jews were too new to emancipation to have divested themselves of anti-Christian suspicions. They had ample historical proof from which to deduce that anti-Semitism was endemic to all forms of Christianity.

While the Jews independently combated legal disabilities, a new wave of intolerance was gathering momentum. The same Protestant zeal sparking the agitation for Sunday laws and a legally recognized Christian state spilled over into nativist drives against the immigrant and the Catholic. Unleashed bigots were swept along in a wave of hysteria punctuated by riots, church burnings, and exposés of lurid

Catholic "plots." The movement culminated in the Know-Nothing party of the 1850s that worked to bar Catholics and the foreign-born from the equal enjoyment of civil rights.[54]

Although Jews were not the prime targets, they, too, suffered nativist and Know-Nothing attacks. One scholarly account has claimed that anti-Jewish prejudice was neither a consistent nor a uniform pattern among the Know-Nothings, and that it was matched by similar sentiments among the political opponents of the nativists. Customary prejudice aside, however, the Democrats, un-like the Know-Nothings, never boasted a constitution or party plat-form that discriminated against non-Protestants and the foreign-born or that called for the legal recognition of Christianity as "an element of our political system."[55] Moreover, American Jew-ish spokesmen, quick to respond to popular slurs as well as to legal discrimination, never reacted so noisily to any individual's insult as they did to the Know-Nothing outburst by William Stow against the Jews.

In 1855, during a debate in California's state legislature on a bill to forbid trading on Sundays, Speaker William Stow, who was repor-tedly seeking the Know-Nothing nomination for governor, vulgarly attacked the Jews. According to the report in the *Sacramento Dem-ocratic State Journal*:

The Speaker was in favor of the bill and had no sympathy with the Jews, who ought to respect the laws and opinions of the majority. They were a class of people who only came here to make money and leave as soon as they had effected their object. They did not invest their money in the country or cities. They all intended or hoped to settle in their "New Jerusalem." He was in favor of inflicting such a tax upon them as would act as a prohibition to their residence amongst us.

Stow's accusations, the stock-in-trade of anti-Semitic imagery for centuries, were aired and rebutted in the Anglo-Jewish periodicals and by Jews in California. Since the immediate need was to defend the Jews against Stow's charges of economic parasitism and dis-loyalty, and since the secondary purpose was to counter the Sunday agitators, the Know-Nothing question was largely eclipsed. Only the *Asmonean* of New York used the occasion to step up its cam-paign for the repudiation of the nativist party by Jewish voters.[56]

A minority of Jews thought differently about the Know-Nothings. Bitter memories of persecutions by Catholics ran deep—Crusaders' excesses, yellow badge, Inquisition, and autos-da-fé. Liberal anticlericalism also rubbed off on some who experienced at close range the European revolutions of 1830 and 1848 and who, like Max Lilienthal, Reform rabbi and contributor to Wise's *Israelite*, held the Catholics reponsible for provoking the Know-Nothing agitation.[57] Doubtless for some insecure souls, support of the anti-Catholics, who, incidentally, gladly accepted Jewish votes and even some Jewish participation in their ranks, constituted incontrovertible proof of unalloyed Americanism.

A well-known politician of the day who championed nativism was Lewis C. Levin, a Jew by extraction but not affiliation. He had left his native Charleston at the age of sixteen and moved around various states until he settled in Philadelphia in 1839. His biographer described him as a demagogue, an inveterate agitator unstable and alienated from his surroundings, a crusader at different times for the causes of antidueling, temperance, and, above all, nativism. In addition: "He seems to have tried to escape from his religious past. Though there is no evidence that he ever religiously affiliated himself with any of its sects, he became an advocate of Protestantism." Aping the extremist clerics who fused moralistic interests with narrow Americanism, Levin used his privately owned newspaper and then a six-year stint in Congress to spew forth his venom against Catholics and foreigners. His activities ranged from charges of papal conspiracy to actual incitement of popular hysteria. Levin's public career burned out in 1850 when he lost his seat in Congress. He died in 1860 after several years in hospitals for the insane.[58]

As a Jewish nativist propagandist, Levin was the notable exception. Neither he nor most Jews who sympathized with the nativists could claim any position of leadership within the Jewish community. In the 1850s the editors of the Anglo-Jewish press as well as prominent rabbinical and lay figures stood squarely against the Know-Nothings and nativism. Outspoken in their denunciation of injecting religion into politics, they cogently reasoned that the abridgment of any religious minority's rights put their own rights in jeopardy. But they stopped short of suggesting any cooperative venture with the victims of the persecution. Seventy-five years later, when Louis Marshall entered the famous *amicus curiae* brief for the American Jewish Committee on behalf of state toleration of Catholic schools, the Jewish community signaled that it had broadened its active defense of religious equality to include non-Jews. Until then Jews generally followed the crude rule of thumb formulated by Leeser's *Occident:* "We should neither be anti-catholic nor anti-protestant; but the moment that either of these factions endeavors to make headway in the state, that moment it is made our duty to become its opponents."[59]

Religion in the Public Schools

"Our sires came from the lowly condition of the . . . Judengassen of the Old World," Rabbi Henry Berkowitz of Kansas City said in 1889. But, he continued: "They sent us to the public schools, and there we found realized the great ideal truth of the absolute equality of rights and the brotherhood of all men." The public school was the great equalizer, "commingling . . . the children of the rich and poor, the high and low, putting the Teuton and the Celt, the Aryan and Semitic, the believer and the unbeliever on the same footing, a free race and no favors, merit alone to win."

By the time of Berkowitz's address, American Jews had embarked on their passionate love affair with public schooling. Their Enlightenment heritage had led them to believe that secular education shaping young impressionable minds was the surest way for society to capture the humanistic absolute truths of which the philosophers spoke. As the clouds of ignorance lifted, irrational prejudice, like that directed against the Jew, would also vanish. A common school system hastened Americanization and fostered good citizenship. Jewish participation would prove the patriotism of that minority and their desire for full integration. The opposite, a society of competing denominational schools, would disrupt national harmony. The small numbers of Jews, caught between rival contenders for power within the state, were sure to suffer as they had in European religious conflicts. In public schools even the erstwhile ghetto Jew could perform more than creditably. He might not be able to compete with the Americans on the farms or in the mines, but his traditional reverence for learning well equipped him to show his proficiency and his values in the educational arena. If merit determined success, the Jew confidently believed that it lay within his grasp. Above all, however—and Berkowitz articulated what most affirmed—public schools held out the promise of true equality, equality and not mere toleration, equality before the law and, just as important, equality in social attitudes and usages.[60]

The case for equality through state-supported schools rested on the condition that the schools be nonsectarian. From men like Gabriel Riesser and Moses Mendelssohn, Jews had learned that full emancipation required the separation of church and state in civil affairs. Since Jews always believed that the hatred they encountered sprang from religious hostility, separation was axiomatically locked into their blueprint of freedom. With respect to education, Reform rabbis deduced the principle from Mendelssohn's *Jerusalem* that the state had no right to teach or enforce special religious principles.[61]

The situation that obtained in American public schools in the second half of the nineteenth century fell short of that ideal. Their character was nondenominational Protestant rather than nonsectarian. Since Protestantism was woven into the fabric of American culture, the Protestant orientation of the schools was inevitable. Timothy Smith has explained: "An evangelical consensus of faith and ethics had come so to dominate the national culture that a majority of Protestants were now willing to entrust the state with the task of educating children, confident that education would be 'religious' still." Nor did local authorities mask the religious intent of the schools. In 1843, when Jews in New York City objected to the use of the New Testament and religious-flavored textbooks in the classrooms, the newly organized Board of Education had several answers. First, books that inculcated Christian principles were by definition good; second, the Bible was not a sectarian book; third, the Jews might be taxpayers, but, since this was a Christian country and since the public schools' existence antedated the presence of the Jews (a gross inaccuracy), Jews did not deserve the same consideration as Christians.[62]

Individual Jews who attended public schools in the 1860s recalled the distinctions if not the slights that they, non-Protestants, were forced to endure. In the same address calling heavenly blessings down upon the public schools, Berkowitz testified to the alienation of the Jewish pupils:

The bell rang and the school came in order. The opening exercises consisted of a reading from the Bible, followed perhaps by a repetition of the so-called "Lord's Prayer," and the singing of one or more hymns, in which all were required to join. I remember very well how strange all this seemed to me at first, and how out of place I felt. Along with my brothers, I was among the first of the Jewish children in my native city in Pennsylvania to attend the public schools. When we brought home information about these religious exercises which we were required to participate in, and also about certain passages in our readers, histories and geographies which spoke about Jews in a way that brought the blush of confusion and shame to our cheeks, one of our leading Jewish citizens made an appeal in our behalf to the principal and the school board, but we were not allowed to be excused from these exercises, nor in later years from the devotions held in the high school.[63]

The reality of the school situation disclosed a basic dilemma confronting American Jews. Could they—or indeed should they—aspire to integration within a society whose cultural complex was inextricably tied to Protestantism? While the question in abstract form was not discussed, it underlay Leeser's debate with Isidor Busch, a journalist turned businessman, about Jewish attendance in public schools. The Philadelphia rabbi argued that both public and private schools were "essentially Christian," that their very atmosphere subjected Jewish children to Christian influences and scorn that weaned them away from their own faith. Whereas Leeser thought separate Jewish schools were the answer, Busch argued that Jewish separatism would only exacerbate the anti-Jewish prejudice. Jews who went through the public school system, he maintained, were better equipped to handle the problem of bigotry. Besides, he optimistically expected that the schools would in time become religiously neutral.[64] Leeser, the traditionalist in matters of religion, was troubled about the retention of a Jewish identity. Busch, the newer arrival seasoned by the European ferment for emancipation, intended to fight prejudice. For him the goal of acceptance as equal Americans transcended the importance of Jewish studies.

The Jewish community endorsed Busch's position. In 1855 the Cleveland conference of rabbis went on record in opposition to all-day Jewish schools. By 1860 the trend was well under way toward closing down the public and congregational schools established by the German Jews in which both Jewish and secular subjects were taught.[65] More acclimatized now to the concept of common schooling, Jews heard the stirrings of Reform Judaism, whose leaders were preaching an interconnection between American and Jewish ideals and hence an almost religious commitment to American institutions. Doubtless they had also been frightened by the anti-Catholic movement, which gained middle-class Protestant support on the very issue of Catholic discontent with public schools and the establishment of parochial schools. According to Rabbi Berkowitz, Cincinnati's Jews investigated sectarianism in the public schools in 1856—the very year that the Know-Nothing party ran a candidate for the presidency—and concluded that their fears of Christian influence had been very much exaggerated.[66]

Most Jews disapproved of Know-Nothingism, but Jewish partisans of nonsectarian education would scarcely entertain the thought of an alliance with the Catholics on the school issue. Their long-standing grievances against the Roman church had been newly exacerbated by the Mortara affair of 1858. Moreover, some Protestants counted on Jewish endorsement of anti-Catholic measures. In 1858 the Order of United Americans shocked its Jewish members by calling for the election of Protestants to New York's Board of Education. Asked to explain, the order cited the Mortara case as good reason for the Jews to support the literal (i.e., antipopery) meaning of the word *Protestant*.[67]

Max Lilienthal, a rabbi in Cincinnati, openly criticized the ruling of the Vatican Council of 1869 on papal infallibility, which he interpreted as a qualification of Catholic loyalty to the United States and as a dangerous interference in civic affairs. He reported that when Cincinnati tried to bring the Catholic children into the public school system, the archbishop was asked on what conditions he would agree. The latter's answer—that he would first consult the pope—incensed the school board and ended the deliberations. In practical terms too, Lilienthal explained, nonsectarian schooling could never satisfy the Catholic clergy, "the sworn enemies of our free schools." If the schools retained their Protestant forms, Catholics disputed their sectarian nature. But if the Bible and religious instruction were eliminated, Catholics called the schools "godless" and "atheistic." Suspicion that the Catholics were bent on destroying the public schools aroused a counterfanaticism from the Protestants. "On one side of this controversy are the Protestants and on the other side are the Catholics," Lilienthal said. "Where in heaven's name are the Americans?"[68]

For their part, the Jews compromised. Distasteful as the sectarian features were, Jews decided against maintaining their own schools. "Bible or no Bible," Lilienthal said, "our children will visit the public schools. Our Sabbath schools and synagogs give us ample room and time to impart to them the required religious instruction."[69] Hence, Jews assumed the task of ridding the public schools of those religious trappings that put non-Protestants on a less than equal basis.

With the same intensity that marked their persistent concern with Sunday laws,[70] Jewish leaders and the press in the fifty years before World War I kept close check on sectarianism in the schools. In this instance the task was even more cumbersome, because policy was often fixed by administrative decisions of local school boards as well as by town ordinance or state law. The overall issue involved a broad range of grievances: Bible readings and prayers, religious hymns, Christological textbooks, and the right of teachers to wear religious garb. Jews also challenged rules that penalized students who missed classes or examinations on Jewish holidays.[71] While all agreed that public funds should not support denominational schools, the Jewish community divided on what nonsectarianism in the public institutions meant. When, for example, the Cincinnati Board of Education debated the question of whether Bible readings from the King James version violated the pupils' liberty of conscience, the two Jews on the board took opposite sides. Reformers tended on grounds of principle to be most consistently purist, demanding the elimination of all practices that brought religious doctrines of any sort into the classroom. Their leading newpaper, the *American Israelite,* forthrightly insisted that in order to safeguard human rights Jews had to work for a secular state and secular free schools. The *Jewish Spectator* of Memphis agreed, but the moderate New York *American Hebrew* cautioned against the undesirable result of identifying the schools with agnosticism. The more traditionalist *Jewish Messenger* also sought a middle ground. It preferred before 1900 to keep the Bible in the schools, albeit in a form inoffensive to any believer. The paper turned more apologetic at the end of the century, explaining, for example, why it opposed religious hymns. It feared too much clamor by the Jews on the sectarian issue, particularly at a time when anti-Semitism was growing stronger. The Jew believed he was in the minority, the *Jewish Messenger* said, and, therefore, he accepted the Lord's Prayer, New Testament, and hymns without loud objections.[72] For the insecure in particular, considerations of expediency and image tempered principle.

Until the Supreme Court ruled that the Bill of Rights was binding upon the states, legal challenges to religious school practices were based on state constitutional guarantees respecting freedom of conscience and worship. In 1875 James G. Blaine, Speaker of the House of Representatives, proposed a constitutional amendment forbidding the use of state tax funds for sectarian purposes, but it narrowly missed the necessary two-thirds approval of both Senate and House. Although President Grant as well as the national party platforms of 1876 also came out in favor of nonsectarian schools, the ultimate arbiters in the school issue remained the state courts. In the numerous cases heard between 1870 and World War I, most dealt with Bible reading or the recitation of the Lord's Prayer, but no single point of view emerged. The Cincinnati case referred to above was an early and signal victory for the separationists against Bible reading. Nevertheless, since the court left the question to the discretion of the school board, it sustained a rule requiring Bible reading some twenty years later. Some courts barred Bible reading outright; in Wisconsin the judges ruled that the provision excusing objectors from class was still in violation of equality among pupils.

Other states held that the Bible was not a sectarian book, if read without comment. Nebraska's court vigorously defended the separation of church and state but justified Bible reading by likening it to the reading of the *Iliad* and the Koran. However, Loren P. Beth observes skeptically that "one may have reservations about how far the judges themselves would have accepted their own doctrine had the Koran, the Book of Mormon, or the speculations of Miss Mary Baker Eddy actually been involved . . . rather than the Bible."[73]

Some cases involved Jews either as petitioners or as points of reference in the arguments of lawyers and judges. One lawyer, contesting Bible reading in the Cincinnati case, insisted that the Jews, although descendants of those who crucified Jesus, were still entitled to complete civil and religious equality. Judge Alphonso Taft, who voted in that case against Bible reading, stated that Jews flocked to the public schools because they were willing to risk a loss in religious feeling for a superior education. He added that the Jews "wisely" left religious education to the home and to their separate institutions. Forty years later in Illinois the court ruled that the Bible was a sectarian book to Jews and to all believers in non-Christian religions as well as to nonbelievers. Since the law knew no distinction among citizens on grounds of religion, the state-supported schools had to remain secular. A Louisiana court in 1915 decided unanimously that the Jews' right of conscience was invaded by readings from the King James Bible or the Lord's Prayer. Distinguishing between the "Rabbinical Bible" and the "Christian Bible," the court ruled, however, that Catholic rights were not similarly violated.[74]

Religion in the public schools was but one issue of a deeper conflict that surfaced in post–Civil War America. On the one hand, with the help of rapid urbanization and new discoveries in science, the appeal of secularism could no longer be dismissed.[75] The believer, formerly despised even more than non-Christians, was winning greater recognition within the pale of respectable humanity. Defenders of religious liberty could even mention the right not to believe. Toleration was a hateful concept, men like *Harper's* editor George William Curtis said; Curtis preferred "soul liberty." That President Grant, the national party platforms, and a widely supported constitutional amendment advocated brakes on the influence of Protestantism in public life revealed how accustomed society had become to view religion as a private affair. Control by religious institutions was slipping, too. The established churches, catering to a comfortable middle class and ignoring the social problems of a modernized economy, lost significant ground among urban workers. With the arrivals of vast numbers of Catholic and Jewish immigrants from southern and eastern Europe after 1875, the threat loomed more seriously that the Protestant component of the American polity might be substantially undermined.[76]

But at the same time that modernism, secularism, economic tensions, and the "new" immigration battered away at Protestant hegemony, a new spurt of religious zeal erupted. Protestant stalwarts braced themselves for the battle to save the cities, and indeed the entire nation, from utter ruination. To renew Sabbatarian legislation, enact prohibition, engraft an amendment recognizing Christianity onto the Constitution, and instill Protestant dogma in the schools were their favorite crusades. Each cause led to the organization of a separate pressure group, but the underlying religious goal united organizations like the Women's Christian Temperance Union, the National Reform Association, the American Sabbath Union, and the National Bible Association. They, the forebears of the Moral Majority of the 1980s, worked together to mend the fraying American fabric. It was no mere coincidence, for example, that Senator Henry Blair, who pushed for a national Sunday law in 1888, sponsored an amendment that same year that provided for the education of all public-school children in the principles of Christianity. Both of Blair's proposals failed, but the religious groups placed new difficulties in the path of the adherents of church-state separation. Perhaps most lasting with respect to the school issue was their charge that secularism bred amorality. Indeed, from 1890 on, educators grappled with the question of how to teach morality without a religious base. [77]

As foremost champions, to whatever degree, of separationism, Jews were put on the defensive by the "godlessness" argument. The *Jewish Messenger*'s cynical comment that skepticism emanated more from pulpits than from schools had no effect. Protestant zealots linked Jews with infidels and Jesuits, who in league together were operating to undermine American (that is, Christian) schools and civilization. If society heeded those charges, Jews again became the outsiders, tolerated at best but vulnerable to persecution and bereft of any hope for true equality. Jews saw how the charge of secularism coupled with materialism assumed ugly overtones as it fed the anti-Semitic agitation in Bismarck's Germany. The conspiracy theme hinted at in the Protestant brief—the Jew as the Antichrist and threat to Christian civilization—was also not qualitatively different from the anti-Semitic propaganda then being peddled in western Europe. By association, Judaism was branded as well as the Jew; it became a creed that imposed no demands on its adherents for moral or religious education.[78]

American Jews disagreed about the feasibility and desirability of teaching "nonsectarian" ethics through the public schools. Felix Adler, the founder of the Society for Ethical Culture, pioneered for the introduction of a program of moral instruction divorced from religious sanction. His book, *Moral Instruction for Children*, appeared in 1892 and influenced educators in Europe and the United States. American rabbis were less convinced, and the question aroused debate at the meetings of Reform's rabbinical association on the eve of World War I. To be expected, rabbis would be hard put to legitimate a morality not based in religion, but their view, if applied to the schools, could only reinforce the Protestant character, which they simultaneously contested. On the other hand, rabbis could not take a stand that could be reduced in the popular mind to antimorality. Besides, if public education were strictly secular, perhaps society did lose. As one rabbi put it:

There can be no question that we must insist upon the exclusion of the Bible from the public school, and wherever there is danger of ethical instruction being coupled with such instruction in Bible or religion, we must insist upon its exclusion also. Yet we must never lose sight of the fact that it is a poor and negative and barren victory that we Jews enjoy in thus keeping the Bible out of the public school. There is something to be said upon the other side.

Some members of the Central Conference of American Rabbis raised other considerations. Could the rabbis insist that nonsectarian ethical instruction was impossible of attainment when educators were garnering public support with opposite arguments? More important, could the rabbis contradict those state constitutions and laws that provided for the moral instruction of children, especially if state governments considered it compatible with nonsectarian education?[79]

At bottom, sectarianism in the schools, like Sunday legislation, was symptomatic of the Christian-state idea which Jewish spokesmen labored to keep out of American law. Their efforts were set back in 1892, when the Supreme Court, for the first time, held that the United States was a Christian nation. The case itself (*Church of the Holy Trinity* v. *United States*) dealt with the question of whether a minister brought over from Europe to serve in an American church fell into the prohibited category of contract labor. Speaking for the Court, Justice David Brewer interpreted contract labor as referring only to manual labor. Besides, he continued, no antireligious intent could be imputed to any federal law, since "this is a religious people." He cited numerous examples dating back to colonial times where, through statute, constitution, and customs, Americans affirmed a religious commitment. According to Brewer, they all added up to the indisputable fact that "this is a Christian nation."[80]

One response to Brewer came from New York attorney Louis Marshall, the man whom Jews and non-Jews soon came to recognize as the foremost national Jewish leader. Marshall argued that the intimate connection between church and state of colonial days was halted by the formative period of American history when the framers of the federal and state constitutions consciously sought to engraft the principle of separation on those documents. Marshall also pointed to the treaty negotiated with Tripoli in 1796 that denied that the United States was founded on the Christian religion. True, the majority of Americans were Christians, but it did not follow, therefore, that the government was linked to any religion. To call the state Christian on the premise of majoritarianism, Marshall warned, could lead to religious strife and persecution. The very nature of Marshall's task demanded that he emphasize America's acceptance of separationism and hence the deviant, un-American character of those who would tie the country's law to Christianity. For his immediate purpose, he was constrained to defend Sunday laws, as well as laws prohibiting blasphemy or Mormon polygamy, as police regulations for civic betterment. However, that line of argument exacted its own price; as discussed above, it made a subject like Sunday laws less open to Jewish attack.[81]

The Christian-nation idea continued to agitate Jewish circles. In 1905 Justice Brewer expatiated upon his earlier opinion in a lecture entitled "The United States—A Christian Nation" in which he carefully detailed state constitutional provisions, statutes, and judicial decisions to substantiate his conclusion. Not only did Brewer consign Judaism to the level of a tolerated creed, but he called separation itself an offshoot of *Christian* views on the personal relation between man and God.[82]

Other Jews jumped into the arena with rebuttals. The Central Conference of American Rabbis (CCAR), which was stimulated to set up a standing committee on church and state, interpreted the Brewer piece as another instance in the lengthy series of episodes involving Sunday and school matters that warned of the necessity to construct a "healthy public opinion" against the Christian-state concept. Since the CCAR had already begun work on a lengthy statement, "Why the Bible Should Not Be Read in the Public Schools," the rabbinical committee limited its initial efforts to that topic. Issued in pamphlet form, the rabbinical statement held that public schools were literally "the public's schools," built and supported financially by the entire community, where different religious views had to be treated impartially. Bible reading could never be impartial; the interpretation or lack of interpretation offered by the teacher, the version of the Bible used, and even the tone in which the selection was read conveyed one particular religious approach. Readings easily led to other religious forms and exercises within the schools, which in turn further divided the pupils. In short, Bible readings obstructed America's assimilating process and the very growth of a democracy that depended on a nondiscriminatory and classless school system. Because Bible reading was a matter of conscience, it could not be mandated by the voice of the majority. Numbers counted for nothing where conscience or "soul rights" were concerned. "To deny the soul right of a single individual is to deny the whole principle of human rights."

Unlike the earlier arguments against Sunday laws, the Central Conference's statement went beyond a specific defense of equality for Jews. In fact, it singled out no particular religious group and could well have been written by any defender of separationism. By building their case in general terms, the framers of the statement testified to their own integration within American society as well as to the changed climate of opinion. Americans in 1906 would be far more prone to heed arguments about Americanization and universal rights than the justice of one minority's grievances.

The CCAR buttressed its statements with a review of state judicial opinions on the Bible issue and with Christian opinions in favor of separationism. Within a year it had distributed 3,500 copies of the pamphlet to Jewish spokesmen in various localities; copies were also available for boards of education, Christian ministers, legislators, businessmen, and the press. The Central Conference also sent suggestions to Jewish communal leaders on how to contest the zealots' methods on behalf of sectarianism; in 1907 the rabbinical statement was used to lobby against a Bible-reading bill proposed in the Oklahoma legislature. In this, an early example of an organized public-relations campaign to influence American opinion, the rabbis followed the tradition of Leeser and his generation and equated religious liberty with equality. They said in 1906:

A right which is not worth fighting for cannot be worth much, and he who is not disposed to fight for his rights does not deserve to enjoy them. One such right, woven into the fabric of our body politic, is equality before the law. . . . [T]his preeminent right of religious freedom has been trampled upon time and time again. . . . But only of late has it been evident that a concerted effort to disregard this right is being made in the attempt to introduce Bible readings in the public schools. . . . As Americans, then, who wish jealously to conserve all that the founders of our Republic have in their wisdom set down for the welfare of this country, . . . it is our duty, if we at all deserve to enjoy the right of religious liberty, to demand that this menace to one of the fundamental institutions of our commonwealth be laid low.[83]

More than fifty years later, when Lyndon Johnson's Great Society activated the role of the federal government in education, some Jewish agencies very guardedly endorsed limited public aid to parochial-school students. Nevertheless, the Jewish establishment remained steadfast in its unqualified opposition to the injection of religion into the classroom. The ideal of the public school, the agent of Americanization and the medium for dispelling prejudice, had for more than a century reinforced the Jews' determination to defend jealously this particular symbol of civic equality.

Disability by Treaty

It was one thing for the Supreme Court to rule that the federal government was helpless when state laws impaired the equal rights of citizens but quite another when the federal government itself was a party to discrimination. On various occasions from the middle of the nineteenth century to the present day—from the Swiss Treaty of 1850 to restrictions by Arab countries on American Jews—the American government sacrificed the rights of Jews on the altar of international politics. It seemed a small price to pay for foreign goodwill or commercial favors, especially when so few American Jews were directly involved. Besides, diplomats could bend rules and make exceptions in individual cases. American Jews, on the other hand, fixed on the principle. At stake was the essence of their struggle for emancipation and integration. Their government's acquiescence to politics that distinguished between them and other Americans meant that the United States, like the prejudiced countries it dealt with, thought of them first as Jews rather than as equal citizens of the body politic. From 1850 on, therefore, American Jews devised strategies to force the government to abide by the rules of the American game.

A treaty of commerce negotiated in 1850 by the United States and Switzerland explicitly stated: "On account of the tenor of the Federal Constitution of Switzerland, Christians alone are entitled to the enjoyment of privileges guaranteed by the present Article in the Swiss Cantons." Since Switzerland's constitution guaranteed the right of religious freedom only to Christians, and since Switzerland was a federal republic, its cantons had the right, which some put to use, of refusing entry and commercial privileges to foreign Jews. A. Dudley Mann, the American minister who negotiated the treaty, explained to the State Department that the Swiss restricted Jews because they feared the influx of the unpalatable Jewish peddlers and usurers from Alsace. He thought that individual Jews from America would probably not be turned away. Nevertheless, since the central government was powerless to countermand the cantonal regulations, it could make no official exception for American Jews. To the latter's chagrin, the United States accepted the draft treaty with its discriminatory feature, thus setting the Jews apart from their fellow citizens.[84]

One Jew who resolved to protest was Sigismund Waterman. Waterman was born in Bavaria in 1819, the year of the anti-Jewish "Hep! Hep!" riots. Of a well-to-do family, he received a good education in Jewish and secular subjects. Like many fellow Jews, however, he despaired of a future in Germany and looked for his freedom in America. Arriving in the United States in 1841, he lived for a few years in Connecticut. He paid his way through Yale Medical School by teaching German at the university; in 1848 he received his M.D. degree, the first to be awarded by Yale to a Jew. In 1844 his brother Leopold joined him in New Haven, where the Watermans were respected as both liberals and Jews. Leopold frequently preached at New Haven's Temple Mishkan Israel, and in 1850 he was chosen to serve on the municipal committee that welcomed the popular Hungarian revolutionist Louis Kossuth.[85] To those like the Watermans who gave up material comfort for the sake of freedom, even a small matter of a treaty was tantamount to a betrayal of their trust in America.

In January 1851 Sigismund Waterman wrote an article on the American-Swiss treaty which appeared in two installments in the *Asmonean*. Describing the document as an insult to America's 50,000 Jews, Waterman blamed Mann for ignoring the patriotic and law-abiding community that had made its contributions to America's wars. The Jews, he said, were being deprived of "their due and guaranteed rights": "We stand under the constitution as citizens, fully and permanently qualified to bear this proud title irrespective of our religious principles." The German-born liberal grounded his argument in a work of New York's former chief justice, Chancellor James Kent. According to Kent's *Law of Nations*, Waterman argued that treaties should be used to overcome rather than foster bigotry.

American settlers and colonies had entrusted their rights, among which was that of religious liberty, to a representative government. The compact thus formed forbade the government from disabling a portion of its citizens. It could not barter away the rights of Jews to religious liberty and equality for commercial or political advantage.[86]

The *Asmonean* and a number of individual Jews endorsed Waterman's position. No one contested Switzerland's right to regulate the status of Jews in its own land. The fault lay with the United States for agreeing to that discrimination, thereby tacitly recognizing "a dominant or superior religion" in the United States. In the popular climate of 1850, Jews readily linked the treaty episode with their grievances about Thanksgiving proclamations and Sunday laws. A Jew from Savannah, Georgia, for example, who urged that the treaty be rejected since the Constitution "is as blind as justice herself regarding church, mosque, or synagogue," alluded to Richard Johnson's report on the Sunday-mail question. He was surprised, he added, that there were still attempts after that to undermine the justice of the Constitution with religious superstition. As with the other issues that troubled them, Jews treated this as one of religious liberty, when in fact they meant religious equality.

In two ways, however, the treaty matter was different. First, it involved the federal government, which unlike the states was limited by the Constitution on matters pertaining to religion. One John Samuel of Philadelphia in a letter to Secretary of State Daniel Webster argued that a treaty by which America recognized distinctions among religions was tantamount to a prohibition of the free exercise of religion—specifically mentioned in the First Amendment—and hence unconstitutional. Second, in a manner different from their responses to Sunday laws or Thanksgiving proclamations, Jews forthrightly made this a public issue. Waterman urged the fragmented Jewish community to take up his protest. He also appealed to the Senate and to all Americans to opt for justice and reject the treaty instead of accepting a convention tinged with "tyranny." The *Asmonean*, like Waterman, emphasized the principle at stake. It was not a Jewish but an American question, for if discrimination were tolerated against one, it could be directed against another.[87]

Waterman and Robert Lyon, editor of the *Asmonean,* sent strong messages to leading political personalities. The famous Whig leader and senator from Kentucky, Henry Clay, agreed in a letter to Waterman: "This is not the country nor the age in which ancient and unjust prejudices should receive any countenance." Daniel Webster responded similarly to the Jewish petitioners. No doubt the American officials also took seriously the Jewish argument about the role of the United States as the exemplar of freedom for the rest of the world. Clay, for example, had been an active proponent of American recognition of the newly created South American republics in the 1820s. And hadn't Webster, as secretary of state, publicly endorsed an independent Hungary patterned on the American model? Since President Fillmore and the Senate also sided with the Jewish position, the treaty, with the objectionable clause removed, was returned to Bern.[88]

Once having made their cause public, the Jews were brought closer to those Americans who were pressing at that time for the rights of American Protestants in Catholic countries. When a Senate committee recommended that the United States in future treaties seek to secure the right to worship for its citizens (citizens, and not merely Christians), Senator Lewis Cass, who steered the resolution to its passage, invited the Jews in 1854 to add their petitions on the matter. Captain Jonas P. Levy, a prominent Washingtonian, organized the response, and a Jewish memorial, insisting that other countries reciprocate the privileges that the United States afforded foreign nationals, was forwarded to the Senate. While the Jewish petition did not point up peculiarly Jewish needs, Cass, who presented it to the Senate, did. The senator said in part:

Exposed as the members of this persuasion yet are in portions of Europe and America, both Protestant and Catholic, to the most illiberal prejudices and to religious disabilities, the position of our citizens abroad who belong to it has peculiar claims to the consideration and interposition of the government. Beside their legal right to equal protection there is no portion of our population whose peaceable and law-abiding conduct better proves than theirs does, that they are well entitled to all the privileges secured to every American by our system of government.

Favorable action on the resolution defending religious rights of Americans abroad did not inhibit the Senate from consenting to the second draft of the Swiss treaty. Formally ratified in 1855, it deleted references to exclusively Christian rights but provided that the rights of domicile and commerce obtained only where they did not conflict with cantonal law. The persistent inequity which still left American Jews at the mercy of the individual cantons had been noted by Wise's *Israelite* and Leeser's *Occident*. When Leeser brought it to Cass's attention, the latter made reassuring sounds but in reality skirted the issue. A few secular papers also commented on the amended treaty's violation of equal rights, but apparently the eventual passage of the new draft went unnoticed by most Jews.[89]

Interest was sparked anew when Jews learned that A. H. Gootman, an American Jewish merchant, had been ordered to leave the canton of Neuchâtel just because he was a Jew. Although the American minister to Switzerland succeeded in getting an exemption made for Gootman, the principle that cantons could exclude Jews at will remained unchanged. The Gootman case evoked a new round of agitation in 1857 within the Jewish community. At protest meetings in various cities, Jews, sometimes joined by Christians, loudly denounced the treaty. They drew up resolutions of petitions to the government and formulated plans to send delegations to President Buchanan. Plagued by a lack of communal unity, the Jewish periodicals worked actively to generate and sustain an effective opposition. The *Asmonean* boldly counseled that the Jews be uninhibited about using their numbers, wealth, and commercial position to proper advantage. The *Israelite* pushed more vigorously for a concerted public drive:

Agitate.
Call Meetings.
Engage the Press in your favor!!!!
Israelites, Freemen and Citizens! let not the disgrace of the Treaty between the United States and Switzerland remain upon the history of our country. Do not stand [for] the insult heaped upon the *Jewish citizens,* by unprincipled diplomacy. Hold Public Meetings; give utterance to your sentiments, resolve upon a proper course of actions against that mean and illegal instrument made in violation of the constitution of the United States. Try to win the Press in favor of your cause, and rest not until this outrage is blotted from the United States' records. Slaves and cowards only will submit to such an outrage; we are men, and must be treated as such. Decide, in your meetings, upon efficient measures to have your voice heard, publish your resolutions in your local papers, and send us a copy thereof, that a concert of actions be ensured.

The chorus of indignation exceeded that of 1851 but the principal argument remained the same. From the Midwest, the South, and the Atlantic seaboard the Jewish cry for equality reverberated. The discriminatory treaty, according to its critics, violated the spirit if not the letter of the Constitution and merited the opposition of all Americans. Some argued that by permitting Switzerland to screen American citizens, the federal government was acceding to a test oath, which was expressly forbidden by the Constitution. Others charged unconstitutionality by claiming that the treaty violated the general-welfare clause! It was suggested that those who actually experienced discrimination at the hands of the Swiss sue the American government for damages and test the treaty's constitutionality before the Supreme Court.

Understandably the Jews were more bitter than in 1851. Despite assurances to the contrary by Senator Cass, who was now secretary of state, discrimination had somehow been "smuggled in." The Senate could not be excused; we were sold out, some lamented, perhaps, as Rabbi Isaac Leeser explained, because the government did not think us important enough. The non-Jewish press repeated the conspiracy charge, and the administration's political foes had a field day in attacking the Democrats.

Most Jews refrained from making the issue a partisan one. Those in Easton, Pennsylvania, calling themselves good Democrats, were an exception when they lashed out against their party. Timidity and the habitual reluctance of nineteenth-century Western Jews to inject Jewish interests into politics restrained the others. They preferred to describe the issue as American and nonsectarian, and they bemoaned America's betrayal of its international image. They, a group of loyal and law-abiding citizens rooted in their "second Canaan," were being deprived of rights under a treaty that brought only little benefit to the United States. Their logic demanded that the treaty be abrogated or at least its objectionable clause nullified.

Jewish leaders faulted their coreligionists for helping to bring about a deplorable situation. Had the Jews been attentive to the diplomatic negotiations in 1854, had the community been united or prepared to take concerted action, the damage might have been averted. The traditionalist *Occident* injected its running feud with the Reformers into the matter by insinuating that the community had been lulled into a false security by the "reform doctors." While the latter behaved as if the redemption of the Jews had arrived, the rights of Jews even in America were yet in danger. "[W]e are in *Galuth*," Leeser wrote. "[W]e have our theoretical rights; but practically they are dependent on the will of those who have numbers on their side; and if we make all the noise in the world, and brag aloud after our heart's content, *we are yet strangers* in stranger lands."

In October 1857 a national convention of Jewish delegates on the treaty was held in Baltimore. A breakdown in communication and severe internal bickering prevented the emergence of any body that could really be called representative of American Jewry, but the truncated convention, made up of Jews from only four states, dispatched a delegation to the president. They found Buchanan most gracious. He assured the delegation that had the treaty's inequities been understood properly, his predecessor would not have approved it. The Jews readily accepted that explanation as well as the president's promise to resolve the problem. Rabbi Wise, who took part in the meeting, advised then that the communal agitation cease.

While the episode smacks of Jewish timidity, it did have a positive impact. Alerted by the Jewish pressure, the secretary of state informed the American minister to Switzerland, Theodore S. Fay, that the president was most anxious to have the discriminatory clause removed. Fay in turn agreed with the Jewish demand for equality, and in a lengthy note to the Swiss government he rebutted the arguments underlying Jewish disabilities. The minister claimed on the eve of the Civil War that his note was perceptibly changing opinion in the cantons, and he confidently expected a removal of the restrictions.[90]

American Jews were less sanguine. Their primary goal—to wrest an admission from the government that it could not sanction foreign discrimination against American citizens—would not have been achieved even if the cantons eventually retracted. To their further dismay, the government entered into a treaty with China in 1860 which, while establishing the right of all American citizens to residential and commercial privileges, specifically provided for the protection of the Christian religion. The newly organized defense agency, the Board of Delegates of American Israelites, noted almost wistfully in its first report that equal protection for Jews had "up to this time, been very feebly recognized by the treaty-making power."[91]

In 1866 the board announced that the Swiss restrictions had been lifted. It was at best a partial victory, for the United States by not denouncing the treaty hedged on the rectitude of the Jewish plea for equality. That humiliation continued to rankle. Fifty years after Sigismund Waterman's initial protest, a young Jewish lawyer who wrote the first historical account of the Swiss affair injected the following sentence into an otherwise dry and emotionless narrative: "It was demonstrated to us that while we were American citizens, our citizenship was distinctly qualified—we were and we are American-Jewish citizens, at least as far as our international rights were and are concerned."[92]

Jewish agitation over the Swiss treaty marked several new tactics in the fight for equality: an alliance (albeit foisted from above) with American Christians suffering similar disabilities in foreign lands, a quasi-representative delegation to the White House to plead the specific case, a direct appeal to American public opinion. Jewish efforts to fight the passage of the treaty and then the treaty itself were crude and carelessly executed, but they set the example for the successful campaign undertaken by the American Jewish Committee some fifty years later to abrogate the Russo-American treaty of 1832. By then, Jewish guardianship of the principle of equality was reinforced by an astute grasp of the methods of political lobbying.

3

THE PROPER AMERICAN JEW

A lasting effect of emancipation was to make the now legally free Jewish citizen more self-conscious than ever before. As long as the premodern Jew had accepted a way of life divorced from the dominant society—in essence, a condition fixed by his refusal to embrace Christianity—he worried little about the image he projected. His religious literature taught him how a proper Jew behaved toward his God, fellow Jews, and even faceless political authorities. He knew the dangers to himself and his community were he to cause a scandal in his dealings with Christians, but he never really believed that consistently virtuous deportment on his part would endear Jews to their host country or significantly alter the course of Jewish-Christian relations. Only when the modern Jew strove for social integration did the thought "Mah yomru hagoyyim?" ("What will the gentiles say?") become well-nigh an obsession, coloring his behavior both within the Jewish community as well as within the larger society. The figure he cut by his manners and morals loomed all-important.

For the German Jews who came to America in the nineteenth century, that self-consciousness eclipsed the normal insecurities plaguing an accommodationist immigrant group. The latter sought to reconcile the differences in social mores that distinguished them from the native-born. Jews bore the added burden of living down the ugly stereotypes nurtured by Christendom for more than two thousand years. Those images that refused to die—the Jew as Christ killer, Shylock, eternal alien—strengthened the ethnic force within the Jewish community. Since nineteenth-century Americans generally regarded them first as Jews rather than as capitalists, laborers, or professionals, Jews, too, could not easily slough off the Jewish tag or treat it peripherally. More than class interest, it colored their public posture on all sorts of issues, from philanthropy to politics, while it perpetuated the group's inner cohesiveness.

Manners and Virtues

American Jews adopted a two-pronged approach in response to the unfavorable stereotypes. One was defensive: spokesmen exposed and rebutted isolated specific accusations. The second was active: communal leaders labored to steer their constituency to a course of behavior so impeccable that none could seriously invoke the hateful images. Both approaches rested on the assumption that reason and empirical evidence were the best antidotes to irrational prejudice. French writer Anatole Leroy-Beaulieu echoed that belief even after the Dreyfus affair had severely jolted emancipated Jewry: "Let the Jews of [America] perform their duty to their fellow-believers and to the Republic, let them be steadfast in their faith, and their neighbors will appreciate the spirit which has elevated the ideal above the material."[1]

Besides "proving" their moral virtue, Jews labored to absorb American social tastes and habits. While moral codes applied equally to all classes, manners varied according to socioeconomic status. On the subject of manners Jews looked beyond their teachings and adopted the criteria for proper behavior set by those whose acceptance they craved—the upper middle class. It was natural for the Jews, an urban people distingushed for its commitment to mobility, to pick a reference group that represented the economic and social attainments to which they could realistically aspire. Indeed, from the first stirrings of emancipation in eighteenth-century Europe, the all-consuming move for Jewish self-emancipation, for "civilizing" (i.e., cloaking with civility) the ghetto Jew, invoked the educated bourgeoisie as models. Although many American Jews stayed within the ranks of the working class, communal leaders, generally unsympathetic toward labor, purveyed a message reflecting the tastes of the upper middle class. The dictates of that class with respect to overall style—from upholding the traditional homemaker role of the woman to supporting cultural institutions like museums—commanded respectful attention, and their overtones echoed in Jewish sermons, editorials, and even fiction.

Between morals and manners lay the area of civic virtue—the qualities that marked the proper American citizen. Ever eager to conform, Jewish leaders carefully scrutinized non-Jewish opinions for what they revealed about American expectations of the Jews. There were both positive and negative commandments. Where specific contingencies were not spelled out, Jews attempted to anticipate the gentile response. They weighed the factor of "how it would look" with respect to all sorts of issues, even when public opinion had not surfaced. Was it proper to establish a Jewish defense organization or a university under Jewish auspices? Was it proper for Jews to call for an anti-Grant vote in 1868? Was it proper to set up a separate relief fund for Jewish victims of the San Francisco earthquake? Was it proper for an American Jew to be a Zionist? The answers not only spoke to the immediate questions, but also reflected the struggle to create positive counterstereotypes about the modern Jew. Imbued with nineteenth-century optimism, some even looked forward to the next stage, when all group labels would be erased and Jews would be singled out neither for praise nor damnation.[2]

According to the roster of civic virtues formulated by Jewish spokesmen for their community, the proper American Jew was at least as good as everybody else. He was sober, industrious, and law-abiding; his family life was pure and his business dealings were honest. He fulfilled his responsibilities as a citizen in time of war as well as peace; his patriotism was unimpeachable. Through philanthropy and an interest in education and the arts, the Jew displayed a proper concern for the human condition. Eschewing radicalism of any stripe, he remained loyal to his religion and its institutions. At the same time, he kept his Jewish interests within the confines of his community and never called attention unnecessarily to his Jewishness politically or in other public fashion. In overall civic deportment he looked to models inspired by Emerson and Lincoln; with respect to Jewish conduct he emulated the "old guard," ancient and modern Jews—from Mordecai to Sir Moses Montefiore—who combined patriotism, refinement, justice, and charity with a devotion to Judaism.[3]

So outlined, the prescibed behavior could scarcely have antagonized native Americans. Rather, it sought to assure them that Jewish values coincided with the cardinal tenets of the American creed. Since Americans always accepted the legitimacy of religious differences, they were asked to view Jews merely as another sectarian body.

The list of proper behavioral traits took cognizance, too, of Jewish sensibilities. The "representative men" that the *Jewish Messenger* regularly called for had to be good Jews as well as virtuous citizens. Although definitions of a good Jew varied, particularly with regard to level of observance, all agreed that it meant an affirming Jew, loyal to his religious heritage and sensitive to the needs of his fellow Jews. Communal leaders insisted upon Jewish self-respect, arguing that its opposite made the group despicable in the eyes of the majority. Unarticulated but understood was the realization that only a very fine line separated indiscriminate aping of the gentiles from renunciation of Judaism or even Jewish acceptance of anti-Semitic prejudices.[4]

The importance of proper Jewish behavior was coupled with a warning from rabbis and lay leaders that the individual Jew reflected upon the group.[5] That warning was not new in Jewish history; nor were the designated virtues themselves. Time and again Jews and their compatriots pointed admiringly to the long-standing Jewish reputation for philanthropy and family purity, the low numbers of Jewish criminals, and the traditional Jewish urge for learning. Therefore, as the *Jewish Messenger* and *American Hebrew* explained, to live virtuously was inaccurately defined as Christian behavior.[6] To be sure, Jewish spokesmen who sought to inculcate proper manners suggested some departures from the European Jewish style. (The subject of how Jews dressed, conversed, or amused themselves assumed greater importance when, after 1875, Americans justified social discrimination on the grounds that the Jew was rude and uncouth, and when, at the turn of the century, the east European immigrants presented critical Americans with the spectacle of a great unwashed mass.) For the most part, however, the community overwhelmingly accepted the general guidelines laid down. Serious differences of opinion arose only with respect to the particulars of what constituted *religious*—and, therefore, proper—behavior as opposed to questionable displays of a separate *ethnic* nature.

Exaggerated as it may sound to modern ears, the "how does it look" syndrome cannot be dismissed as mere hysteria or paranoia. In part the heritage of a persecuted people whose fears lived on even in free America, it drew reinforcement from the harsh spotlight that focused continuously on contemporary Jews. Throughout the Western world of the nineteenth century, the question of the emancipated Jew—did he or did he not belong in the body politic?—engaged men of distinction as well as ordinary rabble-rousers. The enormous energy spent and amount of ink spilled over the issue attested to the persistent irritation of the very many by the very few. The "Jewish question" rose to a new high in the last quarter of the century with the appearance of racism, the progenitor of the Nazi fury.

"Applied," as opposed to "ideological," anti-Semitism rarely erupted in the United States, but that did not guarantee that the combustible elements inherent in the ugly stereotypes would never be ignited. Even Christians who interpreted the negative images as the inevitable results of centuries of persecution still admitted their validity. In 1883 a local B'nai B'rith leader in San Francisco answered a newspaper article that talked about a secret Jewish "kahal," loopholes provided by religious law enabling Jews to dodge their legal responsibilities, the dishonesty of most Jewish merchants, and the refusal of Jews ever to fight for their country.[7] The charges and rebuttal indicated first, the enduring strength of the old myths, and second, the Jewish belief that a rational response was effective.

In order to gain the desired goal of social acceptance, many nineteenth-century Jews were even willing to accept the harsher standards which they realized early on were imposed upon them. For example, Rabbi Isaac Leeser of Philadelphia wrote that the Jewish employer had to treat his workers decently and pay them the highest wages, "if possible . . . a little more than non-Israelites." As the editor of *Harper's* admitted, it might not be fair to employ different yardsticks for judging Jewish behavior, but that was an incontrovertible fact of life. After 1880 the contradictions appeared more arbitrary in the eyes of the Jews. Why should they alone be criticized for separatism when other groups also established their own social institutions? Why should they be accused of unmannerly behavior when non-Jews had a proportionately equal share of vulgarians? In 1903 Leo Levi, president of B'nai B'rith, bluntly summed up the double standard in manners: "[The Jew] must be . . . thrice better than a Gentile to be as good." Even more exasperating was the evidence of the differences among critics over proper Jewish deportment. For example, some Americans criticized Jews for separatism and social exclusiveness, and others condemned them for "a general obtrusiveness that is frequently disgusting."[8]

Jews noted how qualities seemingly virtuous could be turned around to become faults. It might be noble of American Jews to aid oppressed Jews, but that lent substance to non-Jewish fears about the order of Jewish loyalties. Jews (quite properly) took advantage of higher education, but in so doing they aroused criticism for becoming overintellectualized and for succeeding disproportionately, often at the expense of their non-Jewish peers. The Jew might be commended for his intelligence, but, as sociologist Edward Ross maintained, he used that power to escape detection for the crimes he committed.[9]

In their eagerness to pinpoint exactly what non-Jews wanted of them, Jewish spokesmen returned to the one thing that separated the two groups—Jewish refusal to accept Christianity. Reflecting an approach that overlay Jewish thinking after the Civil War, Rabbi Max Lilienthal appraised Jewish behavior in 1870 and found nothing wanting. Since Jews were loyal patriots, charitable, of good moral character, and contributors to the arts, he could only conclude that they incurred hatred because they had rejected Jesus.[10] To men like Lilienthal conversion was anathema, and if his analysis was correct, it followed, therefore, that the barriers to total acceptance in a Christian society were permanent.

Some Jews intuited the basic irrational quality of anti-Semitism,[11] which had an existence of its own apart from what present-day analysts call "conflict of interests" situations. But despite the hopelessness inherent in that feeling or, for that matter, in the pseudoscientific answer of racism that reached the United States at the end of the century, most refused to abandon the belief that Jews, by their behavior, had a voice in shaping their destiny.

Workings of Philanthropy

Speaking in 1887 at a dedication ceremony of the New Orleans Jewish Widows' and Orphans' Home, Leo Levi calculated the yearly contributions of the American Jewish community to charitable causes. He estimated that B'nai B'rith and the three other national fraternal orders had donated $250,000 for charity and the local benevolent societies another $250,000. The major institutions for orphans and the aged, along with the free-burial, fuel, and school societies of the larger cities accounted for at least $500,000, while miscellaneous Jewish causes drew about $300,000. All told, then, Jews were spending annually $1.3 million or, on the basis of the estimated adult male Jewish population of 50,000, about $20 per capita on charity. Since, Levi added, Jews also gave generously to non-Jewish causes, the overall expenditure probably reached $2 million, or $40 per capita. Levi's list did not include congregational expenses, which he put at an average of $20 for each male adult, or sickness and endowment benefits. The totals confirmed the speaker's pride in the Jewish record. "If the same generosity were displayed by the people at large, the charity of the whole country would reach the enormous amount of four hundred millions per annum, a sum larger than the national revenues, and almost equal to the value of two cotton crops."[12]

From the standpoint of proper behavior, Jews stood only to gain by chalking up an impressive record in philanthropy. A long-touted American virtue, philanthropy was nourished by religious and secular roots implanted in colonial society by men like Cotton Mather, William Penn, and Benjamin Franklin. It became a necessary and legitimate occupation for the various American religious bodies, particularly when commitments and contributions by government lagged sorely behind social needs. American Jews took care of their needy through their synagogues and later through independent charitable agencies, confident that their activities were eminently American. As if to underline that quality, Jewish philanthropic institutions stressed Americanization; orphanages and later settlement houses celebrated holidays like the Fourth of July and Washington's Birthday almost religiously.[13]

Jewish philanthropy appeared especially praiseworthy when it benefited non-Jews. Indeed, the Jewish press liked to report instances of Jewish bequests to non-Jewish institutions, sometimes with a self-righteous comment that such gestures went unreciprocated. Christian churches as well as secular institutions had received support from the Jewish community ever since New York's Jews raised £5 12S. in 1711 for building the steeple of Trinity Church. One hundred years later, Judah Touro of New Orleans contributed tens of thousands of dollars to the different churches of his city long before he rightfully earned the reputation of a philanthropist for Jewish causes. Humanitarian drives in particular, foreign as well as domestic, elicited a positive response. Jews raised money for the beleaguered Christians in Syria, for the victims of an earthquake in Guadeloupe, and for the famine-stricken in Ireland despite—in the words of the *Occident*—the "undeserved wrongs" that they themselves had suffered at the hands of non-Jews. Not surprisingly, nineteenth-century Jews were also among the liberal contributors to German American welfare organizations.[14]

Between the distinctly Jewish and non-Jewish causes lay the broad private sector which catered to all faiths. Nineteenth-century Jews contributed to general institutions of culture and learning, although perhaps not to the degree that some within the community desired. There were also ventures supported by Jewish money whose benefits extended to non-Jews as well as Jews. Jewish hospitals, for example, quickly adopted nonsectarian admissions policies. In the wake of the Russian pogroms of 1905, when a special committee of leading American Jews was hastily organized to tackle the relief problems of the thousands of victims, the issue of aid to Christian sufferers arose. Opinion was divided, with some arguing that the committee's first duty was to the Jews. The final decision was left to the executive committee, whose guiding figures, Oscar Straus and Jacob H. Schiff, both supported the broader point of view. Schiff had said that a nonsectarian distribution to aid the "suffering Russian people," and indeed there were victims other than Jews, might attract contributions from Christians. More important, Jews had to be liberal-minded, Schiff added, and liberalism knew no religion. To some, Schiff's stand was eminently fair, since among the casualties were Russian Christians who had defended the Jews against the pogromists.[15]

The humanitarian reason always appealed to the emancipated Jews. It cloaked their causes with respectability and even nobility, while it simultaneously relieved the ever-suspect element of Jewish separatism. The values of broad humanitarianism underlay the critique of Jewish philanthropy by Morris Jastrow, who in 1896 advised against Jewish exclusivity in any undertaking.[16] Not until the mid-twentieth century, however, did communal agencies seriously debate the pros and cons of the rectitude of limiting Jewish institutions to Jews.

Christians admired Jews for their generosity both to fellow Jews and to non-Jews. "The Jews take care of their own poor and contribute to poor of all religions," the *Baltimore American* wrote in 1856. While some unfairly criticized the Jews for how they made their money, Mayor Abram Hewitt of New York stated, few could dispute their reputation for knowing how to spend their wealth wisely. He added that no other people had done so much "to relieve distress, give education and elevate the standard of morality in our midst." Christians also invoked the Jewish philanthropic spirit as a model for the larger community. An object of particular attention was Jews' Hospital (later Mount Sinai) of New York, established in 1855. On that subject, German Americans noted that their community, the more populous, lagged far behind "the followers of the Old Testament [who] have a far keener sense of communal responsibility," and a Baptist newspaper in Chicago commented ruefully that "few Christian churches or denominations do as much." In 1900, when Montefiore Hospital in New York dedicated a new building, Theodore Roosevelt pointed to the lesson implicit in that Jewish venture:

I have come to express to you the debt of obligation that the people of the United States are under to you, not only for the deed itself but for the example of the deed. There is an appropriate lesson to be learned in the citizenship which limits only the source from which it draws and leaves unlimited that to which it gives.[17]

The plaudits they received convinced Jews of the efficacy of philanthropy as a weapon against anti-Semitism. Charity silences the Jew hater, according to the *American Hebrew* in 1880. Particularly sensitive that year to debates then engaging Germans on whether the Jew could ever be a proper citizen, the journal maintained that charity proved the civic responsibility of the Jew and the interest in social betterment that he shared with Christians. Carl Schurz seconded that opinion. Decrying Western anti-Semitism of the 1880s, he said:

[The Jew] might take the clamorous anti-semite by the hand, show him the hospitals, orphan homes, charity schools, founded and sustained by Jewish money, Jewish labor, Jewish public spirit, benevolence and devotion, and say to him: "If you have any sick, any aged, any children who cannot find help elsewhere, here we shall have room for them, and they are welcome." What has the anti-semite to answer? No, no, [anti-Semitism] cannot survive. It must perish in shame.

If the Jew became a distributor instead of accumulator of wealth, Reform leader Kaufmann Kohler wrote in 1900, "then will his material success, instead of rousing the envy and hatred of the foe, evoke the admiration and emulation of all for the sense of equity and righteousness of the Jew."[18]

If philanthropy did not change the anti-Semite's mind, at least it appeared unlikely to tarnish the Jewish image any further. After the turn of the century, however, when anti-Semitism was on the rise, some Jews expressed the fear that an abundance of charitable works might arouse false impressions about Jewish wealth.[19]

Respect from the non-Jews made philanthropy a creative and vibrant force within the Jewish community. Jews confidently mobilized manpower and money to tackle the needs of the poor, the old, the infirm, the widow and orphan, the immigrant, and the foreign-born. Only in those endeavors were women conspicuous alongside the men. All were stimulated by outside approval to a level of intensive activity which they never matched in areas like Jewish education or other cultural endeavors. The most respectable, and hence most comfortable, way in which to channel extrareligious ethnic impulses, philanthropy threatened to become a surrogate for religion. As early as 1849, the *Occident* observed that if Judaism meant only charity and synagogue building, American Jews were the most religious in the world. But while the wide spectrum of philanthropic institutions had stripped the synagogue of much of its power, philanthropy and not the synagogue kept many of the increasing number of nonbelievers identified as Jews.[20]

Jewish pride added another stimulus to social-welfare undertakings. Caring for the needy had been ingrained in Jewish tradition since the very beginnings of Judaism; it was a duty incumbent upon all Jews irrespective of wealth. Talmudic precepts like "All Israel are responsible for one another" and "All those that feel not for the distress of others are not of the Abrahamic seed" were faithfully applied in premodern Jewish communities. The experience of centuries gave the Jews in the New World a head start in philanthropy over other immigrant groups. The predecessors of the German Jews, the Sephardim, fulfilled their obligations mainly through kahal-directed charities. In colonial New York, charity accounted for anywhere from one-tenth to one-third of Shearith Israel's expended income. The German heirs of that tradition felt compelled to prove that they could measure up to their forebears and their fellow Jews in Europe as well as to Christian Americans. Those sentiments accounted in part for the opposition within the Jewish community to public aid for sectarian institutions. Some feared that public funding might weaken communal vitality and destroy the well-founded sense of achievement in having met the ethical demands of the Jewish tradition. "[S]o long as we are well able to educate our youth in the Hebrew, send Passover bread or coals to suffering brethren, preserve our own organizations for dispensing charity to our own poor, we should be proud to decline contributions from any fund that belongs to the public for public purposes."[21]

Pride never permitted American Jews to forget the condition imposed on their group by the Dutch West India Company in 1655, when it grudgingly allowed Jews to settle in New Amsterdam: "Provided," the company had stipulated, that "the poor among them shall not become a burden to the company or to the community, but be supported by their own nation." Two hundred years later, Dr. Arnold Fischel of Shearith Israel cited that stipulation, which "I need not tell you never has been and I feel confident never will be, looked upon by the descendants of Israel as an unwelcome obligation." Men like Jacob Schiff took that challenge to heart. Schiff operated on the conviction that Jews would do their utmost to keep other Jews from becoming public charges; a Jew would rather cut off his hand, he once said, than apply to Christians for charity.[22] Poverty was unfortunate, but public welfare, which stigmatized both the Jewish recipient and his community, was scandalous.

Christians, too, recalled the terms imposed by the Dutch. In 1902 Madison Peters, a Baptist minister and defender of the Jews, said: "If the bigoted authorities of New Amsterdam who gave their permission to a few Hebrews to settle in their city 'upon condition that they should always support their own poor,' could see how well they have kept the promise . . . those old burghers would open their eyes in surprise at the many and magnificent benevolent institutions, covering every conceivable case of need, which testify to the inborn kindness of the Hebrew's heart." Even historian John Fiske, although enamored of "Aryan" institutions, wrote approvingly of how well the Jews had lived up to the bargain: "Such a kind of person as a Jewish pauper has seldom been seen." Testifying to the determination and assiduous care with which Jews cultivated charity, the impression arose in the larger community that Jews were never forced to seek public assistance. An exaggeration even in that form, it fed into a still more inaccurate belief that there were no Jewish poor at all.[23]

The American Christian of the nineteenth century found a wide gamut of rewards in philanthropy. Aside from the divine favor he might earn, he had the satisfaction derived from the very performance of humanitarian acts. He also passed the character test that philanthropy imposed. Not asked to atone for how he made his money, the rich man was expected to demonstrate the judicious use of his wealth. Jews echoed similar beliefs. Charity let the rich express gratitude for the freedom Jews enjoyed in the United States and the wherewithal provided by God and/or the country to amass wealth. Good works elevated the donor's character and proved his sincerity as a loyal Jew. Philanthropy, like synagogue building, not only showed material success, in itself commendable, but also proved that the Jew used his money for proper rather than frivolous or "pernicious" objects. Jews also looked upon charity as insurance for the rich who might be cast by the wheel of fortune into the ranks of the needy.[24]

Undoubtedly, selfish motives fed into the stream of Jewish philanthropy. Philanthropists gained the admiration of Jews and non-Jews as well as a position of leadership in Jewish circles. Since Jews were frequently barred from posts of command in old established civic causes—charity organizations, museums, colleges—that were the purview of the American elite, they could satisfy their drive for power in Jewish institutions. In this connection, the goal of social acceptance was at direct odds with the enduring power of ethnic institutions. Once the Jew succeeded in gaining an appointment, say, to the board of a national charity or a secular university, he would have less time and inclination to devote his talents to comparable Jewish affairs.

Overwhelmingly, German Jews defined philanthropy in a narrow sense: it was a palliative for immediate social crises rather than a basic reform of individuals or institutions. The idea of retooling needy Jews was broached in a limited fashion in mid-century with respect to the few agricultural projects discussed above. Some also advocated a program of revamping the economic structure and habits of the Jewish settlement in Palestine.[25] Only later did the problems of the east European immigrants goad the Jewish establishment into considering more radical approaches to the multifaceted issue of charity. Nor did Jews share the views of some Americans who were led to philanthropy by dreams of refashioning the universe or proving the inexorable march of progress.

The pattern of Jewish philanthropy remained conservative in method and ideology. Jewish leaders called at times for greater efficiency in relief work, usually advocating some form of union or consolidation, and some mentioned the danger of fostering pauperism by indiscriminate charity. However, not until the turn of the century, when Jews were pioneering in the movement for federated charities, was there any pretense at scientific giving.[26]

At no time did rabbis or lay spokesmen seriously challenge the capitalist ethos or the existing social order. They knew that there would always be a class of Jewish poor, but they hoped that self-help along with loans or aid in finding employment would keep it a fluid category that permitted easy egress. Once, in an editorial radical for him as well as his audience, Isaac Leeser ventured further than most. He preached that poverty was not a disgrace and that the wealthy, who in fact owed their success to divine help, were not by definition superior beings. He boldly criticized the "artificial" inequities bred of capitalism, its rigid class distinctions, and the dehumanizing treatment of the worker by the employer. But although he argued that there were good moral reasons for reducing the unnatural class barriers—"even if . . . this means [that] all the great hoards of wealth in the hands of a few overgrown rich were swept away"—he retreated in short order. Capitalism had its compensatory features, he quickly added, and, except for a vague half sentence about bridging the gap between rich and poor, his suggestions for mitigating social ills talked merely of easier access to jobs, moral improvement through synagogues and schools, and sufficient funds to keep poor Jews out of public institutions.[27] Within Jewish circles philanthropy became among other things a vehicle for maintaining the social order and economic mobility of nineteenth-century America, goals which had inspired the very immigration of the German Jews.

In that unusual piece Leeser talked about the "honorable poor," a synonym for "deserving poor." The label distinguished the upright and industrious struck by misfortune through no character flaw of their own from the lazy, shiftless, "stationary mendicants" ready to live permanently on community charity. Only the former, who displayed the proper virtues (and, the implication was, who despised poverty as much as the wealthy), deserved support; the latter, some recommended, should be consigned to public institutions. So deeply rooted was the middle-class view of the Jews that even the destitute were expected to give evidence of subscribing to the behavioral code of that class. At the same time, however, few philanthropists paid attention to the sensibilities of their beneficiaries. For example, although the editors of the *Occident* and the *Asmonean* objected to tablets in Jews' Hospital bearing the names of donors lest the patients be embarrassed, their objections were overruled.[28]

Before the Civil War, German Jewish immigrants established multiple local charity institutions, usually prompted in the first instance by the differences that divided them from the Sephardim. Independent agencies sprang up, from burial and sewing societies to a Jewish Colonization Association for removing immigrants from the eastern seaports. Like Americans, Jews, too, had their plethora of organizations. Although synagogues still engaged in charity, their control over that area was permanently broken. After the mid-century mark more ambitious projects were launched. Cincinnati Jewry set up a Jewish hospital in 1850, and five years later New York's Jews followed suit. In 1868, a national undertaking sponsored by B'nai B'rith resulted in the opening of a Jewish orphan asylum in Cleveland. Plans for hospitals and asylums generally drew strong support, since Jewish religious needs—dietary laws, prayers, and protection from Christian missionaries—were ignored in public institutions.[29]

From the Gilded Age until World War I, Jewish as well as American philanthropy was stamped with the imprint of the large donors, men who made charity into another big business. Some, like Andrew Carnegie, believed that their wealth made them stewards for the less fortunate. It sounded like Carnegie but it was Jacob Schiff, echoing a rabbinic dictum of the second century, who wrote that the "surplus wealth we have gained, to some extent, at least, belongs to our fellow beings; we are only the temporary custodians of our fortunes." Wealthy Jews usually responded to all sorts of appeals, but they, too, had their pet charities. For Schiff it was Montefiore Hospital; for Nathan Straus it was the crusade for pasteurized milk. Such activities entailed more than signing checks; Schiff, for example, regularly visited the patients and entertained them on annual outings. Other Jews found a favorite cause in the non-Jewish world. Banker Otto Kahn was chairman of the board (and later president) of the Metropolitan Opera Company, and Julius Rosenwald of Sears, Roebuck dedicated vast sums for improving the lot of American blacks. Less wealthy and less famous, rabbis also plunged into charity work during that period more aggressively than their successors. Young Edward Calisch, a "graduate" of the Cleveland Orphan Asylum, planned an "alumni" association in support of that institution; Joseph Krauskopf of Philadelphia founded a farm school for Jewish boys in Doylestown, Pennsylvania.[30] One-man crusades threatened to fragment still further the resources of the community and the crazy-quilt structure of the philanthropic maze, but they added a dynamic excitement to philanthropy that the bland, professionalized, and scientifically run conglomerates of later years could never attain.

In the long run, philanthropy served as a unifying force within the community. The entire community usually responded as one—if not in method at least in purpose—for the relief of distressed congregations or foreign Jews. Organizations multiplied and sometimes squabbled over turf, but they all adhered to the basic conservative code on how to give. Even before the federation movement at the turn of the century, charities were linked by interlocking directorates of donors who opened their pockets to the myriads of appeals. Donors may have patronized recipients, and recipients may have resented benefactors, but the latter still set a model for the others to emulate. Since tutelage accompanied welfare, especially in the case of the later immigrants, the Germans were able to inculcate their vision of the proper community to succeeding generations. When federation brought formal consolidation and the power to allocate huge sums among the Jewish agencies, American Jews were the closest ever to overall unity and significant autonomy. The character of the philanthropic power structure, a secularized and Americanized version of the premodern kahal, was a permanent legacy of nineteenth-century German Jews.

In the decade between 1850 and 1860 the number of American Jews rose from 50,000 to 150,000. For most of them the panic of 1857 and the depression it ushered in were the first tastes of a severe economic crisis in the United States. The panic hit in the fall, hardest in the Northeast, the burgeoning commercial and industrial region of the nation. Bankruptcies multiplied, banks suspended operations, bills went unpaid, credit dwindled, and business firms closed down. Activity was arrested in every branch of industry "under the withering breath of a monster *Panic*." Thousands of workers lost their jobs, and even those who may have so desired lacked the means to move out West. Hard times had become the staple fare of New Yorkers, the *Asmonean* said. According to the city's Association for Improving the Condition of the Poor, never before had the number of destitute or outlays by the association reached such high levels.

The panic resulted from overinvestment in railroads, feverish speculation in western lands, an inadequate banking structure, and the shrinking European market for American agricultural products. Marking a halt to a period of confident expansion, the economic collapse provided ample fodder for sermons. The ephemeral quality of human institutions and man's own shortcomings were favorite themes. Morris Raphall of B'nai Jeshurun indicted "mammon worship" and the "inordinate lust of gain" for the human misery of the depression. Arnold Fischel of Shearith Israel blamed man's recklessness and arrogance. "Inflated with success, we acted in the spirit of those men who attempted to build a tower which should reach even unto heaven; but lo! in the midst of our labors we were confounded." He was not opposed to industry and wealth, Fischel said, but only to the "abuse" of commerce. Nor did he consider the panic sufficient cause to sour the immigrant's dream of economic freedom in the New World. He called for a renewal of faith in God, a commitment to the principle of the brotherhood of man, and an outpouring of charity—the vehicle to salvation—on behalf of the poor and hungry.[31]

Jewish spokesmen in New York and Philadelphia, the most populous Jewish centers in 1857, echoed Fischel's appeal. They acknowledged the leveling aspect of the depression; hard times had hit donors, too, and some who used to give had fallen to the level of the needy. Nevertheless, they maintained, there was still enough wealth in the community for combating the unprecedented distress, and all Jews were still religiously and morally bound to give according to their ability. They pointed out that with so many swelling the ranks of the unemployed, the established charitable organizations lacked sufficient funds, especially to uncover those individuals and families too proud to beg for aid. Moreover, even a panic did not obliterate image considerations. Never let it be said, the *Jewish Messenger* admonished, that the Jews did not respond to their poor. Jews had to live up to their reputation for benevolence and keep their coreligionists out of public institutions.

The abject condition of the poor was clearly manifest to the still affluent. They watched people begging on doorsteps of homes and stores. Directors of charity organizations who personally investigated the applicants learned firsthand about the horrible living conditions the latter endured. Their findings were further confirmed by the case records of an overtaxed institution like Jews' Hospital that reported on the disease and filth in the living quarters of its patients. They feared, even if they understood, the possible eruption of crime bred of poverty.

The "deserving poor," or those whose jobs or savings were wiped out by the depression, were of particular concern. Since the "industrious artisan" deserved enough help to save him from pauperism and restore him to independence, the charity problem was further complicated. That type of relief case required more aid than customarily extended to the permanently destitute class, thus raising still further the amount of money needed. However, if relief rates were uniformly raised, the undeserving and professional beggars would reap unmerited rewards—a thought that greatly discomfited the virtuous middle class—while they ate into the resources for the "respectable" poor.[32]

To cope with the new burdens more efficiently, community leaders called for consolidation of charitable agencies in the two cities. In New York, the Hebrew Benevolent Society, a Sephardic stronghold, invited the presidents of four other institutions to consider a unified approach to the crisis, but the separate societies refused to give up their autonomy. Apparently, national differences were still too pronounced, with the older settlers arguing that most of the beneficiaries would be Germans, and the latter defensively protesting their claim to equal recognition from the arrogant Sephardim. Both Anglo-Jewish newspapers of New York, the *Asmonean* and the *Jewish Messenger*, criticized the divisiveness and what editor Lyon of the *Asmonean* termed the inability of Jews to transcend their national feelings and identify only as *American* Jews.

Nevertheless, the charities succeeded in their independent fund-raising ventures. The Hebrew Benevolent Society, for example, economized by charging its lavish annual dinner to the directors. The dinner was required by the society's bylaws, but, as one New Yorker explained, it was unrealistic to expect someone to pay $5 for the meal and then contribute to the society. The society substituted a musical evening from which it made more than $2,000, no mean sum in light of the fact that each charity applicant received on the average $2. For the year of March 1857 to March 1858, the society distributed more than $3,500 in charity to more than 2,000 applicants. The applicants were passed on by the officers or a visiting committee, or by recommendations of friends and members of the society, and benefits were allocated irrespective of birthplace or synagogue affiliation. The leading Jewish agency, the society gained recognition from the larger community as a quasi-public body. The Juvenile Asylum extended the use of its premises to the society as a meeting place for the poor, and different departments of the municipal government referred to the society needy Jews who came to their notice. In a period when the domains of public and private charities were still blurred, the oldest extra-synagogal Jewish philanthropy in New York took a place in its community analogous to that of the long-standing Protestant agencies within American society.[33]

The same needs and values underlay Jewish relief work in Philadelphia, but in that city unity was achieved by the erection of the Hebrew Relief Association. In the eyes of its directors, the panic-induced experiment, uniting Philadelphia's six congregations, more than lived up to their expectations. The new organization operated by dividing the city into seven districts; a separate committee for each district canvassed the area for donors, visited the poor, and investigated applicants. Instead of distributing provisions, the association contracted with grocers, butchers, and bakers, as well as physicians and druggists, to supply the poor who had received appropriate coupons from the association. In order to coordinate communal efforts still further, the association gave modest subsidies to the fuel and sewing societies for coal and clothing supplies. Many individuals received outright cash (averaging $3 each), and some even enough to start small businesses. Proud of its methods and accomplishments, the association, which was originally scheduled to wind up its affairs after six months, recommended the formation of a permanent relief organization. Despite the lingering jealousy for the independence of existing institutions, Philadelphia's Jews adopted the recommendation.[34]

In New York and Philadelphia, the community response to the depression peaked in the winter of 1857–1858 and again in March, at which time a special appeal for supplying the poor with matzoth for Passover was launched.[35] Barely had that crisis subsided when news arrived of a particularly severe outbreak of yellow fever in New Orleans. One reporter to the *Jewish Messenger* declared it the worst that he had experienced in twenty-seven years of residence in that city. Over a three-month period synagogues were forced to bury one hundred victims who during their lives had been unaffiliated, and the Sephardic congregation even provided burials for

Germans. (For that to have aroused comment indicated how deep the divisions among the Jews still were.) Since the Jewish charities of New Orleans had depleted their reserves during the panic, they turned for help to their sister communities. The latter responded with sympathy and cash, but despite religious teachings and group pride the money trickled in only meagerly. Whereas a single charity organization in New Orleans had spent more than $3,000 by November, the total amount from the nation's Jews in that same period reached less than $2,000. As a result, a bitter comparison was drawn between the liberal generosity of the southerners as opposed to the "picayune spirit" of the northerners. Isaac Leeser, a resident of Virginia before he settled in Philadelphia, agreed to that distinction in the pages of the *Occident*, thereby feeding another element into the North-South split of American Jewry on the eve of the Civil War.[36]

Neither the yellow-fever outbreak nor the panic of 1857 gave rise to a nonsectarian national appeal for the victims. In New Orleans, a Christian benevolent association raised large sums of money, as did its Jewish counterpart, the Gentlemen's Benevolent Society.[37] The two ran along parallel lines but did not overlap in services. Fifty years later, in the wake of the San Francisco earthquake of 1906, sectarian relief was overshadowed by the work of the American Red Cross, officially designated by President Theodore Roosevelt to cope with that disaster. As a result, the propriety and even responsibility of Jews to service stricken fellow Jews was far less clear than in 1858.

According to a contemporary article in the *American Hebrew*, San Francisco Jewry on the eve of the earthquake numbered 17,500. Their presence had been felt in the city from early times on; Washington Bartlett, the son of a Jewish mother, who later served as mayor and then as governor of California, reputedly gave the city its name. Jewish religious services began there on the Day of Atonement during the gold rush of 1849, and by 1906 there were ten congregations in addition to a wide array of charitable organizations, schools, and clubs. The German Jews had prospered in trade and industry, and their children, who constituted a large percent of California's university population, gravitated in greater numbers to the professions.[38]

Normal life in the city came to a virtual standstill as a result of the earthquake and fire that struck on April 18. Although accurate reports of the impact on lives and property were difficult to compile, the early accounts were staggering. Most of the synagogues were damaged if not destroyed; the section housing the poorer east European Jews suffered heaviest losses; 90 percent of Jewish business houses were physically wiped out; Jews were among the 200,000 homeless who camped in parks and other public places. The organized Jewish charities whose buildings were spared were nonetheless paralyzed, for their records had been destroyed.

The response of Jews throughout the country was to table sectarian fund raising. Rather, they actively solicited money and supplies for the general relief fund coordinated by the Red Cross. Jacob Schiff, then treasurer of the organization's New York chapter, doubtless set the example for a united philanthropic approach. In New York, a representative of the United Hebrew Charities participated in a relief conference called by Mayor McClellan, and Bernard Baruch served on a committee set up by the stock exchange to tap financial houses for donations. As the *American Hebrew* said, "This is not the time for the special relief of our coreligionists." The first call was for physical aid to the victims; later they could look to Jewish communal losses. True, B'nai B'rith collected some $14,000 for the relief of California members of the order, but that was an expression of fraternity rather than of Jewishness. Separate fund raising appeared particularly inappropriate when, within the stricken city, rabbis worked alongside ministers, priests, and nuns in caring for the unfortunate of all colors and faiths. Some rabbis headed city-wide relief forces. Rabbi Jacob Voorsanger directed the food committee, and Rabbi M. S. Levy supervised the grim task of burying the dead.[39]

After two weeks, however, Voorsanger appealed for special Jewish aid. It was "high time," he wrote, that a Jewish relief fund be established for the 10,000 Jews of San Francisco who needed money and supplies to enable them to start work again. The Union of American Hebrew Congregations and the press took up the call, and donations flowed in from the different sections of the country. The National Conference of Jewish Charities, the umbrella organization of leading philanthropic institutions, suspended judgment. At a special meeting it was resolved first "to ascertain the requirements of the Jewish community of San Francisco, both as to its general future needs and as to the work of reconstruction and support of institutions." If the situation required special funds, the National Conference would then launch a general relief drive. On behalf of the conference, Rabbi Judah Magnes, a native Californian, and Dr. Lee Frankel, superintendent of New York's United Hebrew Charities, immediately set out for San Francisco. Voorsanger insisted that at least $30,000 or $40,000 would have to be raised from American Jews, but after touring the city the two visitors decided against a special fund. The immediate needs of Jewish sufferers were answered by the general relief and Red Cross funds and by help from neighboring Jewish communities. Nor did Magnes and Frankel see any urgency in collecting money for long-range rehabilitation purposes. The Red Cross director in the area assured them that funds would be available on nonsectarian lines for those tasks, too. Communal leaders in San Francisco agreed, adding that they would be able to muster additional required funds from the reserves of the charity organizations and from the wealthy of their own city. Undoubtedly, pride entered into their formally drawn-up resolution declining further offers of aid.[40]

It is likely that Magnes and Frankel wound up their trip with a sigh of relief. To have initiated a separate Jewish appeal augmenting the nonsectarian relief work might have raised serious suspicions about Jewish separatism or lack of civic solidarity. The American Jewish community had but recently organized a national relief fund on behalf of the victims of the Russian pogroms; yet another national project for a "Jewish cause" threatened to undercut the first at the same time that it accentuated Jewish visibility. Magnes and Frankel were also very much involved in relief projects for the Jewish ghetto dwellers of the eastern cities, whose seemingly endless needs steadily drained Jewish charitable resources. How well would it serve the needy as well as the Jewish reputation to fragment contributions to the point of ineffectuality?

Following the National Conference's decision to drop the matter, Jews across the land applauded the independence of San Francisco Jewry. However, reactions by the rabbis of two of San Francisco's most prestigious synagogues, Jacob Voorsanger of Emanu-El and Jacob Nieto of Shearith Israel, indicated that somewhere communication with the Magnes-Frankel relief team had broken down. Nieto, who had seconded Voorsanger's original appeal, vented deep bitterness over the easterners' seeming lack of concern. Not only had funds previously collected failed to reach San Francisco, but national religious organizations like the Union of American Hebrew Congregations and the Central Conference of American Rabbis, whose "sacred duty" lay in reconstructing congregational life, remained inactive. Nieto defended the proper behavior of San Francisco's Jews. (1) They had not wanted charity but merely the means to invigorate the city's economic structure and avoid pauperism. (2) They had attempted to handle Jewish relief cases on their own; only 500 out of 1,200 were referred to the Red

Cross, and the rest received loans against personal insurance policies. (3) Many Jews had been too proud to bring their needs even to a Jewish committee, and those cases still needed to be uncovered. In other words, since San Francisco's Jews had lived up to the behavioral code of American Jewish philanthropy, their more fortunate brethren should have understood the unspoken needs and responded with appropriate help. Moreover, Nieto concluded, in light of the fact that every Christian denomination was supporting San Francisco's churches, "for a paltry hundred thousand [dollars] the Jews of the United States cannot afford to be out of the race."

Jacob Voorsanger, who was also a member of the newly organized American Jewish Committee, voiced similar thoughts at a committee meeting a few days later. He explained that the aid requested of the National Conference for rehabilitation work—for the poorer synagogues and Jewish Educational Society—had not been considered at all by Frankel and Magnes. Since Voorsanger had the foresight to clear his appeal privately with Jacob Schiff, the financial guardian of the committee, that agency resolved to raise $100,000 solely for the purpose of reconstructing Jewish religious and educational institutions in San Francisco. That stipulation warded off any criticism about Jews reaping benefits from both public and private funds. Close to $38,000 was raised—Nieto himself solicited funds under committee auspices from West Coast cities— but since no contributions were received after May 1908, the appeal was dropped that year.[41]

Political Neutrality

A group that was primed for freedom before it left Europe, German Jews were likely to accept eagerly the political responsibilities of voting and officeholding that citizenship entailed. But although Jewish spokesmen commended such acts of civic-mindedness, most laid down strict guidelines circumscribing the political activity of Jews as a group. The basic rules were formulated before the Civil War, and they lingered well into the twentieth century.[42] Politics concerned the individual Jew but not the community. Jewish group interests, if indeed there were any, had no place under that name in any political forum. The derivatives followed almost automatically. (1) It was wrong for Jews to band together in separate political clubs. (2) Rabbis or lay leaders had no right to advise the community on how to vote. (3) Jewish agencies must not use their influence to promote Jewish aspirants to political office. (4) Jews should not support a candidate just because he happened to be Jewish.

Communal leaders aimed their strictures at non-Jews, too. Talk of a Jewish vote was unwarranted; political demagogues or parties erred if they claimed they could deliver that nonexistent entity. A Jew did not merit nomination or appointment on the grounds of his Jewishness, but neither should that fact discriminate against him. Bloc voting by any ethnic group was indefensible, and independent behavior by Jews provided a good example to other minorities.

Such sentiments were enunciated as early as 1832 in South Carolina. In that year of the tariff controversy, Jews of Charleston divided over the nullification issue. Apparently a story circulated in the city that the Jews had petitioned the nullification party for representation "as a *religious sect*" in the state legislature. Eighty-four outraged Jews immediately retorted with a public disclaimer that emphasized their political independence and pointed to their participation in both parties. The resolutions they drew up included the following:

Resolved, That we wholly disclaim any wish or intention to be represented as a peculiar community, and that we discountenance the idea of selecting any individual for office . . . upon the ground that such individual belongs to a particular sect, with the view of securing or of influencing the suffrages of such sect.

Resolved, That the perfect independence of the Israelites of Charleston, is beyond the control of any individual, it matters not to what sect or party he may be attached. . . .

Resolved, That while we are sensible there are gentlemen among us, who would do no discredit to any station public or private, we will not support any man for office who is not selected by the public for himself, his character and his talents.[43]

More than other immigrant groups, nineteenth-century American Jews shied away from injecting ethnic interests into the political arena. Since the days of the French Revolution and Napoleon they had sworn that their political concerns were identical with those of their compatriots. It was the posture axiomatic to the attainment of equal rights. The denial of separate group loyalties also drew from the Enlightenment's emphasis upon the importance of the individual as opposed to the collectivity. In the United States, Jewish insistence on the separation of church and state reinforced that stand. If Jews were no more than a religious group, how could they in all good conscience seek a political role at the same time that they railed against the dangers of the Know-Nothings and the anti-Catholic American Protective Association, or against Sunday laws and sectarian schools? Besides, Rabbi Isaac Mayer Wise's *Israelite* declared in 1858, it would be wrong to downgrade the sanctity of religion by mixing it with low and corrupt politics. The *Occident* agreed; political activity neither dignified the character of the Jew or his religion. "Jews should love their faith too much, to permit it to be dragged into the political arena."[44]

Clearly, the Know-Nothing era left an indelible stamp on Jewish political behavior. The impressionable new immigrants of the 1840s and 1850s saw not only the abuses of Protestant zealotry in politics but also the attacks on Irish Catholics for reasons that included political separatism. In 1856, frowning upon a secret anti-British society organized by the Irish in Cincinnati, a state court specifically cautioned that group against "divided national allegiance." Protestant hostility and suspicions even caused some Irish spokesmen to urge neutrality in politics upon their own constituents. The *Citizen* of New York City wrote in 1854 denying the existence of an Irish vote. We have always argued, the paper said, that the Irish should not act together politically as Irish or allow their votes to be delivered by priests or saloon keepers.[45] The Jews who watched the course of events shared neither the political skill nor the temperament that propelled the Irish into the business of politics. But frightened by what could happen to a non-Protestant minority, Jews drew reinforcement for their inhibitions against group activity.

Nervousness about their hard-won security underlay Jewish thinking. In 1648 the Sephardic leaders in London so feared the potential danger to the community that they threatened excommunication of anyone who voted in an election or took sides on a political question.[46] Two hundred years later most American Jews were still wary of suggesting a Jewish point of view on secular affairs. Even in the United States the need to prove their single and unequivocal loyalty to the country persisted. Unfavorable stereotypes continued to dog the Jew, and spokesmen labored valiantly to lay to rest the concept that a single act or characteristic of an individual could stigmatize the entire group. On occasion American periodicals warned the Jews that political pressure on their part could boomerang and cause a backlash of anti-Semitism.[47] In the last quarter of the nineteenth century, when accusations against a malevolent Jewish money power were multiplying in Europe and at home, an anti-Semitic report in Europe charged that Baron Maurice de Hirsch had poured money into Cleveland's election. To avert such slurs and threats, it seemed safest for Jews to keep a low profile politically. In no way should the minority activate ever-latent suspicions about Jewish patriotism or "political schizophrenia."[48]

The prescription for Jewish political neutrality bifurcated the individual Jew and his interests into two distinct orbits—one political and public, one Jewish and private. Spokesmen insisted that the division was tenable, and they refused to admit in principle to any overlapping between the two areas. Reform Jews were better equipped to maintain that position, for by their definition Judaism was only a religion devoid of any ethnic dimension. The differences between religion and politics, church and state, sacred and profane appeared abundantly clear. According to the *Israelite*, the mission of the Jews, "the redemption of mankind from the obscurity of fiction, the bondage of injustice, and the tyranny of superstition and ignorance," could not be achieved by "political parties, elections, rowdies and slanderers."[49] But the behavior of the Reform Jews, particularly with respect to the needs of foreign Jews, proved that even they could not sunder all their ethnic ties. From the outset, therefore, the attempts to divorce Jewish interests from politics were unreal for all who continued to identify as Jews. The wonder is that despite its unnatural quality, the message that "Jew" did not belong in politics reverberated so long.

A particularly glaring logical flaw stood out in the brief for neutrality. Although Jews were instructed to be no more than Americans in all political matters, they were repeatedly admonished that the behavior of an individual Jewish officeholder reflected upon the entire group. The *American Israelite* added that the Jew had to be better than his neighbor when he competed in the public eye.[50] Thus, those who portrayed an ideal political world free of ethnic interests frankly acknowledged that the Jew could not escape his ethnic identity in politics, and their fantasy world remained just that.

The truth of the matter was that insistence on a politically invisible group was more un-American (in the literal sense of the term) than admitting the propriety of ethnic politics. A political system that Madison had correctly interpreted as reflecting the special interests of contending factions expected voters to express their concerns through the ballot. For Jewish spokesmen to insist that ethnic interests were less legitimate than economic ones was artificial and particularly unrealistic in an immigrant community as yet largely unassimilated. Had the Jews been less bent on currying favor with the native Protestants, they might have seen that the renunciation of group political interests only sheared them of any strength that in the American system was rightfully theirs. Neutrality operated neither to serve the real interests that affected the Jewish group before World War I—nativist and anti-immigrant movements, the struggle for the separation of church and state, the plight of foreign Jewries—nor to convince the native Protestants that the Jews only differed from them in matters of religion. By cutting off recourse to the polls, Jews had to push their interests in peripheral ways—petitions or quiet personal pressure on officeholders, or appeals to non-Jewish opinion molders to take up a particular issue. Such ploys often involved the removal of the word "Jewish" from "Jewish interest" and the substitution of "American" or "democratic" in its place. Nineteenth-century American Jews staked their faith on the rationality and goodwill of fellow Americans. Denying the need for political power, they liked to believe that reliance on enlightened public opinion and the persuasive force of American liberal ideology was sufficient. Seek out the "friends of universal liberty," Isaac Leeser advised, little understanding that even those had to resort to politics to be heard.[51]

Protestations from the Jews did not make that group invisible in politics to the outside. Jewish officeholders, no matter how detached they were from Judaism and the Jewish community, always bore the label of Jew. David Yulee of Florida, who served in Congress and then as governor, was usually referred to by John Quincy Adams as the "Jew delegate." In the fury vented during the Civil War, three Democratic politicians who happened to be Jewish in name only—Yulee, Judah Benjamin, August Belmont—drew added abuse from critics on the grounds of their Jewish extraction.[52]

On a different level, American politicians realized early on the political capital inherent even in the very small numbers of Jews. Federalists injected a note of anti-Semitism in their attacks on the Jeffersonians during the last decade of the eighteenth century, admitting thereby the help of Jews to that party. The attacks paid scant attention to the distinction between "Jew" in generic terms and the active individual Jews within the Jeffersonian ranks. Jews may not have voted as a bloc for Jefferson's party, but Federalist anti-immigration as well as anti-Semitic tones reinforced their loyalty to the Democratic-Republicans (and after them to Jackson's party). Democratic politicians in New York City carefully cultivated that loyalty even with innocuous gestures like attending important Jewish social affairs. In 1857, when American Jews were fighting the discriminatory treaty between the United States and Switzerland, the opposition used the "Jewish issue" to taunt the incumbent Democratic administration. Thus, even if Jews took a neutral, independent political stance, the non-Jews disregarded the lines between individual Jewish voters and a Jewish collectivity.[53]

The fact that leading Anglo-Jewish periodicals reiterated the rules time and again indicates that Jews, too, did not swallow them meekly. For example, Jewish political clubs continued to crop up, especially after the arrival of the more politically eager but inexperienced east European immigrants. In 1895 Rabbi Joseph Krauskopf of Philadelphia sued for an injunction to prevent the founding of one such organization. His efforts aroused a public outcry against the club's bid for a charter, and the bid failed. Apparently some Jews also talked to politicians about a Jewish vote. In 1864 John Hay had to reassure New York communal leader Myer Isaacs about a delegation that had visited Lincoln: "No pledge of the Jewish vote was made by these gentlemen and no inducements or promises were extended to them by the President."

With respect to support for Jewish candidates, the *American Hebrew* was forced to suggest a compromise. If both candidates were fit for office, it was proper to vote for the Jew. But if neither were qualified, Jews should work to defeat their coreligionist. In 1860, when Jonas Levy of Washington, D.C., asked the Board of Delegates of American Israelites to intercede on his behalf with President Buchanan and urge Levy's appointment to a consulship, the board reminded Levy of the community's neutrality laws. We appreciate your consistent cooperation in Jewish communal affairs, the board replied, but we can't help. "Mingling in politics is forbidden to the Board by its constitution. The bare suspicion & insinuation of the probability of its taking part in them, nearly prevented its establishment, & the knowledge of its exercise of its influence even in so meritorious a case as yours, might compromise its very existence."[54]

Nineteenth-century American Jews also preferred that their rabbis steer clear of politics lest any statement be interpreted as the sentiment of the Jewish group. Here, too, political invisibility was unnatural, since it broke with the pattern of close clerical involvement with politics set by the Puritans in colonial days. A Sephardic religious leader, Gershom Mendes Seixas, had been part of that earlier tradition. A fervent patriot in New York during the revolutionary era, he delivered a sermon on the National Fast Day of 1798 that was used by the Jeffersonian forces in their differences with the Federalists over the war with France. Not that Seixas spoke politically; indeed, in accordance with the official purpose of the day, he pleaded for peace through individual repentance. However, since the Federalists had determined to stir up war sentiment through the pulpits, and since most ministers obliged, Seixas's sermon was particularly welcome to the Antifederalists.[55]

Sixty years later Isaac Mayer Wise aroused the furor of some Cincinnati Jews by taking sides on the sectional conflict over Kansas and by his firm endorsement of the Democratic party. Not only had he offended the anti-Democrats, but also the angry Jews who aired their grievance in the city press found another reason for denouncing him: "We had supposed when we subscribed for his paper, that it was his purpose to make it a religious paper, totally eschewing all political subjects; and . . . we have been deceived in this."[56]

On the eve of the Civil War, congregations tried last-minute attempts to muzzle their rabbis on the issue of slavery. Isaac Mayer Wise's board, most of whom were Republicans, ordered their rabbi to turn down the Democratic nomination for state senator. They also resolved to tell Wise "that the Board disapproves of all political allusions in his sermons and to discontinue same." The ardent abolitionist, David Einhorn, upset his Baltimore congregation with sermons that drew warnings from both friends and foes in the strife-ridden border state. Jews hastened to affirm publicly that Einhorn did not speak for them, and even sympathizers within Har Sinai Temple advised the rabbi to flee north. When he finally left, the board wrote him that in the future it would be prudent to abstain from "the excitable issues of the time." Rabbi Morris Raphall of New York's B'nai Jeshurun had created quite a stir with a sermon (also on a National Fast Day) in which he argued that slavery was sanctioned by the Bible. Civil War scholar Bertram Korn wrote that Raphall's sermon "aroused more comment and attention than any other sermon ever delivered by an American rabbi." Widely circulated throughout the country, the sermon made friends and enemies in opposing sections for both Raphall and the entire Jewish community. In New York City, for example, the *Tribune* held the community responsible for Raphall's statements. The rabbi's board of trustees warned him after the fact: "We . . . respectfully suggest to Dr. Raphall the impropriety of any intermeddling with politics, as we firmly believe such a course to be entirely inconsistent with the Jewish clerical character, calculated to be of serious injury to the Jews in general and to our congregation in particular."[57]

Perhaps with the Civil War still echoing in their ears, laymen stuck by the politically neutral rabbi even on seemingly trivial issues. In 1894, Myer Stern, active and respected leader in New York's Temple Emanu-El and in Jewish philanthropic circles, took the time to write a public letter denouncing Rabbi Adolph M. Radin. Radin had spoken at an anti-Tammany meeting at which he disclosed cases of police graft and harassment of east European peddlers, and Stern's anger seemed out of proportion to the rabbi's revelations about herring and soda vendors. But, according to Stern, a rabbi as rabbi could not participate in a political gathering.

Since Jews "take no part in politics as Jews," Radin's behavior was "disgraceful and indecent." Rabbi Gustav Gottheil of Temple Emanu-El was also chided for delivering an allegedly political sermon and attempting thereby to control the congregation's "political consciences." For their part, rabbis defended the right to take political stands. In 1889, according to David Philipson, the clergy had been sent circulars that year asking them to devote their Thanksgiving Day sermons to civil-service reform. It was the rabbi's proper function to heed the appeal, Philipson said, because the clergy's concern for religious welfare legitimately encompassed moral behavior on every level. Rabbi Henry Berkowitz agreed: "'How dare you drag politics into the pulpit?' someone will no doubt ask. 'How dare you drag morality out of politics?' I will ask in return." Addressing his colleagues at a convention of the Central Conference of American Rabbis, Rabbi Aaron Hahn took refuge in ambiguity. While people believed a rabbi must not meddle with politics, "he would be no man if he would allow anybody to interfere with his duties as a good citizen."[58]

The rank and file who heeded the strictures on absolute group neutrality were often hard put to draw the line between that and different forms of political activity. For many, neutrality meant aloofness from political office. An account of San Francisco published in 1876 observed: "Few of them [Jews] have any political aspirations, and it is a rare occurrence to find them occupying any official position, either municipal or state. Yet they take a lively interest in politics."[59] To other Jews, however, neutrality doubtless meant total detachment from politics. Reporting in 1856 on the refusal of a Baltimore lyceum to admit Jews, the *Israelite* attributed the perpetuation of prejudice to the tendency of Jews to steer clear of elections. "Everybody knows," the paper said, "how slightly political wire pullers regard those of whom they have to fear nothing."[60] If the journal did not see any inconsistency between that statement and its simultaneous pronouncements that religious issues in politics and a Jewish vote were anathema, perhaps the Baltimoreans did.

In light of the unreal quality of their political rules, even the spokesmen for neutrality could not help but overstep the boundaries. Editor Isaac Mayer Wise was not the only culprit. The *Jewish Messenger* confessed to inconsistency when it once recommended candidates for public office, but it did so again on other occasions. The nomination and election of Jews wasn't supposed to matter, but the *Messenger*, like the other papers, took satisfaction in those signs of public recognition. The New York *Messenger* and Cincinnati *American Israelite* grumbled that the Jews elected to Congress had not proved to be of help to their community. But hadn't the idea been that Jews would perform in office as Americans and not Jews? The Anglo-Jewish press kept tabs on Jews who ran for office and on elections where prejudice hurt those candidates. It shouldn't have mattered either, but the periodicals occasionally felt impelled to account for the relatively small number of Jews in elective office. Usually their explanations were defensive. It was bigotry that kept Jews from higher elective posts; "manners" and "rowdyism" dampened Jewish willingness to participate in the primaries; if Jews chose to devote their lives to politics, it was not unlikely that they would eventually be nominated for the presidency.[61]

Clearly, it mattered very much even to the official neutralists to see the Jewish community represented in politics. At times, when their ambivalent feelings caught up with them, they looked for ways to smooth over their contradictory leanings. The *Jewish Messenger* and *American Hebrew* decided that partisanship and a Jewish vote were justifiable in an election if anti-Semitism was the issue. The *Israelite* (later the *American Israelite*) found a different but equally large loophole. It urged Jews to take an interest in politics on the side of American liberty and justice. Since Jewish causes—e.g., equal rights, separation of church and state—could easily be defined in those terms, they became American causes entitled to the political support of all loyal citizens, including Jews. Thus, for example, when Max Lilienthal of the *Israelite* called on North Carolina's Jews to work for the removal of the anti-Jewish disabilities in that state, he termed the disabilities affronts to America. "It is a holy duty, imposed upon all our brethren, to efface on this soil of religious and civil liberty, the last stain of intolerance, imported in past times from illiberal Europe." A year later the *Israelite* admonished Jews in Baltimore to protest openly against the injustice of the city's Sunday laws: "It is all right to be no demagogue, no office-hunter and no public cryer; but it is not right to be imposed upon, and bear it with lamb-like meekness."[62]

A traditionalist like Isaac Leeser of Philadelphia also groped for answers to the basic questions posed by emancipation: Jewish belonging, visibility, and "groupness" within the body politic. He, too, propagated an individualist and a non-Jewish approach to politics, but since he held on to a belief in Jewish peoplehood, he had greater difficulty than the Reformers in justifying a repudiation of ethnic politics. In a lengthy editorial of 1855 he presented his views:

With politics, however, Jews have little concern, except to vote for those whom they individually may deem most fitting to administer the offices created for the public good. To do this, they require no national organization, nor to be told by their leaders how to proceed. In the Synagogue and congregational meetings we want Jews; in public matters, only American citizens. By this we do not mean to counsel a mean submission to insult, nor an acquiescence in party drill to vote for men who have offended Jews in disregarding what is due to them. . . . It would . . . be the height of absurdity for us to mingle in the strife of parties, and say, "We Jews will give victory to such or such a one"; for in this manner we would not only expose ourselves, justly, to the hatred of the party defeated by *our* influence, but would also do the very thing which we condemn as wrong in others, to permit our religion to enter as a party question in political struggles. We have done well enough, hitherto, by keeping out of the strife of parties; Jews indeed vote; and we hope they will always continue to exercise the elective franchise, quietly and unostentatiously voting for all kinds of men, and with all kinds of parties; thus giving a practical proof that Israelites are men of the country, notwithstanding they are true to their religion. But only when they should become aware that any party threatens the liberties of the country; only when it should become evident, which God forbid, that traitors to justice and freedom would endeavor to overthrow the glorious constitution of the country, by introducing religious tests and abridging the rights of conscience; yes, then let Israelites unite with the friends of the constitution, of equal rights, of freedom, not as Jews, however, but as true citizens of America, and vote for the preservation of the noblest monument of human, God-guided wisdom, . . . established for this happy land.[63]

Laden with contradictions—be an American publicly and a Jew privately; don't submit to insult, but don't stir up popular excitement; rejoice in the blessings of the Constitution, but watch out for the persistence of bigotry—Leeser's statement betrayed a fear of the gentile world along with a determination to belong to that world. Like the *Israelite*, Leeser affirmed that Jewish causes of significance were identical to the principles of Americanism. But even when called upon to defend such principles, Leeser's proper Jews responded more circumspectly; they neither acted as Jews nor took any stand apart from others.

Another thread in the tangled web of political behavior was the traditionalists' fear that religious apathy and secularism almost automatically accompanied politics. For those reasons alone, Leeser would scarcely have counseled Jews to plunge into politics or, even less, to identify politically as a separate group. Leeser was sufficiently close in time to have seen how European Jews, on the brink of emancipation, devoted themselves to the struggle for equal rights with religiouslike fervor and how their attachment to traditional

Judaism simultaneously weakened. For some Jews salvation shifted from its religious moorings to a secular, this-worldly plane, now a goal that man could attain by human and political methods. Leeser said he saw parallel signs in the United States, where Jews thought only about their political equality. No different from the biblical Esau who sold his birthright, some Jews kept their religion under wraps lest it bar their way to political office.

Thus, another problem arose for traditionalists in a modern world: Was it possible to work actively for and enjoy equal participatory rights in a democracy without compromising the ties to Judaism or the nature of traditional Judaism? Leeser thought yes, but nevertheless he worked to mute the appeal of politics. It was the principle involved rather than the benefits derived that justified agitation for equal rights, he explained. He denigrated office hunters who "seek to acquire their daily bread by running after the populace, to flatter them for their vote, or to wait upon those in power to drop graciously into their hungry mouth a few cast-off crumbs from the public table." He also argued that the world would despise those who sacrificed their religion on the altar of political power. If it ever became an either/or question—i.e., Judaism or equal political rights—he, Leeser, was prepared to forgo the rights. "We can do without voting at elections; we can live without holding offices; but we are nothing without religion, we die without our faith." On one occasion the *Occident* reacted to setbacks in the Jewish struggle for political equality with seemingly perverse joy. Those failures proved the hollowness of the fantasy about man-made redemption through the modern national state.[64]

Despite the ambivalences and contradictions, the neutralist position in politics was the norm by the 1850s. The short-lived *Asmonean*, the first Anglo-Jewish weekly of New York (1849–58), found cause to challenge that view and the political apathy it seemed to generate. In 1851, when New York City feted Hungarian hero Louis Kossuth at a public banquet, the *Asmonean* smarted under the insult that no Jews had been invited. Since Jews made up about 20 percent of the city's population, it was an "outrage" to have ignored them. At bottom, however, the fault was the Jews'. Their behavior had convinced the city fathers that Jews were too weak politically to show resentment over slights. Although legally Jews possessed equal rights, the editor of the *Asmonean*, Robert Lyon, maintained that they still lacked true equality. Only if they used their rights to their advantage, like other groups who indulged in politics, could

Jews wield an influence commensurate with their numbers. Lyon recommended an activist approach as a united group:

[U]nless they cultivate their talents, unless they gain the confidence of their fellow-citizens, unless they unite to make their weight as a body duly felt; unless, like all other denominations, they cooperate so as to promote the general influence of that class of citizens called Jews; they may flourish in Wall-street and prosper in Chatham-place, they may keep holy the Sabbath of the Lord, by parading on horseback, or rush to the ballot-box, along with some drunken, shouting, son of Erin; political equality, they will achieve none.[65]

During the next two years Lyon reported on the views of different state and federal candidates about the Jews. By 1854 the *Asmonean* was ready to take sides in the election and advise its readers on how to vote. We don't usually mix in politics, the paper said twice (thereby acknowledging the laws of political neutrality), but at a time when the Know-Nothings were gaining power and notoriety, the *Asmonean* felt constrained to condemn the intolerance and fanaticism of that anti-immigration movement and to side with the Democratic opposition. Voting rather than loud speeches was the best way to show opinions, the paper said. It reserved special criticism for those Jews who, despite the evidence, continued to support the Know-Nothings.

The paper carried its anti-Know-Nothing campaign through the elections of 1856. Critics inside as well as outside the Jewish community found fault with its political role, and publicly the paper backed off. It denied that it had called on American Jews to act together politically; in fact, "We should for many reasons regret to see the Jews of America combine as a political body to support any faction." The paper would have continued to abstain from endorsing political candidates, it claimed, if not for the menace posed by the nativist party to American principles. Its mission in 1856 was merely to prevent those who had supported the nativists two years earlier from repeating their error, and to recognize that the interests of the Jews coincided with the election of Buchanan and the Democrats. In point of fact, the *Asmonean*, like the more timid Jews, was ambivalent. On the one hand, it admitted the validity of the criticisms it had evoked, but on the other, it continued to endorse political candidates even after the 1856 elections. In 1857 it advised that Jews unite and use their numbers and wealth against the Swiss treaty, but sharing the worries of the minority group, it cautioned them to keep the issue free of political partisanship. Without the backing of the community, Lyon hedged his views on the group's political activism.[66]

Half a century later and three thousand miles away, the *Emanu-El* of San Francisco also deviated from the purist code. It had no inhibitions about expressing itself on politics, particularly those of the city, and during the campaign of 1908 it openly canvassed for support of the Republican party. In the issue preceding the election it devoted one page entitled "Vote Right Next Tuesday" to pictures and capsule biographies of preferred candidates. Nevertheless, the paper firmly drew the line against Jewish political clubs and those who called for a solid Jewish vote. The *Emanu-El* probably would have explained its behavior by saying that it only appealed to Jews as American citizens. It had never read specifically Jewish issues into the election, nor did it ask its readers to vote *as Jews,* singly or in a bloc, for certain candidates. Jewish political clubs, however, indicated the existence of a Jewish point of view on current affairs and were, therefore, irregular.[67]

The neutralist political code, often honored in the breach, stunted the group's normal development in politics. Jews lagged behind Protestants and Catholics, Irish and Germans, in sounding the Jewish voice—be it religious or ethnic—in the political marketplace. Not until the twentieth century did they turn more comfortably to politics as a medium for registering group interests and for forging alliances with other minorities.

From the earliest days of the republic Jews had found their way into political office. On municipal, state, and federal levels they served at appointive and elective posts—as legislators, judges, administrators, consuls. By 1830 their record was sufficiently rich to be studied in England during debates on the right of that country's Jews to sit in Parliament. Some American Jews carved niches for themselves within the party machines and, like those who had participated in the organization of New York's Tammany Hall in 1794, enjoyed power and influence without officeholding.[68] The nineteenth-century Jews were also visible in areas of public service. From their ranks came the first Jewish cabinet member and the first Jew on the Supreme Court. Like most minority groups, they were represented in both major parties. They sent fewer men into politics than did the Irish, but the motives and campaign methods of those Jews who sought office were indistinguishable from the others.[69] Although later writers have noted the penchant for political moralism that characterized the east European immigrants—i.e., the belief that politics had the higher purpose of creating the good society—German Jews did not abstain from politics as a way of personal advancement. August Belmont, the banker and agent of the House of

Rothschild, collected marks of political recognition as he did art and horses—to be part of the American non-Jewish scene. Simon Guggenheim and his brothers decided it was fitting for a scion of the mining family to be represented in the Senate, and, as their election methods in Colorado proved, price was no object.[70]

The way in which the self-conscious Jewish spokesmen watched a coreligionist in politics reflected various tensions generated by the three-way interplay of political neutrality, ethnic loyalty, and non-Jewish opinion. They preached independence, but they hoped for a display of ethnic sensitivity on the part of the officeholder. They generally assumed the responsibility of defending the Jewish politician from anti-Semitic abuse, whether the politician desired such defense (or even association) or not. When Belmont, then on the Democratic National Committee, asked Pennsylvania's treasurer about the repayment of the state's debt, the answer was: "We are willing to give you the pound of flesh, but not one drop of Christian blood." The *Jewish Messenger* held up the remark for public attack, but there is no evidence to suggest that Belmont would have appreciated such unsolicited support.[71]

In the case of Judah Benjamin, the "brains" of the Confederacy, the Jews could have found ample reason for dissociation. Benjamin had neither identified with the community nor taken an interest in Jewish affairs while in Congress. His wife and child were Catholic. During the Civil War he drew abuse from both northerners and southerners, and often was excoriated because he belonged to the "accursed" people. But although he evoked charges that impugned the virtues and patriotism of the entire group, the Jews did not read him out of their camp. They took pride in the achievements of the Sephardic Jew, lawyer, and plantation owner whose political career led from Louisiana's state legislature to the Senate and from there to the cabinet of the Confederacy. Before the war the *Israelite* had suggested Benjamin's appointment as minister to Spain, calling it a proper rejoinder to anti-Jewish comments that appeared in the press. It seemed fitting, too, that an American Jew go to Spain, the country which had exiled its Jews the same year that Columbus reached the New World. Benjamin's war "crimes" operated to strengthen ethnic solidarity. The honor of the entire community was on the line when Senator Henry Wilson of Massachusetts accused the Confederate official of conspiring against the government that had extended equal rights even to those guilty of crucifying Jesus.

Benjamin's reputation climbed to greater heights after the war, when he took up residence in England. By attributing to him the story usually told in Disraeli's name about the Jews in the vanguard of civilization, some made him a legend in his own time.° When Benjamin died in 1884, one obituary proudly enumerated his talents and likened his career to that of Disraeli. "He was undoubtedly the most successful statesman of the Jewish family in this century and country, and deserves a special memorial in the Jewish annals." At the end of the century, the *American Israelite* proudly reprinted a letter from Jefferson Davis in praise of his Jewish cabinet officer's brilliance and loyalty.[72]

Unlike Benjamin, the less well-known Abraham Ruef of San Francisco gained a reputation that lacked any redeeming features for the Jewish community to embrace. Born in 1864 into the family of a wealthy merchant of French origin, Ruef was an honors student at Berkeley who went on to earn a law degree. His early urge to political-reform causes was soured by the apathy and corruption that he met with in his initial encounters with municipal politicians. His taste for politics became a veritable addiction, and his path to his coveted goal, a seat in the Senate, propelled him to the organization of the Union Labor party and to campaign in 1901 for his own handpicked mayoral candidate. During Mayor Schmitz's tenure, Boss Ruef, the pivotal figure behind the elected officials, handled the lucrative business of municipal contracts, licenses, and rate fixing. As Ruef himself later recounted, the amount of graft continued to increase, and Ruef shared the take with many elected officials. His power steadily rose and reached a high point after the 1906 earthquake, when he capitalized on the reconstruction of the city for his personal gain. On his way up Ruef made many enemies among prominent men, and the latter finally succeeded in having him indicted for graft. Ironically, the trials of Ruef and others were conducted in two synagogue buildings, which served after the earthquake as makeshift courtrooms.

In December 1908 Ruef was sentenced to prison for bribery, thus ending a two-year period in which the boss's Jewishness was

---

°Benjamin reputedly said in answer to anti-Semitic slurs: "I glory in the fact that my ancestors were waging a war for the true God, for Liberty and Religion, when those of the gentleman who now seeks to reproach me were tending swine in Bohemia, and worshipping stocks and stones as their only embodiments of Deity."

more widely noted than ever before. Like Benjamin, Ruef had not identified with the Jewish community, but after his indictment some newspapers referred to him as a Jew. While he was under arrest two rabbis, Jacob Nieto of Congregation Shearith Israel and Bernard Kaplan of Ohabei Shalom, worked out an arrangement between the prisoner and the prosecution. Ruef would plead guilty, confess, and, as the rabbis understood it, receive full immunity by revealing information to the prosecution. According to the rabbis, it would be Ruef's chance at moral atonement. As it turned out, the prosecution interpreted the agreement differently, and no immunity was forthcoming. The Jewish community of San Francisco joined the mounting public chorus of opposition (political and financial) to the prosecution as the proceedings dragged on. When the *American Israelite* criticized Nieto and Kaplan for having gotten mixed up with a "cur" and a "rascal," letters from irate Californians defended the rabbis. The *Emanu-El*, San Francisco's Jewish weekly, kept up a running attack against the prosecution, implying that the latter for its own low motives had hounded Ruef unfairly. Rabbi Stephen S. Wise of New York's Free Synagogue aroused the paper's anger when he called upon the Jews of San Francisco to clean house. The *Emanu-El* hotly retorted that there were no guilty Jews to be thrown out. It charged the prosecution with purposely disqualifying Jews as jurors, thereby making the entire Jewish group appear responsible for Ruef. Non-Jews also thought that Ruef was the object of persecution, and from both quarters came allusions to the Dreyfus affair.

As in the case of Benjamin, Ruef's notoriety reflected upon the entire group. But whereas outside San Francisco American Jewish leaders criticized or ignored the boss, whom they considered a blot upon the Jewish name, the majority of the Jewish community within the city was critical of Ruef's prosecutors. Ethnic pride and self-image colored both types of Jewish response, proving that even when Jews reacted as Jews on political issues they did not necessarily respond uniformly.[73]

Oscar S. Straus,[74] scion of the merchandising family, rejected the business world in favor of a career in government service. A proud Jew and very much involved in Jewish affairs throughout his life, he was one of the small handful of communal stewards who directed American Jewish secular affairs before the ascendancy of the national defense agencies. As part of the Jewish establishment, Straus, too, preached the neutralist political code, but like Benjamin and

Ruef, he could not shrug off the Jewish label which marked him to the outside. To the extent, however, that Straus's political career was associated with his Jewishness, it differed significantly from that of the other two. First, Straus himself believed that his public performance reflected upon all Jews. For example, when offered the post of minister to Turkey in 1887, he knew that the administration had consulted the powerful missionary groups with interests in the Ottoman Empire about his appointment. Obligated to show the Christians that a Jew could champion their rights, he thought he might also instruct them in religious toleration. Second, in those areas where no blatant conflict of interest existed, Straus used his official position for the benefit of his coreligionists. During his first two missions to Turkey he worked quietly for the rights of Jews in Palestine. While in Theodore Roosevelt's cabinet as secretary of commerce and labor, his defense of free immigration undoubtedly stemmed in large measure from his concern for the hounded Jews of eastern Europe who so desperately needed a refuge. Indeed, charges that Straus was "soft" on immigrant Jews were brought by prominent restrictionists to the attention of the president. Third, Straus's Jewish sensitivities which led him in the first place to support the neutralist political code conflicted with his personal political needs. Ironically, the concerned and involved Jew was honorbound not to request a show of appreciation at the polls from an admiring Jewish community. Benjamin and Ruef may not have requested favors from fellow Jews, but then again they had never earned that right.

Straus's handicap emerged in 1912, when he ran on the Progressive ticket for governor of New York. Though in theory the candidate disapproved, his party made capital out of his Jewishness. The Progressive journals waxed eloquent about the Jew who was nominated while the delegates sang "Onward, Christian Soldiers." The "destruction of religious and racial prejudice in this campaign," the *Outlook* called it. In "splendid accord with the true spirit of this new democratic party which knows the prejudice of neither race nor religion," the *Chicago Evening Post* chimed in. "The Progressive movement is a development of the same aspirations for justice and human betterment that animated . . . the Hebrew prophets," the *Kansas City Times* said.[75] Party workers prominently displayed endorsements of Straus by religious leaders of other faiths, and Progressives outside New York called for statements or appearances by Straus to attract the Jewish vote. True to his convictions, Straus ignored the Jewish issue in such statements. He turned down a request from a congregation in Buffalo for a letter to be read during the Jewish High Holidays. Politics and religion were separate areas, and he wanted no Jew to vote for him out of religious considerations.

Straus's candidacy helped to secure the nomination of the Democratic candidate for governor, William Sulzer. The Democrats needed someone who could offset Straus's popularity with the Jews, and in Sulzer they had a man honored by the Jewish community for his labors while in Congress on behalf of abrogating the Russo-American treaty of commerce. Indeed, Straus, too, had joined in public praise of the congressman, and his words were quoted by the delegate who nominated Sulzer. The colorful Sulzer, known both as a demagogue and a progressive reformer, took the offensive in appealing for the Jewish vote. Straus should stop preaching against Tammany, the candidate taunted, and "tell us what he ever did to aid his race at home or abroad." He told Jewish audiences that his work for abrogation had convicted the czar in the court of public opinion and that by stopping persecution in Russia he, Sulzer, had the praise of Russian Jewry. Only two people hated William Sulzer: the czar and Oscar Straus. Before you vote for Straus, he advised the recently naturalized Jews from eastern Europe, "go and ask him how many Jews he sent back to Russia to be murdered by the Czar while he was Secretary of Commerce and Labor." Sulzer shrewdly intuited the nature of his opponent, and his gamble that Straus could not be goaded into answering back paid off. Democratic partisans also circulated a public letter signed by heads of several minor Jewish organizations asking Straus, in recognition of the Jewish debt to Sulzer, to withdraw from the race. Tammany's hold on the newer immigrants, particularly when strengthened by Sulzer's clever strategy, seemed to be unbeatable. Straus evoked great enthusiasm by his appearances on the Lower East Side, but his arguments that abrogation served the need of all Americans and that Jews were no more than American citizens sorely lacked the touch necessary to arouse ethnic passions at the expense of the Democratic candidate.

Straus suffered a grave blow when two of his circle, foremost figures of the Jewish establishment, wrote letters to a Yiddish newspaper endorsing Sulzer. Jacob Schiff and Louis Marshall claimed that Sulzer's work for abrogation, especially since he was not Jewish, obligated Jews to support him. While some hinted that personal gain underlay Schiff's move, the two Jews probably feared the waste of Jewish votes for a losing party and, more important, the spectacle of Jews massing behind a fellow Jew. Rabbi Stephen Wise, although a loyal follower of Wilson, deplored the disservice to the community by Schiff and Marshall. Hoping to "lay the ghost" of a Jewish vote, they had in fact invoked it. In Wise's opinion: "As a result of a continued emphasis upon the Jewish vote, such as we did not imagine could ever be in American life, the nomination of [Straus], through no fault of his own, became a source of grief to every right-minded and truly earnest Jew."[76]

Not only was Straus deserted by his close associates, but the latter flouted the rules of the political game which Straus, despite the personal cost, continued to respect. The candidate called Marshall's letter an insult to the intelligence of the East Siders, who didn't require advice on how to vote from the uptown "silk stockings" Jews. On election day Straus ran second to Sulzer in the city but behind both Sulzer and the Republican contender in the state. Surprisingly, the pro-Sulzer tactics had no dramatic effect on the outcome. According to an analysis of the Jewish vote in New York City, in four out of five assembly districts where the Jews predominated, Straus received a majority of the votes.[77]

The Civil War and its immediate aftermath tested the self-imposed rules of political neutrality on two levels. One concerned the Jews themselves—how well they had abided by the rules in times of crisis. Another involved outsiders: Were non-Jews convinced of Jewish neutrality, and had they, with the help of the Jewish political posture, learned to receive the Jew fully in American society?

There was no one Jewish position on slavery or the political problems it spawned. Because of the slavery question, some Jews who emphasized the quest for full political liberty moved with many fellow German Forty-Eighters into the ranks of the newly formed Republican party. But for the most part Jews lined up on the questions that divided the country according to their section. During the war, geographical location determined which army they fought in, for whom the women rolled bandages, and for which side rabbis invoked divine aid. True, a few rabbis deviated—most notably abolitionist Einhorn of Baltimore, slavery sympathizer Raphall of New York, and Union protagonist Bernard Illowy of New Orleans. Isaac Leeser of Philadelphia tried to ignore the controversy completely. But overwhelmingly, Jews responded as did their compatriots, demonstrating both how integrated they really were and how regional loyalties during the crisis eclipsed ethnic politics.[78]

The idea of a Jewish position on slavery and the Civil War was not beyond the realm of possibility. The mid-nineteenth-century Irish overwhelmingly condemned abolitionism and as a bloc remained loyal to the Democratic party. In 1853 the American and Foreign Anti-Slavery Society criticized the Jews specifically for not having adopted a group position in support of the antislavery movement. "The Jews of the United States have never taken any steps whatever with regard to the Slavery question. . . . The objects of so much mean prejudice and unrighteous oppression as the Jews have been for ages, surely they, it would seem, more than any other denomination, ought to be the enemies of CASTE, and the friends of UNIVERSAL FREEDOM." Indeed, to the extent that there was a Jewish interest in the sectional conflict, it revolved mainly about the abolitionists. Some rabbis like Isaac Mayer Wise feared the Protestant religious zeal that underlay abolitionism. Always apprehensive about the danger of religious crusades in politics, they suspected the abolitionists of anti-Jewish prejudice, which, if the zealots were so inclined, could also be politicized. Nevertheless, such suspicions failed to undermine northern Jewish support of the Union and the war against slavery.[79]

Despite the sectional loyalties of the Jews, neither side eagerly accepted that group as brothers-in-arms. The war years sparked a violent outburst of Judeophobia in both the North and South. The stereotypes of Christ killer, Shylock, and eternal alien were dredged up in ugly attacks by bigots and even more respectable elements, who accused Jews of disloyalty and of harmful, antisocial behavior. Nor were civil or military officials immune to the popular anti-Jewish bias. In the Union, always more tolerant of ethnic differences than the South, Congress originally disregarded the need for Jewish chaplains even though the matter was raised in debate. A proclamation by President Lincoln ordered the strict observance of Sunday upon the army and navy but failed to exempt Jewish Sabbath observers from some unnecessary duties on their day of rest. The extremes of southern and northern prejudice coincided in one drastic weapon, expulsion. Bertram Korn's in-depth study cites two instances of Jews being banished from towns in Georgia—Thomasville and Talbotton—on the grounds that "the Jews" caused the shortages of goods and inflation. Similar charges of economic chicanery impressed northerners, too. Even in Cincinnati, where Jews enjoyed sufficient influence to demand and receive public retractions, the Jewish clothing houses were accused of having organized to corner the market on blankets, so desperately needed by the Union forces.[80] Clearly, the same pattern of accusations had penetrated to different corners of the country by the time General Ulysses S. Grant issued his notorious Order No. 11 in December 1862, expelling Jews from the military zone under his command (Mississippi, Kentucky, Tennessee).

Its first sentence gave Grant's brief order the distinction of being the "most sweeping anti-Jewish regulation in all American history." It read: "The Jews, as a class violating every regulation of trade established by the Treasury Department and also department orders, are hereby expelled from the department within twenty-four hours from the receipt of this order." The order reflected the problems faced by Washington and the Army in coping with the illicit exchange of northern goods and specie for southern cotton across the battle lines. Jews no doubt engaged in the lucrative trade, but so did other merchants and even military personnel. Given the charges current in both South and North, it was not surprising that the Jews became the scapegoat. Nine days before Grant's order, Colonel John DuBois had expelled from Holly Springs, Mississippi, *"all Cotton Speculators, Jews, and other Vagrants"* as well as northerners without Army connections. The immediate effect of the order carried overtones of a medieval nightmare—Jews hurriedly forced to evacuate their homes, Jewish civilians banished despite the presence of Jews in Grant's army, Jewish spokesmen armed with affidavits on the group's loyalty appealing to the head of state to countermand the edict. Lincoln rescinded the order, but Jews received little support from other officials in Washington. In Congress, the Republicans refused to censure the general, who never did apologize. Across the country, sympathy for the Jews came almost exclusively from the Democrats, eager to use the affair for their political advantage.

The irrational Jew hatred, the one ground on which North could meet South in agreement, generated shock and despondency within the Jewish community. Rational counterarguments did not rouse Americans to a sense of outrage, and the Jews believed they had no other weapons. The Jews of Thomasville, Georgia, compared the town's order of banishment with the ways of the Inquisition, but, they said, "we have no remedy but in an appeal to an enlightened public opinion." In later years nineteenth-century American Jews would single out the Civil War years as marking the onset of serious anti-Semitism in the United States. With that idea went a growing worldliness, a waning of Jewish faith in a future free of Jew hatred. Zionist leader Max Nordau wrote in 1912 that Grant's order and its acceptance by Americans showed "how thin the floor between Jews and Hell was (and most probably still is) even in enlightened free America. . . . What an object lesson to Jewish optimists."[81]

In the immediate aftermath of the order, and contrary to Democratic expectations, the ideal of political neutrality prevailed. The *Jewish Messenger*, for example, warned its readers not to let themselves be used by "designing politicians" seeking to turn the Jews away from the Union cause. The proper Jewish defense lay not in politics but in a strong union of all congregations. "Gen. Grant would *never* have issued an order expelling 'all Jews' from his Department, if he were conscious that the Jews were an influential, a powerful community." (The paper neglected to explain just how a Jewish union that steered clear of politics would convince officials like Grant of Jewish power.) During the campaign of 1864, the *Messenger* would not comment on parties or candidates. It merely urged the Jews, in light of the libels circulated by the press, to support the Union.

In the first flush of anger aroused by Order No. 11, the New York paper had called Grant "*a marked man.*" It hinted darkly: "When the war is at an end, the Jewish community will claim and receive full and complete satisfaction." [82] The community and the *Messenger* had their chance in 1868 when Grant ran for the presidency, but both sidestepped the opportunity. The fear of visibility, and hence the need for official neutrality, was uppermost.

Many months before the 1868 election the nation's press raised the issue of the Jewish vote in the event that Grant headed the Republican ticket. In all parts of the country and with greater attention than in 1863 the order was examined anew. Political partisans rehashed the episode—the Democrats to appeal for Jewish repudiation of the tyrant Grant, the Republicans to explain and hold on to Jewish voters. Catapulted into the public's eye, the Jews felt the urgency of an election in which their image loomed large. Overall, the group was divided. Many former supporters undoubtedly deserted the Republicans, but to match the Jewish anti-Grant meetings in Memphis and Nashville were the Hebrew Grant Club and the public pro-Grant confessions of prominent individual laymen. Simon Wolf, for example, a loud and active critic of the order in 1863, now defended Grant's act and exonerated the candidate.[83]

To the cautious *Jewish Messenger*, which consistently advised low visibility, the sudden thrust of the Jews into the public limelight was uncomfortable. The same paper which had warned five years before that Jews would exact their revenge now took the position that the election did not concern Jews as Jews. Only for a grave reason could the Jewish vote be appealed to, the paper said, but that reason did not exist in 1868. At present there was "*no* religious issue"; the affair of the order had ended in 1863. It was revived not out of any love for the Jews but for political capital. No doubt some Jews would be alienated from the Republican party, but that would be their private decision and not because they were members of the Jewish group. The paper announced firmly: "In the coming campaign, Hebrews will work, and talk, and vote, precisely according to their convictions as citizens, and in no respect will their political action be dependent upon their religious character as a body."

The *Messenger* hit out at politicians who used the episode for partisan gain, at Jewish leaders—lay and rabbinical—who participated in politics under a Jewish masthead, and at Jewish citizens who thought that Grant's candidacy merited a group reaction. Jewish voters must not be guilty of mixing church and state even by such trivial matters as political clubs and stump speeches. The paper repeatedly recited the laws of political neutrality: the divorce of religion from politics, no Jewish views in politics, no Jewish politicians (as opposed to politicians who were Jewish), the impropriety of meddling in politics by communal spokesmen. Jewish independence in politics would gain outside respect, the *Messenger* claimed, and the opposite view, that Jews voted as a class, only confirmed the group libel propagated by Grant's very order expelling Jews "as a class." The paper also subscribed to the views of two anonymous letter writers who sought to minimize Grant's original misdeed. The whitewashers insisted that Grant intended no attack on the Jews as a religious body but erred out of carelessness and ignorance. When Grant's explanation—which was not an apology—finally appeared a few weeks after the election, the paper was completely satisfied. During his campaign for reelection in 1872, the paper could more easily dismiss any anti-Grant feelings. "While some Israelites may not forget an action which was, indeed, indefensible, there are very many who have long ago forgiven the offender, and who have buried their private feelings in consideration of the eminent public services of the General."

Clearly, the *Messenger* had cooled off considerably since 1863. Some in the community accused it of downright cowardice, a charge the paper claimed not to mind. It defended its stand on the grounds of the neutralist political code. Undercurrents in its editorials also suggest other reasons why it feared to deviate from the traditional course. The *Messenger* understood the wide popularity that Grant, the military hero, enjoyed among the voters. Not one Christian, it stated, would be persuaded to vote against him just because of Order No. 11. Since some Republicans defended Grant by vilifying the Jews for worse crimes than those of the war years, prudence advised that a Jewish anti-Grant vote would not defeat the candidate but might well leave the Jews out on a limb, alienated from the administration and its supporters during Grant's entire term. In addition, Republican campaigners claimed that the revival of discussion about the order was a copperhead scheme. By waving the bloody shirt, they impressed Jews, like the *Messenger*, that a vote against Grant would be tantamount to a confession of disloyalty to the Union.[84]

Not all Jewish periodicals agreed with the *Messenger's* stand, but the more prominent ones did. In Philadelphia, young Mayer Sulzberger, who assumed the editorship of the *Occident* after Isaac Leeser's death in 1868, carefully refrained from voicing any opinion about the election other than to chide those Jewish papers actively engaged in political campaigns.[85]

For a few months it looked as if the *Israelite* might jettison the rules of political neutrality. In February of 1868, editor Wise, a Democrat, rehashed the entire story of Order No. 11 when he discussed the possibility of Grant's nomination. He had no intention of meddling in politics, he said, but the *Israelite* had always defended Jews against men who abused them. Urging the Jewish press in particular to protest Grant's candidacy, he announced that if the general ran for the presidency, it would be his duty to oppose the perpetrator of "shameless justice." How Wise drew the line between political meddling and his preconvention editorials is difficult to comprehend. He believed that if any other minority—e.g., the Baptists or the Germans—had been the target of Grant's order, a united protest from that group would be rightfully expected. However, when letters urging him on to active political leadership as well as those counseling restraint poured in from Jewish readers, the editor realized the division within the community. He aired some of his own considerations publicly: to ignore the issue would be cowardly; to deny the fact that there was a "Jewish interest" involved was inaccurate; for Jews to vote en masse after the entire group had been injured by Grant would not be unseemly. But when poised on the brink of calling for an organized Jewish vote and a frank suspension of political neutrality, Wise retreated. He lamely concluded that the *Israelite*, a religious journal, would say no more on the politics of the day. Memphis Jews who had organized a protest pleaded that Wise honor his original promise, and a Cincinnati Jew asked that the rabbi arrange an anti-Grant rally in that city. To both, Wise gave his answer about the impropriety of a religious journal or its editor in the actual campaign. He had done all he could to prevent the nomination and he would still defend Jews against bigots; but now that he had injected the Jewish complaint into the public forum, it devolved upon "offended citizens" to take it from there.[86]

In light of the attention that the Populists received after World War II as the activators of American anti-Semitism,[87] one could expect recognition of a "Jewish issue" in politics by communal leaders in 1896. That year those who advocated free silver captured the Democratic party and gave the presidential nomination to William Jennings Bryan. The rhetoric mouthed by the Populists equating Jew with the gold conspiracy, and the very metaphor employed by Bryan in his Cross of Gold speech, hinted at a potentially grave outburst of political anti-Semitism. For what it was worth, Bryanites also had the support of Hermann Ahlwardt, the notorious German Jew-baiter who had come to America in 1895 for a lecture tour. The next year he circulated a campaign sheet called the *Gentile News* directed principally against the House of Rothschild and the gold clique.[88] Since no other election after 1868 implicated the Jews so directly, it would not have been surprising had the Jewish press, those who filtered the news to the community, totally abandoned the neutralist political code.

Because the *Jewish Messenger* and the *American Israelite* were the only two periodicals whose lives spanned the elections of both 1868 and 1896, and who over the years had consistently defended the neutralist posture, their reactions were particularly illuminating. Self-praise aside, there was truth in the *American Israelite*'s statement in 1896 that its longevity and the prominence of its editor, Rabbi Isaac Mayer Wise, led non-Jews to regard it as the foremost national mouthpiece of American Jewry.[89] The *Jewish Messenger* was similarly entrenched in New York, where it successfully withstood the competition of younger rivals. The editorship had passed from the founder, Rabbi Samuel Isaacs, to his son, Rabbi Abram Isaacs. While the paper now leaned more toward Reform, it retained its customary conservatism on social questions and its worried caution about Jewish visibility.

Quite out of character, the *Jewish Messenger* expressed itself loudly and asseveratively throughout the 1896 campaign. Never had the paper responded so impassionedly to elections; even in 1868 the response had been a counsel of timid inaction. Now it argued almost weekly, from July until November, on the crucial need to defeat the Populists. Its concern was *not* anti-Semitism; it dismissed that question in two short items ridiculing the bigoted statements of Populist leader Mary Ellen Lease. Rather, in an unusual display of economic above Jewish interest, the *Messenger* hammered away at the cheap-money issue in life-and-death terms. The demand of the silverites upset the laws of economic honesty, imperiled the nation's credit, and challenged private property. The Democrats were the party of dishonesty, lawlessness, and national dishonor who paraded their demands under the red flag of communism and anarchy. Not since 1860 had the country faced a moral crisis of similar proportions. While Bryan and his party appealed to the lowest instincts, the voters who stood for honesty, patriotism, morality—and were devoted to their children!—would uphold the "party of honor." The *Messenger* supported the organization of honest-money clubs and urged other ways of disseminating the facts to the electorate. Upon McKinley's victory it said "to God be the praise!" for the vindication of America's integrity. So engrossed was the paper in the money issue that it ignored the customary strictures about a Jewish group's abstention from politics.[90]

Isaac Mayer Wise remembered those strictures, but he was torn along other lines. A loyal Democrat, he nevertheless recoiled from economic radicalism and the free-silver panacea. He blamed the silverites for the depression of 1893, calling them demagogues who were worse than labor leaders. Nor could Wise, the aggressive defender of the Jews, ignore the bigotry manifested by the candidates and journals that represented his party. He faithfully culled and reported examples of anti-Semitic slurs that were voiced in different parts of the country by those "demagogs [*sic*], blatherskites and fanatics." Incensed by the "vermin" who descended to Jew baiting in order to inflame the masses, he realized simultaneously how distant the Jews still were from their goal of integration. When the sound-money side charged that the free coinage of silver was "an old Jewish swindle," it was clear that the Jew, caught in the middle, was sooner attacked for being Jewish than for any views he might hold about currency. True, the *Atlanta Constitution*, when called to justify its accusations, denied its anti-Semitic animus, but it revealed to Wise by "the unusual patronizingly laudatory slop about Jews that we are so sick of reading" that the Jews constituted a very distinct and separate group.

Wise openly castigated national figures like Senator Ben Tillman of South Carolina, and he urged the defeat of state candidates who resorted to anti-Semitic tactics. At the same time, however, he continued to argue for the independent Jewish voter and against Jewish political clubs or those who claimed the ability to deliver the Jewish vote. He warned the Democrats that they would lose the support of individual Jews, but he never advised that Jews organize in opposition to that party. Wise appeared to resolve his own ambivalences by adopting the posture that the Populists, the "rawboned asses," were the illegitimate offspring of the true Democratic party, which, he insisted, had extended more favors than the Republicans to the Jews. He also asserted that the anti-Semitic display did not really hurt. Only a small minority within the country, the Jew baiters "are not lions to rend and tear; they are only mosquitos to annoy us with their buz [sic] and tiny sting." Besides, the Jews were long accustomed to shouldering the blame for society's ills. Yesteryear's poisoners of the wells became the fomenters of economic distress in the modern secular world.[91]

Immediately after the election, Wise basked in self-congratulations. He had avoided political partisanship and thus fulfilled his contract with the community. He never accepted a subvention from any political fund, nor did he discuss the issues of the campaign. He did not overstep the boundary between church and state, and he never created the impression that Jews shared the same political outlook. Finally, he kept his personal views well hidden. None knew, he concluded triumphantly, that he considered McKinley the best the Republicans had to offer or that on election day he cast his vote for Bryan.[92]

The performance of the *Messenger* and *American Israelite* in 1896 indicated a decided shift away from the rigid aloofness on political affairs that usually characterized their editorial pages. Both papers discussed aspects of the campaign, and even the *American Israelite* counseled against whom to vote for. However, the *Jewish Messenger*, in whose case the shift was especially dramatic, reacted to economic rather than ethnic interests. So did a Yiddish election pamphlet of Chicago which stressed the advantages of a gold standard and of the "king-savior" McKinley for laborers and businessmen.[93]

Jews in various parts of the country rallied to Bryan's support, and the candidate himself noted that fact. "I am grateful," he wrote Wise, "to the many thousands of your people who supported our ticket. My appreciation of their services was expressed at Chicago on receipt of a beautiful badge presented by the Hebrew democrats."[94] The evidence proves that American Jewry did not perceive the Populists as a major menace worthy of a Jewish group response. Indeed, the lesson of 1896 cautions against overplaying the Populist strand in American anti-Semitism. Purveying traditional anti-Semitic images that cut through class and sectional lines, the Populists added no new ideas about Jews. They harnessed ever-latent hostility to an economic and political campaign, but not until Henry Ford's activities in the 1920s did agrarian-based anti-Semitism command a significant national following.

The "proper American Jew," like the stereotypes he aimed to refute, cut through economic classes. Irrespective of wealth, the Jew who knew he was being judged as a Jew fashioned his behavior accordingly. How well his efforts succeeded was another matter.

The private diary of William L. Wilson, postmaster general during Grover Cleveland's second term as president, offered one kind of evidence. Wilson had formed a close friendship with Isidor Straus when the latter was appointed to fill a congressional vacancy in 1894. About the owner of Macy's, who was also a member of Cleveland's kitchen cabinet, Wilson wrote:

Not only has my acquaintance with him and his whole family been a joy to me, but as it brought me into contact with other Jews, it has cleansed my mind of whatever prejudice my early training and association gave me against the Jew and taught me that besides being people of great business sagacity, they have as fully as Christians their share of honorable, philanthropic men, and of cultivated women.

Aside from admitting that negative stereotyping of Jews was endemic to society—even with respect to Straus and the "better class of Jews"—Wilson's remarks amply justified Jewish concern about propriety. Not only did the individual Jew reflect upon the entire group, but Straus's proper behavior had undone Wilson's prejudices.[95]

In other areas proper behavior had less effect. Jews had always been inordinately proud of the low incidence of criminals among them, indeed to the point that they turned their back on the religious needs of those Jews within prisons. Americans occasionally made complimentary references to that record, but it did not inhibit them from adding the label "Jew" when members of that group were arrested or convicted. From pre–Civil War days through the first decade of the twentieth century, the Jewish press consistently but unsuccessfully fought that practice.[96] Nor did proper behavior, including military service, scotch doubts about Jewish patriotism or rootedness in the United States. The Jewish community patiently tabulated numbers and recounted anecdotes of wartime servicemen, but the images of slacker and traitor remained. Similarly, although Reform Jews diligently excised references to Palestine from their prayer books, they could not erase the charge of alienism. More inexplicable, on the surface at least, was the exclusion of Joseph Seligman from Saratoga's Grand Hotel in 1877. Since Seligman had previously stayed there and no charge of impropriety was ever leveled against him, behavior had clearly made no difference. Equally disheartening, the evidence of the last quarter of the nineteenth century and early years of the twentieth century cast increasing doubts on the efficacy of reason and education in countering prejudice. If anti-Semitism was a function of ignorance, how was one to explain, for example, the biases of the university-trained patricians who succumbed to the spell of Aryanism or who fought to restrict Jewish immigration?

Despite numerous disappointments, the German Jewish establishment never gave up its insistence on proper behavior. Nor did it stop to ask, as modern students of anti-Semitism do, how important in practical terms the negative stereotypes were. Irrespective of what the gentiles thought about Jews, that argument goes, the very tone of the American experience gainsaid legally "applied" anti-Semitism. No official ghetto had ever existed in the United States, and once political disabilities were removed by state governments they were never reinstituted. Negative stereotypes could be blamed for private anti-Semitism, but how significant was that if Jews earned livings commensurate with their talents or enjoyed homes, education, and recreation on a par with their Christian neighbors?

Such considerations would have sounded alien to Jews of the nineteenth century. Too new to America to have lost their European fears about rescission of rights, they witnessed Grant's order, a vivid reminder of the persecution they had recently fled. More important, the line between ideological and overt anti-Semitism was sufficiently unclear to have escaped them entirely. The "Jew risks" in insurance, for example, with less grounding in fact than in myth, were a case of both ideological and applied prejudice; so was much of the later opposition to Jewish immigration. Nor did one have to experience a pogrom in order to see how images automatically triggered painful results. The "polite" discrimination encountered in schools, resorts, or clubs not only dealt psychological wounds, but also kept Jews out of positions of power inextricably woven into the social perquisites of the native Protestant upper middle class. Finally, even if the negative images were never ignited or applied, the knowledge that they existed was a constant source of bitterness and tension that took a significant toll of the community's emotional energy.

If at bottom Americans regarded Jews no differently from the way European Christians did, the United States still afforded that minority a level of security heretofore unmatched in the history of its dispersion. The Enlightenment-inspired creed of the young republic and its still fluid social structure gave American Jews, more than those in any other country, better reason to hope for success as they chipped away at the foundations of Jew hatred. They minimized neither the importance of those foundations nor the possibilities of progress through proper behavior.

4

THE AMERICANIZATION OF JUDAISM

The Jews have survived persecution, Maurice Harris of Harlem's Temple Israel stated, but he asked, "can we survive emancipation?" One of New York's leading Reform rabbis at the end of the nineteenth century, Harris stressed the dangers to religion posed by freedom, for, as he explained, there were two sides—"freedom to observe, freedom to neglect." From the time that the newly liberated Hebrew slaves built the golden calf in the desert, Jewish history provided Harris with numerous examples of how freedom had weakened faith. Even Mendelssohn, who aimed to emancipate the ghetto Jew, sacrificed his family in the process. Succumbing to the lures of a gentile culture, his children eventually turned to Christianity. In the United States the pressure of the outside upon the legally free Jew was equally strong:

This is a Christian country in all but name; and some judicial authorities have declared it Christian in name too. . . . The Jews are forced, by all but law, to keep the Christian Sabbath, even though they may keep their own too. Their children are drawn into the participation of the Christmas festivities, by being taught to sing the Christmas hymns, and by being led to look forward gleefully to that time as their Mid-Winter holiday, when too, the world is at its gayest; while they cannot stay away from school during their own festivals, without inconvenience, or even sacrifice, which often they and their parents are unwilling they should make. And even when they do stay away, it does not seem a holy day, for the noise and bustle of the world goes on; while there is a holy hush and all is still on the feast days of the Gentiles. They are not permitted to be ignorant of the doctrines of the Church, of its founder, its apostles or its teachings generally, for this information is presented to them in some form in every book they read and study, with occasional contemptuous reference to their own faith. They see that the Fast Days of the Church influence the food markets, that the Easter regulates the fashions of the world, that Christianity marks the turning point of chronology and decides the Calendar—in brief, that they must adapt themselves largely to the institutions of another religion.

In the small town or village the problem was worse; isolated Jews, forced to mix in a non-Jewish milieu, quickly lost their Jewish knowledge and interest in religious practices and almost automatically married outside their faith.[1]

Harris's theme was not new. One hundred years earlier, European Orthodox leaders opposed to emancipation had voiced similar considerations. Thereafter, both concerned Jews as well as non-Jews who longed for the disappearance of Judaism acknowledged, with despair or glee, the deleterious effect on Judaism of the absorption of the Jew into the body politic.[2] Persecution endangered the Jew, but freedom menaced the survival of his religion.

Thus, American Jews were in the throes of a spiritual crisis long before their Christian compatriots felt threatened by the popularization of Darwinian thought, the spread of biblical criticism, or the inroads of materialism and secularism. Before 1850 American rabbis were preaching about defections from religion and the common phenomenon of intermarriage. In 1845 Samuel Isaacs of New York described the changed synagogue, where cold ceremonials and financial matters were the typical fare and where, it was thought, only the poor were supposed to attend.[3]

If the forces at work on Judaism in mid-nineteenth-century America were divided between those contributing to survival and those to extinction, the balance tipped toward the latter. Political freedom had destroyed the construct of a separate corporate existence, and Jewish civil law was no longer needed to regulate the daily activities of American Jews. Since the government neither mandated religious affiliation nor recognized Orthodox control of the Jewish community, pressures for religious identification and conformity were removed. The law was "religion-blind," but important segments of public opinion still held Judaism to be an inferior religion—a factor that contributed to the undermining of Jewish pride in religious identity.

Jews themselves contributed to the weakening of their religion. Their German heritage led many to equate the Orthodox life style of the ghetto with political servility; the Judaism they had known was contemptible and its social stigma debasing. Abandoning themselves to the "spirit of the age," Rabbi James Gutheim explained in 1844, they impatiently looked to throw off the customs that made them appear unfit for civil rights. A founder of B'nai B'rith summed up the feelings of immigrants he had encountered—"a youth would rather not be recognized as a Jew, and never thinks of visiting a synagogue."[4] Ambivalent at least about their religious heritage, the German Jews, as Harris had recounted, elected to spread out across the land into both large cities as well as smaller villages removed from Jewish life. If the former suffered from a lack of properly trained rabbis and teachers or of Jewish books and religious articles, how much slimmer were the latter's chances for proper worship and education. Only the singular Jew outside the large cities built a private ritual bath, learned how to slaughter animals, or supported live-in Hebrew tutors to educate his children.[5] Besides, the German Jews overwhelmingly committed themselves to the ideal of the public school. An indicator of their prime concern for rapid Americanization and integration within society, it meant, however, a radical setback to Jewish education and a higher level of religious ignorance and indifference.

European Orthodoxy seemed, to all intents and purposes, immediately doomed in America. Nevertheless, other factors pointed to the probable survival of some form of Judaism. First and foremost, the psychological and emotional needs of the immigrant Jews kept them within the fold. Nineteenth-century Americans also preferred immigrants to identify with any religion rather than with none at all. Since the government never limited occupations or professions to Christians—there was even a Jew in the first graduating class of West Point[6]—conversion was not a real threat to survival. Jews had the right to public worship and, since the autonomy of each congregation was respected, the right to create new religious forms of expression. Untroubled by legal surveillance or the vested rights of any particular group within the Jewish collectivity, Judaism, in theory at least, could flourish in the United States.

As was the case throughout the history of the Jewish dispersion, survival of a minority religion depended on the balance it struck between its independent traditions and the forms of the host country. Tradition without acculturation spelled fossilization; indiscriminate absorption of the majority's ways led to extinction. A vibrant Judaism in America required both continuity with its historical Jewish heritage and sufficient Americanization to render that tradition intelligible and respectable to Jews and non-Jews alike. The Reform movement in America, the best example of conscious and purposeful Americanization of Judaism, took up just that challenge.

Growth of Reform Judaism

Reform Judaism, which ultimately blossomed into the major cultural contribution of nineteenth-century American Jewry, was born in Germany.[7] There, in the early 1800s, Reform awoke to the need of modernizing the beliefs and practices of Judaism within a fixed structure. It denied that the totality of Jewish life could be governed any longer by the religious law of ghetto days—a multi-layered edifice of biblical ordinance, Talmudic precept, post-Talmudic juridical interpretations, and custom hardened into law. Furthermore, how relevant to modern faith was the study of endless regulations concerning temple worship, food taboos, ritual hygiene, or the ox that gored a neighbor's ox? Of greater immediate concern was the desire of Reformers to dust off the image of the Jew and prove his readiness for full emancipation and social acceptance. With that goal in mind, how prudent was separation on civil matters like marriage and divorce or prayers for the restoration of Jewish national life? Napoleon's government had posed just such specific questions to Jewish religious leaders in the first decade of the century.

Reformers had still another aim. Witnesses to the waves of frustration that swept the European Jewish communities and sent many into the arms of the church, they hoped that an altered Judaism in tune with modernity would stem the tide of desertion. If it did not lead to outright conversion, defection by individual Jews from religion held out a different kind of threat. The haphazard, eclectic choice of which practices to abandon and which to retain threatened Judaism with utter anarchy.

As the intellectual child of the Enlightenment, Reform approached Judaism with a scalpel honed by the tenets of reason, progress, and universalism. By cutting away the unnecessary baggage accumulated over more than two thousand years, it determined to uncover and cultivate the spiritual essence of Judaism. Reform would replace doubt with a reinvigorated faith and formal disarray with modern institutions. The result would enhance both the self-respect of the Jews as well as the respectability of the Jew and Judaism to the outside world.

Unlike their German brethren, American Jews enjoyed legal rights, but their spiritual crisis and their zealous push for social acceptance prepared the way for Reform to take hold. Thrown into a setting where the separate Christian and Jewish premodern worlds had never obtained, German Jews in the United States consciously and sometimes painfully recognized the religious differences that set them apart from fellow Americans. Sabbath and holiday observance, for example, handicapped them economically, particularly when the law enjoined them from laboring on Sunday. The Sabbath and dietary laws also put limits on free association with their non-Jewish neighbors, while simultaneously rebuffing those gentiles who genuinely extended hands of friendship. The latter, who visited the synagogues on occasion, could also come away perplexed if not contemptuous of services where decorum was nil and religious honors were sold, where men wearing hats and prayer shawls swayed as they chanted unintelligible Hebrew prayers aloud and independently of one another. Families did not pray together, for synagogues consigned their women to galleries or side benches, and the interminably long services were not even relieved by an engaging sermon or dignified organ music.

Bowing to considerations of image as well as their own social goals, Jews began implementing changes in religious forms to narrow the gap between them and Protestant America. Conscious steps at imitation had been taken by early German Reform in the first three decades of the century and, hence, the process was not alien to them. Isaac Mayer Wise's *Israelite* encouraged such moves, asserting that one principle of Reform was "Whatever makes us ridiculous before the world . . . may safely be and should be abolished." A group of Jews in Charleston instituted organ music on the Sabbath; another in New Haven tried mixed seating; New York's Temple Emanu-El introduced family pews and discontinued the wearing of prayer shawls.[8] In some cases the innovators articulated the need to win gentile approval. Disaffected members of Charleston's Beth Elohim had asked as early as 1824 for a shorter service, improved decorum, and English prayers—in order to see the synagogue "elicit that regard from Jew and Gentile, which its great character deserves." In New York the Cultus Verein, progenitor of Temple Emanu-El, stated in its prospectus:

We would occupy a position of greater respect amongst our fellow-citizens of different faith and would better deserve of it, if in faithful attachment to the precepts of our fathers, we would remove all the abuses and desecrations from our sacred cultus, and use in public worship the customs handed down in their original venerable simplicity, without the confusing ceremonies added by later periods.[9]

That statement, like that of the Charlestonians, proved, incidentally, that laity, too, sketched out blueprints for change and did not slide casually and without forethought into Reform.

At the beginning of the twentieth century the historian of Reform, Rabbi David Philipson, summarized the outstanding changes of modern synagogue worship. He mentioned English prayers and sermons, organs and mixed choirs, family pews and the abolition of women's galleries, a confirmation ceremony for boys and girls in place of the traditional bar mitzvah for boys, and uncovered heads during worship. All of those testified to the success of Reformers and especially to the adaptation of Judaism to American Christian forms. So thoroughly had the synagogue been Americanized that Rabbi Judah Magnes of Temple Emanu-El, a harsh critic of the overly zealous Reformers, included the following anecdote in a sermon of 1910: "A prominent Christian lawyer of another city has told how he entered this building at the beginning of a service . . . and did not discover that he was in a synagogue until a chance remark of the preacher betrayed it."[10]

Two streams fed concomitantly into the development of American Reform, one pragmatic and one philosophical. A case has been made for the pragmatic side exclusively[11]—i.e., that not until American Jewish congregations reached a certain level of acculturation and economic affluence did they entertain and accept deviations from Orthodox practice. According to that argument, the formal piety of the German immigrants eroded under the impact of the American social and economic environment. Reform came from the bottom up and not from rabbinical engineering or manifestoes; congregations ripe for change took their rabbis along with them while those not sufficiently Americanized ignored Reform pronouncements. Early Reform was hardly radical, the argument continues. Even those synagogues that identified with that movement before the Civil War—Beth Elohim of Charleston, Har Sinai of Baltimore, and Emanu-El of New York—adopted changes only very slowly. The conclusion: Reform was a gradual grass-roots process in response to socioeconomic factors that paid scant attention to ideology.

Qualifications to that interpretation are very much in order. In the first place, the fact that the German Jewish immigrants on their arrival willingly settled in places far removed from established centers of Jewish life indicated a basic readiness to modify traditional religious practices. Their admitted laxity in personal observance further facilitated the alacrity with which they dispensed with customary ceremonials. However, as Max Lilienthal pointed out early on, the very same laymen habitually denounced rabbinical opinions that operated to loosen religious requirements but accepted more stringent regulations without dispute.[12] In other words, attitudes and habits fixed in Germany as much as Americanization determined the evolution of Reform. If Americanization alone accounted for Reform, the wealthy and oldest congregation, Shearith Israel of New York, would have long abandoned its traditionalist rites.

Second, the ideological contributions to Reform of men like David Einhorn, Samuel Adler, Samuel Hirsch, and Kaufmann Kohler cannot be overemphasized. Those thinkers supplied a structured theoretical framework to Americanized Judaism which otherwise might have disappeared entirely. Inspired by the development of Reform in Germany (Einhorn, Hirsch, and Adler had participated in the famous rabbinical conferences convened there in the 1840s), they hammered out the ideology of an American Jewish religion in which creed as well as form linked Judaism to Americanism. At least as important were the contributions of Isaac Mayer Wise, architect and builder, who translated the Reform vision into religious institutions. Without active rabbinical guidance there might well have been anti-Orthodoxy but never Reform. Tutelage gave those Jews, admittedly sufficiently Americanized to move away from Orthodoxy, a purpose and direction. Leadership from the top injected order and unity into the course of religious change, which in its home-grown state could differ from congregation to congregation, and brought Reform stature and recognition in the United States.

Third, the gap between the ideologues and the rank and file was not that wide. Rabbis spoke to the people as well as to each other. Synagogue attenders listened to Sabbath and holiday sermons and to lecture series by their rabbis. Rabbis also reached nonmembers when they addressed the YMHAs, B'nai B'rith audiences, and the Jewish Chautauqua assemblies. Rarely could ideas about religious change or Reform not come across if the subjects dealt with Jewish history, education, or Jewish-Christian relations as well as with matters of worship. Once, when Reformer David Einhorn spoke in New York, a member of the audience became sufficiently enthusiastic to ask for a "platform of principles."[13] Furthermore, most of the influential popular journals of the century were edited by rabbis, both traditionalist and Reform—Isaac Leeser's *Occident*, Samuel Isaacs's *Jewish Messenger*, Wise's *Israelite* and *Die Deborah*, Einhorn's *Sinai*, Emil Hirsch's *Reform Advocate*, Jacob Voorsanger's *Emanu-El*. They printed sermons, editorials on Reform beliefs and practices, reports of theological works and conferences both in Europe and the United States, accounts of growth and experimentation in single congregations or cities, and attacks on their religious opponents. Readers learned about the currents of religious opinion and even participated in the ongoing debates with letters to the editor. Like all movements, Reform Judaism needed both leaders and followers. In America neither group was passive, nor were the two independent of each other.

The founding of Chicago's Sinai Congregation demonstrated the collaboration between laity and ideologues to fashion a Reform Judaism where practice derived from principle. The Chicago story centered about Bernhard Felsenthal, a schoolteacher from Bavaria whose extensive Jewish knowledge was largely self-taught. Felsenthal came to the Midwest in 1854 and after a few years of teaching took a post as bank clerk in Chicago. His commitment to Reform, reflected in several articles he had written for American Jewish periodicals, preceded him, and he attracted a small group of laymen interested in the modernization of religious life. Not content with a few external reforms, they wanted to discuss the theory that underlay ritual. At a meeting held in June 1858 in Felsenthal's office on Clark Street, the Jewish Reform Society was organized. Felsenthal presented to the group twenty-seven theses in which he outlined the mission of Judaism to spread the doctrines of universal truth among all mankind. Those precepts were ascertained, according to Felsenthal, by the use of reason, which distinguished between eternal verities in the Bible and primitive, ephemeral concepts, and by the individual's free investigation into the literary creations of Judaism. He called the practice of moral duties the essence of worship; the proper ceremonial rites were those that promoted the cognition of the universal truths and strengthened love of Judaism and morality. The society debated Felsenthal's theses at a few meetings—showing lay input into scholarly matters—and adopted them with only slight modifications. The group then proceeded to discuss the content and form of the liturgy for Sabbaths and holidays.

With the encouragement of prominent Reform thinker Rabbi Samuel Adler of New York's Temple Emanu-El, the group turned its thoughts to the organization of a Reformed congregation. Their cause was aided by the publication in 1859 of Felsenthal's small pamphlet "Kol Kore Bamidbar" ("A Voice Crying in the Wilderness"). In it Felsenthal, now appealing to the larger community, explained his theses as well as the other principles passed on by the society. He urged his fellow Jews to take on the pioneer and constructive work of Reform—it was the season to build and not to tear down. In America, the blessed land of freedom, where legally recognized and paralyzing Orthodoxy did not exist, nothing hindered Jews from embarking on their mission of modernity. In the same tenor Felsenthal addressed two public meetings called by the society. Finally, in 1861, Sinai Congregation was organized, and Felsenthal, until then a learned layman but still only a layman, was unanimously elected rabbi.[14]

As the history of early Reform in Europe showed, it was inevitable that changes in form would bring about changes in substance. In the German temple at Hamburg, for example, the introduction of an organ and prayers in the vernacular led almost automatically to the excision of passages related to a return to Palestine in the messianic age. Albeit part of the overall desire to make the Jew and his religion conform to outside tastes and pressures, in this case proof of the unalloyed patriotism to the national state, that alteration was a radical theological deviation. Again, at the famous German rabbinical conferences of the 1840s, Reform-minded rabbis debated both form and substance: use of an organ, Sabbath observance, mourning customs, the substitution of a universal messianic age in place of a national messiah for the Jews.[15] The line between fundamental precepts and the "abuses" and "confusing ceremonies" of which the New York Cultus Verein had complained was not clear-cut in the organic evolving tradition that was Judaism. Strong differences in interpretation arose among the Reformers. What bound them together was a determination to forge a Judaism consonant with modernity and one that would both revitalize the religion and assure its respectability.

From its earliest days Reform acknowledged its debt to the Enlightenment by insisting, first, that reason had to temper faith and religious behavior, and, second, that universalism transcended ethnic or parochial national creeds. The platform adopted by nineteen American Reform rabbis assembled in Pittsburgh in 1885 reflected that approach in its synthesis of the theological beliefs that crystallized in Germany and the United States. The platform affirmed the "God-idea" and the compatibility of the fundamentals of Judaism with science and biblical criticism. Emphasizing the goal of spiritual elevation, it rejected those ceremonials discordant with modern civilization, specifically those laws relating to diet and priestly purity. It stressed the universal mission of Judaism—"a progressive religion, ever striving to be in accord with the postulates of reason"—which stood for the propagation of monotheistic and moral truths among all men. Universalism precluded both the national dimension of Judaism and the traditional views of the messianic age:

We recognize, in the modern era of universal culture of heart and intellect, the approaching of the realization of Israel's great Messianic hope for the establishment of the kingdom of truth, justice and peace among all men. We consider ourselves no longer a nation, but a religious community, and therefore expect neither a return to Palestine, nor a sacrificial worship under the sons of Aaron, nor the restoration of any of the laws concerning the Jewish state.

Underlying all plans was the optimistic belief that a rational faith could prevail, that "the spirit of broad humanity of our age is our ally in the fulfillment of our mission."[16]

The Pittsburgh platform, or Reform's Declaration of Independence as Kaufmann Kohler called it, fixed Reform squarely in the Enlightenment tradition. Since America also took pride in its Enlightenment heritage, Reform demonstrated its ideological kinship with the country. But more than a common source linked the two. Dwelling on the theme of freedom, Reform ideologues and preachers found in America the place where Judaism could achieve its highest fulfillment. There, Judaism, as well as Jews, enjoyed religious freedom. In a land where church and state were officially separate, and where the civil arm could not be invoked on the side of Orthodoxy, Judaism had the right and opportunity to carve out new directions.

Rabbi and scholar Samuel Hirsch of Philadelphia went a step further. He postulated that freedom was the essence of Judaism. It followed that since the American government, in his opinion, rested on biblical precepts, the United States had appropriated the universal truths of Judaism for this-worldly use and had translated the ideal into the real. Hirsch's contemporary, and equally important in the annals of Reform theology, was David Einhorn. Like Hirsch, Einhorn saw an ideological link between America's and Judaism's commitments to freedom; both, in fact, were engaged in similar missions. America was his personal Canaan, Einhorn added, following his exodus from European slavery. He believed that scriptural teachings would be fulfilled in the United States and, indeed, that it was the land where the kingdom of God could be established. Einhorn put a religious halo around American heroes and symbols; Washington, Franklin, Lincoln, as well as the Declaration of Independence and Constitution transmitted messages of religion and morality.[17] Men like Einhorn and Hirsch successfully circumvented the apparent contradiction between Reform's universalism and American nationalism by predicating humanity's advancement upon an American base.

Other rabbis took up the theme of the ideological ties between Judaism and American democracy. The Fourth of July frequently led Isaac Mayer Wise to comment on liberty and independence, the birthright of Israel. The United States, according to the rabbi, "embraced our long cherished principles"; the American Revolution

to Old World cultures and loyalties. Furthermore, in an era when Americans touted their manifest destiny, they could feel a greater affinity with Reformers' religiouslike patriotism and the Reformers' concern with a mission made consonant with America's.

In language, forms, and ideology, Reform embodied the American spirit of the nineteenth century. Perhaps the one whose career best captured that spirit was Isaac Mayer Wise. Wise did more than preach the affinity between Judaism and Americanism. Affinity, according to Wise, afforded a singular opportunity to root the institutions of an American Judaism (a term he preferred above Reform) in fertile soil. He aspired to a religiously unified American Jewry which would blend the variegated rites and customs of the immigrants into a specifically *American* rite. His revision of the traditional prayer book, which appeared in 1857, was called just that—*Minhag America,* or American rite. An indefatigable worker, Wise ministered to a leading congregation in Cincinnati and found time to lecture, cultivate friendships with American politicians, write history and novels, and edit two popular weekly newspapers. Through his writings and at rabbinical conferences he labored over many years for congregational unity and for a seminary to train American rabbis. Never a theologian like Einhorn, Hirsch, or Kohler, Wise was the pragmatist, the salesman, and the builder. Often ready to compromise doctrine for the sake of unity, he elicited both scorn from the radical (Einhorn) wing of the Reform camp and bitter enmity from the Orthodox. A moderate Reformer, he saw the future of that movement in the western communities, removed, as he said, from Orthodox ignorance and radical Reform fanaticism. His intellectual shortcomings aside, it was Wise who designed and steered to fruition the lasting institutions built by Reform: a union of congregations (Union of American Hebrew Congregations—1873), a seminary (Hebrew Union College—1875), and a union of rabbis (Central Conference of American Rabbis—1889).[22]

By 1890 Reform's institutions dominated the American Jewish religious scene. The religious census of 1890, the only one that distinguished between Orthodox and Reform, revealed that the latter had outdistanced its opponents in membership and especially in synagogal property.[23] Although the traditionalists were gaining in numbers with the new Russian immigrants, their ranks were divided and their religious creativity was prompted almost exclusively by a negative, anti-Reform stimulus. Reform encountered serious ideological challenges at the turn of the century, principally in the forms of secularism and Zionism, but until the 1900s its hegemony was undisturbed.

How well Reform had succeeded in guaranteeing survival for Judaism was another matter. Somehow the vague concept of a universalist mission as the raison d'être of Judaism and the negative approach to traditional ritual could neither fire nor sustain massive enthusiasm or devotion. By the turn of the century serious Reform leaders were acknowledging their failure to command the loyalty of Jewish youth, and they put forth new schemes to halt further defections. Rabbis talked about missionaries to the Jews, about the advisability of changing the synagogue from the cultic to a social center, and about the need to work on campus with college students. Most thought that the answer to Maurice Harris's question— can Jews survive emancipation?—lay in education. Toward that end, Rabbi Henry Berkowitz, inspired by the American Chautauqua movement, spearheaded the organization of the Jewish Chautauqua Society, which from 1893 on operated to popularize knowledge of Judaism through home reading courses and summer assemblies.[24]

Defection from organized Jewish life stemmed perhaps less from Reform's inadequacies than from the American principle of religious voluntarism. A radically new element in the Jewish experience, it permitted Jews the choice of institutions with which to affiliate and the very option of affirming or ignoring their Jewish identity. At the Central Conference of American Rabbis convention of 1895, Rabbi Isaac Mayer Wise gave a candid résumé of the negative impact of voluntarism: "Many deserted the old standard and fled to the camp of the Nothingarians while others sank into the indifference and lethargy of the thoughtless masses, that eat, drink, work, sleep and die in common with the beast of the field."[25]

According to the findings published by anthropologist Maurice Fishberg in 1907, it was essentially unfair to expect Reform, or for that matter any other modern religious movement, to reverse the signs of a decreasing Jewish population in western Europe and the United States. Fishberg examined the marriage and childbearing patterns of acculturated Jews, indices primarily of social, economic, and intellectual conditions, and found a lower birthrate, fewer and later marriages, and more mixed marriages. The environmental forces generating such conditions defied containment, and Fishberg predicted that the number of Jews, if not augmented by the influx of the east Europeans, "would dwindle away at a rate appalling to those who have the interests of their faith at heart." He concluded: "The Jews are thus paying a high price for their liberty and equality—self-effacement."[26]

Reform's progress in the nineteenth century, though never seriously impeded, was challenged by traditionalists every step of the way. The latter relied solely on their own resources, for in America the government did not, as it did in Germany, lend its protection to the Orthodox. During the second half of the century, the opposing camps engaged in two significant disputations, one in 1856 and one in 1885. Unlike those of medieval days when Jews, generally against their will, crossed swords with representatives of the Catholic church over the "true" religion, the informal American debates involved no direct confrontation, and the adversaries were Jews. But at stake was the same issue of legitimacy, in this case what form of Judaism was valid in the postemancipation world.

The defender of Orthodoxy in 1856 was Isaac Leeser.[27] Born in Westphalia in 1806, Leeser was educated in Münster in secular subjects and in the Hebrew language, Bible, and rabbinics. His formal Jewish education ceased when he was fourteen, but the young man continued to read avidly and grow intellectually. Family tragedies marked his early years, and in 1824 Leeser left Germany to take up residence with an uncle in Richmond. Of a scholarly temperament, he was more attracted to Jewish religious affairs and to writing than to his uncle's business. He assisted the hazzan of the Richmond synagogue at services and in teaching the children of the congregation. He rapidly mastered the English language, and he took the first steps in a long journalistic career when he published articles rebutting an anti-Semitic essay that had appeared in a London journal. Those articles brought him to the attention of Mikveh Israel, the old established synagogue of Philadelphia's aristocratic Sephardim. Although Leeser had never been ordained, he was appointed hazzan in 1830, a post that he filled for twenty years. By 1856 he was well known for his books and his numerous activities relating to Jewish charity, education, and defense. As editor and publisher of the *Occident,* the first Anglo-Jewish journal of national significance, he gained recognition and respect from Jews throughout the country as well as from Christians.

Leeser opened the pages of the *Occident* to Reformers, but there was never any doubt where his sympathies lay. While still in Germany, he had witnessed early contests between Reform and traditionalism and, under the influence of the anti-Reform rabbi of Münster, had committed himself to the preservation of traditionalism. His long ministry at Mikveh Israel undoubtedly reinforced that bent. True, Leeser pushed for decorous services and defended the use of the vernacular; nor was he averse to adopting Christian forms (like the Sunday school) that would directly serve to invigorate Judaism. But tampering with substantive Jewish customs, let alone religious dogma, aroused only bitter negative responses.

Leeser's adversary in 1856, and his junior by nine years, was Bavarian-born Max Lilienthal.[28] After earning both a university degree and rabbinical ordination in Munich, Lilienthal turned down an appointment to the diplomatic corps because it required conversion to Christianity. In 1839 he became superintendent of the government-sponsored Jewish school in Riga. Committed to the ideal of modernizing Jewish education, Lilienthal remained in Russia until he learned that the czarist regime's purpose was to convert and Russianize its Jewish population through the state schools. The young rabbi in 1845 arrived in New York, where he first ministered to three loosely allied congregations and then ran a boarding school for boys. Ten years later his career took a radical turn. He was called to a pulpit in Cincinnati, and there, in close association with Isaac Mayer Wise, actively enlisted in the cause of moderate Reform.

Like Leeser, Lilienthal had seen the split between Reformers and traditionalists in Germany, and he, too, had sided with the latter. His inaugural sermon in New York stated his opposition to Reform innovations, and he went only so far as to insist upon decorum at services and to initiate the ceremony of confirmation. However, according to his biographer, Lilienthal came to realize that the condition of American Jews demanded Reform. He shocked his new congregation in Cincinnati by not appearing for services on Tishah b'Ab, the fast day commemorating the destruction of the Temple. The gesture signaled his belief in the providential loss of Jewish nationality and in the universal spiritual mission of the Jews. Lilienthal's change of heart in mid-career and his later appearance on the American Jewish scene stood to Leeser's advantage, but Lilienthal matched his opponent in writing skills and surpassed him in rabbinical learning. As an associate editor of Wise's *Israelite* in 1855-1856, Lilienthal, like Leeser, enjoyed both the authority attached to a berth in a flourishing periodical and a platform from which to air his views. Perhaps just because Lilienthal lacked Wise's vitriolic tongue and was known as a man of peace, his barbs were all the more telling.

Reformers and Orthodox had exchanged words long before 1856. Leeser and fellow traditionalists wrote against changes in synagogue forms in the early issues of the *Occident.* The introduction of an organ into Beth Elohim's services in Charleston and Rabbi Poznanski's equation of America with Zion elicited especially bitter comments. Charleston's synagogue was also the setting for a debate between Isaac Mayer Wise and Poznanski on the one hand and Orthodox defender Morris Raphall on the other. In 1850 and again in 1854 Leeser published three series of long editorials challenging Reform ideas; the title of one, "Reforming and Deforming," summed up his views. The *Israelite*, upon its inception in 1854, readily entered the fray with counterattacks alongside a defense of Reform. Personalities, too, became involved, and Leeser and Wise in particular exchanged insults and criticisms of each other's writings.[29]

A decisive episode in the widening rift was the Cleveland conference of 1855. Since Leeser's aim for a union of American congregations—one that would promote and bring order into matters of religion, education, and charity—transcended his differences with Reform, he joined the conference of rabbis convened by Wise. Initially Leeser was elated, for the conferees, most of whom were moderate Reformers, posited the authority of both the Bible and Talmud over religious practices. After Leeser left, however, the conference moved from that general reconciliation of traditionalism with Reform to specific issues of the prayer book and Jewish education. Its decisions, and the continuation of innovations in the synagogue after the conference, proved that the Reformers had not yielded their purpose for change and that they would not be inhibited by Talmudic precepts or later rabbinic commentaries.[30]

Leeser felt betrayed by Wise's faction, especially since the Orthodox assailed him for having associated with the enemy. He defended himself publicly, and for the next several months the *Occident* abounded with attacks on Reformers from him and other right-wingers. When in May the *Israelite* printed a letter from a Jerome Cohen of Hyde Park, Maine, advocating radical Reform measures—even the abolition of kashruth and circumcision—the Orthodox accused Wise of having invented a fictitious straw man. His strategy, they reasoned, was to imply that only his brand of Reform could keep the swelling popular demand for religious change within moderate bounds.

Tactically, Leeser erred, however, when in July 1856 he raised the question: "Are all the measures of the reformers wrong?" Although he refused to take a stand, except for scorning the arbitrary innovative approach by individual men and congregations which only brought about anarchy, he suggested that an international assembly of rabbis decide the issue. He added:

That we see ourself something in our mode of worship and ceremonial observances, on certain occasions, which we should be glad to see improved, we do not deny. . . . [I]f peace could be restored by an authoritative alteration, we would not make any opposition on our part.

In Cincinnati, Lilienthal cleverly seized upon those words and welcomed Leeser to the Reform camp. The Philadelphia rabbi, forced once again to defend himself, charged the editors of the *Israelite* with misrepresentation. Lilienthal in turn accused Leeser of self-contradictions and of refusing to confront the pressures of the time and the needs of the community. Indicating a profound understanding of the Jewish attachment to the principles of voluntarism and congregationalism that governed American religious life, he made short shrift of Leeser's proposal for an international rabbinical synod. Lilienthal demanded religious harmony with the spirit of the age, but Leeser, who said he would welcome a religious debate without the customary "vulgar invective"of Wise, answered, "We wish to improve, not to please the spirit of the age, but the spirit of religion." And so the fight was on.[31]

Lilienthal fittingly called his first three letters to Leeser, printed in the *Israelite* of December 1856, "The Spirit of the Age." His thesis affirmed the centrality of the "spirit of the age," or the ideas that governed all aspects of social life, and its inescapable impact upon religion. Judaism in the Middle Ages, bowing to the temper nurtured by the Catholic church, which outlawed free investigation, reason, and science, also hardened dogma and made study subservient to religious authority and blind faith. From the spirit of the age that began with the Protestant Reformation, reason and free inquiry gradually penetrated the thinking of Christians about Jews and of Jews themselves. Mendelssohn and his group, like the later nineteenth-century Reformers, drew fire from the fanatical antirationalist Orthodox but could not be subdued. What they absorbed from their time and applied to Judaism contributed to the upward spirit of progress that forever governed the course of general human history as well as of Judaism. The spirit of the modern age attempted to realize more completely the ideas set in motion by the Reformation that flowered into political liberalism. And just as the impact of those ideas embodied in emancipation was accepted joyfully, so should their religious form—namely, Reform Judaism. In sum, Lilienthal made religious change that was inspired by the spirit of the age essential to the progress and very preservation of Judaism.

In three succeeding letters to Leeser, Lilienthal considered the charges Leeser had brought against Reform: of destroying Jewish unity and of violating rabbinical codes. The Cincinnati rabbi argued that given the basic principles of Reform, unity on Orthodox terms—i.e., abiding by all the rabbinical strictures—no longer was a real possibility.

Your party rests on the medieval principle of authority; the reform party on the acknowledgment of reason, as declared by the spirit of the age. Your party is founded on the unlimited belief in tradition; the reform party on the results of critical and historical investigation. Your party claims equal right and title for all our biblical, traditional and rabbinical codices; the reform party denies this. Your party asserts that Judaism must remain confined within the limits of its national particularity; the reform party maintains, that acording to its messianic ideas, Judaism has to lead the van, in order to accomplish the acknowledgment of the only "One" by the whole human race. Your party expects the fulfillment of this prophetic promise from some supernatural occurrence; the reform party asserts, that in the general development of the human race and the dutiful cooperation of men, the ways and means are given for attaining this sublime aim and end.

Instead of living in the past, Reform fired the imagination of the "rising generation" and signaled "the bright anticipations of the future." Since Reform was a legitimate by-product of the temper of the times, so was disunion.

Leeser's position on which customs to retain was full of contradictions, Lilienthal continued. The spirit of the modern age repudiated arbitrary rabbinical ukases, and even the Orthodox, he insisted, were influenced by that spirit. Would Leeser dare, for example, to get up before American Jews and demand that women cover their hair or defend the prohibitions on drinking wine made by gentiles? Such habits had broken down, but Leeser, ostrichlike, refused to admit it. Furthermore, the very dicta on the importance of custom that Leeser quoted in resistance to change had been formulated by the sages in order to permit the evolution of Judaism and free it from legalistic chains. Finally, although Leeser held the legal code, Shulhan Aruk, to be inviolable, Lilienthal recited examples where that work contradicted the Bible and the Talmud. Disputing the binding quality of the Shulhan Aruk, Lilienthal summed up Leeser's dilemma: you can maintain that legislative power in religious matters ceased with the Bible or Talmud, or you can admit that it was bequeathed to later generations. Either way, however, the nineteenth-century Jew had the right to deviate from the decisions of the post-Talmudic rabbis.[32]

Not surprisingly, Leeser remained unmoved. He declined to respond point by point, and he referred his adversary to his previous lengthy editorials in the *Occident*. He stood by the conclusions he had long held: (1) Purporting to strengthen religion, Reform was in reality destructive; it bred infidelity, destroyed the unity of Israel, and held out the danger of schisms and sectarianism. (2) Its repudiation of Jewish nationality and the traditional beliefs of the messianic age, like its disregard for ceremonials, betrayed the essence of Judaism and threatened its survival. (3) Reform's insistence on innovations ignored the underlying questions of the purpose and degree of change as well as the proper mode or authority for emendation. (4) Reform encouraged a willingness by Jews to refashion their faith in order to win gentile approval, and yet a Jew who rebelled against his religious duties could not be a good citizen. (5) The idea of the universal mission to convert mankind, no less ambitious than that of Jesus or Mohammed, was deluding and self-destructive. (6) Reform's arrogance and smugness, and its ridicule of Orthodoxy, were as misleading as they were unwarranted:

They [Reform Jews] have a complacent method of regarding themselves as marvels of intelligence and probity. They alone are learned, refined, and not imbued with the faults which distinguish the old Jews. If you see an old orthodox, ten to one that he is cold, selfish, bigoted, unacquainted with any modern improvement or science; addicted to making money by all means, unwilling to labor, and deaf to the voice of history and reason. But a reformer is warm, generous, liberal, cognizant of astronomy, philosophy, engineering, the natural sciences, and all the arts that embellish life; he eschews traffic as a contamination; is scrupulous to pursue mechanical arts and agriculture; and is thoroughly identified with the progress of history and a servant alone of reason.

Lilienthal's letters caused Leeser to reconsider anew "the spirit of the age." But even as he examined it more seriously, he raised weightier objections to what heretofore he had dismissed as flighty and whimsical. He disputed Lilienthal's belief in the idea of progress, at least with respect to morality, and the relativistic implications of the Cincinnati rabbi's formula for change. The march of history did not necessarily elevate human behavior, nor did material advances undo the need for eternal laws on right and wrong. Similarly, neither time nor place could legitimately change the "elements and basis of religion." Leeser called the desire for reform an indication of self-interest, self-indulgence, and expediency. Change of any sort could not be lightly undertaken and was unthinkable for "the well-established customs of Israel," which were "the landmarks of a Jewish life."

Leeser raised two other points with respect to "the spirit of the age." Despite what Lilienthal said, how desirable was it to conform to the prevailing temper? He cited example after example from biblical and ancient history of Jews—Abraham, Moses, the prophets, the Maccabees—who forged Jewish practices and beliefs out of a rebellion *against* the spirit of the age. Furthermore, even if one attempted to conform, it was well-nigh impossible to seize the meaning of "the present." That was a fluid category, ever moving into a new phase.

On the topic of customs and rabbinic authority, Leeser added little to what he had previously written. He replied that the nonobservance of the usages cited by Lilienthal—drinking wine prepared by gentiles or mandating covered heads for married women—made them neither wrong nor absurd. Pleading with Lilienthal to be more specific, he presented a list of direct questions on various issues, from the Reformer's belief in a personal messiah to his opinion on the wearing of phylacteries. Lilienthal refused to air his own observances and advised Leeser to keep to the central issue of the legality of overhauling both customs and codes. Since Leeser had no answer to the question on legislative power as posed by his opponent, which was indeed Lilienthal's strongest point, Lilienthal resolved that the "chit-chat" exchange had gone far enough. He would publish his letters in Germany, he said, where he was assured of more learned opponents and an enriching debate.[33]

Although both Leeser and Lilienthal admitted the same need— i.e., to decide how to preserve Judaism in the postemancipation world—the disputation succeeded, like the Cleveland conference, in widening the distance between the defenders of Orthodoxy and Reform. It lessened the power of the moderates, drawing Leeser further to the right and men like Lilienthal and Wise further to the left, and thus lowered the chances for overall unity. It pointed in the direction of the Philadelphia and Pittsburgh conferences of 1869 and 1885, where Reformers alone would formulate their creed. The debate marked the traditionalists as mere standpatters, without the proper organization and educational institutions to back up their words. Reform, too, still lacked an institutional framework, but its very talk of change evoked a positive image of vitality and constructive activity.

On the scale of Americanization, Lilienthal's position scored higher. It reflected the optimism and belief in progress that America had long symbolized; it echoed Americans' cherished belief that men make law, that they could not be eternally fettered by the legal dictates of previous generations. While Leeser thought of a world body guided by an international conclave of learned rabbis, Lilienthal's antiauthoritarian system better suited the independent mold of American church organization. Leeser upheld a Judaism independent of a time or place, but Lilienthal emphasized a religion calculated to fit the behavior of emancipated and especially American Jews for whom faith had lost its once paramount position.

By 1885, American Reform, now more solidly entrenched, boasted its own rabbinical seminary and union of congregations, and its ranks had been strengthened by the immigration of intellectuals like Samuel Adler, Samuel Hirsch, and Kaufmann Kohler. Although Reform's opponents were still in disarray, the young movement confronted serious problems. The Darwinian challenge to religion, as one rabbi recalled, played havoc with the synagogue as it did with the church, and movements like Ethical Culture, Christian Science, and different forms of spiritualism attracted significant numbers of American Jews. Religious indifference and ignorance, especially among the youth, continued to grow, and even Reformers admitted their failure to counter that trend. Within the Reform movement individual congregations and rabbis often struck out on their own, veering further away from the traditional Jewish practices and the moderate course staked out earlier by Wise and Lilienthal. Thus, Reform and Orthodoxy were sorely in need of reinforcements—the former to produce direction and positive content for what was fast turning into anarchy and a spiritual vacuum, the latter to come up with a positive alternative to Reform.[34]

For their needs, the anti-Reformers eagerly hailed the arrival to the United States of Alexander Kohut. Born in Hungary, Kohut came from a poor but learned and Orthodox background. He was formally educated at Budapest and at Breslau Theological Seminary, and he received a doctoral degree at the University of Leipzig. While still a student, he embarked on his lifework, a multivolume dictionary of the Talmud, through which he revealed his grounding in languages and philology. By the time he was invited to New York's Congregation Ahawath Chesed in 1884, the forty-two-year-old rabbi had established a name as a good orator and erudite Talmudic scholar. In addition to his rabbinical duties he had lectured, published, and served as a district school superintendent. He was elected to the Hungarian parliament as a representative of the Jews, a post that he never filled because of his decision to emigrate.

Three weeks after his inaugural sermon, Kohut began a series of weekly discourses centering on *The Ethics of the Fathers.* Displaying a confidence unusual in a new immigrant, particularly one called to succeed a beloved leader of a congregation that was far less observant than he, Kohut set out to do more than preach. In learned fashion without invective he boldly and incisively challenged American Reform. His sermons quickly roused the enthusiasm of the anti-Reformers, and his message was aired week after week through the Anglo-Jewish press. The traditionalists had found a worthy defender and the Reformers a worthy adversary.[35]

Kohut's opening sentence on *The Ethics of the Fathers* was an assertion of the unbroken chain of Jewish law from Moses through successive generations of Jewish leaders and sages. "On this foundation," Kohut said, "rests Mosaic-rabbinical Judaism to-day." He continued: "He who denies this, denies this on principle, disclaims his connection with the bond of community that unites the house of Israel." Pinpointing the guilty, Kohut said: "A Reform which seeks to progress without the Mosaic-rabbinical tradition is a deformity—a skeleton without flesh and sinew, without spirit and heart. It is suicide." Reform which distilled religious truths into mere principles made Judaism bodiless and caused its evaporation. "If we would burn the bridges behind us which unite the present with the past," and yield to every whim for change propagated by irresponsible religious leaders, our end would be chaos and death.

Kohut also lambasted that Orthodoxy which he described as narrow, fanatic, or "blind letter-worship." If Judaism were a "closed book," the result was petrification. Disdaining the formalism of both extremes, Kohut called for a faith that blended past and present, spirit and body, that was bound to the Mosaic and rabbinic tradition but recognized the exigencies of modern times. He termed it a "Mosaic-rabbinical Judaism, freshened with the spirit of progress, a Judaism of the healthy golden mean."

Jews had the right to make changes in religious usages, Kohut insisted, and interpretations which constituted the "non-essentials" could be modified in accordance with changing opinions and mores. One example was the right to change the traditional prayer book; retaining the Hebrew, one might still excise passages in order to make the prayers more meaningful to modern worshipers. As another example Kohut cited the traditional ban against mixed seating in the synagogue. He would not oppose its removal, he said, if it enhanced the piety of the congregation. Those modifications, however, had to be based upon the Torah as interpreted by rabbinical law and introduced by learned men aiming thereby to bring Jews closer to the word of God.

As a newcomer to the country Kohut would not presume, he said, to pass judgment on the state of American Judaism, but he deplored the glaring degree of religious indifference and the lack of unity. The key to the religious problem as he saw it was the dearth of proper rabbis. The typical American rabbi preached too much and studied too little. Congregations needed to respect the authority of their rabbis, but they first needed to appoint "recognized authorities as teachers; such men . . . as acknowledge belief in authority, and who . . . with comprehension and tact, are willing to consider what may be permitted in view of the exigencies of the time, and what may be discarded, without changing the nature and character of the foundations of the faith." Kohut had barely fired his opening salvos when Kaufmann Kohler jumped in with a defense of Reform. Undeterred by his challenger's ability and seniority in the American pulpit, Kohut kept on insisting that the opportune time for building the Judaism of the golden mean was at hand. "Only when the Rabbis of this country shall be moved by a common endeavor for wise moderation, unaffrighted at the 'Backwards' cry . . . only when conservative progress rather than ungovernable speed shall characterize our religious movement, can the outlook for Judaism be hopeful."[36]

In scholarship and intellectual acumen Kohut found an equal master in his Reform adversary, Kaufmann Kohler. Born in Bavaria in 1843, Kohler was raised and educated in a strictly Orthodox environment. His spiritual mentor was the renowned leader of German neo-Orthodoxy, Samson Raphael Hirsch. Introduced to philology, psychology, and anthropology at the Universities of Munich and Berlin, Kohler underwent a spiritual crisis that marked his break with traditionalism. His thesis, in which he suggested the evolution of the "God-idea" among the ancient Jews, also argued for freeing religion from a stagnant past. Kohler opted for a rabbinical career instead of pure scholarship, but since the Orthodox had banned his book, he had no prospect of obtaining a post in Germany. Establishing contacts with Reform leaders in the United States, he was called in 1869 to a pulpit in Detroit. There, and at his next two congregations—Sinai of Chicago and Beth-El of New York—he expounded the legitimacy and relevance of Reform for modern man. He associated himself with the radical wing of American Reform and its champion, David Einhorn; the latter became his father-in-law as well as his new spiritual father.

As Einhorn's successor at Beth-El, the learned Kohler was the logical respondent to Kohut's charges. He respected Kohut's intellectual powers, and in fact the two had discussed aspects of their theological differences privately. But realizing that Reform was now seriously on the defensive, Kohler sought a wider audience. He delivered a counterseries of five sermons entitled "Backward or

Forward," which was translated into English and given wide coverage in the Jewish press.[37]

Kohler constructed his exposition of Reform as the true Judaism on Kohut's flat axiom that those who in principle denied Mosaic-rabbinical Judaism were no longer Jews. To that statement, which called upon Reform to admit its errors and to backtrack, Kohler replied indignantly:

Must we, after having . . . worked for thirty five years in this country for the emancipation from the yoke of Mosaico-Talmudical Judaism, again bend our neck to wear it in order to be complete Jews in the sense of orthodoxy, or may we persist in claiming . . . to stand on a far higher ground?

According to Kohler, Reform's claim to the title of authentic Judaism rested on several premises. First, since Judaism was a re ligion of reason—or, as Kohler put it, "reason is the light of God in the soul of man" the irrational myths and usages of ancient times suited to a semibarbarous people were inessential excrescences upon the true faith. Reform had to sift out what was meaningful to the free mind of the modern age and translate it into appropriate modernized forms. To turn away from reason by clinging indiscriminately to the old not only obscured the light of Judaism but held out the threat that modern Jews would be forced to seek a rational faith through the Christian churches.

Second, Kohler defined Judaism as a living and constantly unfolding revelation. The past could not be ignored, but ancient cere monials and laws had to be understood in the cultural context of their times. Reform, the vitalizing power within Judaism, carried the faith to progressively higher forms. Indeed, rabbinism, before it petrified into dry legalisms, was the reform of Mosaic Judaism during the Talmudic age. Optimistic and progress-oriented, modern Reform recognized Israel's mission to spread the truths of monotheism and prophetism and looked to "the Messianic era of humanity," the highest stage in Judaism's evolution.

Third, Judaism, as the sages themselves explained, was a religion of freedom. Therefore, it went against the grain of Judaism to read out of the community those who did not believe in supernatural revelation or to assign a lower status to women, slaves, or heathen. Freedom promised more:

[F]reedom from all restrictions which curb the minds and encroach upon the hearts in their craving for all that is beautiful, good, and true . . . freedom from all fences and hedges which prevent the unfolding of the full truth; freedom from all rust and mould of the past, which disfigure and obscure our bright heritage before the world and check its wholesome growth.

It was that doctrine of freedom that appealed most to the emancipated Jew and kept him loyal to his faith. In America, where Reform beliefs harmonized with the national creed, Reform was the most fitting of Jewish expressions.

Fourth, Judaism proclaimed the divine individuality of every man. In order to endow man with ever greater "liberty and grandeur," it had bequeathed the legacy of prophetic teachings to the world. Reform understood that prophetism was the essence of Judaism, and Reform made Judaism a practical religion relevant to the worldly problems of mankind.

Since those were the tenets of true Judaism, Kohler's conclusion was self-evident. Reform was positive, constructive, and forward, while Orthodoxy (or Conservatism) was negative, destructive, and backward. True, Reform had its weaknesses. It had overemphasized reason and sacrificed religious warmth and emotion. But Orthodoxy erred more grievously, for it blinded Jews by a maze of legalisms to the true meaning of their faith and their purpose as Jews. Kohler buttressed his case with arguments drawn from Jewish law, but he used loaded images as well—ghetto, Oriental, liberty, progress— well calculated to arouse American Jews in favor of Reform and against traditionalism. Most unfairly, however, he completely ignored Kohut's plea for moderate progress and a "golden mean" Judaism. Kohler slanted the debate to either/or terms, Orthodoxy or Reform.[38]

The public issue in the 1885 debate boiled down to that of the Leeser-Lilienthal interchange. But the superior intellectual level of the second disputation testified to the erudition and sophistication of the two contestants. It also revealed how far the quest for an American Judaism had moved from its raw, frontierlike stage of pre– Civil War days. Indeed, the very fact that America had attracted rabbis like Kohut and Kohler proved the maturation of the Jewish community. As in 1856, the Kohut-Kohler disputation hardened the differences between the Reformers and their opponents, but it had more positive results. The middle-grounders found a champion in Kohut, and his presence contributed to the founding of the Jewish Theological Seminary in 1886. That institution became the mother of the Conservative movement in America, the attempt to blend progressivism and Americanism with a commitment to rabbinical Judaism.[39]

For its part Reform was challenged to clarify its position further.

With the encouragement of several of his colleagues, Kohler called for a conference in Pittsburgh in the fall of 1885 "for the purpose of discussing the present state of American Judaism, its pending issues and its requirements, and of uniting upon such plans and practical measures as seem demanded by the hour." At the meeting, Kohler stressed the need for a platform *"broad, comprehensive, enlightened and liberal enough to impress and win all hearts, and also firm and positive enough to dispel suspicion and reproach of agnostic tendencies, or of discontinuing the historical thread of the past."* It was Kohler's paper, outlining the beliefs of American Reform and reiterating much of his reply to Kohut, that culminated in the adoption of the Pittsburgh platform.[40] The highlight of American classical Reform, the creed remained unchanged for fifty years. But the fortunes of Reform steadily eroded as the face of the Jewish community slowly changed under the imprint of the more numerous and nationalistic east European immigrants.

New Religious Forms and Roles

Aside from the purposeful changes enacted by Reform, Judaism inevitably assimilated American, in many cases Protestant, forms. The first Jewish translation of the Hebrew Scriptures in the United States, for example, copied the design and print of the standard King James version of the Bible. In traditionalist congregations, too, the use of Hebrew yielded more and more ground to English; translations of the prayer books and sermons in the vernacular became increasingly common. Traditionalists, like their Reform counterparts, worried about the lack of decorum, and they also raised questions about modifications in prayer and the role of the woman in the synagogue. In 1847 Orthodox rabbi Samuel Isaacs charged Jews with indiscriminate and sometimes destructive imitation of Christians and Christianity. Among the examples he gave were the substitution of Christian dates for the Jewish calendar and the ceremony of confirmation—both of which were shortly appropriated by the anti-Reformers.[41]

Isaac Leeser, the most vocal of the traditionalist camp, was a moderate innovator. The Philadelphia rabbi introduced regular English sermons into the service, translated prayer books and the Bible into English, and prepared catechisms and a Hebrew speller for Jewish Sunday-school students. Although Leeser warned against social or educational situations that might weaken Jewish loyalties, he did not hesitate to adopt those Christian methods that succeeded in invigorating Christianity. He insisted that Jews could apply with benefit the same fervor that Christian missionaries displayed, and, taking a lesson from the numerous Protestant tract and Bible societies, they would be well advised to distribute inexpensive books and pamphlets among the community to propagate knowledge of their heritage. That motive underlay his efforts to establish a Jewish publication society and a Jewish Miscellany, or anthology, series. Those ventures failed, but Leeser's work on behalf of the Jewish Sunday school, which directly copied the Protestant model, was eminently successful.[42]

The founder of the Jewish Sunday school was Rebecca Gratz. The grande dame of Philadelphia's Jewish society decided in 1838 at the age of fifty-seven that since "we had never yet had a Sunday School in our congregation, . . . I have induced our ladies to follow the example of other religious communities." The American Sunday-school movement to which she referred had begun in Philadelphia in 1790 and mushroomed rapidly over the next forty years. Within that time the purpose of the school had changed from one of providing rudiments of education to poor working children to that of nurturing religious piety among children of all classes. Leeser, who in 1830 took the post of spiritual leader in Philadelphia's Sephardic congregation Mikveh Israel, closely associated himself with the project. He had thought of a Sunday school while he was still in Richmond, and three years before Miss Gratz's venture he had publicly appealed to Philadelphians for support of such an undertaking. In his view the school would also serve to build up Jewish defenses against the active missionaries.

If Leeser's fervor contributed to the establishment of the Sunday school, it was Rebecca Gratz's personality that was stamped on the memory of her pupils. Her grandniece left a vivid description of how her aunt presided over the one-room classroom with ladylike but iron discipline. In the free school that was open to children of all classes and which followed the curriculum form of Christian school, she and her students recited prayers, read chapters from the Bible, studied catechism, and sang hymns. For want of Hebrew teaching materials, they at first used the King James Bible and books issued by the Christian Sunday School Union; Christological passages were appropriately erased or pasted over. As was the custom, outside visitors came to test the children annually, and the examiners apparently were quite satisfied with the performance. The Philadelphia school grew rapidly and soon branched out to other cities. Ultimately the Sunday school became the most popular form of Jewish education in the United States.[43]

Jewish educators did less well in attempts to provide good books of Jewish content for juvenile readers. Several attempts in the nineteenth century at publishing a children's magazine failed for financial reasons. Julia Richman, active in one venture to produce a paper similar to those used in Protestant Sunday schools, recognized "how far behind our Christian friends we Jews are in providing proper ethical reading for children of our own faith." She added: "We have learned or borrowed from our friends of an alien faith so much of what is good in our present Sunday school system; can we not also learn from their practices how to give our little ones a taste for Jewish religious literature?"[44]

The Sunday school raised opposition within the community from the newly organized German congregations, who saw it as a distasteful imitation of the gentiles. Irrespective of their own questionable piety, the more recent Jewish arrivals expressed shock over the laxity in communal observance that they encountered in America. The word went back to Germany, where, as Rabbi David Philipson reported, observant Jews came to believe that religiously, "in Amerika geht alles!"[45] But as acculturation rapidly peeled off layers of European practices, the newer immigrants overwhelmingly appropriated the changed customs. The sociological pattern illustrated in Abraham Cahan's classic novel, *The Rise of David Levinsky,* was already well entrenched.

One less well-known item borrowed from the Protestants was circuit preaching. Instituted at the end of the nineteenth century by the Union of American Hebrew Congregations, Jewish circuit preaching dispensed with the horseman who carried Bibles in his saddlebag, but fed on the image of clergy who had saved the West for the church. Circuit work was directed at small and isolated communities of the interior too poor or too few in number to support a permanent synagogue. To shore up the Judaism of those living away from the centers of Jewish life, neighboring rabbis were asked to volunteer their time to visit the outlying settlements, to hold services and help organize schools and congregations. In their visits they distributed pamphlets of holiday sermons—an attempt to provide the means by which concerned Jews could hold services even in the absence of rabbis. During the first decade of the twentieth century, the union's committee in charge of circuit duty, now a part of a broader Department of Synagogue and School Extension, proudly pointed to the numerous Jews it had reached and the enthusiasm it had aroused. Department director Alfred Godshaw reported in 1908, for example, on his work in Ardmore, Oklahoma, "a sparsely settled section of Indian territory." He established a congregation there in 1904, and four years later returned to find that a school in addition to the congregation was well kept up. The union's work also inspired small towns to organize their independent circuits, which permitted them to share the expenses of acquiring religious materials and personnel.[46]

The wave of radical Reform crested between 1870 and 1890, but despite the clamor for Americanization, the radicals failed to change Jewish weekly worship from Saturday to Sunday. Neither economic pressures nor the desire for conformity tipped the scales in favor of adopting the Christian day of rest. On the matter of the Sabbath, like the retention of circumcision and the opposition to intermarriage, nineteenth-century Reform put limits on its submission to the dictates of reason and modernity.

The decline in synagogue attendance on Saturday, an American working day, generated compensatory experiments. An attempt was made at Sunday services in Baltimore in the 1850s, but although the sponsors, the Hebrew Reformed Association, designed them as supplementary to, rather than in lieu of, the Sabbath, the venture failed. Traditionalists, of course, shrank back in disgust. The *Occident* charged that a Sunday Sabbath obeyed the Christian community and not the Bible. If it meant to be religious, it was a violation of Judaism; if it weren't religious, it was a mockery of Jewish worship.

By the time the Reform rabbis convened in Pittsburgh, supplementary Sunday services had been adopted by only three congregations—Baltimore's Har Sinai, Chicago's Sinai, and Philadelphia's Keneseth Israel. Moderate Reformer Isaac Mayer Wise opposed Sunday worship but instituted a supplementary late Friday evening service. The Pittsburgh conference, afraid of causing a schism within Reform ranks, neither endorsed nor condemned the Sunday practice. It referred to the "historical" Sabbath as "a symbol of the unity of Judaism the world over," but it found nothing in Judaism to prevent the introduction of Sunday services in congregations where that need was felt.[47]

Shortly thereafter, Sinai Congregation, under the leadership of Rabbi Emil Hirsch, discontinued Sabbath services entirely in favor of Sunday. Both Hirsch and his father, who ministered at Keneseth Israel, warmly supported the idea. The elder Hirsch had argued in Germany for a "post-ghetto" Sabbath, on which the Jew, under a religious commandment to work six days and not five, would rest on the same day as the larger community. Father and son insisted on the sanctity of the Sabbath idea but denied that it was chained eternally to a particular day. To pray and preach on Sunday was not sinful, and to utilize society's day of rest, "which alone would give us again a real Sabbath, without landing us in a social Ghetto," was not treason. Conditions of life had turned Jews away from Sabbath observance, and the realistic options were Sunday or no religious day of rest at all. Emil Hirsch's change to Sunday, the first of its kind in the United States, appeared to flourish. One enthusiast reported that the weekly services drew audiences of 2,000, both Jews and non-Jews. But Hirsch's success apparently derived more from his personal appeal than from the social need that Sunday services filled. Essentially a practice that reflected the leanings of individual rabbis and congregations, it could not be mandated across the board for Reform's entire constituency.[48]

In 1888 the *Jewish Tidings,* a Rochester paper that spoke for radical Reform, launched a major crusade to abolish services on the "antiquated" and "inconvenient" day of rest and switch to Sunday. Triggering a controversy that engaged Jewish journals in different parts of the country and echoed in the secular press as well, the paper quickly modified its stand to one of supplementary Sunday services. Two years later it polled about fifty leading rabbis and laymen and elicited a decidedly mixed response. Those who opposed Sunday services argued for the "historical" Sabbath and against a step that some believed would legitimate further nonobservance. An interesting comment came from Solomon Schindler, a Reform rabbi of Boston; he had tried Sunday services for two years but had failed, and he pessimistically concluded that services on any day of the week were doomed.

Kaufmann Kohler explained in 1895 why he, a former advocate, felt conscience-bound to abandon the Sunday service. Earnestly seeking at that time the reasons for the decline of religion among American Jews, Kohler admitted that Reform "with no other principle but that of progress and enlightenment has created a tendency to treat the past with irreverence and to trifle with the time-honored institutions and the venerable sources of Judaism." The Sunday innovation, which he called a "patricide," was a case in point. It destroyed the Sabbath and failed to erect a Judaism loyal to its historical institutions.[49]

The Central Conference of American Rabbis took up the discussion in the first years of the twentieth century. By then the movement was seriously examining the alienation from Judaism that

Reform had not been able to stem. Whether the cause was material affluence, Darwinism, Zionism, biblical criticism, the secession movement of Felix Adler's Ethical Culture, inadequate education, or the inability of Reform to reach the new wave of Russian immigrants, both critics and defenders agreed that American Jewish youth was well on its way out of the fold. Since debates on how to revive Reform Judaism drew first priority, it was understandable that radical proposals on the Sabbath issue would command little enthusiasm. Reform could not afford the charge that it was out to destroy the Sabbath. The matter was discussed seriously at the 1902 rabbinical convention, where the general tone was one of cautious moderation. Jacob Voorsanger of San Francisco delivered the working paper in which he set forth the social, economic, and spiritual reasons for Sabbath nonobservance. But in this instance, which pointed logically to the phasing out of Saturday worship, the "spirit of the age" was not invoked. Rather, Voorsanger said:

The non-observance of Sabbath by millions of Jews does not invalidate the fact that, as an historical institution, it represents principles that are part of the life blood of our religion. Upon the face of this presentation it might be easy for some to readily pronounce the impending doom of the Sabbath and its ultimate extinction. . . . The Sabbath is one of those powerful elements that have given our religious system that distinct individuality that has made it the source of other systems and I question whether the elimination of so great an element does not involve the gravest danger to the system itself.

The few radicals were outvoted, and the conference, not specifically referring to Sunday services, went on record in favor of strengthening observance of the "historical Sabbath." The next year, fighting hard to retain its sway over the community, Reform went only so far as to reaffirm the resolution of the Pittsburgh conference.[50]

For both Reformers and traditionalists America radically changed the office of the rabbi. Without the quasi-official status which a rabbinic post enjoyed in a legally recognized community or in a religious network headed by a chief rabbi, the stature of the American rabbi depended primarily upon the power he wielded over his own congregation. In most cases that meant subservience to the lay officers headed by a president or parnas, who controlled synagogue ritual and discipline as well as finances. Some Jews may have had unpleasant memories of rigid, clerically dominated European com-

munities, but initially the laity had no other option. European ordained rabbis did not immigrate with their flocks, as did many
Christian ministers, or even appear in the United States until the
1840s; for men of rabbinic learning, America, bereft of Jewish
books, seminaries, or circle of scholars, was a cultural wasteland.
The "reverends" or Sephardic hazzanim who functioned as spiritual
leaders of the early congregations were frequently poorly trained in
rabbinic lore. In New York's Shearith Israel some were part-time
workers with mercantile establishments on the side. The few
Sephardic "rabbis" like Leeser who wielded leadership earned
their power by their personal force and commitment, scholarly attainments, or innumerable communal enterprises.

The first rabbis to immigrate in the German period failed to
reverse the pattern, for more often than not they lacked impressive
credentials or records of significant experience. In 1846 the newly
arrived Isaac Mayer Wise reported that only two in New York knew
how to read unvocalized Hebrew. The absence of learned religious
leaders and the habit of doing without them eroded traditional Jewish veneration for religious expertise. According to Wise, American
Jews looked down upon men of culture, considering them "impractical and helpless." Instead of a minister or preacher, the congregations preferred a jack-of-all-trades—a "teacher, butcher,
circumciser, [shofar] blower, gravedigger, secretary." The subor-
dination of the rabbi to the laity cannot be explained as an indicator
of democratization within the religious community. On the contrary, the nineteenth century witnessed hardening social stratifica-
tion, as synagogue building, membership dues, and rates for pews
increasingly divided rich Jews from poor.[51]

German congregations grew accustomed to treating the rabbi
often as shabbily as hired help. They muzzled their minister on
political issues and required him to obtain permission before he
preached. Leeser testified to how they also muted the rabbi's voice
on extrasynagogal affairs:

[T]hey are, as a rule not admitted to public meetings; and if they are,
prudence teaches them not to touch upon any subject which might
perchance be unpleasing to their flocks; for sad experience has proved to
them how little they gain who have an independent opinion of their own.

The same Leeser was forced to sign a contract that provided for
penalties should he default on his duties.[52]

The autocratic parnas, and not the rabbi, controlled the synagogue. Wise, who was counseled by two rabbinical colleagues not

to pursue that profession, called the parnas the ruler of "the quick and the dead." The handful of lay officers determined salary and tenure. Except in the established congregations, the rabbi usually received only a one-year contract; salaries were low and disability or death benefits nonexistent. In 1853, when congregation B'nai Yeshurun of Cincinnati offered Wise $1,500 a year, the rabbi reported that the figure exceeded by $500 the salary earned by any other rabbi. The situation turned into a vicious cycle. The less the authority or material rewards, the less the rabbinical office attracted capable men; and the more that mediocrities filled the office, the more the congregations looked down upon their rabbis.

Wise bemoaned both the low intellectual level of the rabbis and the treatment meted out by the laity in the early volumes of his weekly, the *Israelite*. Time and again he called for an American rabbinical seminary to raise the quality of the office and thus counteract the decline in synagogue attendance. Reformers and traditionalists agreed on the importance of a native and well-trained ministry, but three early attempts to establish such programs failed.[53]

The low status of the rabbi persisted after the Civil War despite the arrival of erudite and well-known men from Europe. One educated observer, the son of a rabbi, blamed the state of affairs on the age of materialism, when pretense and extravagance infected both church and synagogue. Emil G. Hirsch, another rabbi's son, vented some grievances in 1885 on the occasion of his father's seventieth birthday:

The bread of the Jewish Minister is but seldom buttered. I, who have been privileged from earliest infancy to share the intimacy of such a life, I know . . . that the bread—the mere bread—of the Rabbi is not compensation for the would-be-entailed loss of manhood! . . . Bread, indeed! As though he who is fit to occupy a Jewish pulpit was too stupid to cast his lot in other lines, as though he would not be as successful a merchant, as skilful a physician, as eloquent an advocate, as the philosophers who assail him!

In a sermon to the Central Conference of American Rabbis in 1904, David Philipson, a member of the first graduating class of Hebrew Union College, also commented on the indignities that many rabbis suffered at the hands "of rich vulgarians and upstart parvenus." He discussed other reasons that discouraged possible candidates for the rabbinate and caused some practicing rabbis to leave the ministry entirely. But whatever the cause, the vast majority of American Jews found the profession unattractive for them and their children. "Time was," he said, "when a Jewish parent considered it the greatest blessing if his son became a rabbi . . . and when the Jewish Croesus regarded it the highest honor to ally himself by the marriage of his daughter with a noted rabbinical family."[54] On that issue, even Reformers looked back longingly on the past.

In some cases a rabbi's stature was enhanced by the attention and respect he gained from non-Jews for his sermons and for the figure he cut within his local community. That, too, attested to the changing role of the Jewish minister in a free society. Like his Protestant counterpart, he prayed for the welfare of the government, held special services for Thanksgiving or government-designated fast days, and was concerned with the practical social problems that beset his congregation. No longer required by his community to adjudicate civil disputes or to interpret Jewish law for daily living, the rabbi became primarily the preacher as well as the pastor and the public functionary.[55]

For many Jews whose religious education was scanty or nil, the sermon constituted the single source of Jewish edification. A perceptive comparison between the "ancient rabbi" and the "modern minister" published in 1900 reflected on the function of the sermon and the skills demanded of the modern preacher:

The pulpit then had to take the place formerly occupied by the school, and instead of *Derashoth*, which were no longer understood or appreciated, sermons had to be delivered, which were freely compared with those of ministers of sister creeds, and which had to run a competitive course. Nor was the theme of the sermons confined any longer to the discussion of dogmatical subjects and the elaboration of theological disquisitions; the sciences and the arts, philosophical questions and social problems, Jewish history and Biblical exercises had to have room and place in it; the progress and advance made had to be brought in harmony with religion, if the latter was not to be brushed aside. Neither was the congregation composed of the old material. The belief in Divine Providence, in Revelation, in Immortality, the obligation of ceremonial practices were questioned, and the weapons with which the doubter could be refuted, had to be taken largely from the armory of reason, history and logic, outside of Jewish thought and literature. The congregations no longer consisted exclusively of believers, but were largely sprinkled with skeptics, who did not keep their doubts to themselves. Altogether, the rabbi, to obtain any influence among his people, or the world at large, as a representative of Jewish ideas, had to possess all the varied accomplishments demanded of the scholar of modern times.[56]

Thus, by the turn of the century, rabbis frankly admitted to another opponent in addition to the "well-fed Parnass"—the arrogant and antireligious university-trained professional.

The Central Conference of American Rabbis considered the problem of the rabbi's role in modern society at its very first convention in 1890. Aaron Hahn read a paper dealing with the historical evolution of the rabbinical office, and to that he appended suggestions on how the modern minister should preach, what subjects his sermon should avoid, and the new responsibility of pastoral work. Thirteen years later those issues, but particularly that of the rabbi's status, were treated in a frank and illuminating report written by a special committee on the relation between rabbi and congregation. Pleading for mutual confidence rather than a relationship of employer to employee or master to servant, the report emphasized means of elevating the dignity of the rabbinical office. It advised against "trial sermons," short-term contracts that put the rabbi on probation, and the exclusion of rabbis from the boards of directors. Congregations should not judge the rabbi's worth by his success or failure to bring in new members, nor should they expect him to devote all his time to social functions that passed for pastoral work. The report insisted on the rabbi's supreme authority over matters of ritual and education. However, his chief concern and his exclusive domain was the pulpit:

The congregation has the right to expect *Jewish* sermons from the pulpit. The pulpit is not a platform for the discussion of miscellaneous themes of an encyclopediac nature. Conversely, the pulpit is the rabbi's domain; it is sheer presumption for any officer or member of the congregation to dictate to him what to preach.

At the same time, the rabbi had to serve as representative to the larger community:

In our American life the rabbi is a citizen of his community as well as the spiritual head of his congregation. As the representative of the congregation, it should be his pleasure as well as his duty to represent his congregation in the various charitable, municipal and social activities that interest the community at large. His congregation expects this, for he must be not only in the world but of it.

The unanimous approval that greeted the committee's report indicated how accurately it mirrored the rabbis' concerns. Yet, genuine fear of lay reaction kept the Central Conference from officially adopting or publishing the document.[57]

Social Justice Movement

One of the characteristics of present-day Jewish religious institutions is their involvement in social issues, usually on the side of progressive reform. Although it is commonplace now to see rabbis in synagogues take stands alongside their liberal Protestant and Catholic counterparts on matters of domestic and foreign policy, Jewish institutions largely ignored such matters until the 1900s. In time, however, they followed the lead of the Protestant pioneers of the Social Gospel and, like them, broadened the preoccupation of religion with social ills.

The American Jewish reputation for liberalism, in the sense of welfare capitalism, stemmed from the ideologies and political activities of the east European wave of immigrants. It is misapplied if read back to include the Germans of the nineteenth century. As a group, the latter steered clear of the reform movements of the 1840s and 1850s, in large measure because of their link with Protestant zeal or what some called Christian religious fanaticism. On the crucial issue of slavery, most Jews lined up with their geographic section, arousing criticism from abolitionists for nonparticipation in the antislavery crusade. After the Civil War the rapidly rising Jewish middle class overwhelmingly supported conservative and pro-business economic policies. Since the German Jews never spawned a clearly defined proletariat, few were involved in labor unions and even fewer in the radical protest movements of the farm groups and the Populists, the socialists, or the popular followings of Henry George and Edward Bellamy.[58] The vision of America which had prompted their immigration in the first place remained one of untrammeled economic liberty alongside political freedom. Tampering with the laissez-faire system frequently drew sharp protests. The *Jewish Messenger,* always a bastion of conservatism, not only equated the free-silver movement with communism, but had argued early on against an eight-hour day for labor that would most certainly encourage "indolence and wrong."[59] Given the mood of the Jewish community, where with very few exceptions rabbinical sermons ignored concrete social issues until after 1870, it is not surprising that individual Jewish critics of the social order—Ernestine Rose and her work for women's rights, socialist Daniel De Leon, and American Federation of Labor founder Samuel Gompers—had for all intents and purposes dropped their Jewish identity.[60]

Felix Adler, who substituted "natural ethics" for religion as the base for his Society for Ethical Culture, turned that organization and the Free Religious Association (founded by the Unitarian minister Octavius Frothingham) to practical reform measures as early as the 1870s. In advance of the Social Gospel movement, the son of Rabbi Samuel Adler had also severed his ties with Judaism. Although his society and lectures attracted mostly Jews, the leaders of the community branded him "a heretic, traitor, and apostate Jew."[61]

In no way would they take a cue from him on social reform or any other type of action.

Not until after the turn of the century, when churches were caught up in the Social Gospel movement, when Theodore Roosevelt and Woodrow Wilson stamped progressive reform with middle-class respectability, and when the rapidly acculturating Russian immigrants added their voice on public issues, did the organized Jewish community consider necessary amendments to the capitalist structure.

Just as "new liberalism" in the Western world challenged the legitimacy of laissez-faire, so did the social-justice movement in American religion, feeding into pre–World War I progressivism, modify the established canons of philanthropy. Philanthropy as charity was no longer sufficient; the literal meaning of the word, love of mankind, required middle-class America to think in terms of altered institutions and of adjustments in the balance between the haves and the have-nots. Religion demanded such changes not as marks of noble virtue or divine favor on the part of the affluent, but as the just response by society to the rightful demands of the unfortunates. Social justice never replaced traditional charity, but it radically broadened the horizons of welfare thinking.

The Social Gospel movement, which insisted that the churches assume active leadership in fighting the evils unleashed upon society by rapid industrialization, gathered momentum in the last two decades of the nineteenth century. Penetrating the seminaries, the religious press, and the pulpit, it reached its peak in 1908, when the Federal Council of the Churches of Christ went on record in favor of labor's interests. The Social Gospel, which cut across denominational lines, spelled optimism, environmentalism, and confidence in man's ability to improve society, perhaps even to bring about the Kingdom of God on earth. It flowered in tandem with the liberal currents in Protestant theology, which deemphasized the individual and his relation to God and stressed the social aspects of good and evil as well as the social setting of divine workings. The primary focus of the movement in the twenty-five years before World War I was on "victims" of capitalist exploitation, who, according to the Social Gospelers, could be saved by the proper application of religious teachings of humanity and brotherhood to everyday marketplace situations.[62]

Since a Jewish proletariat did not take shape until the east European immigrants numbered a sizable group, rabbis and synagogues lagged behind their Episcopal and Congregationalist counterparts who pioneered in the Social Gospel movement. In 1886, for example, the American Congress of Churches discussed the worker's alienation from the church. The same subject was not aired until twenty-three years later by the Central Conference of American Rabbis, the only organized group of Jewish clerics, and one which at first assigned labor questions to a committee in charge of the education of the blind, deaf mutes, delinquents, and other dependents. In 1909 Rabbi Solomon Foster raised the humanitarian issue as well as the practical consideration that church and synagogue attendance on the part of labor was steadily declining. Gompers had long since indicted the churches for their callous indifference to the plight of the workers and for their alliance with the "money interests." He had maintained that the typical Jewish worker from eastern Europe viewed the synagogue as an institutionalized form of industrial tyranny and another abridgment of his liberties. Through a discussion on how to bridge the chasm between the immigrants and the established synagogues, the Central Conference was led to take a stand on the specific socioeconomic issues pertinent to the Jewish worker. Those principles, similar to what both Protestants and Catholics were propagating, were not enunciated until 1918.[63]

Rabbi Emil G. Hirsch of Chicago was different. Untroubled by synagogue attendance figures, he stood for social action by religious institutions before there was a significant Jewish proletariat or a pronouncement by the Federal Council of Churches. A serious student of Bible, philosophy, and history of religion who contributed to the development of Reform thinking and practices in the United States, he simultaneously identified with numerous reform causes of the pre-Progressive and Progressive eras—rights of labor, women's suffrage, international peace, penal reform, education, and good government. The title of the newspaper he founded in 1891, the *Reform Advocate,* had a double meaning; like its founder it represented religious as well as social reform. Hirsch interpreted Judaism to be a practical, worldly religion whose nature dictated social justice. His posture reflected the influence of his father and father-in-law, Samuel Hirsch and David Einhorn, both prominent radical Reformers in Europe and the United States who stressed the social responsibility of religion and its task of bringing about human brotherhood. The younger Hirsch's talents as rabbi, scholar, and speaker permitted his independence, even though progressive views ruffled his wealthy parishioners in Sinai Temple. Hirsch recognized the unpleasantness he heaped upon himself—"Let the preacher today venture to breathe however faint a suspicion that the prevailing social system is not altogether right, [and] his most ardent admirers will begin to shake their heads in ominous fashion"—but he persisted.[64]

Far ahead of his colleagues, Hirsch preached the need of social justice—*"justice,* mark you, not charity"—from the 1880s on. At the Pittsburgh conference of rabbis in 1885, where Reformers drew up a platform that summed up their interpretations of God, Jewish nationhood and mission, Mosaic legislation, and the messianic era, Hirsch insisted that one plank deal with social action. The industrial evils of contemporary society required rabbinical attention, particularly since the laws of Moses and the voices of the prophets, the first socialists according to Hirsch, had stressed social betterment. "It was high time," he said, "for the Hebrews to take a stand against the prevailing sentiment that Hebrews as a class were merely migratory in disposition and mere money-makers, possessing neither moral nor social influence in the community." Since in 1885 the social-justice movement within the Protestant churches was still in its early stages, Hirsch was probably responding less to that than to the currents of the new anti-Semitism then sweeping western Europe. Since he insisted that ethics be grounded in a religious base, he apparently also hoped to blunt the appeal of movements like the Society for Ethical Culture, which preached the importance of deed without creed. The rabbi sneered at the intellectual cowardice of Ethical Culture and its supporters—"women of either sex who have never thought." At the conference Hirsch won out, and the eighth plank of the Pittsburgh platform, the unamended creed of Reform Judaism for fifty years, read:

In full accordance with spirit of Mosaic legislation which strives to regulate the relation between rich and poor, we deem it our duty to participate in the great task of modern times, to solve on the basis of justice and righteousness the problems presented by the contrasts and evils of the present organization of society.[65]

The rabbinical commitment to social justice remained a dead letter until the immediate prewar years, but Hirsch continued to work for reform on his own. Sinai Temple, for example, was the first to invite a woman to speak from the pulpit. For Hirsch, as for the pioneers of other faiths, the industrial scene loomed most important. The major upheavals of the 1880s—particularly the Haymarket affair—were followed by more disturbing signs of popular unrest and disaffection in the early 1890s—the rise of the Populists, the depression of 1893, the Pullman strike and socialist "conversion" of Eugene Debs, Coxey's Army's march on Washington. Hirsch also kept abreast of the criticisms and theories of economists and reformers, men like Henry George, Thorstein Veblen, Edward Bellamy, Richard Ely, Debs and other socialists, and he doubtless knew of the progress made by the Social Gospel movement.

In 1895 Hirsch gave two major addresses that set him squarely alongside the liberal theologians and Social Gospelers of the Protestant churches. One, "The Philosophy of the Reform Movement in American Judaism," was delivered before the Central Conference of American Rabbis. Here Hirsch stressed the ethical dimension of Judaism and the moral duties imposed upon the individual because he bore the stamp of divinity. Another theme was that of social organization; Judaism rested on the principle that each man was his brother's keeper and was thereby responsible for all humanity. The third postulate made God's kingdom a this-worldly goal, by equating the messianic age with social redemption and regeneration.[66]

The second address, delivered in two parts as sermons before Sinai Temple, explained Hirsch's stand on the industrial problems of the day. The rabbi began by challenging the doctrine of "inalienable rights," so long the watchword of Western liberals. Under its banner, Hirsch maintained, a new kind of tyranny had been bred. Instead of a society cognizant of human needs, individualism running wild under capitalism had given rise to selfish atomistic units. The rich refused to see the inequities that dragged down millions and that caused despair and unrest. The fault, however, lay not with the capitalist but with capitalism, against which "my religion, the religion of Isaiah and Jeremiah, the religion of the best among all men—has everything to urge." Hirsch did not suggest the repudiation of inalienable rights but serious qualifications to the concept. The economic individualism of the Adam Smith school had resulted in grave wrongs if, as Hirsch pointed out, the courts in the name of liberty could side with the rich and strike down an income tax and legislation limiting the work day of women. The question had assumed crisis proportions, Hirsch warned, and isolated palliatives like the income tax or single tax were not enough. It could be solved only when all groups, even the deprived, recognized that rights carried with them duties and responsibilities to others. Logically, the doctrine of "inalienable duties," the title of Hirsch's sermon, bound poor as well as rich, imposing a sense of moral obligation upon all classes. But since the rich already had the full enjoyment of rights, their duties were clearest. Hirsch, the rabbi of an upper-middle-class congregation, stated with respect to private property:

To own the fruit of one's labor is an inalienable right; to dispose of one's earnings by will and testament may even be included in this category. . . . Yet, property is our own only to do therewith what shall prosper the common life. The right to possess is limited by the duty to utilize one's own for the social good. . . . Nor is property ever more sacred than humanity.

Wherever the right of property clashes with a duty to humanity, the former
has no credentials that are entitled to consideration. . . . Where wealth is
rooted in the ruin or the degradation of men, it is a usurper that should be
accorded the shortest shrift. Moloch competition shall never feed on
human sacrifices.[67]

Hirsch's critique of classical economics echoed that of the Christian social reformers, whose attack on laissez-faire "was to attain
the prestige of academic sanction during the 1880's" and forever
remain at the heart of the Social Gospel movement. The concept of
a mutually dependent capitalist and working class, with both rights
and duties, also became the stock in trade of those reformers. When
Hirsch said on another occasion that labor was not a commodity to
be bought and sold on the open market, he was repeating what
Bishop Henry Potter had first underscored in 1886. Other than
making Judaism rather than Christianity the base of ethical behavior, Hirsch's social-justice philosophy did not deviate from the
teachings of his Christian contemporaries. The rabbi, however,
found a link between the need for social justice and specifically
Jewish interests. In 1885 at Pittsburgh he had alluded to the images
purveyed by the anti-Semites which a Jewish creed of social justice
could undo. His sermon ten years later interpreted the new European anti-Semitism as an anticapitalist protest, a sign of the pervasive social unrest.

Against impersonal capital and the capitalistic organization of society this
new crusade nominally purposed against the Jew is . . . directed. As all
social movements of whatever kind are first tested by trying the experiment
with the Jew, so anti-capitalism takes on naturally the guise of anti-
Semitism.

Jews might be blamed unfairly for the evils of capitalism, but the
logic of Jewish as well as of humanitarian considerations ordered
them to the side of reform.[68]

Hirsch was conspicuous in defense of the worker. He condemned sweatshops, child labor, inadequate wages, and inhuman
hours. Calling for state aid in protecting labor, he also supported
unemployment insurance and collective bargaining. He stood by his
distinction between justice and charity and demanded righteousness, the true meaning of the Hebrew word tzedakah. Justice was
the virtue, but charity that used the poor "as a stepping stone to
Heaven" was not.

Hirsch's teachings inspired a handful of younger rabbis. Perhaps the most famous of those was Stephen S. Wise, a man whose name was associated with countless reform campaigns and whose Free Synagogue in New York drew inspiration from the institutional churches of the Christian reformers. It was Wise who eulogized Hirsch after the latter's death in 1923, calling him the giant who had reinfused Reform Judaism with the fire of religious ethical imperatives. Hirsch lived long enough to see the flowering of the social-justice movement in Judaism, and in his later years he warned the zealous converts to the cause against its abuse and against reducing religion to mere ethics or sociology.[69]

Not surprisingly, the Jewish community lagged approximately twenty years behind the Chicago rabbi. The rank and file of the German congregations were primarily those who had risen rapidly up the social ladder. Since they had become successful, the capitalist structure probably appeared to them as a fair test of ability that brought deserved rewards for merit. Why penalize them by pro-labor legislation just because they were successful businessmen? Their record of generous charity proved their virtuous character, and, besides, the pitied poor would no doubt behave just as ruthlessly in the economic marketplace if they had the chance. Rabbis who nagged about social justice were unwise to find fault with the American system and to disregard the barriers between religious and sociopolitical issues.

While such arguments could have been heard in most conservative affluent Christian churches, Jewish interests probably also played a part in the response to social justice. On a deeper level, nineteenth-century Jews may have sensed an attack on the underpinnings of emancipationist ideology. They had seized upon classical liberalism—i.e., the absence of restraints—as the surest way for the newly emancipated Jew to catch up to his compatriots and become an equal member of the modern state. Now social justice in the name of reducing inequality called for reforms that set limits on economic freedom. Once started, that process might easily get out of hand. Furthermore, for the government to decide whose freedom needed restraining on behalf of whose opportunity posed a serious problem to any minority. In the long run, if the group's share of perquisites and power were determined by the numbers of votes at their command, they stood only to lose.

When rabbis and synagogues allied themselves with the Social Gospel forces, they took on the coloration of their liberal Protestant counterparts. The fact that rabbinic Judaism was consistently more preoccupied with social questions than was orthodox Protestantism—thereby making the new focus of the synagogues less radical than the Christian movement—was immaterial. Liberal Protestants had fathered the new doctrines, and their adoption by Jews owed more to Christian influence than to any concerted Jewish interest in adapting the ethics of their heritage to the contemporary world.

For their part, liberal Protestant theologians and Social Gospelers, imbued with a new interest in biblical criticism, reexamined the historical Jesus and linked his message to that of the Old Testament prophets. Some openly and with sincere praise acknowledged the debt that their movement owed to Jewish teachings. As they, on the one hand, elevated the importance of the ethical roots that had nurtured Jesus the Jew, and liberal Reform Jews, on the other, argued against antiquated layers of rabbinic dicta that obfuscated the universal truths of Judaism, it did not appear farfetched to conceive of a possible merger of liberal Protestantism and liberal Judaism. An ecumenical spirit manifested itself in speeches at the World's Parliament of Religions in 1893, in interfaith services—for which both rabbis and ministers in New York prepared *A Book of Common Worship*—and in the increased popularity of exchanging pulpits.

Nevertheless, as one incisive study has shown,[70] neither Social Gospel nor its propagators was devoid of the old-fashioned Christian conditioning that kept anti-Jewish sentiments alive. No different from their conservative forebears, liberal Protestants held the crucifixion story (with the Jews as the deicides) central to their teaching. Indeed, they introduced a new element that compounded that Jewish crime. In their eyes Jesus was the Social Gospel leader of his day pitted against Pharisaic conservatism and corruption. Furthermore, if Jesus embodied all that was noble in Mosaic legislation and the books of the prophets, it was appropriate to wonder anew why Jews, especially those who took a stand against the evils of capitalism, persisted in rejecting Jesus. Requiring the application of ethical teachings, the modern age needed the support of a religious tradition that went beyond Pharisaism, and hence Jewish beliefs in the superiority of their faith and its contributions to the cause of humanity were misapplied. The Social Gospelers may have personally shunned anti-Semitism, but they saw no reason for Jewish "separation." Their very tone evoked echoes of nineteenth-century Christian reformers who expected emancipation to bring the Jew ultimately to Christianity. Thus, while the Social Gospel addressed itself in progressive fashion to the economic problems born of capitalism, it may have actually reinforced conservative prejudices and the conservative religious underpinnings of anti-Semitism.

An American Jewish Scholarship

The Judaism of the German Jews mirrored its American settings in forms, ideology, and social concerns. Even the failure to come up with a unified, single religious structure was eminently American. The unbridgeable chasm between Orthodox and Reformers on theology and ritual, and the marked divisions that set off congregation from congregation within each of those two broad groupings, reflected the congregationalist principle governing American religious life. "What's 'American' about American Jewry?" Joseph Blau asked in a recent book, and one of his answers is "protestantism" and "pluralism." The recognition of the legitimacy of different religious conclusions arising from the same starting points (protestantism) and the validity of basing religious systems on differing premises (pluralism) characterized the development of American Judaism as it did American religious life generally.[71]

While the Jewish community argued incessantly about how best to balance traditional religion with American life, Judaism as a subject of scholarly study was a low priority. But those who pioneered in that area also recognized the need to adapt to an American environment. As in the case of religion — or, for that matter, any ethnic undertaking—survival depended upon earning the stamp of legitimacy from the host country.

Cyrus Adler, then librarian of the Smithsonian Institution, used the occasion of the fifteenth anniversary of the *American Hebrew* in 1894 to take an inventory of serious Jewish intellectual activity in the United States during that same period. He optimistically looked forward to a revival of Jewish learning, or what he called "A Jewish Renaissance," in the English-speaking world. Nevertheless, Jewish scholarship required careful nurturing, he said, for American Jews still lacked the basic apparatus of libraries, scientific publications, and independent scholars.

It is plain, therefore, that Jewish science is without those opportunities in America for research now afforded every other scientific activity. To remedy this defect and to focus our intellectual activity, I propose the establishment of the Jewish Academy of America. This academy should collect a library, should publish scientific researches, provide facilities for students, be the central point of meeting of all of our learned men, and last, but not least, have connected with it a staff of men who would themselves be constantly engaged in advancing Jewish science.[72]

Adler's lifelong goal, to develop Jewish studies into a scientific discipline in the United States, was the product of several factors. Partly, it mirrored his personal contentment in his career as a Semiticist. The native-born Jew, whose father had emigrated from Germany to the unlikely destination of Van Buren, Arkansas, had completed his undergraduate studies at a time when American universities, responding to influences emanating from German institutions, were developing serious graduate programs for the training of professional scholars. Adler enrolled in Johns Hopkins, where, in the newly organized Semitics department under the direction of Paul Haupt, he was tooled in philology and archeology, fields whose rapid advances after 1850 radically altered the study of ancient culture and religion. The first American to earn a Ph.D. degree in Semitics from an American university, he taught at Johns Hopkins until his duties at the Smithsonian required full-time attention. At both jobs he was among the pioneer builders. As instructor and associate professor he contributed to the growth of Hopkins' Semitics Seminary. At the Smithsonian he developed the departments of Historic Archeology and Historic Religions and arranged government-sponsored exhibits of biblical and Near Eastern objects. His enjoyment of pure scholarship operated in tandem with a desire to bring the products of scientific research before the public.

Although professionally Adler belonged to a loose confederation of scholars of various countries engaged in the *Wissenschaft des Judenthums,* or Jewish science, movement, his paramount concern was for Jewish studies in the United States. An ardent patriot and second-generation American who never boasted of cultural ties with Germany, Adler envisioned America as a major center of world Jewry. As a result of the heavy immigration from eastern Europe, it could even become *the* world center. To be sure, Jews formed a kinship group whose ties crossed national boundaries, but American Judaism needed to look to the development of its own resources. The rapid growth of the community argued forcefully against its living off the cultural bounty of European Jewry. In 1891, when Adler visited England, he was impressed by the intellectual lights of the Anglo-Jewish community as well as by their schools, publications, and the study of rabbinics at Oxford and Cambridge. The signs of a "renaissance" there encouraged him to think of similar developments in his country.

A deep pride in his Jewish heritage underlay Adler's goal. Nothing could better fuse his scholarship, love of country, and loyalty to Judaism than securing for Jewish studies a legitimate place on America's scholarly agenda. Never an ivory-tower scholar, Adler was also alert to the needs of his coreligionists. In an era when prejudice blossomed in the Western world, he believed that Judaism, Americanized according to the canons of modern scholarship, could raise the level of knowledge and respect on the part of both Jews and non-Jews for the ancient but still vibrant culture. Years before he became associated with the Smithsonian, his family had donated a shofar and tools of shehitah (ritual slaughtering) to the museum. The gesture, like Adler's later activities, bespoke a pride in Jewish practices and an assumption that Judaism enriched American civilization.

A science of Judaism in America also served Adler's traditionalist background and life style. A member of Philadelphia's Mikveh Israel, he was a lifelong disciple of its rabbi, Sabato Morais. Adler's very decision to study Semitics arose from a desire to counter the attacks of biblical criticism on the truth of the Hebrew Scriptures and on the singular contributions of Jewish monotheism. From a traditionalist point of view, Jewish studies could reawaken an interest in the ongoing development of a total culture that was not the mere spiritual faith to which Reform had reduced it. Furthermore, it might prove the relevance of an unbroken evolving legal tradition and the invalidity of Reform's distinction between essential law and expendable usages.[73]

By the time Adler called for a Jewish academy, he had taken several significant steps to further the development of Jewish scholarship. His teaching career and museum work, albeit under the rubric of Semitics or Near Eastern studies, contributed to an appreciation of ancient Jewish civilization. Fixing Jewish studies in a larger orbit helped to free Hebrew and Jewish religion from the limited confines of Christian theological schools. At the formal opening of Harvard's Semitic Museum in 1903, Adler explained:

It is coming to be more and more recognized that in everything which makes for the higher life the modern man derives directly from a few groups of peoples that lived about the Mediterranean, and that a knowledge of their civilization is essential to an understanding of the history of human thought. It had been supposed for a long time that religion was the only important product of the Semitic mind and soul, and the study of these important peoples was confined to the theological faculty or pursued from the point of view of the divinity student, thus limiting to a profession what should have been the property of all cultivated men.

But as Semitic researches advanced through the digging up of buried cities and the uncovering of hidden parchments, it was seen that the rudiments of the sciences and the arts as well were to be found in Western Asia; that not only must the student of Bible know his Semitic history and archaeology, but that every educated man should be cognizant of the fact that when he used his alphabet, he was going back to the ancient Phoenicians; that when he examined the face of his watch, with its combination of sixes and tens, he was employing the number system of the ancient Babylonians; that when he spoke of the stars in the heavens or uttered some of the commonest terms known to mathematical and chemical sciences, he was speaking in the language of mediaeval Arabia; that when he prayed to his God, he was employing the concept handed down from Palestine.

The dispassionate scholar, Adler eschewed apologetics or defensiveness, but he doubtless shared the views of Jacob Schiff, who had endowed the museum. The latter put it more bluntly:

Indeed, the Jews, the modern representatives of the Semitic people, may well be proud of their origin and ancestry. Anti-Semitism in Europe, social prejudice and ostracism in free America may for a time be rampant. . . . To combat . . . these unsound currents in an efficient manner, opportunities should be created for a more thorough study and a better knowledge of Semitic history and civilization, so that the world shall better understand and acknowledge the debt it owes to the Semitic people.[74]

Adler helped organize the Jewish Publication Society in 1888 and, as an active member of its executive and publications committees, volunteered his services to read and proofread manuscripts. Dedicated to spreading the knowledge of Jewish history and religion, the society aimed at providing authoritative works in English to a community sorely in need of such books. To raise the intellectual level of English-speaking Jews, it translated works from foreign languages for both its fiction and nonfiction lists. By 1894, three volumes of Heinrich Graetz's monumental *History of the Jews,* a standard reference in any language, had been published. Through Adler's mediation the society also obtained a manuscript from a struggling British writer, Israel Zangwill, whose *Children of the Ghetto* appeared in 1892.

At Adler's insistence the society later undertook to publish the *American Jewish Year Book,* a compendium of yearly statistics on the number and distribution of Jews throughout the world and facts about their communal life and services to their country. Adler himself prepared and edited the first seven volumes. A reflection of the rapidly changing American Jewish scene, the *Year Book* assembled raw data for the use of future scholars.

Another legacy of the society was the translation of the Hebrew Scriptures into English. In that laborious project, Adler functioned officially as chairman of the board of editors and unofficially as diplomatic arbiter between the Reform and traditionalist editors.[75]

In September 1888, Adler publicly discussed the desirability of an organization that would collect source materials and encourage scholarly research on the history of the Jews in the United States. While Adler developed the scheme along academic principles, it appealed to Jewish leaders concerned with the growing threat of anti-Semitism. They concluded that a society which could prove the continued involvement of American Jews in their country's history would help dispel the image propagated by anti-Semites of the eternally "alien" Jew. Thanks to Adler's canvass of prospective supporters, and spurred on by the four-hundredth anniversary of Columbus's discovery, the American Jewish Historical Society was established in 1892. Secretary and then president, Adler contributed numerous articles to the society's *Publications.* Especially proud of this first attempt by American Jews to establish an organization solely for the purposes of scientific investigation, he called it "an oasis of earnestness in the desert of frivolity." But for its existence and its publications, Adler later claimed, many articles in the twelve-volume *Jewish Encyclopedia,* published in America at the turn of the century, could never have been written. Needless to say, that venture, a testament to the advances of modern Jewish scholarship and American Jewish cultural independence of Europe, also engaged much of his time and labor.[76]

Although Adler ferreted out multiple avenues through which to entrench Jewish studies in the United States, he objected to a separate Jewish university that taught secular as well as Jewish subjects. That idea had cropped up sporadically since 1843, when Mordecai Manuel Noah wrote a prospectus for a school that would combine classical education with instruction in Hebrew and religion. Noah's motive was to ward off the allegedly pernicious influences of Christian private schools; he called his school a college, but it was meant to serve children from the age of six years and up. The short-lived Maimonides College of Philadelphia and Isaac Mayer Wise's Zion College of Cincinnati also planned to include languages, mathematics and sciences, history and philosophy along with their Jewish curriculum. At the end of the century, others advocated a secular Jewish university divorced from theological training. Some said that perhaps Jews had carried their ideology of nonsectarian schools too far. If Catholics and Protestants had their universities, why shouldn't Jews? The *Jewish Messenger,* still fearing exposure of Jewish students at Christian institutions, thought a Jewish university would be a contribution to American higher education. However, not until anti-Jewish discrimination on campus grew more blatant after 1900 did the idea take greater hold. Its supporters reluctantly agreed that prejudice necessitated the establishment of a Jewish university, but they usually insisted that such an undertaking be nonsectarian. Critics still claimed, however, that universities privately funded by religious groups of any stripe were un-American.[77]

A variation of the university theme was the idea of endowed chairs in Judaica at American colleges. One proponent, Emil G. Hirsch, stated in a sermon of 1895 that "by giving Jewish science a home in our great universities," Jews could best counter modern anti-Semitism. "One Jewish professor," he said, "especially if he teaches Jewish science and teaches the history of Judaism and the philosophy of Judaism, does more for the generations to be than all other movements to combat prejudice combined."[78]

Adler argued in 1892 that since the trend was under way for the secularization of higher education, a Jewish university was academically unsound. Endowed chairs in Hebrew were equally bad. The study of Hebrew was moving out of religion departments into Semitics, and exegesis belonged exclusively to rabbinical schools. He suggested that funds could be better spent in having the Jewish Publication Society promote and publish original research. Copies of those publications could then be distributed to every college, library, and seminary in the United States. Another possibility, he said, was to underwrite a library on Jewish science run by the Library of Congress or the Smithsonian.[79]

Apparently Adler preferred to see the study of Hebrew and Judaism on the university level woven into the broad tapestry of the humanities. Implicitly, he drew a line between what was academically appropriate (language and culture) for the general university and what was parochial (religion). For Judaism to gain acceptance and respect as a valid component of intellectual study, it had to be taught by scholars committed to the canons of dispassionate science. Chairs in Hebrew purchased by Jewish money and likely to be filled by rabbis might enhance Jewish separatist inclinations or create a veritable ghetto within the university. Moreover, they could well cast doubt on the academic legitimacy of the subject matter. Jews first had to promote scientific research and thereby train a corps of scholars whose labors in the totality of Jewish culture could pass critical examination by any serious modern humanist.

A major venture for the advancement of Jewish science was the establishment in 1907 of the Dropsie College for Hebrew and Cognate Learning in Philadelphia. The man who made it possible was Moses Aaron Dropsie, a watchmaker and businessman who at thirty turned to the study of law. He won renown for his successful legal career and writings and for his financial and civic interests. Born of a Christian mother, Dropsie formally converted to Judaism at the age of fourteen. He actively participated in Jewish communal and religious affairs, but his special concern was Jewish education. He worked closely with the Hebrew Education Society of Philadelphia and Maimonides College, and he served as president of the board of Gratz College, a school established in 1893 for the training of Jewish teachers. In his will, Dropsie left the bulk of his estate, about $1 million, for a college to promote and teach "the Hebrew and cognate languages and their respective literatures and . . . the Rabbinical learning and literatures."

Dropsie did not have a yeshiva in mind. True, as Adler explained, the lawyer was a traditional Jew who bitterly condemned Reform's efforts to strip Judaism of its postbiblical legal accretions. He even wrote a pamphlet that argued the cogency and relevance of rabbinical commentaries on the Bible and Talmud and that drew a parallel between Jewish patristic literature and British common law. Not only was the corpus of Jewish law essential for the survival of Judaism, but representing as it did the accumulated wisdom of all ages on matters of science, history, and philosophy, it constituted a vast field worthy of scientific research. The college he envisioned would foster that dual perspective; it would teach the necessity of an evolving oral law, and it would instruct students, irrespective of creed, race, or sex, in the scientific study of Judaism and related disciplines.

The governors of the college named in Dropsie's will looked to Adler as the ideal person to head the first Jewish graduate nonprofessional school. He embodied, perhaps even inspired, what Dropsie wanted. In the words of Abraham Neuman: "Religious in motivation, but dedicated to pure research, designed to promote the knowledge of the sources of Judaism, but aiming to spread the light of that truth to all the world, the College program was typically Adlerian."

Nondenominational in purpose and in student body, Dropsie College was an eminently American institution to Adler. He even thought of adding a department that would train men for consular posts in the Near East. For thirty years Adler labored to build up the college, its library, and a faculty of scholars. During most of those years he also served as president of the Jewish Theological Seminary. Associated with the New York seminary since the days of his revered mentor, Sabato Morais, he had successfully engineered the reestablishment of that institution at the turn of the century under the leadership of Solomon Schechter. Adler worked closely with Schechter, and he was particularly proud of the seminary's library and the achievements of its faculty, but his special love was

Dropsie. When in 1910 he revived the *Jewish Quarterly Review,* a scholarly journal originally published in England, he housed it at Dropsie. He thus added greater prestige to the college at the same time that he secured the intellectual organ which he believed American Judaism needed so desperately.[80]

At the seminary's commencement exercises of 1907, Adler discussed "A University for Jewish Studies." He explained it as a further step capping the establishment of separate colleges and theological schools. Not a school but merely an aggregate of individual corporations under a central governing body, it would direct Jewish education throughout the country. Its major function would be to administer one single fund for propagating Jewish studies evenly and efficaciously among Jewish and non-Jewish institutions and individuals:

The Jewish colleges and schools of this country, the Jewish scholars, and Semitic and Oriental departments of our secular universities, the professors engaged therein, their libraries and their museums all need aid, varying according to circumstances. Sometimes an additional professor is needed; sometimes a fund for publication; sometimes a scholar should go for a year to work at Oxford or Paris or Berlin or Rome; sometimes there are students for whom there are no scholarships and whose studies would be cut off without such aid; photographs of manuscripts are needed for comparison; museum collections . . . are scattered . . . at forced sales. Colleges and institutions, which have not the means to provide lectureships on Jewish . . . culture, feel the need of adding this subject to their curriculum, and are debarred therefrom by the lack of a few thousand dollars a year. All these and many other things . . . could be done if there existed a fund.[81]

An outgrowth of his 1894 vision of a Jewish academy, his ambitious overall plan was never fulfilled.

Moses Dropsie once wrote of his hope "that the . . . sun of the golden age of Spanish-Jewish literature may again shine in the United States," but it was Adler who worked through Dropsie College and other means to realize that dream. The objective underlying his numerous scholarly activities was summed up in the purpose he outlined for a scholarly journal: to promote learning and original research, and to awaken the public's interest in matters concerning Judaism or the history of Jews. Adler believed that "for everything vital to the spiritual world, . . . our own little narrow piece of the Orient, Judaea, furnishes the deepest and the most universal inspiration."[82] Jewish science, planted firmly in American soil, would translate that message to the modern world while it enhanced the respectability of Judaism and its believers.

5

"ALL ISRAEL ARE RESPONSIBLE FOR ONE ANOTHER"

THE handful of Jews living in San Bernardino, California, in 1860 who donated thirty-eight dollars for the relief of Jewish refugees in North Africa had by their own admission grown lax in religious observance. Nevertheless, their ethnic sense had not dulled. "All Israel are brethren," they wrote in a letter that accompanied the donation,

[and] although we differ in several insignificant matters and quarrel upon some important ones; yet we are brethren, we are Jews, and the Jews, like the God they worship, are immortal. The enemies of Judaism need not the flattering unction to their souls, that we are less faithful than our forefathers; apparently we are so, we may even be somewhat lethargic, but let circumstances abide requiring us to manifest the integrity and solidarity of our faith, and we are as ready to manifest it, as our forefathers were.[1]

That ethnic consciousness above all other factors inhibited the disappearance of Jewry as a collective group. American Jews recognized that they were the bearers and guardians of a corporate memory, of a sense of peoplehood which most were not ready to relinquish. Tied in a common heritage with Jews in other lands, they were steeped in a tradition that imposed upon them the responsibility of one for all. Responsibility as taught by Judaism throughout the ages entailed more than relief or philanthropy. It included agitation for the rights of foreign Jews, protests against persecution, and concern for the preservation of a vibrant Jewish tradition in far-flung communities. Responsibility also assumed an underlying emotional empathy that bound together members of the group. Boston's Jews who celebrated the passage of England's Jew Bill in 1858 described those ties in a resolution formulated for that occasion: "It is manifestly ordained by the Supreme Ruler of the Universe that the children of Israel, however widely dispersed, living under different governments, in different climes, and speaking different languages, should still feel united in sympathy and sentiment; that the woes, joys and triumphs of one or a few of them, finds a 'ready response' in the bosoms of the whole race."[2]

Freedom and equality within American society never totally obliterated ingrained ethnic bonds no matter how Americanized the Jew or his religion became. Isaac Mayer Wise expounded Reform Judaism, an ideology that consciously strove to cast out the ethnic component from Judaism, but he, too, upheld the precept of *kol Yisrael arevim zeh ba-zeh* ("all Israel are responsible for one another"),[3] a teaching irreducible to mere matters of faith. From the Damascus libel of 1840 through the continuing crises that beset the state of Israel in the twentieth century, American Jews displayed more unity in responding to the needs of their fellow Jews than on any other issue. The tasks they undertook joined Orthodox with Reform, synagogue member with freethinker. They resolutely affirmed their loyalty to their foreign brethren on two levels. First, it was incumbent upon the Jews in free countries to display exemplary conduct—to prove, as it were, that freedom for the Jew was a safe investment for all nations.[4] Second, just because they enjoyed a more fortunate position, their responsibility for ameliorating the plight of the less advantaged was if anything increased.

Happily for American Jews, the United States, a nation of immigrants, saw nothing amiss with Jewish concern for fellow Jews in foreign lands. Still decades away from sustained involvement in world affairs, America had no reason to fear any conflict between its own interests and those of the Jews. Other minorities, too, engaged in relief drives and different forms of agitation to secure the freedom of coreligionists or coethnics. On occasion some might grumble that Jews were sending too much money in the form of relief out of the country,[5] but for the most part Christians commended the fervor with which Jews responded to their less fortunate.

Moreover, the interest of American Jews in the conditions of foreign Jews dovetailed with the concept of the American mission. During the Revolution, Benjamin Franklin had summed up America's belief in its appointed role to serve as the exemplar of liberty for the entire world:

[O]ur cause is esteemed the cause of all mankind. . . . We are fighting for the dignity and happiness of human nature.

Establishing the liberties of America will not only make that people happy, but will have some effect in diminishing the misery of those, who in other parts of the world groan under despotism.[6]

Against that canvas, Americans who called upon Old World governments to desist from tyranny and to recognize human rights were only acting out the national creed. The belief in the American mission accounted for the optimistic hope in the first half of the nineteenth century that revolutionists in other lands—the Spanish American colonies, Greece, Hungary—were seeking to emulate the American example. American Jewry found encouragement in the outpouring of public sympathy for those causes and for the suffering of rebels at the hands of despotic regimes. True, the government avoided direct intervention in the conflicts, but the idea of humanitarian diplomacy, that the United States had the right if not the responsibility to speak out on behalf of political freedom and in defense of human rights, persisted.[7] Jews invoked that tenet time after time and, in a sense, became its self-appointed guardians. Just as they defended and broadened the principles of religious freedom and separation of church and state, Jews labored to keep America faithful to this universalist component of its creed.

Humanitarian Diplomacy and Self-Interest

Rebecca Gratz, the Philadelphian who purportedly inspired the portrait of the Jewess Rebecca in Sir Walter Scott's *Ivanhoe,* enjoyed letter writing. The most famous American Jewish woman of pre–Civil War days, she actively participated in Jewish philanthropic and cultural affairs and, at the same time, cultivated a wide circle of friends within Christian society. At home in both communities, she had the perceptiveness and leisure to comment knowledgeably on the events and personalities of the period. In a letter of 1840 she discussed developments in the Damascus case and noted its impact on Philadelphia Jewry: "The Damascus persecution has fallen in a time to put down all petty strife and make us all desire to act & pray for the oppressed. May not this 'partial evil prove a universal good'?"[8]

While inspiring American Jews to a singular display of unity, the Damascus blood libel of 1840 also illustrated the workings of humanitarian diplomacy. The libel arose when a priest in Damascus and his servant mysteriously disappeared. The Ottoman government, believing that the Jews might have killed the two Catholics, immediately entered the Jewish quarter and tortured several Jews until confessions to murder were elicited. The Jews supposedly admitted that the blood of the two victims was drained to use in the baking of matzoth for Passover; the bodies were then hacked into small pieces. The Ottoman government stepped up its tortures, determined to find the bottles of Catholic blood. At first report, seventy-two Jews were sentenced to be hanged, but the entire Damascus Jewish community, perhaps as many as 30,000, was under suspicion.

Upon hearing of the British protests against the persecution of the Jews in Damascus, the American secretary of state, John Forsyth, informed the American representatives in Egypt and Turkey of America's dismay over the revival of the barbaric charge and of its sympathy with the victims. Forsyth wrote that President Van Buren desired the repression of "these horrors," and, tying humanitarian diplomacy to the mission concept, he justified America's intervention in the affair:

The President is of the opinion that from no one can such generous endeavors proceed with so much propriety and effect, as from the Representative of a friendly power, whose institutions, political and civil, place upon the same footing, the worshippers of God, of every faith and form, acknowledging no distinction between the Mahomedan, the Jews, and the Christian. Should you in carrying out these instructions find it necessary or proper to address yourself to any of the Turkish authorities you will refer to this distinctive characteristic of our government, as investing with a peculiar propriety and right the interposition of your good offices in behalf of an oppressed and persecuted race among whose kindred are found some of the most worthy and patriotic of our citizens.

The government's reaction cannot be dismissed merely as a political favor to the 15,000 American Jews; the executive responded *before* the Jews petitioned for intercession.

American Jews learned of the Damascus affair from Jews abroad. At several mass meetings which took place weeks after the administration had acted, Jews also cited America's mission as reason for official protest. Since they called the blood libel a blow against enlightenment and civilization, and thus a threat to humanity at large, they insisted that it rightfully deserved the condemnation of Jew and Christian alike. Buoyed up by a sympathetic public and by the government's response, the Jews of Richmond confidently interpreted Van Buren's action as a hopeful sign for the future. His "voluntary act," they said, "assures to us his sympathy in whatever may hereafter be attempted or done toward extending to the ancient race of Israel, wherever dispersed, the civil and religious privileges secured to us by the Constitution of this favored land."[9]

For Americans, the Damascus affair turned out to be one of

those rare occasions on which all participants won. The government, free of conflicting pressures or interests in the Middle East, advanced its image as a protector of universal freedom. Concerned Christians could reap satisfaction insofar as the public outcry from the free world halted the persecution in Syria. American Jews, too, emerged victorious. Their faith in the beneficence of their government and in the efficacy of rational appeals to public opinion was vindicated. They were proud of, as well as gratified by, the expression of Christian sympathy, for it meant that the cause of Jews rated as important in the eyes of their compatriots as the causes of other oppressed groups. They preferred to ignore the fact that Van Buren may also have been rewarding the fealty of most Jews to the Democratic party,[10] but his favor in 1840 doubtless reinforced that loyalty.

The component of American Jewish self-interest in the Damascus affair, albeit low-keyed, was not absent. At the meeting of Philadelphia's Jews, the speakers called the blood libel a "calumny" against Judaism. One of them ventured further: "If such a calumny is not nipped in the bud, its effect will not be limited to any particular place, but will be extended to every part of the globe."[11] Even if most American Jews could not imagine being subjected to torture, the charge that Jews used Christian blood for their Passover rites constituted a blot upon their faith and called for vigorous denials.

The few who feared that the libel's influence could reach American shores were proved correct a decade later. On April 6, 1850, the *New York Herald*, which had originally sympathized with the Jews of Damascus, reopened the charges with a lurid front-page story of how an atrocious murder had been perpetrated by the Jews, acting according to mysterious Talmudic injunctions, and how the investigation had been squelched by the devious manipulations of the House of Rothschild. The *Herald*'s account was potentially far more dangerous to American Jews than the original episode. As the *Asmonean*, the New York Jewish weekly, pointed out, not only could the story "kindle afresh that latent bigotry which may be smoldering in weak minds," but also it linked the "mysteries" of the Jewish religion with the archsymbol of nineteenth-century Jewish secular power. It thereby made the Jewish peril this-worldly, immediate, and a potential danger to Western society—and hence more credible to an American audience.[12]

Eighteen years after the Damascus affair the Jews again appealed for humanitarian diplomacy. This time they pleaded the cause of

Edgar Mortara, a six-year-old Jewish boy of Bologna, Italy, who was forcibly abducted from his home by papal authorities after a Catholic servant confessed to having had him secretly baptized. In Europe, individual Jews and Jewish organizations, with the help of Protestants, raised a storm of protest. Even heads of Catholic countries—Prime Minister Cavour of Sardinia, Napoleon III of France, Franz Joseph of Austria—pressed for Edgar's release. The venerable Sir Moses Montefiore, president of the Board of Deputies of British Jews who later traveled to Rome to intercede personally with the pope, alerted the American Jewish congregations and called for their collaboration. The request electrified press and pulpit, and Jews throughout the land took up the fight. From Boston to New Orleans, from New York to San Francisco, they organized local protest meetings, formulated resolutions, and signed petitions. Frequently joined by Christians and by the non-Jewish press, they roundly condemned the church's act. Some also called upon the American government to register its official sympathy for Edgar and his family with the Holy See.[13]

The Jews were quick to acknowledge that the government had no right to interfere or resort to coercive measures in the internal affairs of another state. But this was different, they said. Humanitarian diplomacy was eminently justified where the universal principle of religious liberty was at stake. Besides, no other country had raised the humanitarian issue directly with the pope. All the Jews wanted from the government, Isaac Leeser wrote, was a "simple act of humanity." "[O]ur government," said the president of Savannah's Congregation Mickve Israel, "has the right to interpose its moral influence in favor of oppressed humanity, everywhere, and at all times." Boston's Jews pointed out that the impropriety of meddling in matters of religion did not apply to cases where one church sought to deprive individuals of their "inalienable rights":

We therefore declare, that our citizens and government have a right, both at home and abroad, to vindicate the great principle of *liberty of conscience*, whether it be in the benighted region of China, or in the equally benighted focus of the most frightful intolerance of Rome.[14]

Much as the Jews worked to build up a case of humanitarian diplomacy, their petitions on the Mortaras' behalf were denied. President Buchanan considered them to be unwarranted meddling in a foreign country. Despite his expressions of personal sympathy, neither he nor Secretary of State Cass would be budged. They asserted that nonintervention was the policy of the country, that the

Damascus case had been a "single act" involving torture and loss of life, which did not alter that basic concept. A three-man delegation from Philadelphia armed with a mass petition and flanked by two congressmen from Pennsylvania went to Washington in January 1859 to enter a final personal plea with the president. They begged for government action which would perhaps induce European governments to treat their Jews more kindly. This, the second Jewish delegation to be received by Buchanan within two years and still raw in the ways of political bargaining, lowered itself to pitiable groveling and defensiveness. The delegation said:

The Israelites were in many countries cruelly treated. . . . It is therefore no wonder that abroad we are cramped in body and mind, since oppressors keep down our natural energies. But let us once be free, and we could show that we are not inferior to the best races of mankind in all respects. We asked, "Is not the representative belonging to our people here present [the Hon. Henry M. Phillips] fully equal to the duties of the trust reposed on him? is he not up to the high standard which may be demanded of the representatives of the people? And so also in literature and other mental pursuits, we have shown in America that we are inferior to none; because we had nothing here to check our energies and mental development; and give us the same opportunity elsewhere, and we would soon prove that it was not our fault that we lagged behind in the race of advancement."[15]

The year 1858 was far different from 1840, and the administration had cogent reasons for turning down the Jewish request. Buchanan presided over a party and a country split on the issue of slavery and moving ever closer to armed conflict. Intervention on behalf of Mortara could have alienated the Irish Catholics, loyal Democratic supporters ever since their heavy immigration in the 1840s, and it might have invited European criticism of the slave system. True, the number of Jews had increased almost tenfold since 1840, and their votes counted, too. But their commitment to the Democrats was less certain than in 1840. No doubt some resented the competition of the Irish, who clustered in the major eastern cities and were so eagerly absorbed by the local Democratic urban machines. Others were repelled by a party that defended slavery and, like other liberal immigrants from Germany, joined the ranks of the Whigs and then the Republicans. Besides, by having promised the Jews action on the Swiss treaty, a problem of simultaneous concern, Buchanan had already extended himself on their behalf. "I have not been regardless of their [i.e., American Jews'] just rights in foreign countries," the president said, and for that favor alone he could consider them in his debt.[16]

Failure in the Mortara case revealed the ever-uncertain position of the supplicant minority. It also disclosed the woeful immaturity of the newly emancipated nineteenth-century Jews in the give and take of democratic politics. They witnessed the politicization of the Mortara affair—how the Know-Nothing partisans used it to build up their bogey of the Catholic menace, how the abolitionists bitterly compared public sympathy for the kidnapped victim with popular indifference to the lot of the slaves, how Republicans seized upon the issue as a means of prying Jews away from the Democrats. Jewish Republicans joined the political game and tried to channel Jewish resentment into support for their party. On the other side of the political spectrum Rabbi Isaac Mayer Wise, a consistently loyal Democrat, discounted Buchanan's official reason for noninterference and sharply criticized the administration for deferring to the Catholic vote.[17] But the Jews all skirted the real issue—a willingness by the group to air Jewish interests collectively in the political marketplace. The proper Jewish Americans, as has been discussed, refrained from any activity that smacked of Jewish group politics even if such behavior doomed the attainment of their goals. But in the world of politics, Rabbi Sabato Morais's defiant gesture of discontinuing prayers for the government's welfare made little impression.[18]

Too late did Jewish leaders agree that unity among American Jews, instead of scattered and duplicatory efforts, would have brought about a different result. In 1859 a small number of Jewish congregations joined themselves into the Board of Delegates of American Israelites, the first serious attempt of the community to establish a defense agency. Although its architects disclaimed the purpose of creating a Jewish *political* body—and, indeed, the agency, patterned upon the British Board of Deputies, was supposed to serve the internal religious and philanthropic needs of the community at least as much as to protect the rights of American and foreign Jews—some Jews demurred. The very idea that they might need a defense agency in a free land could be interpreted to mean that their faith in the United States was imperfect. Temple Emanu-El of New York even suggested that a board would raise the anti-Jewish charge of a state within a state.[19]

Paulson Dietrich's death gained greater attention than his life. Dietrich, a Jew, died in a Catholic hospital in St. Louis in 1858 after having been involuntarily baptized. The Jewish community learned of the baptism from another patient, but Catholic and hospital authorities refused to discuss the case or to permit visits to the dying man. Dietrich was buried in a Catholic cemetery, and only after determined efforts by the Jews was the body exhumed and reburied in a Jewish cemetery. Since the event occurred when the reaction to the Mortara case was reaching its peak, Jews across the land discovered their own counterpart to the Italian affair. The presidents of the two congregations in St. Louis were particularly upset, as their letter to Buchanan disclosed: "The Roman Church has its priests, its asylums, its hospitals in our midst; and if the Pope gives his sanction to such acts of fanaticism [i.e., the Mortara kidnapping]—the Roman Catholic clergy here, obeying his laws as supreme, will be guided by the same principle, and similar acts will occur in the U.S."[20]

Despite a few such isolated warnings from the Anglo-Jewish press on the dangers posed by the Catholic church even in free America,[21] American Jews generally did not feel menaced by the Mortara affair. As a group they responded primarily out of feelings of kinship. Had they been less optimistic about the goodwill of enlightened men or the promise that America held out to them, they would have paid more attention in 1858 to a number of gratuitous comments which appeared in the nation's press. Some newspapers easily went from expressions of sympathy for Mortara to casual statements about Jewish clannishness and money power. From those stereotypes—themselves the grist for anti-Jewish mills—a few took the logical next step and charged the Jews with dual loyalty, avarice, and anti-Christian sentiment. The House of Rothschild, as in the *Herald*'s story of 1850 on the Damascus affair, again was singled out. Now, the unfriendly journals called it the Jewish medium for buying Edgar's release or for wreaking vengeance on the pope.[22]

Despite the evidence that revealed how average Christians could invoke deeply embedded anti-Jewish stereotypes and apply stock myths to American as well as foreign Jews, American Jews before the Civil War were reluctant to admit that their own security was jeopardized when bigotry erupted in a distant corner of the globe. They had settled in a New World, which non-Jewish ideologues since the eighteenth century had hailed as the Promised Land. Jews wanted to believe that their history had turned a corner when it reached the United States, that just as America had broken away from a decadent Old World to establish the ideal free society, so would America be the noble experiment in the Jewish experience. Many of their foreign brethren were still unemancipated, but they, because of their country's exceptionalism, enjoyed a seeming immunity to the torments and tortures so familiar in the Jewish past. True, American Jews found occasion to assert that freedom was contagious, that the passage of England's Jew Bill, for example, would advance Jewish interests in other countries of Europe.[23] However, they still preferred to ignore the obverse of the same coin—i.e., that anti-Semitism, like freedom, could transcend national boundaries.

For those who cared to take note, the case of the Swiss treaty of the 1850s illustrated the indivisibility of anti-Semitism. American Jews were barred from certain Swiss cantons, as Minister Dudley Mann explained at the outset, because those cantons feared the influx of "undesirable" Alsatian Jews and would make no exception for others. Here, the Americans were regarded first and foremost as Jews, a category that figured more importantly than nationality or level of westernization. American Jews, as has been discussed, were primarily concerned, however, with America's agreement to a treaty that set them apart in the United States as less-than-equal citizens. Cognizant of the hardships foisted upon all Jews by Swiss discrimination, they nonetheless steered clear of merging their private fight with that of the Alsatians. A few, like Isaac Mayer Wise, urged that American Jews, in conference, petition the government to raise its voice on behalf of Jewish freedom generally in Switzerland.[24] But their sympathy and even their expressions of mutual responsibility never included an admission of equal vulnerability.

The one who faced up squarely to that proposition was Theodore S. Fay, American minister to Switzerland. In a long note prepared for the Swiss government urging removal of disabilities against American Jews, Fay argued the latter's case in a broader context. Singling out the Alsatians for particular attention, he defended the rights of all Jews in the modern world.[25] He thereby admitted that the acceptance of American Jews could not be divorced from the acceptance of other Jews.

Fifty years later, in the case of Russian discrimination against American Jews, a new generation of communal leaders built a campaign on that very principle. In the Russian episode an obvious issue was again one of American Jewish equality. Despite a treaty of 1832 which guaranteed reciprocal rights to Russians and Americans in each other's countries, the czarist government imposed economic and residential restrictions on American Jews. Since the United States passively accepted Russia's actions, American Jews were stigmatized as second-class citizens. Accordingly, under the leadership of the American Jewish Committee they launched a fight for the abrogation of the treaty.

Temple Emanu-El,
New York, 1868
Courtesy of The Library of Congress
and The American Jewish
Historical Society

Rodeph Shalom Synagogue,
Clinton Street, New York, 1853
Courtesy of The Library of Congress
and The American Jewish
Historical Society

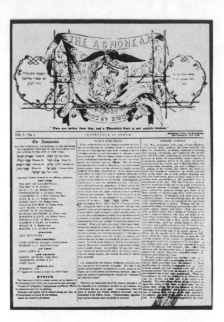

The Asmonean:
First issue of Robert Lyon's publication, October 26, 1849
Courtesy of The American Jewish Historical Society

Excerpt from a Jewish
petition to the U.S. Senate
Courtesy of The American
Jewish Historical Society

The Israelite, 1854,
*first issue of Rabbi
Isaac Mayer Wise's publication*
Courtesy of The American
Jewish Historical Society

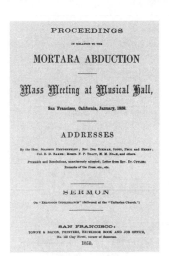

*Announcement for
a meeting regarding
Edgar Mortara's abduction*
Courtesy of The American
Jewish Historical Society

*Jewish Hospital announcement,
Philadelphia, 1864*
Courtesy of The Library Company
of Philadelphia
and The American Jewish
Historical Society

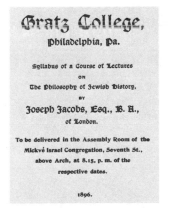

*Gratz College
lecture announcement*
Courtesy of The American
Jewish Historical Society

*Some results of the Galveston Plan
to direct Eastern European Jews
away from the East*
Courtesy of The American
Jewish Historical Society

German Jewish immigrants peddle their wares
Courtesy of The Library of Congress
and The American Jewish
Historical Society

Adler and Brothers, Chicago, 1866
Courtesy of The American Jewish Historical Society

The Peddler's road leads to a department store
Courtesy of The American Jewish Historical Society

Filene's advertisement, Boston, 1909
Courtesy of The American
Jewish Historical Society

Feustmann & Kaufmann, a Philadelphia dry goods business
Courtesy of The American Jewish Historical Society

Lasting from 1908 through 1911, the campaign drew from the earlier techniques of Jewish agitation. Albeit in a more planned and refined fashion, it, too, made use of public protest meetings and resolutions, Christian allies, visits to the president and other public figures, and contacts with foreign Jewish groups. Most important, however, the activists knowingly or unknowingly took a leaf from Fay's book. Although they highlighted the discrimination against American Jews, their primary objective was to compel Russia to emancipate its own Jews. They reasoned that if the Russian government, under the threat of abrogation, granted rights to American Jews, it could not do less for the Jews of Russia. Thus, just as Fay had fought for Alsatians in order to get rights for Americans, the American Jewish Committee fought for Americans in order to get rights for the Russians.

The campaign for abrogation showed that the link between the status of native and foreign Jews was growing clearer. Russia's very actions supplied the evidence, for restrictions on American Jews increased during the years that the government actively plotted the destruction of its own Jewish population. The obvious deduction on the interdependence of Jewish rights had been made even earlier, in 1881, by Secretary of State James G. Blaine: "[A]n amelioration of the treatment of American Israelites in Russia could only result from a very decided betterment of the condition of the native Hebrews. . . . [A]ny steps taken toward the relief of one would necessarily react in favor of the other." Jacob H. Schiff, a prime mover behind the abrogation campaign, openly spelled out the same principle in 1911:

Our anxiety to see our Government take action should not be misunderstood. It is not because the Jewish people lay stress upon the admittance into Russia of a few hundred of their number who may annually wish to go there, but because of the conviction that the moment Russia is compelled to live up to its treaties and admit the foreign Jews into its dominions upon a basis of equality with other citizens of foreign countries, the Russian Government will not be able to maintain the pale of settlement against its own Jews.[26]

Seasoned by events of the half century between the Swiss and Russian affairs, American Jews in 1908 to 1911 were not consumed by the single passion to uphold their own status. They were aware of the successes scored by racial anti-Semitism in Europe in the last quarter of the nineteenth century in the enlightened West as well as the East. In the United States they themselves were buffeted by a tide of social anti-Semitism which began to swell after the Civil War and showed little sign of abatement. Developments on both continents taught them that hatemongering and anti-Semitism could and did spread their poison from one country to another. They still believed that America was the ideal place for Jews, but they sensed that it, too, could not remain immune. Nineteenth-century anti-Semitism had steered them to a more realistic view of their vulnerability and to the lapses that they might expect even from their government. No longer would they give vent to the same hurt feelings which their predecessors had displayed in the 1850s. In an increasingly businesslike attitude, they established new organizations to cope with the ongoing problems of Jewish rights and acceptance in the United States and abroad. Slowly they were learning that self-interest, and not merely the noble sentiments of philanthropy, demanded that they defend their foreign brethren.

Trans-Atlantic Ties and Anti-Semitism in Western Europe

In December 1876, between fifty and seventy-five distinguished Jewish delegates from European countries and the United States assembled at Paris to draw up a memorial pleading for the rights of Jews in the Ottoman Empire. The *Jewish Messenger* of New York enthusiastically reported on their deliberations over which the renowned French leader Adolphe Crémieux presided: "The presentation of their Memorial marks an era in modern history. It suggests, what cannot be long deferred, the 'universal alliance' of Israelites for the enfranchisement of their race wherever held in moral or social thraldom—for the restoration of Judaism to its true place among the religions of the world."[27]

As the Paris conference proved, American Jews reserved their appeals for government intervention to extraordinary matters. The ongoing tasks of physical relief for the victims of poverty or of natural and man-made disasters were customarily handled by societies and ad hoc committees. In 1880, the Board of Delegates (by then affiliated with the Union of American Hebrew Congregations) even sent its own agent to Tangier to report to the American consul on wrongs that might be perpetrated upon the Jews in Morocco.[28] The conference also illustrated how Americans often worked in tandem with European Jewish leaders. As early as 1843 Crémieux had appealed for American Jewish support for Jewish schools in Egypt. In the antebellum years, funds for Palestinian Jews were usually forwarded through Sir Moses Montefiore of London.[29] Western Jews, closer to the center of international diplomacy and to the chronic trouble spots, served as sources of information for the Americans on crises like the Damascus and Mortara affairs.

The transatlantic connection grew stronger between the Civil War and World War I. The Board of Delegates and the later American Jewish Committee cooperated with the established Jewish organizations in England and the Continent on virtually all foreign affairs. Complementing the formal institutional operations, and frequently more efficacious, were the ties of family, business, and friendship that bound together the Jewish communal stewards of the different countries.

Cooperation, however, did not mean self-effacement. Americans may have welcomed the appearance in 1860 of the Alliance Israélite Universelle, an organization dedicated "to work[ing] actively everywhere in behalf of the emancipation and moral progress of Israelites," but they gave only lukewarm support to alliance branches in the United States. In the first place, the Board of Delegates refused to yield its initiative to the dictates of an international umbrella society. Second, in the last decades of the nineteenth century, all Western lands experienced an upsurge in nationalist sentiment. Like their counterparts in Europe, American Jewish communal leaders preferred to tailor their "diplomacy" in conformity with their government's, rather than with the alliance's, foreign policy. Third, since the alliance became for all intents and purposes a French organization, the rivalries that erupted between that society and its sister organization in Germany usually inclined the German Jews in America to the anti-French side.[30] Despite their need of Europe for religious and cultural inspiration as well as for diplomatic aid, American Jews determined long before the turn of the century that they would forge a communal policy of their own making.

In one atypical episode in foreign affairs before the Civil War, Isaac Leeser was prepared to venture further than most other American or European Jews. When Britain opened up China to Western trade, news of the existence of an ancient but decaying colony of Jews at K'ai-feng began to trickle out. Leeser's *Occident* in 1843 reprinted extracts from a book published that year in England describing the Chinese Jews. Nine years later, tantalized by missionary accounts of the exotic community and disturbed by the Christian zeal and apparent success in ferreting out the survivors, Leeser suggested that Western Jews attempt to establish communication with their Asiatic brethren and send them literature on Judaism or, better still, a teacher. The Philadelphia rabbi pictured the K'ai-feng Jews as in a state of siege, stubbornly guarding their faith despite persecution and ignorance, and beset "by the insidious hunters after precious souls." Since, according to one missionary account, two Jews had asked for instruction in Hebrew, Leeser wrote: "Is it not dreadful that our brothers should be compelled, in order to learn Hebrew . . . , to resort to those who merely accede to their wishes for the purpose of eradicating Judaism out of their hearts?"[31]

Only a handful of supporters responded to Leeser's initial plea for an organized crusade to ransom those modern-day captives. The *Occident's* editor lashed out against the casual indifference he encountered, and for a while he persisted. He revealed that there was an American Jew (whose name he purposely withheld) who would be willing to travel to China, if deputized by the Jews of England and America, and devote a few years to teaching the Jews of K'ai-feng. The costs would not be high; the religious books would be available, and, as Leeser learned from a San Francisco Jew who had lived in Shanghai, the difficulties of traveling through China were not insurmountable. Leeser called for the chief rabbis of England, along with the congregational leaders in America, to organize committees to collect funds for sending several teachers, "restorers of the faith," to the Chinese. It would be a noble gesture, proving the vitality of Israel's modern-day faith, and it would obviate the shame of losing Jews to the more zealous Christians.

One American congregation and a few individual Jews pledged donations to Leeser's Jewish missionary campaign. In November 1853 a meeting was held in New York at which representatives of different congregations met to organize a missionary board. Nevertheless, Chief Rabbi Nathan M. Adler of London, relying on a report from the Sassoon firm in Canton, thought that the revolutionary turmoil in China would militate against a successful Jewish mission. Since the Americans did not generate enough enthusiasm of their own, the scheme fell through.[32]

Until the twentieth century American Jewry was generally the junior partner in ventures that joined it with Jews of western Europe. Although the former may have boasted that American citizenship made them the most fortunate Jews in the world, they readily acknowledged their subordinate role in Jewish affairs. Their very young community was less affluent and cohesive; its traditions were more fluid; and its cultural resources, both Jewish and secular, vastly inferior. American Jews had neither prestigious seminaries or libraries nor official or unofficial nationally recognized leaders—no chief rabbis, Rothschilds, or Montefiores. Since Jews and Jewish institutions of England, France, and Germany frequently served as models for Americans, the latter customarily deferred to the Europeans.

It was particularly upsetting, therefore, when the emancipated and established Jews of modern Europe themselves became the targets of discrimination.[33] The tide of political and racial anti-Semitism in western Europe in the fourth quarter of the nineteenth century caught American Jews unprepared. To them as to all Western Jews in the post–French Revolutionary era, anti-Semitism was a throwback to medieval barbarism, a hatred nurtured by rigid ecclesiasticism, and, therefore, a condition that would disappear when society was exposed to the rays of enlightenment. Then, socially and politically emancipated, Jews would contribute alongside their compatriots to the culture and economic prosperity of their respective countries and thus to the advance of civilization generally. With reason and liberalism as the passwords to continuing progress, nineteenth-century Western Jews looked forward to the future with unqualified optimism. Events after the Franco-Prussian War leading in Germany to the emergence of anti-Semitism as a political movement and in France to the Dreyfus affair broke the spell. Those countries were light-years away from autocratic Turkey or despotic Russia, where the Enlightenment had not yet penetrated and anti-Semitism could still be accounted for. In France, the fount of liberty and equality, and in Germany, the birthplace of "modern science and scholarship," anti-Semitism was an unexpected development.

American Jewish faith in the inexorable unfolding of material and spiritual progress was badly shaken. By 1892 Isaac Mayer Wise's newspaper, the *American Israelite*, which had confidently predicted the universal triumph of liberty, changed its tone. "How could the nineteenth century," it wrote, "with all its grand achievements, thus deny and belie its glorious predecessor, the eighteenth century? How could the civilized world so retrograde in moral principle and humane sentiments?"[34]

No doubt many American Jews felt personally as well as philosophically betrayed. Overwhelmingly German in origin, they had taken great pride in their heritage. Often allied with non-Jewish Germans, they sought to perpetuate different German cultural forms in America. Now, rebuffed in Germany and even at times by those German Americans who took their cue from the fatherland, could or should German Jews in the United States, as the *American Israelite* and the *Jewish Messenger* admonished, repudiate their German customs?

The new anti-Semitism was fraught with psychological trauma as well. Since western European Jewry served as the religious and cultural reservoir for the young American Jewish community, what American Jews were witnessing was the humiliation of their Jewish parents, a spectacle that could shake their faith in Judaism itself.

Finally, as long as American Jews considered themselves inferior to the western Europeans, the latter's plight tended to paralyze rather than goad them to countermeasures. It was one thing to intervene directly on behalf of the less "civilized" Romanian and Russian Jews, which in fact Americans were readily doing at that very time. It was quite another, however, to assume control over those who usually gave the directions. In 1881, at a time when German anti-Semites were agitating for the rescission of Jewish rights, the Board of Delegates on Civil and Religious Rights (the successor to the Board of Delegates of American Israelites and the one body within the fragmented community that could call itself a defense agency) resolved to take no action on the situation. The board's statement in its own defense was an ominous harbinger of what would be parroted during the Hitler era: "This course was . . . desired by the leading Israelites of Germany. They were fully competent to maintain their position, having confidence in the essential justice of their cause and the returning reason of the German people."[35]

True, American Jews had been warned off by their brethren in Germany. The latter, severely jolted by the intensity of the "respectable" anti-Semitism erupting after 1871, were themselves in a state of shock. On psychological, emotional, and political levels, as Jehuda Reinharz has described, they were unprepared to defend themselves. Apologetic and defensive, German Jews opted for inaction rather than confrontation.[36] When Rabbi Max Lilienthal of New York wrote leading Jews in Europe asking what Americans could do to help, the answer was an emphatic "Nothing." German Jews also told the Alliance Israélite Universelle not to interfere. A cable dispatched from Berlin in January 1881 reported that news of public agitation in the United States on the anti-Semitic question produced a wave of anti-American sentiment. No doubt the German Jews feared that national resentment over foreign intervention would be directed into the anti-Jewish crusade.

Most American Jews heeded the counsel from Germany and refrained from protest meetings or petitions to the government.

The cry for humanitarian diplomacy, in which some non-Jews joined, mustered little support. When a B'nai B'rith member suggested that the order take up the German question in light of the board's inactivity, his resolution was tabled. Even the action of the Texas legislature, instructing the state's delegates in Congress to work for some official statement against the German anti-Semitism, did not encourage the Jewish leaders to change their minds.

American Jewish noninterference dovetailed with the government's policy. Minister Andrew D. White in Berlin was requested to give an account of the German Jewish situation, and official reports revealed that he was instructed to do what he could for the German Jews on an *informal* basis. President Hayes's administration was apparently prodded by American public opinion and by the problem posed by naturalized American Jews residing in Germany who might be affected by the anti-Semitic agitation. But reluctant to touch off an international incident or a discussion in Congress which might bring out American anti-Semitic opinions, the executive sidestepped any public action.[37]

True, Jewish spokesmen appreciated unsolicited government favors that could redound to the benefit of the Jews abroad. When President Cleveland was considering Oscar Straus for the ministerial post in Constantinople, the Jews, joined by a few Christian clergymen, urged the appointment as a lesson to European governments. In 1893 Max Judd was consul general to Vienna, and Austrian Jew baiters voiced their opposition. The *New York Times* commented that the government should pay no attention unless Austria raised the matter directly. The paper advised Judd not to resign, for thereby he would be facilitating the persecution of Austrian Jews.

Trapped by their self-inflicted paralysis,[38] American Jews depended more than ever on non-Jewish allies. The same Jewish newspapers that debated whether publicity about foreign persecution would be counterproductive and serve to spread anti-Semitism more pervasively expected a sympathetic public response from the clergy and the secular and Christian press. Anti-Semitism constituted a blow against humanity, civilization, and progress; persecution of the Jews, like persecution of the Christian missionaries in non-Christian lands, demanded unequivocal denunciation. When the *Nation* described the German Jewish situation of 1880 in a matter-of-fact manner, the *Jewish Messenger* was outraged. The *Messenger* charged that the *Nation*'s tone was "almost as passionless as if the subject had been potatoes." The religious weeklies were even worse, the *Messenger* asserted. Inclined to dwell on the charges against the Jews and to dismiss the Jewish defense, they "discussed the situation with an air as though 500,000 cattle [rather than people] were concerned."[39] The *American Hebrew* was more outraged when the *Independent* (a Congregationalist periodical) described the anti-Semitic agitation in western Europe but concluded that it could not pass judgment on the justice of the persecution.

American Jews were grateful to ministers who preached against German anti-Semitism. Apparently someone did approach New York's clergy, and on the last Sunday in December of 1880 two liberal preachers, Henry Ward Beecher and Robert Collyer, discussed the conditions in Germany. Collyer, a long-time defender of the Jews,[40] likened the German anti-Semitic party to the Know-Nothings of the United States, and pointed out how anti-Semitism directly betrayed the liberal spirit of Germany's heritage. Beecher called for a remonstrance by the United States, and he, too, expected better of Germany. "No nation," he said with nineteenth-century confidence, "can commit with impunity the crime which will be charged to the Germans if they continue to persecute the Jews."[41]

As they watched the anti-Semitic currents in Germany, Austria, and France gain momentum, American Jews grew more conscious of their own vulnerability. Some who concluded that German anti-Semitism sparked the Russian pogroms of 1881 could see the epidemic spreading westward. In an address delivered at a conference of the Jewish Ministers' Association in New York in 1890, Rabbi Marcus Jastrow said:

A drop of poison has been instilled into the blood of Western nations causing a distemper contagious in its nature, and, there is no use in denying it, the contagion has reached our beloved country, and the poison, too, has been imported, and it works its way into the heart of our community, destroying the social peace which heretofore has been its just pride.[42]

Since the anti-Semites did not usually sort out Jewish traits according to geographical location, it was clear that their brief against the physically and morally degenerate Jew, who was an economic parasite and a swindler, a disloyal citizen, and a plotter of the downfall of Christian civilization, could apply to those in the United States, too. Within a very short time after the new anti-Semitism became popular in Bismarck's Germany, American Jews talked about prejudice in general terms, thus admitting that they stood in the dock with their European brethren.

Americans learned about the new anti-Semitism mainly through the writings of Jew baiters—from the sensationalist diatribes of a Wilhelm Marr or an Edouard Drumont to the more respectable prose of a Goldwin Smith or an Edward Freeman. For each stratum of society, from the intellectuals to the masses, anti-Semitic propaganda found an appropriate conduit. The British historian Goldwin Smith assailed the tribalism of the Jews in the columns of the *North American Review* and *Nation.* Madame Z. Ragozin used *Century Magazine* to blame the Russian pogroms of 1881 on the repellent and immoral beliefs and behavior of the Jews. Some of the more popular magazines, like the comic weeklies, drew inspiration directly from European anti-Semites for their caricatures of Jews. Those who did not read the anti-Semitic pamphlets or articles were clued in by American newspapers and journals, where reports of charges, rejoinders, and counterrejoinders were presented.

Edouard Drumont's monumental contribution to Jew hatred, *La France juive,* cut across class lines. The book apparently influenced novelist Lafcadio Hearn to turn from philo-Semitism to anti-Semitism; it also encouraged the mounting Judeophobia of Henry Adams, frustrated scion of the patrician establishment. Another respectable follower was a professor of Greek and theology in Columbus, Ohio. In an article written for the prestigious *Andover Review,* he cited Drumont as his source for attacking the morals and the evil economic power of Jewry. A Catholic bishop writing in the *New York Sun* also referred to Drumont when he charged the Jews, specifically the Alliance Israélite Universelle, with working to establish Jewish domination of the world.

For the less erudite, Drumont's book appeared in a popular American version as *The Original Mr. Jacobs* by a certain Telemachus T. Timayenis. Timayenis acknowledged his debt to Drumont in the preface to the book, but only a reading of the two books side by side reveals the enormity of that debt. Not only did Timayenis quote from Drumont, but he summarized, paraphrased, and lifted entire paragraphs and pages from the two-volume French work. His contribution was to condense the book to a 300-page volume, to expunge Drumont's sections critical of Freemasons, Protestants, and Americans, which would alienate American readers, and to include material on American Jews. Untroubled by the dictates of logic, he attacked Jews for their money power as well as for their "socialist" designs aimed at undermining civil order, the national fiber, and the American worker. Adumbrating the later *Protocols of the Elders of Zion,* Timayenis's *The Original Mr. Jacobs* sketched a Jew (whether in capitalist or Bolshevik garb) bent upon destroying Christian civilization.

The new anti-Semitism propagated by Drumont and Timayenis updated the older negative stereotypes. The nineteenth-century Jew charged with demoralizing society by circulating smut or preaching socialism was no different in kind from his premodern ancestor who allegedly desecrated the Host or poisoned the wells. Like their predecessors, the new images born in Europe found nesting places across the Atlantic.

Two dedicated European anti-Semites appeared in the United States in the persons of Adolf Stoecker and Hermann Ahlwardt. Stoecker, the ex-court chaplain of Berlin who was known to the world as the "leader of the Jew baiters," was the more circumspect. He visited America in 1893, officially in connection with a Lutheran missionary convention. Perhaps to reassure a hostile press which had warned him to refrain from Jew baiting here, he announced that he would not discuss anti-Semitism. Nevertheless, in two speeches in New York he explained his hatred of Germany's Jews, charging them with absorbing the wealth of the country while simultaneously fomenting the spirit of Marxist revolution. When he stated that Germany could not live by the Jewish spirit any more than America could, Stoecker revealed that he was not averse to spreading the anti-Semitic gospel at least among his German-speaking audiences. In a statement published by the *New York Times*, Stoecker added that Americans were too clever for the Jew, because they refused to permit him to push himself where he was not welcome.

Ahlwardt arrived in New York two years later with the openly admitted purpose of disseminating propaganda. A pamphleteer and demagogue whose influence contributed to anti-Jewish riots in Germany, he planned a lecture tour for the purpose of organizing an anti-Semitic movement in America. His arrival was denounced by prominent German Americans. Leading American Jews, when interviewed by reporters, would admit to no concern, and a group of New York Christian clergymen in a public resolution condemned Ahlwardt's bigotry and his attempt to transplant German hatred to American shores. Ahlwardt's initial appearances in Manhattan, Brooklyn, and New Jersey were marked by near riots. The German himself was assaulted and beaten up a few months later by ruffians allegedly hired by the Jews. He managed, though, to found a short-lived American Anti-Semitic Association and newspaper, *Der Antisemit*, both in New York, before he faded from the scene.[43]

The anti-Semitic reverberations from Europe could not have come at a worse time. The last quarter of the nineteenth century in the United States brought grave economic and social upheavals.

Coupled with an upsurge in immigration and heightened nationalist fervor, they coalesced into what John Higham has called a "likely context for anti-Semitism." Within that context American Jews had begun to feel the hardening of social discrimination. Joseph Seligman's exclusion from the Grand Union Hotel in Saratoga in 1877 was not the first incident of its kind, but that episode seemed to trigger an ever-widening acceptance of fixed boundaries which Jews could not cross. The European message of anti-Semitism found an increasingly receptive audience in the United States, and it, in turn, reinforced American bigotry. Dean Nathaniel Shaler of Harvard University testified at the turn of the century to a new and palpable dislike of Jews among the students. He blamed the changed mood in schools and hotels on the European "epidemic of hatred." In 1906 the *Independent* wrote that anti-Semitism in the United States had "not yet" reached the same level of intensity as in Europe, but it foresaw the possibility that "race hatred might flare as fiercely as in Paris or Vienna or even Kishenef."[44]

The new anti-Semitism demonstrated again the indivisibility of Jew hatred as well as the impact of European intolerance upon Americans. It also raised the specter of racism, the core of the modern "Jewish question," that challenged the promise of emancipation in the Western world.

Rights for Russian Jews

At the close of a decade of intensified anti-Semitism in czarist Russia, the *Jewish Messenger* canvassed selected members of the American Historical Association on the question of what measures the Jews of that land should adopt to secure civil and religious freedom. Of the few who expressed a point of view, Harvard professor Josiah Royce was least optimistic: "[W]hat means can be suggested to the lamb in his controversy with the wolf? Against irrational prejudice and oppression, the wise, who have no earthly weapons in their hands, have never been able to oppose anything but patience and the dignity of their wisdom itself." Several respondents, like Professor Herbert Baxter Adams of Johns Hopkins University, suggested more constructively that exposés of czarist brutality would arouse public opinion and force Russia to alter its anti-Semitic policies.[45] In reality, Adams was merely advising what the American Jews were already doing. The motive behind the very questionnaire was doubtless to publicize Russian persecution. Expressions of sympathy from American intellectuals, even if they had little else to say, would put the seal of respectability on the efforts of American Jews who declared their private war against the czarist regime.

In the twenty-five years before World War I, the Russian question in its many ramifications dominated the thought of the Jewish communal leaders. To halt the persecution, to relieve those Jews victimized by physical violence or economic strangulation, to find refuges for the hundreds of thousands who sought to escape were their major goals. Undeterred by feelings of inferiority such as impeded their efforts on behalf of Jews in Bismarck's Germany, they worked on all fronts simultaneously. While Jewish organizations like B'nai B'rith and the American Jewish Committee played a part in the drawn-out struggle, the initiative and planning came mainly from individuals. This was high tide in the era of the communal steward, the man who believed that his economic or political power entitled, and obligated, him to take on the burdens of the community. Jewish stewardship could find parallels in Andrew Carnegie's famous essay setting forth the gospel of wealth. Indeed, Baron Maurice de Hirsch, prominent European railroad builder and financier whose Jewish philanthropies spanned continents, once remarked admiringly that Carnegie had shown the rich how best to enjoy their wealth through its proper distribution.[46] Equating material achievement with ability and leadership, stewardship glorified the successful individual and was thereby well suited to the climate of an individualistic society. The Jewish version, which derived its primary strength from the responsibility of kinship mandated by Jewish law and tradition, simultaneously fit the needs of an ethnic minority striving to balance the American creed of individualism with Jewish group interest.

The American Jewish stewards at the end of the nineteenth and beginning of the twentieth centuries were those who by virtue of economic standing, official post, or access to power brokers and opinion molders were able to command attention and favors for their fellow Jews from the government and Christian America. Within the Jewish community they determined policy for the philanthropic and defense organizations as well as strategy for singular crises. The names of Jacob H. Schiff, Oscar S. Straus, Jesse Seligman, Louis Marshall, and Simon Wolf stand out among the most prominent. Bound to each other by ties of friendship, business, and marriage, they formed an intimate circle. Individualists all, they operated surprisingly well together, able to work out a natural division of labor by which each utilized his special advantages for a common goal. Most assumed responsibilities on their own initiative; others were co-opted. All shared a strong commitment to their ethnic group and, like American stewards, interpreted personal status and wealth as indicators of their right and duty to lead. They made little pretense of consulting the constituency they represented. Undemocratically, but out of a sense of noblesse oblige, they defined the needs of the American Jewish community.[47]

The stewards had no magical formulas for solving the Russian problem. Rational men in an era that still believed in the ideals of universal freedom and progress, they, like Professor Adams, relied principally on enlightened public opinion and on American humanitarian diplomacy. As early as 1880 representatives of the Union of American Hebrew Congregations called America's attention to Russian barbarism. Two years later Myer S. Isaacs, active worker in communal philanthropies, forwarded a lengthy memorandum to the House Committee on Foreign Affairs describing the Russian persecution and defending intervention by the United States.[48] Concomitantly, the Anglo-Jewish press had begun its detailed reports of Russian persecution and its victims.[49]

As the Russian situation continued to worsen, and since the American minister to Russia, Charles Smith, in 1890 denied the reports of oppression, the stewards made more concerted efforts to bring the plight of the Jews before the State Department and the civilized world. A committee including Straus, Schiff, and Seligman called upon President Harrison in 1891 and persuaded him to appoint a special commission to investigate the causes of European immigration to the United States. Briefed by the stewards before they left, and armed by them with letters of introduction to prominent Jews abroad, the commission reported back most sympathetically on the plight of Russian Jewry. A year later Straus, Schiff, Seligman, and Isaacs pressed the State Department to appoint Andrew D. White, former president of Cornell University and ex-minister to Berlin, to the diplomatic post in St. Petersburg. They were determined to undo Minister Smith's "blindness," and in White they found a sympathetic witness. Shortly after he assumed office, White, agreeing to a suggestion from his Jewish friends, prepared a lengthy memorandum on the situation of the Jews in Russia. Like Fay's report on anti-Semitism in Switzerland, it combined a probing analysis of the persecution with an able defense of the victims. At the same time the American Jewish leaders underwrote a trip to Russia by correspondent Harold Frederic of the *New York Times*. Frederic's articles, which consequently appeared in a book entitled *The New Exodus*, described the Russian situation most feelingly to a wide readership in New York, Boston, St. Louis, and Chicago.[50]

While the emphasis on publicity was not new, the determination to ensure accurate reports from American diplomats and the American press was. When in 1911 the American Jewish Committee was agitating for the abrogation of the Russo-American treaty of 1832, it exposed the ways in which the Associated Press distorted the news from Russia about Jews. Ever since the AP's general manager had been decorated by the czar and had promised the Russian ministry favorable coverage, the news service's stories had been pro-Russia as well as anti-Semitic. The committee presented an airtight case in special hearings on its charges, but biased reports and reporters persisted. As late as 1914, president of the committee Mayer Sulzberger wrote that the news stories from Russia were probably lies. Jacob Schiff added that somehow the Russian government could always bring the American ambassador around to its point of view.[51]

Schiff, the German-born American banker, occupies a special place in the annals of American Jewish stewardship. Starting a career in banking in New York after the Civil War, Schiff joined the firm of Kuhn, Loeb in 1875. Ten years later, at the age of thirty-eight, he became its head. His ability and acumen, respected in European and American financial circles, contributed to the rapid rise of the firm. By the turn of the century, with manifold operations at home and abroad, Kuhn, Loeb ranked among the top investment houses in the United States. At the same time that he was carving out his own empire, Schiff actively participated in civic and philanthropic (non-Jewish as well as Jewish) causes. He applied the same energy, forcefulness of purpose, and personal involvement in those areas that he displayed in his business affairs. He did not merely sign checks; he faithfully attended meetings, steeped himself in the running of the institutions he supported, and frequently visited his favorite charities. A prominent and respected citizen of New York, Schiff was seriously considered in some circles for the mayoralty nomination in 1905. On Jewish matters his fellow stewards called him the "Jewish primate."

A proud Jew of a prominent family of Frankfurt, Schiff affiliated with Temple Emanu-El but contributed to Conservative, Orthodox, and secular Jewish ventures as well as to Reform institutions. An intense commitment to the security of Jews and the survival of Judaism throughout the world underlay his choice of beneficiaries and, more important, dictated a tireless involvement in "Jewish diplomacy."[52] More affluent than the other Jewish stewards, and endowed with a brusque manner and quick temper, he never hesitated to request official help on behalf of fellow Jews. On the Russian problem, only a Schiff could have badgered presidents and bargained with the czar.

Schiff's approach lacked tact and conventional niceties, but it was downright refreshing. He never flaunted his power in the banking or Jewish worlds; it was a fact of which he and the official he turned to needed no reminder. On the other hand, he never fawned, groveled, or tried to ingratiate himself with powerful Christians. Fritz Stern's description of Gerson Bleichroeder, Bismarck's Jewish financier—"He begged when he could have petitioned; he petitioned when he could have demanded; he proved yielding when he should have been obdurate"[53]—did not apply to Schiff. To Schiff, emancipation was not a favor to the Jew, and hence it did not saddle him with an eternal debt of gratitude that so easily led to subservience. Besides, Schiff was much too secure in his Jewish heritage and in his closely knit Jewish circle to worry unduly whether the same Christian bankers who dealt with him during the business day would socialize with him after hours. Even had he so desired, which is highly doubtful, Schiff knew that grants of political freedom neither automatically integrated the Jew into Christian society nor bridged the differences between Jew and non-Jew. Practical and confident, he strove for the possible. For himself and for Jews generally, he preferred justice and respect above indulgent affection.

The Kishinev pogrom of 1903 captured the world's attention. Despite the ensuing protest, physical atrocities against Jews in Russia continued. Schiff turned time and again to President Theodore Roosevelt to "do something," oblivious to the president's mounting indignation over Schiff's sustained pressure and "hysteria." Roosevelt, not the type who enjoyed admitting his helplessness, had responded positively to some requests, but he believed that repeated verbal protests by the United States—which the Russian foreign office on occasion refused to receive—served only to humiliate him and the country. In typical style he wrote to Schiff:

[W]here we can do nothing I have a horror of saying anything. We never have taken—and while I am President we never will take—any action which we cannot make good.

It is not unlikely that Schiff purposely indulged in forceful language, even at the risk of appearing hotheaded, in order to convey the intensity of his purpose and the urgency of the situation. At the same time that he prodded Roosevelt he calmly agreed in letters to his friends that there was little the president could do and that there was a danger in "crying wolf."[54]

Horrible as the pogroms were, Schiff knew that it was futile to focus exclusively on them. The deeper problem was to secure legally recognized rights for Russian Jews. Emigration might be the solution for vast numbers, but even then millions would still be left under czarist rule. The steward-banker used his position in the financial world to bargain for Jewish rights. For many years he labored stubbornly and successfully to keep American money markets closed to Russian loans. The czarist regime felt the pinch of Schiff's actions. V. K. von Plehve, the Russian minister of the interior, invited the American Jew to St. Petersburg for conversations about financial cooperation, a mission that evaporated when von Plehve was assassinated. The minister of finance, V. N. Kokovtzev, sent feelers out to Schiff, but again the latter stood firm. Equality for Russian Jews was his fixed price. Russia also resorted to face-to-face bargaining through Gregory Wilenkin, a special financial agent dispatched to the United States. Wilenkin's endeavors for more than half a dozen years failed miserably to win Schiff over with descriptions of the profits that would accrue to Kuhn, Loeb.[55]

During the Russo-Japanese War of 1904–5, Schiff, as one American diplomat put it, "went out of his way to help Japan." In a market that was initially unresponsive to Japan's desire to float its bonds, Schiff's firm performed crucial service in underwriting five Japanese bond issues. Motivated by the hope that the war would bring about constitutional government in Russia, Schiff also promised Japan the help of his banking associates in Germany. For his service Schiff was decorated in 1906 by the emperor of Japan.[56]

When Theodore Roosevelt was negotiating the treaty that ended the Russo-Japanese War, Schiff and four other Jews met with the Russian representative, Count Sergius Witte, at Portsmouth. Officially at least, the subject of financial aid was ignored, but the Jews told Witte that Russian goodwill in the United States was endangered so long as his country's Jews were denied equal rights. No uncensored account of the three-hour conversation remains, but apparently Schiff, true to form, was sharp in his interchange with the czar's deputy.[57] As one of Schiff's colleagues said on another occasion when the banker shrugged off the dictates of diplomacy and openly spoke his mind, the Jews did not necessarily suffer because of his display of temper: "On the general principle that every successful business needs and has a wicked partner, there is no occasion for tears or regrets. Nagging and dunning are sometimes more effective than genteeler methods."[58]

Russia's refusal to recognize the rights of American Jewish passport holders led Schiff to an alternative route on behalf of Russian Jewry. He believed—and the czarist government concurred—that Russia would be hard put to permit foreign Jews the freedom it withheld from its own. That presumption, as mentioned above, underlay the American Jewish Committee's fight to abrogate the Russo-American treaty of commerce. Schiff, who had been invoking the same logic years before the abrogation campaign,[59] appreciated the tactical advantage of merging the Russian cause with that of American Jews. To pressure the American government on what rightfully belonged to its Jews held out a greater chance of success than to beg the Russians for favors to their Jews.

The passport issue became Schiff's favorite weapon in politicking with both Roosevelt and President Taft. In July 1904 he urged Roosevelt to mention the passport question in his letter accepting the Republican nomination. It was not unlikely, he reminded Roosevelt, that New York City's Lower East Side vote could decide the state and possibly the national election. Four years later Schiff repeated the exact same message to William Howard Taft. Since I hope you win, the banker wrote, I am worried lest your Democratic rival capture the Jewish vote by promises on securing the recognition of Jewish passports. Schiff was not too pleased with Taft's letter of acceptance, but the Republican standard-bearer assured him of "special attention" on the passport matter if elected. Since Taft denounced Russian discrimination against American passport holders in his campaign speeches, Schiff insisted that the administration accept the logical implications of that rhetoric and repudiate the treaty. "He knows exactly . . . what we expect him to do in redeeming his pledge," Schiff wrote to Cyrus Adler, and "if, after all we have told him, he leaves this matter go to sleep, he is not the man I have taken him for." Refusing to be put off by hollow platitudes when the public issue at stake was the right of American Jews to equal treatment at the hands of their government, Schiff was more impatient than circumspect when he urged the American Jewish Committee to "build a fire in the rear of the President."[60]

As the pressure for abrogation began to mount, the committee's campaign also became a personal skirmish between the president and the Jewish steward. At the conference with Taft in February 1911 when the president informed the Jewish delegation that he would not go along with abrogation, Schiff lost his temper. He, along with Marshall, rebutted Taft's arguments and gave Taft "a most unhappy half hour." Marshall testified subsequently that he had never seen Schiff so "worked up"; according to reports, the banker stormed out of the White House without shaking the presidential hand.[61] A few months later Schiff publicly disclosed that Taft's ambassador to St. Petersburg, who was supposedly working to change Russia's Jewish policy, had said in a newspaper interview that too much had been made of the passport issue and that the American economic interests in Russia were more important. In addition, Schiff revealed that Russia had arranged with John Hays Hammond to form a syndicate of American manufacturers for the purpose of strengthening the economic ties between the two countries. Hammond was chosen, according to Schiff, because of his friendship with Taft. Schiff privately admitted that the president had known nothing of Hammond's selection until after the fact, but his disclosures left the impression that the Taft administration was ready to sacrifice principle for dollars.[62]

For his part, Taft was equally resentful. While he would have liked to see Russia recognize the passports of American Jews, he concluded that abrogation would not achieve that objective. Moreover, since substantial American economic interests had developed in Russia under the treaty, he refused to imperil them. After the disastrous meeting in February, the president turned defensive and tried, again unsuccessfully, to justify his decision to Schiff. In letters to his friends, Taft lashed out time after time against the Jewish leaders, an "imperious crowd" threatening 200,000 votes, but he reserved the most bitter words for Schiff. "Of course we are threatened with the Jewish vote," the president wrote to Hart Lyman of the *New York Tribune*. "It is formidable and can be easily roused on such an issue and Jake Schiff is engaged in spending money to rouse it, but he can't frighten me into a useless injury to our National interests, not to advance a principle but to gratify his vanity." Taft confided in a similar vein to Otto Bannard: "[Schiff] had been consumed with fury because he could not control the Administration and sacrifice all national interests to the gratification of his vanity and that of some wealthy Hebrews."[63] In the end, Taft's administration yielded to the pressure aroused by the American Jewish Committee in Congress and the country at large, and it notified Russia of its intention to terminate the 1832 treaty. The Jews won their case in December 1911, but since Russia made no overtures to negotiate a new treaty or to change its domestic Jewish policy, Taft thought that he had had the last laugh on Schiff and his "circumcised brothers."[64] Nevertheless, American Jews had compelled the government to honor their claim to equality. In the end, it was Schiff, the indomitable force behind the American Jewish Committee's campaign, who scored. His actions gave notice that the stereotype of the cringing ghetto Jew no longer fit in America.

Unrestricted Immigration

A few weeks after the Dillingham Immigration Commission had submitted its report to Congress, prominent New York attorney Max J. Kohler warned: "We must recognize that we are in the midst of a new 'Know-Nothing Era.'"[65] Unlike the mid-nineteenth-century eruption of nativism, this episode of Know-Nothingism very much involved the Jews. The economic, social, and ideological forces in favor of restricting immigration had been gathering momentum since the 1890s; the act of 1907 establishing a commission to investigate immigration and offer recommendations to Congress had been merely a holding device. Not surprisingly, at the conclusion of three years of deliberations the Dillingham commission called for a basic shift in government immigration policy from regulation to restriction. Its recommendations, if adopted, threatened to constrict the primary escape route for the Jewish victims of czarist oppression. Close to 1.5 million Jews from eastern Europe had emigrated to the United States during the two decades since 1881, the start of intensified economic, cultural, and physical persecution, and there was little hope that the stream would shortly run dry.[66]

The established American Jews resented and feared the entry of such vast numbers. For ten years after 1881 they advocated selected immigration,[67] which would have permitted them to decide which Jews and how many should enter the country. Different from the non-Jewish restrictionists who feared the threat of heavy immigration from southern and eastern Europe that allegedly endangered the living conditions and, indeed, the very essence of the American Protestant way of life, American Jews had their own reasons for preferring selected immigration. They knew that the problem of the Russian Jew did not automatically end with immigration, and they assumed—testimony again to their ingrained sense of ethnic responsibility—that the burden of the destitute, the sick, and the unemployed among the new arrivals would fall upon them. Second, beset as they were by a rising tide of social anti-Semitism in the United States, they reasoned that substantial numbers of foreign Jews with their "outlandish" practices would only exacerbate American prejudice against all Jews. But even as they pressed for orderly immigration of able-bodied workmen instead of mass stampedes, ambivalent notes crept in. The *Jewish Messenger*, the prestigious and oldest Anglo-Jewish weekly in New York, offered a case in point. On the one hand, the journal shuddered when it contemplated the conditions of the new urban ghettos and the overwhelming task of Americanizing the hordes of newcomers. It ventured at times that the Russian Jewish problem should be solved in Russia, even suggesting that it might be more advantageous to send American Jewish missionaries to Russia to "civilize" the Jews there. At the same time, however, the *Jewish Messenger* was quick to retort to any negative criticism, particularly by the press, of the east European immigrant in the United States. It also spoke out against nativists while it praised those who defended the right of immigration. Never did it let the Jewish community forget its responsibilities to the east Europeans. As early as 1882 the paper reminded its readers: "And as to the prejudice which [the immigrants] are likely to awaken, that has already been aroused on these shores by brethren richer and better circumstanced."[68]

Since the situation in Russia worsened in the 1890s and the clamor of the American restrictionists mounted, the Jews altered their stand and closed ranks in defense of free immigration.[69] It was one thing for them to criticize immigration or to argue with their counterparts in western Europe about saddling America with a disproportionate share of the Russian Jewish burden, but quite another when non-Jews, and especially the government, voiced those same points. Selected immigration was a feasible option only if the government permitted the selection to be done by the Jews themselves. Legally mandated restriction, particularly in the racist garb adopted by its advocates, would not only impede the entry of Jews generally but also would mark off even acculturated American Jews, by association, as a less-than-desirable element. Besides, once enacted, restricted immigration would be more difficult to modify if and when graver crises erupted. In sum, then, if the choice on aliens became one of open door or official restriction, the Jews could only opt for the former. Furthermore, so long as the doors remained open, the mass arrival of impoverished refugees might serve to goad the American government into protesting officially the persecution that set the flow of immigrants in motion.[70]

Ideological reasons dovetailed with self-interest to compound American Jewish horror over the prospect of restriction. A nagging fear (usually implied rather than articulated) haunted American Jewish leaders that the United States was repudiating its ideals. They read restrictionist sentiment as a sign that the American creed, with its glorious components of universalism and concern for human rights, was being eroded by the hypernationalist spirit then sweeping the Western world. Thus, just as Jews had denounced the Know-Nothing movement before the Civil War for threatening the principles of Americanism, so, too, were they motivated to combat the antialien forces of the early twentieth century. Only by keeping America true to its promise could they shore up their own security and, at the same time, meet their ethnic responsibilities.

Some American Jews realized even before 1900 that defense of Americanism entailed the defense of other beleaguered minority groups. For those Jews who lived east of the Pacific coast, criticism of American policy toward the Chinese came easily. The *Jewish Messenger*, editorializing against the Chinese Exclusion Act of 1882, urged Congress to remember America's role as the exemplar of enlightened and liberal sentiment to the rest of the world. To enact a restrictive law against any group would have worldwide reverberations. It would not only justify persecuting nations but would end American influence and place the country "among the shams of civilization." Leopold Morse of Massachusetts, one of the two Jews in Congress in 1882, added his opposition to Chinese exclusion, calling it a violation of treaty obligations, "dishonorable," and "un-American." *The American Hebrew*, arguing that the Jews could not afford to support Chinese exclusion and thereby cast themselves into the role of oppressor, reported that the same type of discrimination could well be extended to the Jews. As if to prove that point, the anti-Semitic British historian Edward Freeman wrote in 1882 that every nation had the right to get rid of strangers it considered nuisances; his examples were the Chinese in the United States and the Jews in Russia. Meanwhile in Austria, the Chinese Exclusion Act became the model of racial discrimination for the anti-Semitic agitator Georg von Schoenerer.[71]

Discrimination against the Chinese brought Max Kohler into a career dedicated to the protection of the right of immigration and the rights of immigrants. At the age of twenty-three, after receiving his law degree from Columbia University, Kohler was appointed assistant district attorney for the federal district that included New York City. In the post that he held for four years he frequently was called upon to enforce the Chinese exclusion laws on behalf of the American government. His work developed his keen sensitivity for the rights of aliens and the hardships to which new arrivals were subjected, and after 1898, when he embarked on private practice, he frequently fought on the side of the alien in federal and state courts. Representing Chinese, Armenians, Hindus, as well as Jews in proceedings that in some instances reached the Supreme Court, Kohler became the acknowledged legal authority on the alien and the law. He carried the problem of injustice to the alien from the court to the public, speaking and writing for popular and scholarly audiences. He often volunteered his services to organizations engaged in defending the immigrant—the Board of Delegates, National Council of Jewish Women, Educational Alliance, National Jewish Immigration Council, American Civil Liberties Union—and singly, or in conjunction with other lawyers, insisted on a hearing for the immigrant. In Kohler's obituary in the *New York World-Telegram* of July 26, 1934, it was stated: "He was not a pusher. He

was not loud. He worked for the cause, not for personal publicity."
Known to his friends for his selflessness and his unflagging commitment to the cause of justice for minorities, Kohler grounded his sentiments in the unswerving belief that the United States was intended by its founders to be a haven of refuge for the oppressed. He adopted a sentence from Jefferson's first annual message—"Shall oppressed humanity find no asylum on this globe?"—as his personal creed.[72]

What set Kohler apart from other defenders of immigation was his insistence that the law, and not merely considerations of immigrant contributions to America or even compassion for the plight of refugees, justified both unrestricted immigration and a humane approach to aliens. With regard to the very act of immigration, Kohler pointed to the 1868 law that called the right of expatriation "a natural and inherent right of all people, indispensable to the enjoyment of the rights of life, liberty, and the pursuit of happiness."[73] Further, and a distinctive contribution on his part, he developed more thoroughly than most the idea that due process of law as well as treaties and statutory laws protected the alien from arbitrary administrative proceedings that threatened his right to enter and remain in the United States. Time after time when protesting the treatment of the Chinese, Kohler argued that the methods surrounding the deportation of Orientals violated civil liberties of aliens and legal judicial procedure. He called the "barbarities" of deportation practiced against Orientals "un-American," "inhuman," and even worse than the expulsions of Jews from Russia. Hadn't Russia itself pointed out how America had forfeited its right to condemn the Kishinev pogrom of 1903 by its oppressive treatment of the Chinese?[74]

Kohler continued his defense of the Chinese and Japanese immigrants,[75] but in the ten years spanning the immigration acts of 1907 and 1917 he, like other American Jewish leaders, concentrated primarily on the effect of impending restrictive legislation upon Jews. Appointed in 1910 to the executive committee of the Board of Delegates, Kohler played a major role in the struggle to secure the right of immigration for the east European Jews. While his colleagues from prominent national Jewish organizations like the American Jewish Committee and B'nai B'rith stressed the virtues of the Jewish immigrants and their rapid acculturation, Kohler's thrust was usually different. In articles and statements to government bodies and in legal briefs, he frequently shifted the argument from a defense of the immigrant to an attack on the government for its improper behavior. The need was not to institute restricted immigration, itself a flagrant violation of American traditions, but to improve the administration of existing regulations aimed only at excluding those "who would inflict injury upon the body politic, either physically, mentally, or morally." Kohler strictly construed those categories of inadmissibles, and reverting to points made previously on behalf of the Chinese, he stressed the government's responsibility to ensure due process of law for the aliens. To Kohler those rights included judicial safeguards (e.g., judicial review, right to counsel and appeal) before boards of inquiry determining exclusion and deportation and the easing of financial and physical requirements, often decided without statutory authority by lower administrative officials. The recommendations made jointly by the American Jewish Committee, the Board of Delegates, and B'nai B'rith to the Dillingham commission unmistakably reflected Kohler's authorship; two-thirds of the statement dealt with due process for the immigrant.[76]

Kohler's insistence on the legal rights of immigrants led to an all-out campaign against William Williams, commissioner of immigration at the port of New York. Kohler attacked Williams for his unwarranted and anti-Semitic directives as well as for his intimidation of subordinates on Ellis Island in order to assure their compliance. Secretary of Commerce and Labor Charles Nagel, whose department housed the Immigration Service, tactfully criticized Kohler— "a very young lawyer"—for his rigid legalism, but the latter, rightfully condemnatory of arbitrary administrators, held fast to the axiom that America's government was one of laws and not of men.[77]

Kohler was not deterred in his criticism of those in high places. He openly took on the Dillingham commission, a body comprising members of Congress and immigration experts, for its faulty procedures and for its hastily drawn and often illogical conclusions. Why, for example, did the commission recommend the restriction of unskilled laborers when its investigations were limited to the atypical conditions prevalent after the panic of 1907 and to the atypical conditions of the coal mines? Those recommendations were even contradicted by reports from the Department of Commerce and Labor on wage increases earned by the unskilled. Furthermore, if the commission's own evidence showed that physical traits of immigrants changed after living in the United States, how could it logically suggest annual quotas for different and so-called unassimilable races? Working secretly, without proper deliberation of its drastic recommendations, and flouting its own data, the commission, according to Kohler, was never an objective fact-finding body. In essence it had served to give support to the a priori demands and biases of the restrictionists.[78]

Just as his defense of the immigrant's right to due process was replete with legal and judicial precedents, so was Kohler's case against restriction laced heavily with references to scholarly works. His specific attacks against immigration authorities who were also "respectable" restrictionists—men like Professors Henry Fairchild and Jeremiah Jenks—showed that Kohler, himself a student of American history, was well steeped in the historical and social-science literature that proved the importance of immigration to the country. On well-researched grounds he challenged those popular prophets who preached that the country could not absorb the new waves of immigrants economically or culturally and that the alien influx kept down the birthrate and creativity of native Americans.[79]

While defending immigration in general, Kohler concentrated on the special needs of the Jews. With respect to the exclusionary practices of the lower immigration officials, he stated that Jews faced greater danger than others, for if refused admission, they could return only to the horrors of Russia or Romania. Since large numbers of Jews were refugees from persecution, Kohler believed that those peculiar circumstances warranted treatment different from the blanket stringent measures put forth before Congress between 1911 and 1917.[80] The literacy test for immigrants, a favorite theme of restrictionists that mustered increasing public support after 1900, especially troubled him and other Jewish leaders. Their own surveys checked out the government's findings: more than 25 percent of new Jewish immigrants were illiterate. Kohler was quick to point out that the surprisingly large number—surprising, because once in America the Jews rapidly satisfied their eagerness to learn how to read and write—reflected the oppressive measures in eastern Europe which curtailed educational opportunities for Jews. Indeed, largely because of Jewish endeavors, a clause exempting religious refugees from a literacy test was grudgingly written into the act of 1917.[81]

Congressman Walter Chandler was one of those who opposed the "ludicrous" and "absurd" proposal for a literacy test, calling it a devious subterfuge on the part of the restrictionists. He said in part:

It has been found necessary, therefore, to avoid open declaration of unqualified restriction by inventing a pretext of patriotism and of solicitude for the welfare of the citizenship of the Republic. And, instead of selecting as a test the shape of the head, the color of the hair, or the size of the feet, they have proposed the plan of testing the immigrant's qualifications for good citizenship by his ability to read a few words upon a printed slip which may be handed him.

In a speech whose content appeared to draw heavily on arguments circulated by the informal lobbyists of the antirestrictionists, the representative from New York questioned the justice and reasonableness of the test's effects on both the immigrant and the country. He elaborated, too, on the racial and religious bigotry—specifically directed against the Jews and Catholics—that underlay the literacy provision. As Chandler himself said, the racist current and the desires of the racists were no secret. From the 1890s on, serious writers and social scientists had been linking pseudoscientific jargon about inferior and superior races with an antiforeign bias. In the theories propagated by the believers in the Nordic myth, the immigrants from southern and eastern Europe, and particularly the Jews, the lowliest of them all, were a threat both to American institutions and to the biological superiority of the native stock.[82]

It was a foregone conclusion, then, that the restrictionists who served on the Dillingham Immigration Commission would reveal their racist bent. As one volume of its lengthy report, the commission issued a *Dictionary of Races or Peoples,* which drew upon popular anthropological and ethnological works classifying immigrants according to their physical and linguistic traits. Distinguishing between the old (from northwestern Europe) and new (from southeastern Europe) immigrants, the commission assumed the inferiority of the latter and deemed them undesirable.[83] It even suggested that quotas on immigrants be fixed according to race. In the racially charged atmosphere of prewar America, Kohler and others who argued on behalf of immigration had but minimal effect. A man like Kohler stood for due process of law, sanctity of American tradition, inalienable human rights—all predicated on a groundwork of rationalism and confidence in the basic goodness of man. The tidal wave of antiforeignism, however, sprang from the depths of irrationality—fear, frustration, and hypernationalism. To swim against that current was a losing battle, but the established German Jews in the United States had no alternative. They had staked their own survival on America's exceptionalism, in its adherence to the universalist principles of the Enlightment. In their minds, to give up the fight would mean a betrayal of the American creed and the bankruptcy of their own political faith.

The *American Israelite* coupled its criticism of restrictionist legislation with a statement of the principles that animated the Jewish community:

Jews have always held that it is the inalienable right of every honest, law-abiding man to gather up his family and household and, leaving his native land forever, go to any other where he thinks he can improve his . . .

condition. It is his God-given right to enter and dwell therein, to enjoy life and liberty and pursue happiness on the same terms as the native-born, if he is willing to give his adopted country unequivocal loyalty and to share honestly the burdens and responsibilities it imposes upon all of its citizens. . . . This was the doctrine taught by the fathers of the Republic and it is the duty of every good citizen and certainly of every believing Jew to save the nation from becoming recreant to them.[84]

Faithful to those principles, Kohler refused to surrender. He may not have been overawed by the New England Brahmins who spearheaded the powerful Immigration Restriction League.[85] After all, his family ties were just as impressive, at least in contemporary Jewish circles, as theirs. His father was Kaufmann Kohler, the Reform theologian and president of Hebrew Union College, and his maternal grandfather was David Einhorn, one of the most respected Reform thinkers to emigrate from Germany. A Jewish patrician, Max Kohler continued to inveigh against the ideas of racism and quotas for their scientific inaccuracies and the social bitterness they engendered. Both ideas were un-American; a vote for quotas was tantamount to "voting down the Declaration of Independence." From among the authorities who disputed racism, Kohler invoked the views of Josiah Royce and the teachings of anthropologist Franz Boas. Like the Jewish spokesmen, particularly of the Reform stripe, who had long argued that Judaism was only a religion and not a nationality, Kohler now took the lead in denouncing the proposition that Jews constituted a distinct race. But realizing that his side was no match for the pseudoscientists, Kohler dug his heels firmly into one axiom: Even if scientists should say that Russian Jews were a race, these Jews still had rights under international law and the American Constitution as human beings. "In the law fundamental human rights are fixed so definitely that they are statable in axioms which we hold to be self-evident and incapable of contradiction."[86]

Kohler and his coterie helped to postpone the adoption of racist quotas for immigration, but they could not stave off the immigration act of 1917 with its literacy-test clause. Perhaps, most significantly, they served as gadflies to keep America from forgetting the ideological principles that shaped the nation in its formative years.

6

THE JEWISH QUESTION AND
SOME JEWISH ANSWERS

What was referred to as the Jewish question in Europe had antecedents reaching far back into the past. "The Jewish problem is as old as history and assumes in each age a new form," wrote Emma Lazarus, the American Jewish poet, in 1883. Whether evoking religious intolerance, racial antipathy, or social enmity, Jews "seem fated to excite the antagonism of their fellow-countrymen."[1]

But by the 1880s, the Jewish question had come to mean something different from mere animus toward a minority non-Christian people. In the first instance, the temper of discourse had been secularized. Enlightenment thinkers from the nineteenth century on discarded customary theological explanations of the Jews in the Christian design of the universe. They often held on to time-worn descriptions of the undesirable Jew, but their newly phrased indictments sprang from psychological, social, and pseudoscientific rather than religious roots. Second, the obsession with a Jewish question paralleled the evolution of national states and an intensified focus on national unity. Anti-Semitic ideologues drew sustenance from the hypernationalist temper and rested their formulation of the Jewish question on an apposite premise: the Jews were a discrete group who, although bereft of an independent homeland and common language, stubbornly retained and cultivated their separate identity and social solidarity. With the benefit of hindsight, anti-Semites argued that even emancipation, which tore down the legal barriers between Jews and others, failed to eradicate the sense of groupness. Logically it followed that Jewish loyalty and indeed Jewish assimilability in the countries in which they resided were open to question. Could or should a state committed to the cause of national homogeneity tolerate such indigestible elements? To compound the problem, the Jews appeared to be endowed with capacities and ambitions that propelled them to dramatic economic and social successes after their emancipation and hinted at their ultimate domination of modern society. Fear of the aggressively mobile Jew, who was also the eternal alien, led easily in turn to fantasies of Jewish conspiracies to "Judaize" or destroy the Christian world.

Variations of these themes sounded throughout the nineteenth century, usually in tandem with debates on Jewish rights or with economic crises and social upheavals that accompanied the processes of urbanization and industrialization. By the 1880s—"the seedtime of totalitarian nationalism," in the words of Carlton Hayes—nationalism had been shorn of its earlier liberal and cosmopolitan moorings and joined with conservatism, militarism, and racism. It was racism that added a distinctive conceptual framework to the Jewish question. Carelessly appropriating jargon as well as authority from the developing science of anthropology, it purveyed to the public popular renditions of theories like the immutability of cultural traits and the myth of Aryan supremacy. The alien Jew, of inferior stock but nonetheless a menace to Christendom, was frozen in perpetuity with his undesirable and malevolent characteristics. Seized upon by hatemongers who spun intricate webs of anti-Jewish propaganda, the Jewish question in its racist garb underlay eruptions of political and social anti-Semitism that would peak in the twentieth century.[2]

American Jews who pondered the eruptions of anti-Semitism in Europe and the United States after 1870 feared—and, as has been discussed, their fears proved correct—that European Jew hatred would spread its poison across the Atlantic. While they made that link, they did not connect the components of the new anti-Semitism, or the Jewish question. Joseph Jacobs, the British-trained student of literature and anthropology who directed his energies to Jewish history and contemporary affairs, illustrated the same disjointed approach in a bibliography he published, entitled *The Jewish Question, 1875–1884*.[3] His entries included writings of and about anti-Semites, different aspects of anti-Semitism (from ritual-murder charges to civil disabilities), the socioeconomic conditions of Jews in various countries, and the defense of the Jew. So loosely constructed was his definition of the Jewish question that among his listings were a speech in the House of Representatives denouncing Russian pogroms, the annual reports of the Hebrew Emigrant Aid Society of the United States, and a study of living conditions in Brody—a central depot for emigrants fleeing czarist persecution. In the United States some Jewish leaders, even further afield, appropriated the term *Jewish question* to signify the erosion of religious belief and ethnic identity within the community.[4]

Non-Jews in America were hardly more precise. They spoke and wrote about the modern Jew and his problems; two commencement speeches in 1883 even addressed themselves to that subject.[5] But, again, aside from the hatemongers, they filed disparate items under the general rubric of "Jewish question." The *Readers' Guide to Periodical Literature,* for example, introduced a new category called the "Jewish Question" for the volume covering 1890 through 1899; the articles listed dealt with Zionism and the general condition of Jews in Europe as well as with specific manifestations of anti-Semitism.

Without a consensus on the meaning of the Jewish question, American Jews could not readily agree on explanations or solutions for the multiple subjects—social discrimination in the United States, European anti-Semitism, racism and charges of alienism, Zionism—commonly tagged with that label. The remedies advanced also ran a wide gamut, from apologetics and lessons in self-improvement to appeals to Christian enlightened reason, from religious fortitude to Jewish nationalism. Consistency and logic frequently fell victims to the exigencies of the hour; opinions shifted and arguments changed. Some Jews even denied that it was rightly a Jewish question. "It is a Christian question," Rabbi Emil Hirsch of Chicago preached. "Let Christians become Christians and they will find the solution."[6]

Social Ostracism in the Gilded Age

The *New York Times* reported on June 26, 1877, that forty-six Jewish businessmen of Cincinnati had resolved to sever relations with the A. T. Stewart Company, a national wholesale dry-goods firm. A few days earlier the Grand Union Hotel at Saratoga, owned by that company, had refused accommodations to the prominent banker Joseph Seligman because he was Jewish. Shock and condemnation of the discriminatory act joined Jews with Christians throughout the country. Bret Harte, whose one Jewish grandparent had come to the New World before the Revolution, wrote a poem mocking the behavior of Judge Henry Hilton, the Stewart representative responsible for Seligman's exclusion. The affair was by no means the first or an isolated example of social discrimination against Jews in the United States, but the fact that Seligman was President Grant's personal friend and the head of a firm with ties to the government ever since the Civil War signaled an ominous departure in America's benign acceptance of the Jew. The gravity of the incident was reflected in the reaction of European Jews. Gerson Bleichroeder of Germany, whose significant financial dealings with Bismarck did not protect him from the anti-Semitism then burgeoning in his country, called it "monstrous." Highly placed American government officials apparently worried, too, lest the Rothschilds withdraw from negotiations over an American bond issue because of the affair.[7]

The Seligman-Hilton episode made the American public realize how pervasive was the image of the socially undesirable Jew, even if he was powerful and acculturated, and it brought out into the open the prejudice of other Americans. Resorts and vacation spots, which advertised through railroad and steamboat companies and through newspapers and magazines, were the most notorious offenders. Some announced openly: "No dogs. No Jews. No consumptives." Before long Jews found the same barriers in social and professional clubs, private schools and camps, and campus fraternities. So determined and appealing were the bigots, that their competition, in order to attract students or members, usually followed suit whether or not they were anti-Semitic in principle. Within private homes, where the women applied exclusionary lines, Christians and Jews did not mix. Outside of business, the *Nation* commented, the Jews were not received in "good society."[8]

The most alarming feature of this "bolder, more outspoken, more consistent and systematic" prejudice, Rabbi Max Heller added, "is in the invariable characteristic it had of holding once conquered territory in undisputed possession. The hotel which excludes the Jew may reopen its doors to him under financial stress; the club or fraternal society which has once banished him, looks henceforth upon the matter as settled forever; such an event as the breaking down of the barrier in response to a newly awakened sense of justice is yet to be recorded in a single instance."

Heller perceptively analyzed the problem.[9] In light of what the Jews had suffered throughout their history, social ostracism looked unimportant. An amorphous body of irritating pinpricks and petty annoyances, social exclusion defied statistical calculation or predictable patterns of development. Yet the pernicious atmosphere that enveloped the Jew through school, business, and public life steadily eroded his ambitions and stultified his creative powers. (In studies that correlated the social club or private school with success in the corporate economy, later analysts pointed out more tangible hardships.)[10] Just because there was no dramatic crisis—say, a pogrom, a riot, an edict of expulsion—the victim was denied the opportunity to display bravery or heroism. Diffident, passive, and disillusioned, the modern Jew also lacked the emotional and psychological comfort that his ancestors derived from a culturally autonomous ghetto life.

Troubled by irrational bigotry which fixed upon an entire group and challenged their long-cherished beliefs in rationalism and individualism, Jewish spokesmen in America's Gilded Age reached no clear consensus on the causes for the hardening social barriers.[11] Most believed that religious animus underlay the discrimination. A few also mentioned socioeconomic factors—envy of Jewish affluence on the part of the nouveaux riches; the rising middle class, ill bred and with pretentious pseudoaristocratic values, which employed social exclusivity in its scramble for status. Some noted the influence in America of anti-Semitic ideas then fashionable in Germany, Austria, and Russia. Still others, borrowing opinions then being aired in Christian America, blamed those Jews who retained their foreign accents and mannerisms and especially the loud and flashy parvenus and their jewel-bedecked women who incited popular distaste by their vulgar ostentation. German Jewish leaders knew that the immigrants from eastern Europe had not caused the problem,[12] but they worried lest the latter's visibility exacerbate it. While those reasons were alluded to usually in cursory fashion, others, like racism, interethnic rivalries, patrician status anxiety, and heightened nationalism, were rarely if ever discussed in tandem with social anti-Semitism. On one occasion, the *Jewish Messenger* dismissed all "rational" reasons for discrimination and compared the Jew with Dr. Fell of the nursery rhyme: "I do not like thee, Dr. Fell / The reason why, I can not tell / But I do not like thee, Dr. Fell."[13]

At the heart of the quandary lay the unanswered question posed by emancipation: What was the modern Jew? Not until Jews resolved the meaning of their identity could they draw firm conclusions, right or wrong, about the reasons for Jew hatred. Nineteenth-century American Jews agreed that the Jew was first and foremost a member of a religious body, but that definition was not sufficiently broad. Discrimination proved that the outside world saw a discrete Jewish collectivity embracing more than those who believed in the Jewish religion. Whatever its genesis, prejudice was directed against the group, affecting the secularist and religiously unaffiliated as much as the observant Jew. On the other side of the coin, not all who discriminated against Jews were consciously motivated by religious antipathies. Identifying Jews realized, too, that their heritage included components other than faith. Since the term *ethnic* was not yet in vogue, they used loose labels about themselves—a people, a nationality, a race—with utter lack of precision or consistency.

On one matter Jewish spokesmen generally agreed. Social discrimination may have been more pervasive after the Seligman affair, but it marked no novel departure in Christian behavior. American Jews had noted their exclusion from the "favored circles of society" many years before. The evidence pointed not only to patrician snobbery (which might be argued for the exclusionary practices of college clubs or the New York Bar Association) but to middle-class ostracism as well (boardinghouses, a Masonic lodge in Massachusetts, a German glee club in New York). In an attempt to keep their vision of the United States untarnished, American Jews liked to think that the prejudice they experienced was brought over from Europe by recent immigrants. Even if it had been, which is unlikely, it was not unknown in American circles before the 1870s. The Jewish population in the United States did not reach 250,000 until 1880, but to nineteenth-century Jews that was no reason to minimize the significance of earlier hostility. Since they did not distinguish between ideological Jew hatred and actual discrimination—between a Good Friday sermon which charged Jews with deicide and a school which excluded Jewish students— the existence of anti-Semitism depended on neither numbers nor the visibility of Jews. *Rishus*, as they called it (literally, Hebrew for "wickedness"), cropped up at different times and in various forms.

The thought that nothing qualitatively new had transpired offered a modicum of comfort. Each age produced its persecutors and bigots, but Jews and Judaism continued to survive. The same idea lent credence to the favorite Jewish answer for the upsurge in bigotry: An aggressive, militant Christianity, as in premodern days, was responsible for the new wave of discrimination. The explanation anchored social discrimination within the parameters of experience. Simultaneously it provided a known principle on which to pin the disjointed petty annoyances that Max Heller had described.

Jews could cogently argue that the hatred spawned by Christian religious teachings had not bypassed the United States. The settlers of the New World had brought with them the belief that the Jews, having rejected and crucified Jesus, had become a despised and persecuted people, their faith inferior and subservient to Christianity. Long before the colonists had actual contact with Jews, their opinions of "the Jew" were fixed. They wrote their views into their law codes and state constitutions. History books and fiction as well as sermons and theological tracts kept the images alive, and so did the spellers, readers, and geographies used in the country's schoolrooms. Missionaries who worked zealously to save the benighted souls stressed the pitiable state of Judaism; conversion, they promised the Jews, would purify and uplift them.

Well into the nineteenth century, the Jews had ample reason to fear the influence of Christian teachings on their political rights and status in society. Orthodox Protestants invoked the deicide charge in order to justify the retention of the ban against officeholding by Jews in Maryland. As discussed above, Governor Hammond and Judge O'Neale predicated opinions discriminating against Jews on the Christian character of their society. During the Civil War, Grant's order expelling Jews from the military territories under his jurisdiction and America's willingness to accept it were also proof, according to Rabbi Leeser's *Occident*, of the church's nefarious power. When, as in such cases, public officials acted out the precepts of fundamentalist Christianity in the political arena, it became meaningless to distinguish between ideological Jew hatred and overt hostility.

According to Isaac Mayer Wise's *American Israelite*, the seeds of the intensified social prejudice had been sown during the Civil War. At that time, according to the paper, the mischief was started in the nation's capital by public figures and newspaper correspondents who delighted in vilifying the Jew. This alarming upsurge of prejudice testified to the social upheaval brought about by the war: "A revolution of the government had just been accomplished, and the highest had become the lowest, and the lowest had become the highest. . . . [A] lower stratum had been brought to the surface, and with it all the virtues and vices of upstarts in this world; hence, also prejudices against the Jew."[14] Washington society was infected, and the poison spread throughout the country, leaving long-lasting damage to Jewish-Christian relations. The editor also blamed the religious revival begun during the war and carried over into the political arena for fomenting the new Jew hatred. Wise's line of reasoning points to the need to look beyond social competition or agrarian radicalism, the usual reasons advanced by scholars for an understanding of discrimination. True, in the Gilded Age other doctrines that eroded religious strength—science, secularism, materialism—flourished, but, as Paul Carter has persuasively shown, the same era brought a revival and resurgence of religious fervor.[15]

Isaac Leeser also reported heightened religious sentiment during the Civil War, which he, like Wise, interpreted to mean increased hostility toward the Jew. The war had inflamed religious passion, and Jews, despite their military service in both the Union and Confederacy, were singled out for all sorts of "crimes." In the North, where the churches had thrown themselves into the antislavery movement, abolition was considered a victory for Christianity, and Jews were criticized for not having been sufficiently outspoken against slavery. Their general prosperity nurtured the mounting antipathy, for how could unbelievers enjoy earthly rewards which belonged rightly to members of the saving church? More threatening was the possibility that the new religious fervor would spill over into the political arena and cause dissenters from the majority position to forfeit civil rights. Despite America's tradition of religious freedom, that possibility did not appear too farfetched after a war that signaled a major constitutional and social upheaval, particularly to a people whose history was punctuated by suffering at the hands of churches or church-dominated states.

No wonder, then, that Jews took seriously the growing momentum of the movement to engraft Christianity upon the Constitution. Just before the war, a small group of Presbyterians had met in Allegheny, Pennsylvania, and petitioned the Senate for a constitutional amendment acknowledging the authority of God, Jesus, and scriptural law. After 1861 the group drew support from the belief that the destruction and suffering of the war were marks of God's vengeance against a nation that was not sufficiently Christian. By 1863 the movement was considerably more significant, having attracted other denominations and even some prominent public officials, and it continued to expand from year to year. Jews derived hope for its defeat in the divisions which precluded a unified stand among the multiple Protestant denominations, but Leeser, for one, sketched in the dire results should rights to vote or hold office be predicated upon a religious base.

Leeser's apprehensions, which were shared by the young Jewish defense agency, the Board of Delegates of American Israelites, resulted in a remonstrance to the Senate against the amendment from the board. What is more interesting was the *Occident*'s tacit admission that America was not different. Just as Jews throughout their history had lived with persecution spawned by religious bigotry, so in the United States, too, they would face similar cycles of both tribulation and respite.

The promoters of the constitutional amendment organized themselves into a national association and dispatched a delegation to present their aims to President Lincoln. After the war clergymen and religious periodicals took up the cause and spread the message that it was both "an error and an evil" for the Constitution not to acknowledge God or Jesus. The association, standing for a Christian nation resting on Christian beliefs, pitted itself against those "baneful" views that were being heard in politics: "That civil government is only a social compact; That it exists only for secular and material, not for moral ends; That Sabbath Laws are unconstitutional, and that the Bible must be excluded from our Public Schools." If the stated purpose alone did not prove that the association included Jews among its opponents, the speeches at the national conventions were more explicit. One clergyman uttered a blanket condemnation: "The enemies of our movement naturally draw into their ranks all infidels, Jews, Jesuits, and all opposers of Him who is Lord over all, our Lord Jesus Christ." Another cited the "confederacy of the Jesuit and Jew, infidel and atheist" for attacking the Bible in the schools. Those elements had no common aim, "but they have stricken hands like Herod and Pontius Pilate in the common work of crucifying Christ."[16]

The Jews could not ignore the movement, especially since it was headed in the early 1870s by Supreme Court Justice William Strong and included several governors, state judicial officers, and academicians among its vice-presidents. The *Jewish Messenger* argued several points at once: the greatness of the Constitution and the Founding Fathers just because they eschewed an established religion, the evils of a church-state combination, the fact that Jewish teachings were the base of so-called Christian virtue. When in 1874 the House Judiciary Committee turned down the association's petition for an amendment, the paper happily suggested that the members offer their services to Bismarck (who was having trouble with the church) or to the "valorous women, who expect to conquer the rum sellers by prayer."[17]

The clamor for an amendment abated for a while, but other manifestations of religious intolerance persisted. New Hampshire did not permit non-Protestants to hold office until 1877. In Massachusetts and Pennsylvania Jews were far more numerous, but those states still required all to refrain from work on the Christian Sabbath irrespective of whether they observed Saturday as the day of rest. The Centennial Exhibition held in Philadelphia in 1876 was closed on Sundays in deference to Christian pressure, and Jews felt slighted still further when Bishop Simpson, who offered the opening prayer, referred to America's Christian civilization. It was strange, the *American Israelite* observed, that in the years celebrating a century of progress and enlightenment, such anachronisms, inconsistencies, and hypocrisies could still exist. But Americans had been governed by "rings, cliques and vestrys [*sic*]" since 1861; when priests and deacons decided otherwise, the Constitution and the statutes on religious liberty were not insurmountable. Jews wanted no special legislation, the paper insisted, but merely freedom based upon justice and equality.[18]

The winter of 1875–1876 also marked a high point in the revivalist crusade of the Reverend Dwight L. Moody. The popular preacher who reached tens of thousands through meetings conducted in major cities did not ignore the Jews. Not only did he repeat the accusation of deicide—recounting the story of the Crucifixion in gripping, dramatic detail—but he also once claimed that a thousand Jews meeting in Paris in 1873 had boasted of killing the Christian God. Rabbi Sabato Morais of Philadelphia, the city in which the claim was made, said: "None of us would have believed, before he undertook an ostensibly holy mission, that the attempt to inflame the passions of multitudes against law-abiding Hebrews would have been tried . . . two days before the Centennial year was ushered in."[19] Moody was denounced in the secular and Jewish press and the story of the Paris meeting exposed as a falsehood. Isaac Mayer Wise challenged Moody repeatedly to debate the deicide charge, but the latter took no notice. He later stated that he had been misquoted, that he never passed a Jew without wanting to take off his hat to the people who were destined to convert the world to Christianity. That Moody was interested in converting Jews was true. That he honored them is highly questionable, for years later he had no qualms about inviting Adolf Stoecker, ex-court chaplain and notorious Jew baiter of Bismarck's Germany, to share a pulpit with him.

Moody spelled danger to Jewish spokesmen because he appealed to emotions instead of reason and because he invoked inflammatory images. Furthermore, like all evangelical Protestants, he stood for a religious or Protestant base for American society. But to dismiss him as an illiterate demagogue, the way the *American Israelite* tried to, was inaccurate. Moody was not the stereotypical backwoods revivalist. He was the preacher who brought traditional religion to native Americans on the urban frontier, and his messages bridged their former way of life with the new industrial reality. His audiences were middle class in aspirations and values—he even had the financial support of some postwar millionaires—uncomfortable as yet with the Darwinist and secularist challenges to religion. Moody shared their attitudes; he identified with businessmen and applied business principles to his own revival campaign.

Jewish spokesmen remained alert in the last quarter of the nineteenth century to the causes undertaken by militant Protestants.

The latter were then seeking popular support and protective legislation in a desperate attempt to hold back the sweeping currents of secularization. Their particular concern was the city, where new industrial patterns were undermining fixed social traditions and where hordes of Catholic and Jewish immigrants from southern and eastern Europe were neutralizing the Protestant flavor of established customs. To retain the religious component of Americanism as they knew it, they breathed new life into old ventures—missionary drives, Bible reading and sectarian teachings in the public schools, the religious-amendment movement (which sputtered again in the 1890s), prohibition, and stricter Sunday laws. The last was spurred on significantly in the 1880s by the work of the National Reform Association and the Women's Christian Temperance Union, and reached a climax in Senator Henry Blair's bills of 1888 and 1890 proposing a national day of rest.

On most of those issues the Jewish press had long since recorded its opposition, and its favorite targets remained the missionaries, Sunday laws, and sectarianism in the schools. Since Jews saw how the different causes and their sponsors were connected in the underlying purpose of safeguarding Christian morality through law, they also denounced any incident, no matter how insignificant, which could be construed as an entering wedge. Thus, they criticized the demand to close the 1893 Chicago World's Fair on Sunday, the attempt in New York to make Good Friday a legal holiday, and even a proposal by the congressional representative from the territory of Wyoming for paintings on the capitol walls depicting the life of Jesus! At the end of the century Jews strongly deplored the anti-Catholic activity of the American Protective Association, for they were combating the very same forces of religious bigotry. Some even feared that the prejudice against Catholics might be turned upon them. It is not surprising, therefore, that as they watched the injection of religious issues into politics, American Jews gravitated increasingly into a position favoring a secularist state.

For two decades after the Seligman affair—and indeed into the twentieth century—writers in the Anglo-Jewish press called religious hostility the source of discrimination. As noted above, other reasons were tentatively broached, but none carried the same conviction as that of the ongoing tension between Christian and non-Christian. The free-silver and Populist crusades at the end of the century did not alter the Jewish perspective. The importance of Populism in fomenting anti-Semitism, a theme that later historians popularized, was lost upon nineteenth-century Jews. To the extent that the free-silver faction was anti-Semitic, it was merely updating time-worn economic stereotypes about Jews and harnessing Jew hatred to an economic and political campaign. It is doubtful that it made Jew haters of any who were untouched by the Shylock myth or by Christian religious beliefs about Jews. The free silverites' achievement was to vent the latent antipathy and popularize it. By linking Jews with serious and immediate economic issues, they made the "Jewish menace" more palpable and credible to an increasingly modernized society.

The *American Hebrew,* a New York weekly journal founded in 1879 under the editorship of Philip Cowen, was particularly outspoken in disseminating the message that discrimination rested on religious grounds. The *Jewish Messenger,* more fearful of arousing controversy than its New York rival or Wise's *American Israelite,* also affirmed the connection:

The persistency of popular prejudice against the Jew is due to many factors . . . [but] the most fruitful . . . has been the religious training of the Christian. As most Christians have capacity to understand only the material elements in the crucifixion, they take a grim religious pleasure—a sense of duty done—in crucifying the Jew.[20]

To argue that many who discriminated against Jews were not churchgoers did not alter the case, for their prejudices had been instilled at an early age by religious training in schools and by a traditional Christian environment. Therefore, it was futile to look to churches and schools to end the discrimination, even though, as a few articles pointed out, Jesus and the apostles would also have been barred from the summer resorts.

Writing in the *North American Review* in 1881, Nina Morais pointed to a history of civil disabilities, Jewish manners, and ignorance about Jews as the causes contributing to prejudice. But at least equally culpable were the anti-Semitic Christian teachings repeated in the nursery rhymes, the public schools, and missionary exhortations. As long as Christianity refused "further enlightenment," the results in society were inevitable:

Under the circumstances, it is not wonderful that the ardent church-member should bestow some active hatred upon the criminal, or that an involuntary aversion to the Jew should become a mental habit in the most indifferent Christian. To dislike the Hebrew *per se* is natural, whatever the causes of the dislike may be. . . . [The prejudices against him] have been wrought in the very woof of Christianity.[21]

The religious argument could generate a resigned, passive, or even fatalistic mood; nothing the Jews did could change matters radically. Jewish observers noted, for example, that self-improvement did not guarantee the end of discrimination. This was an imperfect world, Judge Mayer Sulzberger of Philadelphia wrote, and "if all Jews behaved themselves properly there would be more prejudice than ever."[22] In particular, the argument by some Christians that Jewish boorishness constituted the core of the problem appeared to be more a rationalization than a real cause. Vulgarity cut across class, religious, and ethnic lines; Christians also gambled and bet at races, and Christian women also "disport themselves at the seashore in indecent bathing costumes."[23]

The concentration on religious differences that set even acculturated Jews apart from other Americans put anti-Jewish discrimination on a plane different from the antiforeignism directed against other European ethnic groups. Irrational and anachronistic, perhaps, in an age that prided itself for a devotion to modern scientific doctrines, anti-Semitism nonetheless was permanent and irremediable so long as Jews, Americanized or not, remained outside the Christian camp. In a sense, those who discriminated against Jews were blameless, too. They were merely acting out the logic of an omnipresent ideology.

Opinion within Christian circles on Jew hatred was also mixed. Many denied that age-old religious doctrines could be faulted for what was transpiring in the last quarter of the nineteenth century. Some said discrimination was a question of racial antagonism analogous to American hostility to the blacks and Chinese, while others suggested that Christians turned to prejudice because they feared the superiority of Jews.

On the other hand, a good number agreed that religious hostility was a primary cause, even though it might have been reduced to residual or even unconscious significance. George W. Curtis, editor of *Harper's*, wrote about the absence of true "soul liberty" in the United States; the root of anti-Jewish discrimination was the charge of deicide, "a terrible retribution" for what a "Syrian" mob did more than two thousand years ago. The fact that some Christians pointed to Jewish violations of Christian sensibilities—e.g., disrespectful behavior on Sunday—also attested to the importance of the religious factor.

In the 1880s, what with anti-Semitism rife in both western and eastern Europe and social ostracism more widespread in the United States, the Jewish question and the issue of Jewish-Christian relations became favorite topics of discussion. At that time, a new note was increasingly heard from Christians who spoke out on the reasons for discrimination. The fault lay, they said, in the exclusiveness and separatism practiced by the Jews. In a symposium conducted by Philip Cowen in 1890 on the causes and the nature of anti-Semitism, prominent clerics and public figures cited the clannishness of the Jews and their feelings of superiority as the Chosen People. Jewish behavior showed, some respondents said, that Jews were just as prejudiced as Christians.

"How singular," wrote Rabbi Gustav Gottheil, "that, when the Jew attempts to . . . mix freely with his neighbors, he is repelled and unceremoniously shown back to his own tribe; and if he keeps there, he is accused of hereditary and ancestral pride!"[24] The *American Hebrew* echoed that sentiment and argued that those who raised the charge were motivated by a religious animus. Despite centuries of Christian proselytism, Jews retained their "religious autonomy" and refused to merge with the dominant faith.

Nevertheless, just because it was less crude than the charge that Jews as a group were vulgarians, and just because it was voiced by friends of Jews as well as by their critics, the argument of separatism was more troubling. For one thing it contradicted the claim that the religiously observant Jew was accorded greater respect than his irreligious brother. But, more important, it meant that social amenities and cultured tastes alone did not make the Jew acceptable to society, that Jews who held on to religious practices like dietary laws and the ban on intermarriage were still beyond the pale of respectability. The choice was theirs—ancestral traditions or social acceptance—when in fact they wanted to combine elements of both.

The issue of Jewish exclusiveness perforce dashed the hopes of those Jews who called upon the Christian community to shoulder the responsibility for ending the "un-American" discrimination. Although the overwhelming body of church and lay leaders, if asked, would have repudiated prejudice, few had actively campaigned on behalf of the victims. Now the latter were faulted and the responsibility was shifted to them. After all, why should Christians extend themselves without evidence of Jewish goodwill or, in this case, of a desire for total assimilation? The charge that Jews could not or would not assimilate constituted a primary impediment to their acceptance in a Western world whose mood grew increasingly nationalistic at the turn of the century. Whether based on religious, secular, or pseudoscientific arguments, Jewish unassimilability was the heart of what non-Jews meant by the Jewish question.

As Rabbi Heller predicted, social discrimination became more deeply entrenched in the years leading up to World War I, and Jews had difficulty in finding an effective response. Their reactions ran a wider gamut than their explanations for the problem, and many set precedents that lasted well into the twentieth century.

On one extreme there were Jews who adopted the prejudice of the outside. They changed their names (and later their noses) and searched for schools and clubs where Jews were not visible. Critics within the Jewish fold scoffed at their self-abasement and at their pathetic readiness to be tolerated in restricted circles.[25] Of a similar bent were those Jews who renounced Judaism because of the difficulties membership entailed. Some advocated the path of intermarriage,[26] while others, taking advantage of religious voluntarism, found it simpler merely to defect. The swelling number of unchurched Americans eliminated the need to make an either-or choice between Judaism and Christianity, and Jews could abandon their faith without a formal declaration of allegiance to another. The losses that ensued were summed up in the preface of the 1926 edition of *Who's Who in American Jewry:*

Doubtless many names have been omitted which should have been included. . . . Unfortunately, some persons preferred to be omitted rather than associate their names with those of their racial colleagues. A few even rejected with indignation the proposal of being included in a volume where their Jewish identity would become a matter of public knowledge.[27]

Other Jews, although opposed to the extinction of Judaism or Jewry, faulted their fellow Jews for bringing discrimination upon themselves. The *Jewish Messenger*, for example, frequently repeated pleas for improvement in social manners. In time, such arguments implied, the Jew would become sufficiently educated and refined to merit social equality. The paper took seriously the Christian charge of Jewish exclusivity, and it hammered away at the evils of separate Jewish associations and "self-ghettoization." Above all, the journal sought to avoid what it considered to be the undesirable effects of Jewish visibility, and hence cautioned its readers not to exaggerate the prejudice.[28]

Among those who refused to acknowledge Jewish culpability, opinions varied. Rabbi Bernhard Felsenthal, who later became an active Zionist, said that the western Jew could do little more than "live down" the prejudice and work simultaneously to elevate Jewish institutions and Jewish life. "We have to do our duty in this regard, and have to hope that slowly but surely, the day of salvation . . . will come."[29]

Others shared Felsenthal's belief in ultimate triumph of enlightened justice, but they preferred to lend an active hand instead of waiting passively for God's kingdom. Despite the irrationality of bigotry, most activists still believed that rational men could be reached by education, specifically education about the Jew and Judaism. Preferring to ignore prejudice in learned circles, some argued that since Jews had never bothered to dispel the popular ignorance about their tradition, the gravity of their faults was compounded in the popular mind.[30]

A novel opportunity to educate the world about Judaism came in the World's Parliament of Religions, an adjunct to the Chicago World's Fair of 1893. At that unprecedented ecumenical conference, spokesmen for the major religions of the world explained the principles and practices of their faith. The Jewish committee planning for the conference called on a dozen rabbis and a few laymen to prepare papers on Jewish theology, ethics, history, and social institutions. The committee responded enthusiastically to the chance to clear up the popular misconceptions about their faith, which in turn gave rise to discrimination:

Since the existence of our religion no such opportunity has ever been extended to the Jew to set himself right before the whole world. It would, therefore, be criminal negligence did we not embrace this chance to proclaim . . . what our fundamental doctrines, hopes, and aims have ever been, what are the chief spiritual contributions for which humanity is indebted to us, what is our attitude toward other religions, and in what respect Judaism is still indispensable to the highest civilization.

They were also pathetically grateful for the recognition of Judaism as a religion entitled to an equal hearing at the parliament. Even the venerable Isaac Mayer Wise, long experienced in handling public and controversial issues, was overwhelmed by the responsibility foisted upon him as a major participant. He wrote that he felt "like the High Priest on Atonement Day" on this, probably the last occasion to defend Judaism to the entire religious world. He took pride in the favorable reception accorded his words; he said that in presenting the essence of his faith to the international assemblage he had reached "the most triumphant moment of my life."[31]

American Jews had overwhelmingly blamed Christian teachings for generating discrimination, but few dared criticize the majority religion openly.[32] Again, the indefatigable Wise, by no means an authority on Christianity, proved an exception. He would stop carping about Christianity, he promised, only when Christians stopped attacking Judaism and trying to convert Jews. Wise's ongoing battle against Christian missionary work among the Jews dated back to his days in Albany in the 1840s. In the pages of the *American Israelite* he continued to blast the proselytizing movements, which were symptomatic of an aggressive Christianity that saw itself—incorrectly so, according to Wise—as superior to other faiths. Wise also attacked Christianity for its "retrogressive" character. On one occasion, calling the religious persecutors of the Jews enemies of justice and liberty, he candidly asserted that Christianity required radical reform before it could fit with modern ideas of equality and humanitarianism. In his book *A Defense of Judaism versus Proselytizing Christianity*, the rabbi again labeled the "conversion mania" of Christianity as the root of anti-Jewish prejudice and, in light of the misery and destruction it caused, "the direct opposite of true religion." Although their religion was "incessantly" attacked by the would-be proselytizers, Jews would hardly "retrograde" from Judaism to Christianity. The religion of the Jews, the rabbi proudly claimed, was a faith of reason, one that refused to see a sinner in every human being or a hell for nonbelievers.

In 1883 Wise delivered a series of Friday-evening lectures, later published in book form, under the title of *Judaism and Christianity, Their Agreements and Disagreements*. The burden of his thesis was that in essentials both religions agreed; the disagreements, the cause of senseless prejudice, derived from a difference in means and forms. Hailing the freedom that permitted a Jewish lecturer to compare the two faiths publicly and dispassionately—thank God that we have free speech in Cincinnati, he said—Wise neither adopted a polemical tone nor refrained from criticizing Jewish sages who misinterpreted the essence of their religion. Nevertheless, he made no secret of his preference. Christianity could not legitimately claim superiority. Judaism was the source of all that was true and benevolent in Christianity. Furthermore, it was the Jewish affirmation of free will and freedom that underlay the idea of constitutional government and made it a religion eminently suited to the modern world.[33]

Christians, too, offered opinions on how best to counter discrimination. One line of thought urged political activism. John B. Weber, who had investigated the causes of Jewish immigration to the United States in the early 1890s, wrote candidly to Oscar Straus that acceptance of the Jew would not emanate from noble principles like the golden rule. Only when the Jew had the power to hurt, and the power to make and unmake political bosses, would he be respected. Weber advised, therefore, that Jews unite for political purposes in their local communities; after all, the Irish became the rulers of the larger cities through the ballot. Mark Twain wrote along similar lines when commenting on anti-Semitism in Europe. He stated matter-of-factly that the Jew should not expect an end to persecution—the Jew "is . . . a foreigner wherever he may be, and even the angels dislike a foreigner." Nevertheless, he believed that the Jews, particularly in England and America, could improve their situation:

[I]n politics organize your strength—band together, and deliver the casting vote where you can, and where you can't, compel as good terms as possible. You huddle to yourselves . . . , but you huddle to no sufficient purpose, politically speaking. You do not seem to be organized, except for your charities; there you compel your due of recognition. . . . It shows what you can do when you band together for a definite purpose.[34]

Although Weber and Twain were more concerned, respectively, with the prejudice against the east European immigrants and the persecution in Europe, the same advice could be applied to the problem of social discrimination. Slowly but perceptibly the American Jews in the early twentieth century began to cast aside some of their customary restraints and wet their feet in political waters. In 1905 in response to a petition from a group of leading Jews, the New York Board of Regents censured state librarian Melvil Dewey. Dewey's offense was that he operated a summer hotel which baldly advertised its anti-Jewish exclusionary policies. We can't fight private clubs or hotelkeepers, the petitioners said, but "when a high public official . . . can . . . forget . . . the duties which he owes to the entire public as to spread . . . a publication which tends to make of the Jew an outcast and a pariah, the State . . . cannot . . . allow an infamous precedent to be established." Louis Marshall triumphantly reported how he had made a humbled Dewey squirm at a hearing of the Regents' library committee. After the librarian resigned, *Vogue* magazine bitterly warned of dire consequences—denial of Christian philanthropy to Jews, losses to Jewish businesses, and even a race war—should such "race politics" continue.

Undaunted, leading Jews pressed on. Under the leadership of Louis Marshall and the American Jewish Committee, Jews successfully pushed for the enactment of New York's Civil Rights Law in 1913. The law in question provided that all individuals were entitled to equal accommodations in resorts, taverns, restaurants, and other places of recreation and amusement. Owners of such places could neither exclude persons because of race, creed, or color, nor advertise that they followed restrictive policies. The law left many loopholes, but some Jews disapproved of the very principle of invoking state aid in this as in the Dewey affair. Marshall, who likened the Jewish effort in this area to the campaign for the abrogation of the Russo-American treaty, denounced the "cringing, fawning spirit of the Ghetto" which still questioned the rectitude of political action. To Marshall, the issue was one of achieving equality for Jews, eradicating un-American prejudice, and maintaining Jewish self-respect.[35] Such actions multiplied in the twentieth century when the organizational pillars of the Jewish community turned increasingly to legislation as well as litigation in their ongoing defense of Jewish equality.

Different from the activists were those at the other end of the spectrum who found the answer to discrimination in Jewish social institutions. Not many were in the position of Nathan Straus, co-owner of Macy's department store, who built a hotel in New Jersey for Jews right next to, and twice as large as, the one that had refused to admit him,[36] but the same idea permeated more modest attempts. Actually, the withdrawal to a strictly Jewish social milieu had its precedents. One reason for the organization of the B'nai B'rith in 1843 was the refusal of private lodges to admit Jews.[37] The separatists aroused criticism from their fellow Jews as well as from friendly Christians who reasoned that such actions added fuel to the bigot's charge that the Jews were inherently clannish and self-segregating. From the liberal point of view the very principle of separatism was undesirable, for it militated against the ideal of one humanity. But the antiseparatists failed to see the strength of ethnic sentiments. In later years, when Jewish organizations began concerted efforts to tear down Jewish segregation in clubs or residential areas, those concerned retorted that they preferred to live and socialize with other Jews rather than with Christians.[38]

Discrimination in the United States never reached the levels of bigotry in Europe, even in the western countries. Nevertheless, as Rabbi Max Heller cogently observed, the problem had deep and painful consequences. It taught American Jews that their cherished liberal beliefs left them exposed. They rightly saw that constitutional guarantees alone afforded sufficient protection neither to the members of a minority nor to the desire for group survival. Although many Jews continued to mouth a faith in the inevitability of progress, at least in the United States if not universally, the seed of the question—How different was America?—had been sown.

Jewish "Conspiracies" and Racism

European patterns of anti-Semitism, replete with rhetoric and political parties formed to limit the legal rights of Jews, failed to emerge in the United States. Nevertheless, even if one dismissed the argument that American social discrimination or "polite anti-Semitism" was in essence as threatening as the more virulent forms, the spillover of Jew hatred from Europe cannot be denied. By concrete example—the Dreyfus affair in France was only the most dramatic in a seemingly endless series—western as well as eastern Europe fed American opinion about Jews. As has been discussed, European bigots and rabble-rousers, universities and scholars contributed to popular antipathy against Jews and their social ostracism.

Europe also deserved the credit for injecting into America the conspiracy theory—the plot of Jews bound together throughout the world to subvert the Christian order by their economic and political power.[39] Years before Timayenis adapted Drumont for American readers, secular and religious renditions of the European-made conspiracy theme appeared in the United States. One early version was Osman Bey's *The Conquest of the World by the Jews*, translated from the German by F. W. Mathias and published in St. Louis in 1878. Osman Bey was the pseudonym for Frank Millinger, a swindler of Jewish origin who literally peddled his anti-Semitic pamphlets throughout the European continent. His book dwelt on Jewish economic control of the world and the evil designs of the Jewish international organization, the Alliance Israélite Universelle. He advanced a simple solution: drive the Jews out of civilized society to Africa or exterminate them.[40]

Evangelical preachers and missionaries also propagated the conspiracy theme in messages related to the fulfillment of biblical prophecies. For example, in 1879 the Reverend L. C. Newman (probably a missionary for the Society for the Promotion of Christianity among the Jews) lectured in New York on "Jerusalem and Its Future." He lauded the achievements of the Jews in the face of incessant persecution, and he predicted their restoration to Palestine and the emergence of Jerusalem as the "metropolis of the world." In the course of his remarks, which were more matter-of-fact than malicious, he said: "They [the Jews] control the finances of Europe . . . and they are now more prosperous than at any time since the destruction of Jerusalem. The Jewish community throughout the world is united by a bureau of correspondence and they hold conventions, to which delegates come from the outermost parts of the earth." Around the same time a preacher in Washington repeated the theme that Jews, like the Jesuits, were organized into societies throughout the world and that their organization had ordered their return to Palestine. Some twenty years later the Reverend Dr. Isaac Haldeman of New York's First Baptist Church discoursed on the degree of Jewish economic power. Already the financial masters of the world, Jews would soon control all the professions—all this since God promised them the wealth of the gentiles before restoring them to their own land. The next stage prior to their ultimate conversion called for an Antichrist arising from among the Jews who would "devastate the nations of Europe and build up a kingdom in Palestine." Haldeman, like the others, was concerned with restoration to Palestine as a harbinger of Jewish conversion, but in the meantime he joined in spreading charges of an international Jewish secret organization and of Jewish economic domination over the gentiles.

That missionaries readily appropriated the conspiracy charge was not surprising. Evidence cited above indicated that European conversionists had been circulating dire warnings about Jewish power at least since the 1840s.[41] Their objectives may have differed from those who later injected the conspiracy theme into politics, but the two streams, one religious and one secular, reinforced each other. Together they cultivated popular receptivity to the image of the Jewish menace.

Anti-Semitic themes along the lines expounded by German bigots were echoed by Samuel H. Kellogg, a Presbyterian missionary of Allegheny, Pennsylvania (the seat of the movement for an amendment grafting Christianity onto the Constitution), who in 1878 became professor of theology at Western Theological Seminary. In 1881 Kellogg wrote an article about the Jewish question in which he described how emancipated Jews tended rapidly to outstrip Christians and dominate the different European nations. The Jews amassed the capital, controlled the press, and exerted great power in politics and education. He could overlook their economic and intellectual control, Kellogg said, but he could not forgive them their stand against religion. Hostile to all evangelical Christianity, Jews wielded a "pernicious" influence on the Christian life of any people. Allied with radical (i.e., modernist) political parties, they also identified with the antireligious stand of the "radical." Kellogg agreed with Adolf Stoecker of Germany, who called the Jewish question a religious one: Modern Jews, like all rationalists, were "sworn enemies of the Gospel of Christ."

The Jewish question obsessed the minister, and two years later

Kellogg worked out his "facts" into a full-blown exposé of a Jewish conspiracy. In a book entitled *The Jews, or Prediction and Fulfillment,* he postulated that everything that had happened or would happen to the Jews was foretold in Old and New Testament prophecies. According to divine plan, Jews were accumulating the wealth of the world from the gentiles, who had oppressed them, while simultaneously gaining control of the press and prominence in world politics. Kellogg documented those charges primarily from European sources; he drew much from Stoecker and, in his second edition (1887), from Edouard Drumont. More interesting was how Kellogg pinpointed the fulfillment of the prophecy that Israel would be God's instrument for the overthrow of the gentiles. Not only were Jews currently engaged in abusing and denigrating Christianity, Kellogg said, but they were responsible for the birth of pantheistic rationalism (Spinoza) and of socialism and communism (Marx, Lassalle, et al.). The same people who had crucified the Messiah had engineered these deadly assaults upon Christian civilization.

Kellogg's work was used and embellished by the Reverend L. B. Woolfolk of Cincinnati, whose book *Great Red Dragon* also appeared in two editions. The Dragon, drawn from an image in the Book of Revelation, symbolized the evolution of the "Money Power" or the Jewish economic masters of the world. The Money Power operated secretly and underhandedly as it dispossessed honest labor and asserted control over all aspects of commerce and manufacturing. Through organization, political manipulation, and the use of carefully placed agents, it worked solely for its own gain while threatening the survival of republican institutions and Christian churches. A union of the money evil with the devil, the Dragon was the Antichrist and the head of the Money Power the destined Jewish Messiah.

Just how many people were influenced by such clergymen is impossible to estimate, but those who were could not help but fear and hate the Jews. Even if they accepted the view that the Jew's behavior conformed to biblical prophecies and would ultimately bring about the millennium, it was not a cheerful prospect to be one of the generation to fall to the Jew on the way to salvation. More likely there were those who would remember the power and danger of the Jew much sooner than the biblical message.

The preachers and their theories attest to the influence of European thinking about the Jews upon Americans. They also represent a stage in the evolution and public acceptance of full-blown, twentieth-century anti-Semitic ideology. While they legitimized Jewish behavior—God designated Israel to be the "torch of fire" among the gentiles, the "lion among sheep"—they were also legitimizing the anti-Semitic assertions about the incalculable power wielded by the Jews. By fusing religious imagery with selected "facts" from the nineteenth-century industrial world, they made anti-Semitism relevant to the present. They updated the garb of the Jew. But whether he took the form of Satan, Rothschild, Spinoza, or Marx, his threat remained constant: he conspired to destroy Christianity and Christian civilization.[42]

Echoes of the conspiracy theme resounded in American novels and other respectable writings at the end of the nineteenth and beginning of the twentieth centuries.[43] Nonetheless, evidence provided by the Anglo-Jewish press, a reliable barometer to the currents of anti-Semitism, indicated that at least until the turn of the century the charge mustered far less credence in this country than in Europe. Since Americans discerned no imminent danger to the United States from the alleged Jewish conspiracies, Jewish defenders took notice of such charges only rarely, and when they did, they scoffed. The *American Israelite*, for example, reprinted an article by a Reform rabbi arguing that Osman Bey's tract was a parody written by a "friend of truth and fair play" who purposely embroidered upon anti-Semitic propaganda in order to discredit it. Alas, the rabbi concluded, translator Mathias, who added his own scraps to Bey's indictment, had been duped. For its part the *American Israelite*, like the *New Orleans Times-Democrat*, questioned how so small a minority could be charged with the rapid Judaization of society and the attainment of so much power. The horrible persecution in Russia in the early 1880s should have dispelled conclusively the notion of Jewish international power. On the appearance of Drumont's book, Wise's paper commented: "It must be a stupid little world which is governed by a handful of Jews and a handful of Freemasons." It added sarcastically that if the charge of Judaization were really true, it constituted reason enough for Europeans to convert to Judaism as fast as possible.[44] Jewish spokesmen made no serious attempt in the last two decades of the century to play down the importance of the House of Rothschild and the Alliance Israélite Universelle, the made-to-order symbols for the anti-Semitic specter of an internationally organized Jewish collectivity whose economic tentacles spanned the entire globe.[45]

Had the Jewish community been seriously concerned about the charges of Jewish power and conspiracy in the United States, it is doubtful that New York-born Isaac Markens, a writer for the *Mail and Express* and the *New York Star*, would have published *The*

Hebrews in America in 1888. Markens did prodigious research for his book, the first history by a Jew on that subject, and for his efforts he earned the sobriquet of "pioneer writer and investigator."[46] His book traced the early history of the Jews in the urban centers of the United States. In addition the author provided capsule profiles of Jewish organizations and communal leaders and, most important, long chapters about Jewish participation in the armed forces, politics, professions, and business life of the community. Readers, however, would search in vain for proper historical method or critical analyses and judgment. All Markens's Jews were men of conscience and integrity, philanthropists and patriots, who had earned the respect of their communities. Lewis C. Levin, the irrational Know-Nothing agitator, underwent an extraordinary transformation at Markens's hands: "He was a man of genius and remarkable eloquence, and was likewise distinguished for his kind-heartedness and benevolence." Even more outstanding, no poor Jews appeared. From cigars to corset clasps, from banking to butchering, Jews captured a large measure of control of the nation's economy. Their financial successes stretched throughout the union—from New York to Oregon to Georgia. Had Edouard Drumont sought grist for his exposés of Jewish power, he could have well turned to Markens's boastful claims about his fellow Jews. Indeed, Markens's opening remarks were enough to frighten any self-respecting anti-Semite: "Marvelous prosperity and steady progress mark the history of the Hebrews in the United States. In every department of commercial and intellectual activity they are continually making headway. . . . Close observers of the times are of the opinion that within half a century the Hebrews of this country will control the balance of trade."[47]

Seventeen years later Louis Marshall's article written on the occasion of the 250th anniversary of Jewish settlement in the United States reflected a different climate of opinion. The very request by *Harper's Weekly* for a piece from that prominent attorney and dedicated communal worker indicated that the conspiracy charge now loomed more important. Marshall was invited to explain "the financial position of the Jews of the United States, the proportion of wealth of the country that they control, and the part that they play in the financial, political, and social life in America." Concentrating mainly on the economic question, Marshall used the opportunity first to deny that any correlation existed between Jewishness and economic achievement, or that American Jews differed in economic matters from American Protestants, Catholics, or atheists. Second, Marshall labored to disprove the myth that Jews were all wealthy and that the country's economic fate rested in their hands: "As a class they are far from rich." "Among them there are some millionaires, and, unfortunately, a vast number who are poor." "[T]hey control but a small percentage of the wealth of the country." From humble beginnings but with a commitment to the work ethic, Marshall continued, the Jews had spread out into all avenues of the economy. Merchants, skilled craftsmen, professionals and white-collar personnel, peddlers, realtors, and farmers, they contributed in diverse fashion to the nation's economic progress. Far too astute and proud to engage in outright apologetics, Marshall carefully sketched the portrait of a hardworking, self-reliant, and patriotic group dedicated to the preservation of a capitalist order.[48]

Americans also lagged behind Europeans who grounded Jew hatred in racist doctrines. The initial flurry of interest in Count Joseph Arthur de Gobineau's *Essay on the Inequality of Human Races* and similar viewpoints that dovetailed with the defense of slavery had quickly disappeared. It revived only after 1890, when seized upon by the militant proponents of immigration restriction. True, American Christians referred increasingly to Jews as a race in the immediate years following the Seligman-Hilton affair, but, like the Jews, they used the generic terms *race* and *religion* inconsistently and imprecisely. *Harper's*, for example, called the social ostracism an indicator of racial prejudice analogous to American treatment of the blacks, but claimed at the same time that the anti-Jewish prejudice rested on a religious foundation, deicide. Harvard president Charles Eliot spoke admiringly to the Unitarian Club on the "combined force of race and religion." He echoed the Jewish power cry—"The Jews are seizing upon all the best things in all the countries of Europe and Africa"—but unlike the anti-Semites he welcomed the results. When German anti-Semitism peaked in 1880, the *Nation* stated: "[T]here is some leaven of truth in the talk about the contest of Germanism and Jewism—namely, the difference in the national or race character of Jews and Germans, a difference . . . whose existence is one of the most important factors in history." The journal refrained, however, from drawing parallels to the American scene. Only twenty-five years later could the *Independent* envision the rise of racial anti-Semitism in the United States.[49]

Understandably, many American Jews were reluctant to acknowledge the radically new dimension in Jew hatred. Do not be misled by the learned term *anti-Semitism*, Philadelphia attorney Mayer Sulzberger wrote: The movement in Germany is only an attack on freedom of religion. Rabbi Marcus Jastrow explained further that since religion no longer commanded enough respect in a secularized society, science was invoked in the figures of Aryan versus Semite to justify persecution of the Jew. Such men preferred to see modern anti-Semitism as merely another link in the chain of persecution long endured. If every generation had its Haman or its "Hep! Hep!" movement, this, too, would pass. To admit to peculiarly Jewish traits, whether the products of race or of history, and whether admirable or abhorrent, precluded the hope of ever achieving real equality in the modern world.[50]

Just as some Americans adopted the racist vocabulary but stopped short of vilifying the "Jewish race," Jews, too, could not help but absorb the popular jargon of the day. The *Jewish Messenger*, for example, took great pride and comfort in the words and deeds of two who acclaimed Jews as a race—novelist George Eliot and Benjamin Disraeli. Disraeli, the baptized Englishman, became a hero to the traditionalist New York weekly. Although in 1868 the paper said that Disraeli could not be claimed by the Jews, after 1870 he was frequently hailed as the man who remembered and fought for his people, a modern Mordecai. When the paper took perverse satisfaction in the fact that Berlin Jews, despite their assimilation and high social position, could not escape anti-Jewish bigotry, it, too, was accepting the premises of racism.[51]

The *American Hebrew*, the *Jewish Messenger*'s New York competitor, ignited a spirited controversy in Jewish circles when it printed a racist editorial in 1884 entitled "New Jews and Judaism." Arguing that conversions to Judaism for the purpose of marriage could not endow an Aryan with the feelings and aspirations of a Hebrew, the paper insisted that Jewishness meant consanguinity and race in addition to faith. Jewish race purity contributed to civilization: "Whenever the Aryan has stood for pillage the Semitic race has stood for peace. When the Aryans pursued the chase, Semites cultivated letters. The law of fittest surviving, aided by the breeding of hereditary qualities in a pure race, has given the Jews a physiological and mental superiority which can be perpetuated only by the perpetuation of the race purity."

From across the Atlantic, Claude Montefiore, theologian and spokesman for liberal Judaism in England, wrote a bitter rejoinder. If no alien could become a Jew, then no Jew could properly assimilate non-Jewish characteristics or culture. Unless Jews believe that they must integrate fully with their fellow citizens except in matters of creed, they ought not to enjoy the advantages of living and prospering in Christian society or to complain when they are discriminated against or charged with disloyalty.

Cyrus L. Sulzberger of the *American Hebrew*'s board contributed a final rebuttal. He, too, upheld the importance of blood ties (witness the Jewish response to the persecuted in Russia as contrasted to Aryan inaction) and the existence of a "tribal bond" stretching back throughout history. That bond never precluded intense loyalty to the countries in which Jews lived, but it served to keep Jews alive and to permit them to propagate the message of monotheism to all humanity. If Jewish separatism ended, and if Jews were denationalized the way Montefiore and anti-Semites advocated, they would cease to exist and their mission would fail.[52]

From the 1880s on, the American Jewish community abounded with various opinions about a Jewish race. Some used race in an anthropological sense, others in a social, cultural, or religious way. Since point of reference differed, Reformers were not all allied in denouncing race nor traditionalists in defending it. Jews were a "Volk" and Judaism was racial (or tribal) as well as universal, said prominent Reform rabbi Emil Hirsch: "Without 'race' we ossify in dogma, as did Christianity. Without universal tendency away from the merely racial, we are doomed to fossilization." According to Hirsch's colleague Bernhard Felsenthal, Jewishness could be obliterated neither by conversion nor atheism: Disraeli was an Episcopalian in religion, English in citizenship, and Jewish in race. Even Kaufmann Kohler, the president of Hebrew Union College and zealous anti-Zionist, said: "Ethnologically, the Jews certainly represent a race, since both their religion and history ever kept them apart from the rest of the people of the country they inhabit."[53]

However defined, the term *Jewish race* could not be discussed in the abstract. It immediately conjured up concrete questions of the day—anti-Semitism, Jewish separatism, and, indeed, all facets of Jewish-Christian relations. By the turn of the century, phrases like "race purity," "mongrelization of races," and "racial suicide" had entered the American vocabulary, and the government busily tabulated immigrants according to racial origin. When incoming Jews were designated as Hebrews, prominent lawyers like Simon Wolf, Max Kohler, and Julian Mack lodged protests in the name of the community.[54] They were not concerned about the scientific soundness of the bureaucratic procedure; they feared rather that a separate racial classification for Jews could only operate to their detriment. If Jews were recognized legally as more than a religious body, their rights, rooted through the years in the guarantee of religious freedom, would become more vulnerable.

If a racial hierarchy became entrenched, the Jews would not be able to escape the stigma of inferiority. The only way out, some Jews reasoned, was for the Jew himself to eradicate those "racial traits" or "tribal bonds" that were responsible in the first place for the anti-Semitic racist argument. Charles Waldstein, an American-born archeologist who taught at Cambridge University, advanced that point of view in a book, which although published anonymously received serious attention. Part of his message was a defense of Jews, part a refutation of claims that Jews exhibited racial traits, and part a plea to Jews to renounce the "evils" of racial exclusivity. He suggested that Jews could satisfy their need for a separate identity through a "Neo-Mosaic Church" open to all who believed in pure monotheism but free of racial trappings. Like Montefiore, Waldstein warned that emancipated Jews who retained archaic customs invited popular disfavor.[55]

For Jews to cultivate universalism and reject particularism was also the prescription of Morris Jastrow. Born in Poland but trained in Germany in Oriental languages and for the rabbinate, Jastrow left the pulpit for a job in Semitics at the University of Pennsylvania. His reaction to the race issue was just as emotional as scholarly. In a lengthy essay published in 1896, he argued against the concepts of race purity, the unity of either the Aryan or Semitic races, and the inappropriate use of the term *Aryan* (a linguistic designation) to a physical type. He interpreted so-called racial traits to be products of social conditioning and common experiences, and he denied the then-prevalent notion that the mixture of races undermined culture. Not content, however, with faulting those who distorted science to fit their prejudices, Jastrow proceeded to blame the Jews for their "clannishness" and lack of public spirit. Their narrow philanthropies did not adequately extend to the non-Jews; they stayed aloof from civic reform causes, and they did not support American educational institutions. Jastrow called instead for a "broader spirit in the synagogue" and "a closer assimilation . . . between Judaism and *certain* types of Christianity"—goals for which he would have willingly yielded a separate Jewish identity.[56]

By the time the race question was generating serious debate, Felix Adler had already proved his commitment to universalism and had severed his ties with Judaism entirely. The son of the famous rabbi Samuel Adler, who had campaigned for Reform Judaism in Germany and in the United States, the younger Adler carried Reform's cardinal principles of rationalism and universalism to a logical conclusion. In 1876, after a short stay as professor of Hebrew at Cornell, he founded the Society for Ethical Culture, a movement that eschewed all religions in favor of a "practical" religion dedicated to the advancement of the ethical worth of the individual and the ethical standards of humanity. Not surprisingly, Adler's answer to racial anti-Semitism was to propose the "reunification" of the Aryans and Semites and to urge the Jews specifically to "transcend" their religious traditions and racial confines. Confident that racial animosity could be overcome, he organized a Universal Race Congress in 1911 whose object was to discuss the relations among different groups and, "in light of science and the modern conscience," to encourage understanding and friendship among them. [57]

In their concern for Jewish integration into society, Waldstein, Jastrow, and Adler were throwbacks to the intellectual Jews of Germany of the first quarter of the nineteenth century who, in their passionate commitment to the Enlightenment's dream of universalism, were willing to cash in Judaism for acceptance as human beings. Like their German prototypes, those three articulated the faith of the academician, confident that reason and learning would ultimately break down the barriers that divided men. As academicians each of them had inherited the intellectual's scorn for traditional religion and had tasted the intoxicating fruits of free intercourse among individuals of different backgrounds that university life offered qualified scholars. All the more repugnant to them, Jewish separatism bore the taint of the long-vanished ghetto, ever a stumbling block to complete liberation.

Respected though they were for their intellectual expertise, none of the three spoke as a recognized leader of the institutionalized American Jewish community. To the rabbis and laity committed for whatever reasons to the survival of a people, prescriptions that shortchanged Jewish pride were immediately suspect. Jastrow's father, a Conservative rabbi, rejected palliatives to harmonize Jewish-Christian relations that defended capitulation even on matters that his son would have considered archaic. "I . . . was never a believer in a friendship built on bacon and cemented with lard," the elder Jastrow said. Felix Adler, whose actions most closely approximated the earlier German Jews who had flocked to the baptismal font, was denounced in many quarters of the community for his "apostasy."[58] Nevertheless, the three reflected and rationalized demographic trends then in play—the downward trend of the American Jewish population that resulted from intermarriage, conversion, and a lower birthrate.[59] Had the spokesmen for assimilation studied those statistics, they also would have learned that hatred of a group did not necessarily rise or fall in a direct relation to the numbers of that group.

An American Jew who crusaded more effectively against racist distinctions but who had neither Jewish affiliations nor prescriptions for Jewish behavior was the world-renowned anthropologist Franz Boas. To be sure, psychohistorians might well argue that even in his scientific pursuits Boas could not escape his Jewishness. Born to a prosperous family in Westphalia in 1858, Boas grew up in a home committed to the principles of republicanism and individualism. His family's friends included liberals like Carl Schurz, Gottfried Kinkel, Abraham Jacobi, and others who actively supported the revolutions of 1848. It was through Jacobi that Boas met his future wife, Marie Krackowizer, daughter of an Austrian physician who had helped organize the 1848 student uprising in Vienna and was forced to flee to the United States in order to escape imprisonment. Like those Jewish Forty-Eighters whose passion for political freedom and devotion to German culture marched in tandem with anticlericalism, Boas considered himself free of religious affiliation. His university days in Germany, however, coincided with the upsurge of the new anti-Semitism, and as a Jew, even a nonprofessing one, he was subjected to slurs and discrimination on the part of his fellow students. An apocryphal story tells how Boas, on hearing an anti-Semitic insult in a café, threw the speaker out. The latter first challenged him to a duel but subsequently apologized for his remark. Nevertheless, Boas insisted on following through with the match, and, indeed, he bore dueling scars of saber cuts from his student days on. Anti-Semitism would also have impeded a successful academic career in Germany, and it thereby contributed to Boas's decision to emigrate to the United States. In 1896, after appointments at Clark University and the World Columbian Exposition in Chicago, he came to Columbia University, where he taught for forty years.[60]

Boas's response to racism through scholarly and popular writings and lectures was grounded in the wealth of knowledge he amassed as a physical and cultural anthropologist. His signal contribution on that subject was to marshal evidence proving that the environment was a key determinant in shaping and altering man's physical and mental traits. Extrapolating that radical conclusion from immense quantities of empirical data, Boas challenged the scientific accuracy of theories that affirmed race purity, inborn cultural traits, a biological base to race consciousness, immutable physical and characterological properties of human types, and the superiority and inferiority of different races. No wonder, then, that in the words of one of his pupils and admirers, Boas "was honored, on Hitler's accession, by having his books publicly burned."[61]

One of Boas's early forays into the popular race question came in a review of William Ripley's *The Races of Europe* (1899). Ripley, an economist by training, wrote persuasively about the differences among the fundamental European races. Although he judiciously admitted the importance of environment (along with heredity, chance variation, and selection) in determining the prevalent human types, he showed a frank bias for the Teutons. In his chapter on Jews, Ripley fixed on the amazing phenomenon of Jewish "social solidarity." He also discussed peculiarly Jewish physical traits (even separation of the teeth!) and behavioral characteristics. While he admitted that Jews were racially mixed, he saw them as a group seeking to perpetuate a "consciousness of kind"; the east European Jew in particular was a menace to western Europe and the United States. The implications of Ripley's less scholarly observations were discernible, but Boas chose to sidestep the more volatile social issues and judge the work for its scientific merit. The basic flaws, he concluded, were the author's too narrow criteria for classifying physical types and the lack of supportive evidence to corroborate the somewhat cavalier conclusions concerning changes in human races.[62]

While attempting to deflate a book that lent authority to the prejudices of racists and immigration restrictionists, Boas was simultaneously constructing a counterargument. In two addresses between 1895 and 1900, he initiated a serious indictment of the fallacies of fixed racist categories, including the concept of Nordic supremacy. In 1911 he published his seminal study *The Mind of Primitive Man*, the first work to present in cohesive form the scientific arguments of the antiracists. Revised in 1938, the book in its two editions underscored the same conclusions: "There is no fundamental difference in the ways of thinking of primitive and civilized man. A close connection between race and personality has never been established. The concept of racial type as commonly used even in scientific literature is misleading and requires a logical as well a biological redefinition."[63]

What Boas referred to as the "plasticity of human types" was proved by his report for the Dillingham Immigration Commission that also appeared in 1911. With a team of assistants the anthropologist studied close to 18,000 subjects in the New York City area and compared the physical measurements—specifically head forms—of immigrant parents and their children. His findings showed that the head forms of Sicilians and east European Jews born in America differed markedly from those of their foreign-born parents. Thus, even with respect to head shape, whose stability anthropologists had long assumed, Boas demonstrated the response of the human organism to environmental influences. Also measuring differences in stature, cephalic index, pigmentation, and face width among Italian, Jewish, and other ethnic groups, Boas concluded that permanence of types in new environments appeared more the exception than the rule. He posited further that traits of the mind, correlated as they were with the physical condition of the body, would show significant changes as well in response to different environments.[64]

Boas's findings pointed to the influence of the American environment upon immigrants. Like the investigations of a contemporary Jewish physician and anthropologist, Maurice Fishberg, which argued the greater importance of environment over heredity for American Jews, [65] Boas's writings imbued the ideological defense of immigration with new fervor. The Jewish stewards in the front lines of the immigration fight buttressed their arguments with such evidence. However, Boas's labors scarcely dented the appeal of the restrictionist crusaders. The Dillingham commission, despite the contrary evidence it assembled, stuck by preconceived biased judgments. The restrictionists drew rather upon the calculations of Ripley and his ilk, the ideological progenitors of the racist immigration laws of the 1920s, who argued that the Jews and other "subraces" gravely threatened the blood stock and cultural level of native Americans. Bigoted Prescott Hall of the Immigration Restriction League even expounded the racist position from Jewish platforms. He reasoned that Jews above all should sympathize with those who defended the importance of racial purity.[66]

For his part, Boas stayed aloof from the Jewish-interest angle of the race question, at least until after World War I. Among the first to recognize the serious implications of Nazi racial doctrines, he turned his attention increasingly to the public arena after 1933 in denunciations of the Aryan myth. By then he had grown more pessimistic about the ultimate eradication of racial classification and anti-Semitism: "[A]nti-Semitism will not disappear until the last vestige of the Jew as a Jew has disappeared."[67]

Question of Patriotism

The *Independent* in 1906 called Goldwin Smith "the leading and almost the only exponent of Anti-Semitism in the English-speaking world." The journal could have added that as a prominent historian Smith imparted an aura of respectability to racial anti-Semitism. Although considered a liberal on political and economic issues, he served as an important conduit of European anti-Semitic thought to the New World. A wealthy Englishman and formerly professor of modern history at Oxford University, Smith took up residence across the Atlantic, where he first accepted a teaching post at Cornell University. His anti-Semitism was sparked by a feud with Disraeli, and from the 1870s until his death twenty-five years later he vented his fury against Disraeli's "tribe" through British and American periodicals.[68]

Smith's favorite target was Jewish tribalism, which he defined as a mixture of race and religion nourished by the Old Testament and Talmud that set Jews apart as a closed group, a state within a state. Tribalism fostered two evils. First, it prevented Jews from being patriots of the lands in which they lived; Jews responded to racial or "plutopolitan," but not patriotic, motives. If patriotism meant "undivided devotion to the national interest, there is difficulty in seeing how it can be possessed . . . by the members of a cosmopolitan and wandering race, with a tribal bond, tribal aspirations, and tribal feelings of its own." Narrow nationalism was bad enough if it ignored a transcendent humanity, but tribalism which devoured the core of nationality was even worse. "The Jew alone regards his race as superior to humanity, and looks forward not to its ultimate union with other races, but to its triumph over them all, and to its final ascendancy under the leadership of a tribal Messiah." Second, tribal bonds gave Jews the advantage in a free and open society for amassing wealth and power. "[A] wandering and parasitic race, . . . avoiding ordinary labour, and spreading over the world to live on the labour of others by means of usury and other pursuits of the same sort," the Jews conjured up the sinister prospect of world domination and the resultant chaos for Christendom.

In theory Smith distinguished between "liberal" and "strict" Jews. The former had repudiated their tribal practices (e.g., circumcision, endogamy), and, according to his admission, religion divested of race was acceptable. But his excoriations of the baptized Disraeli and the Jew-in-name-only Judah Benjamin contradicted his very words.[69] In point of fact, Smith was less than candid. Jewish religion aside from its ethnic component was by his definition the worship of a tribal god and hence unworthy of survival. His real objective was the *extinction* of Judaism and the removal of Jews from Western society.

Since the goal was effacement of Jewish identity, Reformers closed ranks with traditionalists in denouncing Smith's dicta. Keeping a careful surveillance on his articles, the Anglo-Jewish press took the lead in marshaling the Jewish defense. It used various ploys, from sarcastic taunts to apologetics, to denigrate its formidable adversary and to counter his indictment of modern Jewish behavior. A lighter note was sounded, too, when Wise's *American Israelite* printed a poem summing up Smith's anti-Jewish position:

> To solve the Jewish question,
> And make the Hebrew pause:
> Smith offers the suggestion,
> "Suppress his Book of Laws;
> "If still his fixed division
> "From Gentiles he maintains,
> "Abolish circumcision:
> "'Twill minimize his brains.
> "And if this plan's miscarriage
> "Stops not his nation's life,
> "Enforce his intermarriage
> "With a non-Hebraic wife!"
> All points this drastic treatment clears,
> 'Tis simple, thorough, new:
> The Jewish question disappears,
> *And so, too, does the Jew!*

Frequently the newspapers cited non-Jews or comments from the secular and Christian press that independently took a stand against Smith. That tactic indicated, incidentally, the wide circulation that the historian's arguments enjoyed.

Of all Smith's charges, the attack on Jewish patriotism rankled most. To be sure, it was not a new charge. It had reverberated throughout Jewish history, winding its way through time and space ever since the image of the alien Jew and his questionable loyalty was delineated in the Bible in the words of Pharaoh and Haman. Nor was it unknown in the United States, where Jews had been accused of disloyalty on the eve of the Revolution and again during the Civil War. Usage, however, neither made the charge more palatable nor dulled fears about the security of the community at large. Besides, the allegation was more sweeping now than ever before, for it was rooted in the pseudoscientific axiom that lack of patriotism was endemic to the Jewish character. It threatened to rip to shreds the cherished beliefs that an ideological nexus linked Judaism with Americanism and that American Jews had earned their freedom and equality under a contract sealed in blood. If not effectively squashed, the refurbished image of the alien Jew boded ill for the still unemancipated European Jews as well. It questioned the desirability of enfranchising a group that remained a state within a state, and it undermined the willingness of western European nations and the United States to admit members of that stubborn tribe who landed on their shores.[70]

In 1891 Smith published an essay called "New Light on the Jewish Question" in the prestigious *North American Review.* He added little to what he had uttered before; the *Jewish Messenger,* in fact, emended the title to "Old Spite on the Jewish Question." Again, rejoinders appeared, especially to Smith's sneers about ruthless Jews who proved their base motives and lack of patriotism by a readiness to change their countries.[71] But the larger impact of the article testified to the steady inroads that racism and nativism had made during the previous half decade. The Haymarket affair of 1886 and its backlash, and the organization of the aggressively anti-Catholic American Protective Association in 1887 were but two signs of America's turn to a narrow nationalist cause that paralleled earlier European developments. The growing swell of immigration from southern and eastern Europe, bringing masses of non-Protestants who bore the stigma of inferior races, also contributed to an increasingly hostile temper. At universities, historians like Herbert Baxter Adams of Johns Hopkins were actively propagating the Teutonic theory of American origins, a thesis that accepted the importance of heredity and racial classification. One historian and sociologist, Richmond Mayo-Smith, expressed a notion increasingly popular with First Family Americans when he wrote that "only 'colonists' shared in the 'glory of having established the state,' while immigrants and their descendants forever occupied 'a subordinate position.'" The *American Hebrew* could well ask: "Pray! how many generations does it take to make a native, or . . . is a Jew always a foreigner and an intruder, however many generations back his ancestors may have dwelt in the land?"[72]

By 1891, Smith was no longer the only respectable writer who preached that Jews were unacceptable or unassimilable in Western society. Anna Dawes, an author of juvenile textbooks and the daughter of a senator from Massachusetts, was seemingly puzzled more than viciously anti-Semitic. What, she asked in a lengthy essay that appeared in 1884, was to become of the Jew in the modern world, which rested on the spirit of a "new nationality" and a "renaissance of patriotism"? Could the Jews, despite their talents, virtues, and achievements, which she genuinely admired, hold on to a distinct peoplehood while scattered among hostile nineteenth-century national states? Except for those Jews who were prepared to assimilate completely—and she considered them to be a very small minority—the rest favored Jewish separatism and thereby provided the justification for their persecutors. Perhaps because Dawes was quieter than Smith, her presentation was more ominous. "The Jew himself insists upon remaining a foreign element in every community," she said, "and an indigestible substance must be removed." She laughed off extremist solutions; the extermination of the Jews was as farfetched as a Jewish war against Christendom. The only remedy, and here she resembled Smith, lay in the wholesale colonization of the Jews outside the modern national states.[73]

Since the very climate of the country in the 1890s was attuned to Smith's diatribes, American Jewish leaders looked for fresh ways to erase the image of the religiously and racially alien Jew. In retrospect it is easy to see the handicaps that vitiated their efforts from the start. Committed to a faith in reason and fearful now of arousing suspicions of Jewish power, they were limited to the tools of education. Whereas the new anti-Semites propagated irrational prejudice, the Jews continued to believe that knowledge could influence rational men and blunt the power of the "Aryanomaniacs."[74] However, educational efforts also involved risks. They could easily amount to mere apologetics, projecting a pitiable if not laughable image of the overeager but insecure educator.

The need to present the positive role played by the Jew—neither parasite nor interloper—in American history loomed paramount. The Jewish community still lacked the proper resources to mount that campaign; a contemporary estimate that fewer than half a dozen scholars worked in the field of American Jewish history was overly generous.[75] To coincide with the 400th anniversary of Columbus's first voyage, Oscar Straus arranged for European historian Meyer Kayserling to write the history of the discovery of the New World and prove how Jews were significantly involved with America from earliest times. In 1885 Straus himself had published *The Origin of the Republican Form of Government in the United States of America*, a treatise in which he showed the influence of the Hebrew commonwealth on the early colonists' commitment to republicanism. In 1892 Straus was elected president of the newly founded American Jewish Historical Society. That institution, too, worked to counter the image of the alien Jew. Its original statement clearly indicated more than scholarly objectives:

The object of this Society is to collect and publish material bearing upon the history of our country. It is known that Jews in Spain and Portugal participated in some degree in the voyages which led to the discovery of America, and that there were Jews from Holland, Great Britain, Jamaica and other countries among the earliest settlers of several of the colonies. There were also a number of Jews in the Continental army, and others contributed liberally to defray the expenses of the Revolutionary war. Since the foundation of our government a number of Jews have held important public positions

Open to non-Jews (historian J. B. McMaster was one of the three vice-presidents), the society called itself nonsectarian. President Straus insisted that its activities would benefit the entire country; Americans would learn more about their own history when the Jews' contributions to the settlement of the colonies and the nation's prosperity, heretofore ignored by scholars, were uncovered. Concomitantly, historical research would confirm beyond the shadow of a doubt the right of the Jew to claim equally with any other white man that he was an American.[76] That latter precept appeared to have been uppermost in the minds of those whose articles were published by the society. Untrained and amateur historians for the most part, they concentrated before World War I on ferreting out the facts and documents relating to American Jewish life in the prerevolutionary New World. Their lack of methodology and their apologetic tone have been deservedly criticized, but they nonetheless built an institution that endured and one that over the years contributed to the development of a native Jewish culture.

"Prove our patriotism" appeared to have been the byword among Jews in the 1890s. Rabbi Edward Calisch of Richmond, Virginia, wrote a piece in which he lavishly praised the "indomitable Maccabaean spirit" displayed by the Jewish Confederate soldiers. Max J. Kohler put out a series of articles on "Incidents Illustrative of American Jewish Patriotism."[77] Meantime, Washington attorney Simon Wolf was busily tabulating the number of Jews who had served in American wars. His book, *The American Jew as Patriot, Soldier and Citizen*, devoted more than three hundred pages to Jews in the Civil War, mainly in the form of lists of individual names and regiments. Other chapters dealt with Jews in earlier wars, the contributions of Haym Salomon to the revolutionary cause, and Jewish recipients of the Medal of Honor.[78] Three years later, the American Jewish Historical Society resolved to compile a record of the Jewish soldiers and sailors in the Spanish-American War. That listing, as well as one by Baptist minister Madison C. Peters, was sent on by Oscar Straus to Theodore Roosevelt in 1903. Apparently responding to Roosevelt's query, Straus also informed him that seventeen Jewish sailors had gone down with the *Maine*.[79]

In 1806 the French Jews called by Napoleon to an Assembly of Notables had shouted "Jusqu'à la mort" when asked if Jews accepted the obligation to fight for their country.[80] Now, Americans were supplying chapter and verse to indicate how faithfully emancipated Jews had lived up to that promise.

Even the *Jewish Encyclopedia,* a prodigious twelve-volume work whose high scholarly level guaranteed its lasting usefulness, could not escape the obsession with defense. Published in 1901 through 1906, it marked another significant milestone in the cultural independence of American Jewry, and community leaders hailed its appearance. Joseph Silverman, who in 1901 was rabbi of New York's Temple Emanu-El and president of the Central Conference of American Rabbis, called it "a powerful weapon with which to disarm anti-Semitism and refute its false accusations, as well as correct the errors of a world that has never learned the full truth regarding Judaism and Israel." The British-trained scholar Joseph Jacobs stated publicly that the encyclopedia, on whose editorial board he served, would prove the groundlessness of charges that the Jews were interested only in "money-grubbing" and that they worked "more with the brain than the hands." The truth about Jews, he continued, was obscured by the enemies of cosmopolitanism and by the "new Imperialism" which in every country looked upon Jews as a state within a state. Harking back to the ideals of the French Encyclopédistes, he hoped that the *Jewish Encyclopedia* would carry forward still further the principles of liberty, equality, and fraternity.[81]

By linking Jews with cosmopolitanism and against the new nationalism, Jacobs ignored the changes forced by the new anti-Semitism on the posture of American Jews. On an ideological plane, Western Jews owed their emancipation to the teachings of the Enlightenment. In the free nations they had charted their course of survival along those same principles. The future looked particularly bright in the United States, whose ideological creed owed so much to the Age of Reason. As long as the spirit of cosmopolitanism tempered nationalism, no contradiction emerged between universalist concepts and national allegiance. Jews could and did insist upon equality and respect on the twin grounds of natural rights and their proven loyalty to the state. But when hypernationalism swept cosmopolitanism into disrepute and focused on the Jew as the embodiment of that evil, American Jews felt compelled to choose between the now antithetical currents. They doubtless agreed with Jacobs in principle, but the age-old habit of accommodationism as well as their immediate well-being dictated caution. Overwhelmingly they joined the nationalist side and concentrated above all on touting a consistent and unblemished record of patriotism. Logical precision also succumbed to the pressures of accommodationism: nationalism was good if it was American but bad if it was Jewish; universalism was bad if it drained the strength of political nationalism but good in religion if it propagated truths relevant to the modern world.

Zionism

Strictly speaking, Rabbi Bernhard Felsenthal of Chicago wrote in 1900, there were several Jewish questions. One concerned the form of Judaism; should it retain its traditional mold, or should it be altered? Another asked whether Jews should continue to exist as a separate people or be absorbed by other nationalities. A third, the question *par excellence*, had two parts: Were many Jews suffering just because they were Jews, and what was being done to ameliorate their lot? Felsenthal's answers to the first two questions were understood; a Reformer but one who consistently upheld Jewish racial distinctiveness, he disapproved of Jews plunging into " the ocean of mankind." As for the third question, Felsenthal said, the best answer for persecution lay in Zionism.[82]

For a Reform rabbi to support Zionism publicly in 1900 was exceptional, and in Felsenthal's case it was especially noteworthy. A radical Reformer and the friend and disciple of leaders David Einhorn and Samuel Adler, he had labored arduously from the 1850s on to root the principles of the German pioneer Reformers in American soil. Nevertheless, his turn to Zionism and his repudiation of Reform's mission concept was hardly a glaring about-face. Even in his radical days, Felsenthal had expressed his belief in the racial unity of the Jews. As early as 1883, fourteen years before Theodor Herzl launched the Zionist movement, Felsenthal had urged the colonization of the suffering east Europeans in Palestine. Moreover, the rabbi had come to fear the way in which American Reform, with too much zeal and too little discrimination, discarded traditional Jewish customs and institutions. He had warned in 1859, "Man soll nicht das Kind mit dem Bade ausschütten" ("Don't throw out the baby with the bath water"), and forty years later he worried lest Reform running wild lead inevitably to the extinction of Judaism and of Israel. To preserve "das Kind," Felsenthal the Zionist offered an emendation to the mission concept: Not through dispersion but as one nation among others would Jews serve the interests of humanity.[83]

Despite his age and the intellectual respect he enjoyed, Felsenthal was bitterly excoriated by many Reform colleagues for his disloyalty. If he had little impact among Reformers on the issue of Zionism, it was even harder for the younger men. The outspoken crusader Stephen S. Wise was cautioned by a friend: "No man in his right mind, especially an intelligent young rabbi intent on advancement, should support the Movement." Judah Magnes, who later became the first chancellor of the Hebrew University in Jerusalem, graduated from Hebrew Union College in 1900 and was shortly thereafter appointed to its faculty. Warned that his Zionist views were unacceptable, he served for less than two years. The professional loneliness of those Zionist Reform rabbis was assuaged somewhat by the ties that they cultivated with the newer immigrants, the more nationalist-minded Jews from eastern Europe. The unassuming Felsenthal, for example, won the confidence and admiration of the Orthodox leaders of Chicago for his devotion to the refugees. In New York, Magnes was the modern Maccabee in the eyes of the new immigrants; he learned their language and championed their causes. Unlike most of their German contemporaries, these men saw the east Europeans as fellow human beings and not merely as objects of charity. Stephen Wise described his feelings at the second Zionist Congress in Basel in a more dramatic fashion: "Suddenly, and as if by magic, I came upon a company of Jews who were not victims, nor refugees, nor beggars, but proud and educated men, dreaming, planning, toiling for their people."[84]

The small but impressive handful of Zionists within the established ranks of Reform also incuded Rabbi Gustav Gottheil and his son Richard. The rabbi had identified with the Reform movement in Germany, and after a short stay in England he came to New York to minister at Temple Emanu-El. The new anti-Semitism of the late nineteenth century in Russia, Germany, and the United States steered him to Zionism. He personally had experienced discrimination when he stopped at a restricted summer hotel in New York to request a night's lodging. The owner turned him down but retracted when he learned who Gottheil was. The rabbi, however, refused to take advantage of any exceptional favors. Gottheil enthusiastically endorsed the movement endorsed by Herzl in 1897, and the man who had eliminated all references to Palestine and Jerusalem from prayers now pinned his hopes on Zionism as a cure for anti-Semitism. A few months after the first Basel congress, he took part in organizing the Federation of American Zionists. His son was chosen president, and he and Stephen Wise were made vice-presidents.[85]

Richard Gottheil, who by 1897 was professor of Semitics at Columbia University, shared his father's feelings. "The 'Judenschmerz' rests heavily upon my soul," he wrote, and the Jewish feeling "which has been instilled into me from my youth upward" craved expression. Perhaps because of his academic career he was especially disturbed by quotas or outright bans against Jews set up by private schools. In 1898 he told Herzl that "we are on the brink of very difficult times in this country." Zionism, as he stated at that time in a public address, offered a practical solution to the problem of anti-Semitism. It provided a haven for those seeking to escape oppression, an inducement, he noted wryly, that should appeal to those Western Jews who feared the influx of heavy immigration into the United States. Zionism also had an ideological function. It held out the possibility of the regeneration of Jewry. If Jews had a national home in Palestine, their confidence and self-respect in the Diaspora would be raised. No longer would they feel like pariahs.

More than anti-Semitism accounted for Richard's Zionist commitment. His strong identification with his father seemed also to have bred a resentment against the smug, materialistic upper-class Jew—the vulgar rich of whom Temple Emanu-El doubtless had its share. It is plausible that the rabbi's son felt humiliated by the crass treatment that such people could and did mete out to rabbis, the "hired help." Years later Richard himself recalled in anger how the congregation erred in taking on Joseph Silverman as co-rabbi instead of assistant to Gottheil, and how Silverman operated to the discomfiture of the elder Gottheil. Zionist affiliation was Richard's way of declaring his independence of those circles and yet remaining loyal to his father. Once in office, the younger Gottheil seized numerous occasions to retaliate against the "well-fed dwellers in our golden western ghettos" who supported synagogues, choirs, and "staid church deportment." Lulled by their material comfort (whose level he and his father never approximated) into a mood of false security, they were insensitive to "kicks and hurts." He saw them as harbingers of the destruction of Judaism. Like the Berlin Jews of the early nineteenth century whose children drifted into Christian churches, they cast aside the racial and national bonds which underlay Judaism in favor of assimilation and twentieth-century "Salon-Judaism." Only something dramatic—perhaps the eruption of serious anti-Semitism in the United States—could wake them up. "The ice . . . is exceedingly thick," he wrote to Herzl, "and it will need quite a sharp pick-axe to break it open."[86]

Despite his contempt for the assimilating and materialistic Jew, Gottheil did not repudiate Reform. Rather, he argued that the American Reform movement lessened religious and literary anti-Semitism in the New World by having made the prayers intelligible and having shown the relevance of the synagogue to the modern world. A more elaborate defense of Reform appeared in his full-length book *Zionism*. There he wrote that Reform's motives to harmonize Judaism with the spirit of modernity were sincere. Reform failed, not because of its faults, but because the climate of opinion had changed. In a world that had shifted from the teachings of reason and universalism, Reform was out of place. Anti-Semitism could not be fought by rational arguments, and Reform's destruction of Jewish corporate unity rang hollow in an era that glorified nationalism. Gottheil saw no inherent contradiction between Zionism and the classical Reform mission. First, Zionism did not look to bring all Jews to Palestine. Second, by restoring Jewish unity and keeping more Jews within the fold, Zionism provided greater numbers who might propagate the mission.[87]

In his book and speeches, Gottheil tackled the charge that Zionism fomented dual allegiance and hence aggravated the anti-Semitic taunts of Jewish alienism and disloyalty. As he confided to Herzl, that was the major impediment keeping Jews "of substance" out of the movement. Gottheil's counterargument held Zionism analogous to the ethnic spirit that imbued Irish Americans and German Americans who were still good Americans. Good citizenship did not require racial unity; Germany, Austria-Hungary, as well as the United States were conglomerates of many races. Besides, the patriotism of German and French Jewry had not prevented anti-Semitism or the Dreyfus affair. The popular mood of heightened nationalism forced Gottheil, like Judah Magnes and then Louis Brandeis, to go beyond mere assertions that Zionists were patriots and to argue the rectitude of plural loyalties. Loyalty to the state did not preclude other loyalties, Gottheil said. In that way he and his Zionist colleagues foreshadowed the theory of cultural pluralism usually associated with the philosopher (and Zionist) Horace Kallen.[88]

Until 1904 Gottheil served as president of the Federation of American Zionists and on various committees of the world Zionist organization. His wife joined the movement with him and was one of the founders of Hadassah. In close contact with Theodor Herzl until the latter's death, also in 1904, Gottheil discussed all sorts of matters with the Zionist leader—from the purchase of a typewriter with Turkish characters to the serious obstacles that impeded the movement's growth in the United States. Gottheil was scarcely Herzl's passive mouthpiece; rather did he attempt to guide Herzl to an understanding of the peculiarities of the American Jewish experience. For example, when Herzl suggested that American Zionists use political pressure to gain government support, Gottheil instinctively recoiled. In customary American Jewish fashion, he cautioned Herzl against a course that would involve difficulties and embarrassments, and would prejudice the cause in the United States. Ironically, Gottheil found no inconsistency between that stance and the political character of Herzlian Zionism. The Jewish question needed to be treated as a political, and not a religious or philanthropic, problem, he told American Jews. Don't be put off by the "shibboleth" of mixing religion with politics.[89]

From Herzl's vantage point, Gottheil had the perfect credentials to serve as his lieutenant in the United States. Gottheil's achievements in the intellectual world guaranteed him respect from the new immigrants, the rank and file of the movement, despite suspicions the latter might entertain about his irreligiosity or his Western life style. More important to Herzl, Gottheil had access to that circle of Jews, the men "of substance," to whom the world organization looked for funds. At that juncture it was money rather than manpower that the organization wanted from Americans. Herzl himself interpreted Zionism to the Americans primarily as another philanthropy when he called upon them to remember the plight of the Jews in eastern Europe.[90]

Gottheil expended much time and energy attracting upper-class Jews for the Zionist cause. That need prompted him to advance the scheme of settling Jews in Mesopotamia, a plan elaborated in 1892 by Paul Haupt of Johns Hopkins that caught the fancy of men like Cyrus Adler and Oscar Straus. Straus, in particular, dreamed of an extra-Palestinian Jewish center in some province under Ottoman control. While minister to Turkey he had even broached those views to Secretary of State John Hay. According to Straus, even if the world were to grant the Jews the right to Palestine—which was highly doubtful since both Christians and Muslims claimed it as a holy land—that arid territory held out little chance of practical success. The Mesopotamia plan drew new encouragement in 1903 in the wake of the Kishinev pogrom which underscored the tenuous survival of Russian Jewry. At that time Straus formulated the idea of combining the plan for a refuge with the proposed Berlin-to-Baghdad railroad. He enlisted Schiff's interest, and although American firms were not likely to participate in the financing of the railroad, Schiff spread the idea among some influential European bankers. Meantime, Gottheil advised Herzl to reexamine the Mesopotamia project and to cultivate its supporters. The scheme fell through, but non-Zionists like Straus and Schiff were sufficiently enthusiastic to explore other territorialist plans up until World War I. To their minds, territorialism would serve the double purpose of relieving the east European situation and deflecting part of the immigration bound for America. Gottheil, who found it easier to turn to Cyrus Adler and Oscar Straus rather than to rabid anti-Zionists, also inclined toward a territorialist solution, at least temporarily, if that would secure the flow of American Jewish funds into the Zionist coffers.[91]

Money problems resulted from the active opposition that the nascent Zionist movement encountered under Gottheil's leadership within the American Jewish community. Orthodox Jews, critical of the secular cast of Herzlian Zionism, attacked restoration to Palestine contrived by man that ignored the need for a divinely commissioned Messiah. Socialists adhered to an ideology that repudiated all nationalism in favor of class loyalty. Far more significant, however, was the opposition of the established and acculturated Reform leaders, for they were organized, they controlled the important communal institutions, and they were the spokesmen of the Jews to the outside community. Indeed, the near hysterical attacks by Reform upon Zionism until World War I influenced non-Jews to an anti-Zionist stance.[92]

Despite the weakness of American Zionism until the war (the Federation of American Zionists reported fewer than 13,000 dues-paying members in 1914),[93] Reform took fright and with good reason. Unlike the Orthodox enemy, Zionism could not be dismissed as archaic or in conflict with the modern spirit. Zionism was a child of the modern age and, in fact, more attuned to the secular nationalist climate than Reform. On ideological grounds alone, Zionism constituted the direct antithesis to Reform.[94] Reform defined Judaism as religion; Zionism ignored religion and fixed upon race and nationality. Reform predicated its mission on the dispersion of the Jews; Zionism called for a physical Jewish center and the ingathering of the exiles. Reform, the child of the Enlightenment, optimistically awaited the ultimate triumph of enlightened justice; Zionism gloomily preached the eternal quality of anti-Semitism. Reform found the solution to the Jewish problem in rationalism; Zionism despaired of reason and made "desire" and "creative fancy" the keys to liberation.[95] As the *American Hebrew* summed it up, Zionist ideology "sent the Reform elements to a quick search for the reasons for their existence."[96] Since, as has been discussed earlier, Reform was simultaneously beset by its own spiritual crisis, it had no need of Zionism—a movement that could develop untold strength with the help of the new immigrants—to sap its vitality further.

Reform ranted at Zionism and its leaders through its institutions, pulpits, and press. Backward-looking, of foreign origin, misleading, and impractical were some of its favorite taunts. It scored significantly on two telling if overworked themes. One, that Zionism was un-American, touched an exposed nerve. The very word *un-American* dredged up the fears that crowded in on American Jews who pondered the significance of Bismarckian Jew hatred, the Dreyfus affair, and the spread of European anti-Semitic propaganda in the United States. Those fears had steered them to concentrate in the 1890s on proving their unqualified loyalty to the country. In an atmosphere charged with narrow nationalism abetted by racism, Zionism stood to reverse any progress that Jewish apologists had made. As crusades for Americanization grew stronger and hyphenates came under increasing attack, why conjure up a specter of Jewish Americans whose separate nationalist aims struck a discordant note in the mood of the country? The opening years of the century were far from different from the era of Adams and Jefferson when those statesmen had endorsed the restorationist scheme of Mordecai Manuel Noah. It was hard to conceive of an American head of state in 1900 supporting a this-worldly Zionism in the benign words of President John Tyler:

[T]he United States have adventured upon a great and noble experiment . . . that of total separation of Church and State. . . . The Hebrew persecuted and down-trodden in other regions takes up his abode among us with none to make him afraid. He may boast as well as he can, of his descent from the Patriarchs of Old. . . . He may even turn his eye to Judea resting with confidence on the promise that is made him of his restoration to that Holy Land.

Woodrow Wilson would bless the movement in 1918, but his views sprang from different motives and even then did not signify the country's acceptance of nationalist-minded minorities.[97]

The first argument interlocked with the second. Since Zionism was un-American it was the servant of anti-Semites, validating their indictment of the Jew and feeding them with unimpeachable evidence. Some Reformers also noted the receptivity of anti-Semites to a Jewish settlement in Palestine. Indeed, from Martin Luther in the sixteenth century to Colonel Edward House four hundred years later, there were Protestants who agreed that Palestine was a small price to pay to get rid of the Jews. In the United States, bigots like Telemachus Timayenis and Goldwin Smith, and the more neutral Anna Dawes as well, had absorbed the theory of colonization and argued that it would free the world of an eternally foreign body.[98] Such critics could find in Zionism an admission of Jewish unassimilability and in Zionists compatible bedfellows.

Like the theme of the wandering and alien Jew, that of the unbreakable link between Jews and Jerusalem had made its way into American folklore and popular usage. Invoked usually by Judeophobes, it connoted variously Jewish power, the focus of Jewish eternal longings, and, above all, the indelible foreign stamp that forever separated the Jew from his compatriots. The Know-Nothing agitator William Stow of California complained in 1855 about Jews who were ready to transfer their loyalty to a "new Jerusalem"; so did newspapers reviling the Confederate Jews in the aftermath of the Civil War. Patrician Henry Adams, tormented by the demon Jew, likened his own handicaps and alienation from society to those of a mythical Israel Cohen, "born in Jerusalem under the shadow of the Temple." In *Caesar's Column*, the antiutopian novel by Populist leader Ignatius Donnelly, a Jew who survived the destruction of a futuristic industrialized New York salvaged an immense fortune and fled to Jerusalem. The comic weekly *Judge* used a centerfold cartoon to depict the economic conquest of New York by the Russian Jewish immigrants; the caption read "Their New Jerusalem." The examples can be multiplied. Even the stories that appeared periodically on the purchase of Jerusalem by the House of Rothschild—which may not have been malicious in intent—also implied that those who made their fortunes in the West never shook off their ties to the East or their aspirations for a separate territorial domain.[99] Zionists provided the theme with a grounding in reality. Its opponents feared that a Jewish nationalist movement fixed on Zion could well topple the Reform-built ideological nexus between Judaism and the United States and with it the security of American Jewry.

On the one hand, Reform depicted an imminent and terrifying Jew hatred in order to frighten Jews away from Zionism. On the other, since the raison d'être of Herzlian Zionism was anti-Semitism, Reformers felt impelled to minimize its significance. Not quite sure which line to adopt, some anti-Zionists preached that persecution had a positive side. The Jew who stood up to bigotry developed stamina and vitality and learned a higher faith. Zionism, a counsel of surrender and flight, was the coward's retreat.[100]

When it chose arguments that transcended its ideological competition with Zionism, Reform constructed a forceful case. The thought that by its vilification of the nationalist movement it, too, succored anti-Semitism was not a deterrent. The case against Zionism also showed how gentile criteria for judging Jews could be absorbed unconsciously by the Jews themselves. For example, one of the reasons Gotthard Deutsch, professor of history at Hebrew

Union College, opposed Zionism was that he believed Jews lacked the capacity to govern themselves or build nations. Those same remarks might easily have come from the Teutonist school of American historians, who, at that same time, were attempting to prove the singular talent of Anglo-Saxons for constitutional government and self-rule.[101]

More vehement than any criticism from non-Jews in prewar America, Reform's opposition to Zionism touched off a debate within the Jewish community that raged fiercely until the Nazi era. The controversy divided families—Isidor Straus, co-owner of Macy's, was undeviatingly anti-Zionist; his brother and partner Nathan actively participated in and financed Zionist affairs; the third brother, Oscar, a territorialist, was somewhere in between. Zionism threatened to split congregations—at the onset of the Herzlian movement Rabbis Gustav Gottheil and Joseph Silverman, at dagger points over the issue of nationalism, agreed to ignore Zionism from Temple Emanu-El's pulpit.[102] Zionism also sharpened the lines dividing the religious factions within American Judaism and made Conservatism a more formidable challenger of Reform's hegemony.

Since the days of Isaac Leeser, Reform's antinationalist stance had posed an obstacle to the religious unity of American Jews. Reform's position, patterned on the decisions of the German rabbis at the 1845 Frankfurt Conference, hardened into rigid creed at the conferences of 1869 in Philadelphia and of 1885 at Pittsburgh. Although traditionalists cooperated with Reformers on civil matters, and although some even copied Reform practices in the synagogue, they did not relinquish the Jewish religious hope of a restoration to Palestine. Persecution in eastern Europe added a practical urgency to religious yearning, and when the Jewish Theological Seminary was organized in 1886 as a Conservative or counter-Reform institution, most of its supporters and faculty favored a Jewish nationalist movement.[103]

The reorganization of the seminary in 1902 under the presidency of Solomon Schechter occasioned a short-lived honeymoon between Conservatives and Reformers. The latter admired Schechter for his scholarship and forward-looking views on the evolution of Judaism. In a burst of enthusiasm Rabbi Emil Hirsch of Chicago declared that if his own son desired to become a rabbi, Hirsch would send him to Schechter. The latter reciprocated the display of cordiality and publicly called for a cessation of strife between the two factions.[104]

Basic differences, however, could not be glossed over for long.

Schechter appointed a faculty of outstanding scholars; some were also prominent Zionists. In 1906, the seminary's president in a public confession of faith planted himself squarely within the Zionist ranks. He did not mention Reform by name, but in his endorsement of Zionism he repudiated the ideology that denied a national Jewish consciousness and that welcomed the dispersion of Jewry for the fulfillment of the Jewish mission. Schechter's counterpart at Hebrew Union College, Kaufmann Kohler, responded immediately with a diatribe against Zionism and the Conservative leader. Kohler lashed out at the erstwhile optimist and modernist, now the pessimist and anti-Reformer, for choosing Zionism, "the very counterfeit of Judaism." Schechter and other Conservative leaders voiced their own criticisms of Zionism's secularist bent and its cultural deficiencies. Nevertheless, the rabbis trained by the Jewish Theological Seminary brought Zionism to all parts of the country; "where stood a Conservative synagog there stood a Zionist base."[105] The alliance thus cemented between Conservatism and Zionism endured, and it served both parties well. Combining nationalism with a modern Judaism, Conservatism attracted many of the newer immigrants who could neither go back to Old World Orthodoxy nor swallow the diluted universalism of Reform. By their commitment to Zionism, prewar Conservatives widened the breach with Reform. But their growing base of popular support ultimately enabled their movement to overtake Reform and break the latter's near monopolistic control of the community.

In 1907 Zionism shook the seminaries of both the Reformers and the Conservatives. During that academic year, one-third of Hebrew Union College's faculty—Henry Malter, Max Schloessinger, Max Margolis—resigned. Since all three men had expressed a commitment to Zionism, it appeared to Zionists and the public that they had been forced out because of their nationalist ideas. The three did not resign jointly, but their close association prior to their resignations was a matter of record as was their dislike of President Kohler. Each one charged that the president had attempted to muzzle free expression of Zionist ideas. In Malter's case, an article supporting Zionism was denied publication; Schloessinger was refused permission to participate in a Zionist banquet; Margolis was publicly rebuked by Kohler for having delivered a Zionist sermon in the college chapel. An invasion of *Lehrfreiheit* multiplied by three totaled up to a veritable witch-hunt.

Although technically Zionism was not the immediate issue when two of the resignations reached the board (Malter mentioned tenure and salary in his complaint of "unjust treatment," and it was Kohler who brought Schloessinger before the board on charges of insubordination), the anti-Kohler argument appeared plausible. Kohler's uncompromising stand against Zionism had been set years before he took office, and both the president and the board had found occasion after that to reaffirm the college's anti-Zionist posture. Coincidental or not, Kohler's assumption of office in 1903 had also spelled the termination of the teaching careers of two other Zionists at the college. Most telling, however, was Kohler's explanation of his behavior in the Margolis case, the one in which the Zionist issue was most evident. The president admitted that complete *Lehrfreiheit* could not be tolerated at a rabbinical seminary, that Margolis had infused Zionist ideas "subversive" of Reform theology into his teaching. Before the smoke cleared, two students resigned, alumni of the college divided for and against the president, and Zionists privately and publicly sputtered in righteous indignation.[106]

A few months later, Jewish circles buzzed about a rift at the New York seminary between the Reform-dominated board of directors and President Schechter. At the end of the summer, Jacob Schiff, the seminary's financial angel, made public two letters he had written to Schechter denouncing political Zionism. The core of Schiff's sentiments was summed up as follows:

[S]peaking as an American, I cannot for a moment concede that one can be at the same time a true American and an honest adherent of the Zionist Movement. . . . [H]onest Zionists—I mean if they believe and hope and labor for an ultimate restoration of Jewish political life and the reestablishment of a Jewish nation, . . . place a prior lien on their citizenship. . . . The Jew should not for a moment feel . . . that he is in exile and that his abode here is only a temporary or passing one. If those who come after us are to be freed from the prejudice from which this generation is . . . suffering, we need feel that politically no one has any claim upon us but the country of which, of our own free will, we have become citizens.

Schiff had regretted Schechter's Zionist statement of 1906, but at first he kept quiet. Subsequent events apparently convinced him of the growing menace of Zionism to the community's well-being and of the anti-Semitic backlash it generated. At Hebrew Union College the Zionists not only had the temerity to challenge the president, but the resignations exposed serious divisions within the Jewish ranks. In Germany that same year, the official preacher and teacher (*Prediger*) of the Berlin Jewish community was forced out because of his Zionist views, and a bitter public debate between Zionists and their opponents ensued. One of the anti-Zionist pamphlets from Germany came to Schiff's attention, and he passed it on with his comments to Schechter. Meantime, the banker spent a few days with Kaufmann Kohler and other leading Reformers at the Jewish Chautauqua assembly, where no doubt the Hebrew Union College issue was privately rehashed by the anti-Zionists. Schiff became more troubled when Schechter replied privately to the German pamphlet with a forceful defense of Zionism. The banker respected and admired the seminary's president for his erudition, but he feared the weight that Schechter's name would carry on behalf of the Zionist cause. Although Schechter begged him to give the Zionists the benefit of his counsel instead of attacking them, Schiff was persuaded by a few friends to stand up to Zionism publicly.

Upon the appearance of Schiff's first letter, Cyrus Adler of the Jewish Theological Seminary's board worried about its impact on the school and blamed both men for the controversy. The Federation of American Zionists, under the presidency of Harry Friedenwald, jumped to Schechter's defense, and once more the Zionists had to defend themselves against the charge of un-Americanism. "It is curious," Friedenwald sarcastically commented, "that this charge always comes from Jews who have themselves left Germany, the land of their birth."[107]

The publication of the letters failed to defuse the hot-tempered Schechter or the stubborn Schiff. The latter defended his action; it was his duty as a leading Jew to save his brethren from the dangers of Zionism. Until the messianic age, he insisted to Oscar Straus, "we shall have to remain the Eternal Jew, suffering from prejudice, *you* no less than I and the mass of our coreligionists. Meantime we, in our own generation, have at least this duty to our Country, which we ask to keep its gates open to our oppressed brethren . . . that we counteract [those] influences . . . upon these new Americans, which will keep them strangers in our midst." The president of the seminary promised that Schiff would yet hear from him, and in a long letter to Friedenwald he wrote:

Both Wall Street and the Pulpit have arrayed against us—by us I mean not only the Zionists, but as you rightly point out the Jews who still act and live and believe Judaism. I was and am still contemplating to present a memorandum [to] the Board of the Directors of the Seminary that though I do not make propaganda for Zionism in the institution I recognize and teach no other theology than that given to us by the Prayer Book and Rabbinic

Judaism which is that [Hebrew words: "for our sins we were exiled from our land"], that America is not the final destiny of Judaism, that we believe in the advent of the Messiah who will redeem Israel and bring us back to the Holy Land etc. If they think that these doctrines are incompatible with Americanisation as they understand it and which they believe to be the salvation of the Jews they can have my resignation at once. I would prefer to starve than to keep them under any illusion or to abandon my principles.

Schechter did not resign, and he restrained himself or was restrained from carrying on the exchange further. Except for a statement from board chairman Louis Marshall, the directors closed ranks and maintained a discreet silence. Replying to a taunt by Reform's official organ, the *American Israelite*, Marshall announced that every student and faculty member at the seminary, like every director, had the right to make up his own mind about Zionism. With Hebrew Union College's recent trouble in mind, Marshall countered smugly that the New York seminary never had attempted to stifle intellectual liberty or "to make an auto-da-fé of Jewish thinkers for the delectation of the anti-Semites."[108]

The anti-Zionists who taunted the nationalists with charges of un-Americanism misread the character of American Zionism. Unlike the situation in eastern Europe, where Zionism promised personal salvation to many of the oppressed, American Jews did not latch on to the movement primarily out of selfish considerations. From the beginning American Zionism neither demanded nor expected an existential commitment from its adherents that they give up on the United States and move to Palestine. We are not asking you to go, Richard Gottheil stated many times; "we are striving for a Jewish home and a safe political condition for those Jews who have no such home, and a Jewish environment for those who feel that they need such."[109] Zionists talked of Jewish national consciousness and unity, of the pernicious force of anti-Semitism even in Western society, and of the need to regenerate Jews and Judaism, but the new homeland they proposed to build would be for others. Zionism would strengthen American Jewish cultural resources and ethnic pride but *in America*. Since Zionism in practical terms meant scarcely more than refugeeism, the cry of "either Zionists or good Americans" had little intrinsic validity.

In the pages of the *Maccabaean*, the monthly journal of the Federation of American Zionists, the ambivalent strains of American Zionist thought were manifested. The journal followed standard Zionist theory when it described the abnormal life of the Jews in the Diaspora. Even in the United States, Jews lived an unreal, rootless existence where *Luftmenschen* substituted for productive citizens, where assimilation jeopardized the perpetuation of Jewish values, and where anti-Semitism belied the claim that Jews had found their Zion. Had the *Maccabaean* followed those premises to their logical conclusion, it would have withdrawn in gloomy pessimism from the American scene. Rather, the journal was very much engaged. When it challenged and refuted anti-Semites, when it urged the government to keep to a rigid separation between church and state, or when it encouraged Jews to stand for political office, it showed an unqualified commitment to a Jewish future in the United States. In and of both the American and Zionist worlds, the *Maccabaean* understandably countered the argument of dual allegiance. It saw nothing wrong in United States ethnic nationalities' retaining their special interests. However, in the spirit of nineteenth-century Jewish behavior, it disapproved of the political organization of American Jews as a distinct nationalist group.

Early Zionists also found ways of identifying their movement directly with Americanism. The emphasis on refugeeism was a case in point. To provide for the unfortunate victims of successive pogroms in the first decade of the twentieth century was a commendable, humanitarian purpose in the eyes of Americans generally. To deflect the immigration of the victims away from the United States was at least as laudable. On a different level, the Zionist objective of wresting communal control from the established, anti-Zionist Jewish oligarchs harmonized with American progressivism. Just as Progressives preached the extension of political democracy, so did Zionists battle against the "unrepresentative," and hence un-American, character of American Jewish leadership. When Louis Brandeis assumed control of the American Zionist movement in 1914, he synthesized Zionism with Americanism and made the movement virtually an experiment in progressivism. His leadership assured the successful organization of the American Jewish Congress, an agency chosen democratically to represent American Jewry at the Versailles peace conference and one of the first major defections from German Jewish control.[110]

In sum, then, perhaps the hysteria with which Reform greeted Zionism was justified. By challenging Reform's domination of communal institutions, Zionism in its Americanized form contributed to the ultimate eclipse of the German Jewish establishment.

7

RAZING THE GHETTO WALLS

IN November 1905, American Jews marked the 250th anniversary of their settlement in the United States. The celebration itself was to have been a grand and joyous event. A committee representing Jews of all states and territories and working for the better part of 1905 had prepared special religious services for synagogues and Jewish schools. It had enlisted cooperation of secular institutions as well—Jewish lodges, orphan asylums, the Young Men's Hebrew Association, the National Council of Jewish Women—which scheduled their own commemorative services. Plans also called for the erection of a memorial and for the publication of a popular history of the Jews in the United States. The committee's target date for staging the public celebrations was Thanksgiving Day, a fitting occasion on which to combine gratitude for America's greatness and beneficence to the Jews with retrospective surveys of Jewish achievements and contributions to the development of the nation from pre-Revolutionary days.

But by the time Thanksgiving Day arrived, a discordant note had soured the festive mood. A new wave of pogroms unleashed by the Russian government in October had claimed the attention of the American Jews. Not only was it imperative to raise funds for the victims of czarist brutality, a need which arrested plans for the memorial, but ways also had to be found to ensure the long-term security of the Russian Jews either in their own land or, more likely, through immigration to the West. The anniversary celebrations went off as scheduled, and Christian speakers and newspaper editors joined Jews in extolling the latter's virtues and successes. But the Jewish celebrants could not escape the pall cast by the events in Russia. Many felt constrained to defend the Jew generally against anti-Semitic charges or to extol those Russian Jews who had landed on American shores a few years earlier.[1]

The horrors of Odessa and Bialystok in 1905 confirmed the fears that had long gnawed at American Jewish leaders. Since the 1880s it was clear that their community, and not only those of the victims, would experience serious reverberations from the intensified persecution in eastern Europe. The stream of hundreds of thousands of immigrants to the United States from Russia and Romania showed no sign of abatement. On the eve of the Great War, the total number would reach close to 2 million. Out of practical necessity the established Jews took on the ever-swelling burdens of providing for the adjustment and integration of the new arrivals. Simultaneously they used their influence to keep America's doors open to succeeding waves of refugees. Pressure on Russia, through Jacob Schiff's economic boycott, or the American Jewish Committee's campaign for abrogation, or government statements in defense of human rights, was desirable. But so long as the czarist regime refused to modify its anti-Jewish policies, the first priority was to secure havens for those able to escape. Those were the problems, Schiff confided to Oscar Straus, that caused him sleepless nights.[2]

Ironically, the more the German Jews accomplished on behalf of unrestricted immigration and the more their philanthropies on behalf of the new arrivals succeeded, the more they undercut themselves. By 1900 American Jewry had reached a crossroads. Already outnumbered by the immigrants, the Germans were facing the fate that they had earlier meted out to their predecessors, the Sephardim. It was only a matter of time before numerical superiority would triumph and control of the community pass, this time from the Germans to the east Europeans.

The response of the established American community to the east Europeans in the first decade of the twentieth century captured in microcosm the essence of the Jewish encounter with emancipation. Within one decade the same questions that challenged Jews transplanted to a free environment surfaced all at once. What were the responsibilities of kinship that the Germans owed the immigrants? Were those responsibilities in any way limited, say, by the desire to conform to public opinion or government policy? How was the immigrant to be molded into a proper Jew and proper American? How much of his religious customs could be preserved without danger of hindering his Americanization or social acceptability? If left alone, the east Europeans, on their self-propelled course of rapid acculturation, would have come in time to cope independently with those same questions. However, under the determined tutelage of the Germans, as well as by their example, immigrants were inundated with the precedents and values—and ambivalences—of the established Jews. The latter, telescoping their accumulated experiences into a few short years, inculcated their message of how best to live comfortably and securely as Americans and as Jews. A sense of urgency underlay that message, an urgency reflecting more than the desperate situation in eastern Europe or mounting social discrimination in the United States. Time was running out on the Germans, and if they did not educate the newcomers properly, the latter might well change the face of the community and turn around the course of its development.

New Immigrants and Ghetto Problems

By the end of the nineteenth century the German Jews were well absorbed into most levels of American life. A predominantly middle-class urban group, their economic rise had been rapid and impressive. Poor and untutored for the most part upon their arrival from central Europe, some had actually lived the Horatio Alger myth of rags to riches. Their children attended prestigious American universities; their synagogues, many under the aegis of the newly centralized Reform movement, had penetrated into almost all the states and territories of the union; their ever-expanding network of philanthropic and social organizations serviced the various welfare and leisure-time needs of their kinsmen. In 1906, one of their number, Oscar S. Straus, was appointed secretary of commerce and labor, the first cabinet post ever filled by a Jew.

But despite their progress—or perhaps in some measure because of it—they found themselves after 1880 barred increasingly from American social resorts, private clubs and schools, and professional organizations. Discrimination and hostility drew from a variety of causes, most importantly from the inability of many Americans to come to terms with the radical changes wrought by modern industrialization upon the character of the nation. The Jew who flourished in the urban industrial economy became the symbol of the evils that frustrated Americans of different social and economic classes read into the passage of Old America. From the haughty invectives of Henry Adams to the popular journals or vaudeville acts that caricatured the hooknosed European Jewish merchant, the image of the Jews—compounded of Shylock, avaricious entrepreneur, and anti-Christian—reached all levels of American society. Conspiracy theories and racist doctrines born in Europe found their way to the United States, reinforcing old stereotypes about Jews as a group and making it correspondingly more difficult for the acculturated individual to be accepted on his own merits. American Jews greeted the dawn of the twentieth century with far less optimism than they had expressed earlier. Although the potentially explosive charge that President McKinley had been assassinated by a Jew evoked no significant response,[3] many established American Jews grew more accustomed to explain anti-Semitism as a constant condition. "As long as the Jew is," Rabbi Emil G. Hirsch stated flatly, "there will of necessity be Jew-hating."[4]

Sobered by the growth of discrimination, the Germans could justifiably fear that the arrival of the numerous east European Jews would undermine the status of the acculturated Jews still further. It was bad enough when a Joseph Seligman was denied entry into a summer hotel, or when an Oscar Straus or a Benjamin Peixotto was blackballed by civic clubs,[5] but who would rise to the defense of such individuals if Christians classified them with the "uncivilized" new immigrants? Even friends of the Jews attributed American anti-Semitism at least in part to Jewish clannishness and self-segregation. Now critics could find ample justification for such charges in the spectacle of the Yiddish-speaking "dirty," "diseased," and "shifty" aliens who swarmed to the cheap tenements of the nation's largest cities and established new ghettos on American soil.

It made little difference to the Germans that the overwhelming proportion of other "new" immigrants from southern and eastern Europe also settled in urban ethnic slum enclaves or that native Americans were abandoning their traditional habitats for the action of the urban frontier. The Jew was the most vulnerable, for unlike the Italian, Greek, or Pole he was burdened with the stereotypes of economic parasite, nonproducer, petty trader, and pawnbroker. Always the outsider in Christendom and the eternal alien, he was adjudged, in addition, as being of inferior racial stock. The east European Jew did not cause anti-Semitism in the United States, but since racists and nativists converged to proclaim his unassimilability, his presence threatened to undo the efforts invested by an entire generation in gaining acceptance within American society.[6]

With their own security on the line, German Jews could not help but resent the immigrants. Different languages, cultural and religious forms, and basic life styles as well as prejudices carried over from Europe widened the gap even further between the westerners and easterners.[7] Resentment and fear might have logically led the established Jews to join the mounting public chorus for immigration restriction. At first, they did speak of "selected" immigration, but as the situation in eastern Europe worsened, they could not remain hostile or even indifferent to the need of Jews to emigrate. Imbued with a sense of peoplehood that emancipation could not obliterate, the leaders of the American Jewish community determined to protect the east European's lifeline to freedom, to see that America kept its doors open to the oppressed.

Once the immigrants arrived, there was no question that major tasks of ameliorating the problems of the uprooted and the destitute would devolve upon the established community. Unlike the Italians, who still had some support from the fatherland as well as from sympathetic native organizations to supplement the help from municipal services, the Jewish immigrants could appeal only to private Jewish sources. The earlier arrivals from eastern Europe who had come to enjoy even modest economic success formed their own organizations to help out their *landsleit*, but their resources and fund-raising abilities were severely limited.[8]

Not only was the philanthropic role of the private sector critical in the prewelfare-state era, but American Jewish pride, reinforcing the ties of peoplehood, was also at stake. Nineteenth-century Jews looked back with satisfaction on their tradition of communal philanthropy which they had so assiduously cultivated. Heeding myriads of appeals to help the unfortunate, they had more than lived up to the initial injunction to care for their own imposed in 1655 upon those who landed in New Amsterdam. Often praised by non-Jews for their philanthropy, Jews risked a severe loss of face if they were to dodge the responsibility of the new immigrants. Besides, since the American public and government had expressed their sympathy for the east European victims of persecution and pogroms, the American Jew could do no less. "The American Jew who . . . is less humane and sympathetic than the whole American people is neither a good American nor a good Jew," said B'nai B'rith president Leo N. Levi shortly after the Kishinev massacre.[9]

Admittedly, philanthropy held out selfish advantages for the donors. If handled properly, the immigrant masses could yet be transformed by the established Jews into "civilized" human beings properly Americanized and ultimately acceptable to society at large. With the help of appropriate institutions, the immigrants could absorb the values and behavioral codes, both for individuals and for the community, of their benefactors. Tutored and tamed at the same time that they were being helped, they might even come to recognize the Germans as the leaders and taste makers for the entire community.

After 1880, the established American Jews fought simultaneously for the rescue of the east Europeans and the defusing of

American anti-Semitism. Although the two goals at times appeared to be mutually contradictory, one avenue offered a promise of realizing both. It called for lowering the visibility of the immigrants by breaking down the squalid immigrant ghettos as well as the ghetto mentality of the aliens. The lower their visibility, the less likely were the newcomers, first, to generate nativist drives against further immigration and, second, to sully the image of the established Jews.

Hardly any aspect of immigrant life remained untouched by the German Jews in the antighetto crusade. Even the support of playgrounds and organized forms of recreation stemmed from, among other reasons, a desire to save the immigrant youth from the evils of "alien" radicalism. In a totally unrelated area, the famous cloakmakers' strike of 1910 that pitted Jewish workers against Jewish employers, a similar concern obtained. According to one account, fear of what outsiders might say about Jews involved in labor strife prompted men like Louis Marshall and Jacob Schiff to press for a mediated settlement.[10]

On some matters the immigrant presence contributed to a shift in behavioral patterns of the established community. For example, the customary tirades against Sunday laws which did not exempt Sabbath observers abated noticeably when ghetto residents flagrantly violated those ordinances. No doubt the German Jews recalled their own solemn promises made many years before not to offend public taste by Sunday labor. Now, securing exemption to the Sunday laws appeared less important than educating the immigrants to conform to public opinion.[11] Far more dramatic, as discussed below, was the impact of the east Europeans on the political behavior of the Jewish establishment.

Overall, the most significant change was the rise in ethnic consciousness on the part of the Germans. Signs of heightened ethnicity appeared long before the Russians came to dominate the Jewish community. The process began when the Germans made the multifaceted Russian problem—from the persecution in Europe to the physical and cultural needs of the new arrivals in the United States—their paramount concern. Since the focus was ethnic, so were the responses. In the case of political lobbying and philanthropic work, fulfillment of the responsibilities of kinship automatically reinforced ethnic ties. Other instances, notably the drive to Americanize the immigrants, elicited from some established Jews a conscious recognition of Jewish peoplehood and ethnic interests. Still others, as previously noted, felt impelled to work actively in the nascent Zionist movement, the most extreme expression of ethnicity. On all those levels, the Russian problem revitalized the Jewish sensitivities and creativity of a minority that had heretofore concentrated mainly on its absorption into the larger society.

Corresponding to the ever-swelling wave of immigrants from eastern Europe, the antighetto crusade reached a peak in the decade before World War I. In the 1890s Jews had accounted for more than 10 percent of the more than 3.5 million immigrants; in the next decade, driven by intensified persecution in Romania and Russia, close to 1 million new arrivals raised the Jewish share of immigration to 11 percent. The numbers were staggering, especially since the overwhelming proportion settled in closely confined areas in the nation's largest cities of the North Atlantic states.[12] As it had since the 1880s, the Jewish presence continued to draw comments and investigations by Jews, non-Jews, and the government. Reactions ranged from sympathy to scorn. Some were captivated by the mystery and creative resources of a persecuted people buffeted by misfortune from land to land. Others sneered at the "pariahs," while missionaries rushed in to save the souls of the benighted or at least those of their children. More neutral observers, muckrakers, and social scientists who reported on the curious ghetto dwellers compared their habits with those of other groups or measured their stature and proneness to disease. All agreed, however, that their living conditions were abysmal and that the overcrowded ghetto spawned grave physical and social ills.[13]

While cities like Chicago and Philadelphia were often cited for their problems, New York had the dubious distinction of being the worst. To most east Europeans intent on emigrating, New York *was* the United States. The city that Henry Adams had dubbed "the sink of races" boasted in 1902 a Jewish section on the Lower East Side whose population equaled that of Detroit. President Leo Levi of B'nai B'rith called the Jewish quarter in that year "worse hell than was ever invented by the imagination of the most vindictive Jew-hater of Europe." Cyrus L. Sulzberger, director of New York's United Hebrew Charities, passionately charged at a conference of representatives of Jewish charities that others, even Jews, forgot that the ghetto inhabitants were human beings who were faring worse than cattle.[14]

The chief priority was to provide immediate relief to the destitute, the orphaned, the sick, and the unemployed. Sulzberger once recounted the manifold activities of his agency on a typical day in 1901:

We make 145 investigations. . . . We record 35 applications for employment, and find employment for 17 people. We grant transportation to three people and give half tons of coal to seven. We distribute 150 articles of clothing and furniture. We give two nights' lodging and seven meals. We have fifteen visits made by our doctors, and sixteen calls made upon our doctors in their offices. We have 45 cases for our nurses. Our doctors write 38 prescriptions, and there is one surgical operation. Thirty-six garments are made or repaired in our work room; 125 immigrants are registered at the Barge Office, making a total of 678 different kinds of things done in an ordinary working day.[15]

On-the-spot help for tens of thousands was far from simple to give. The cost alone was staggering, and the number of donors did not increase as the needs multiplied. A contemporary European observer noted that recourse was always limited to the same purses. Despite the periodic exhortations in the Anglo-Jewish press on the responsibility of the entire community, not all Jews went along willingly. Some feared that the very act of giving might cast suspicion upon the level of Jewish prosperity; some argued that refusing charity might discourage the prospective almoner from settling in the ghetto. Others worried lest indiscriminate charity foster the rise of a permanent pauper class. For their part, the east Europeans were often too proud to ask for aid. Some representatives of the newcomers, particularly socialists of the Abraham Cahan stripe, had only contempt for the uptowners' charity and agreed that the immigrant was better off without that humiliation.[16]

The German Jews poured funds and energies into cures and palliatives for the "leprosy of the ghetto walls."[17] Operating at a time when the pragmatic, environment-centered, and optimistic aura of the Progressive mood colored the national temper, they took heart from the prevailing belief that rational man could improve human destiny by structured reform. The social-justice plank of Reform's Pittsburgh Platform spurred on rabbis to join actively in schemes to meliorate the immigrant's condition. Experimenting with different forms of relief, the Germans established new agencies to cope with problems of family desertion, the care and rehabilitation of tuberculosis victims, juvenile crime, mechanical training for the newcomers, Americanization, and the removal of the immigrants from the ghettos to less congested areas. Even the formation in 1906 of the American Jewish Committee, whose express purpose was to defend the rights of Jews wherever they were under attack, reflected the immigrant presence. It attempted to obviate the establishment of a more radical organization, more appealing to east Europeans who were not attracted or attractive to older German associations. Two years later, New York City's Lower East Side Jews set up the Kehillah, an umbrella organization that dealt with community problems of education, crime, philanthropy, and religious standards, but the Kehillah's existence depended upon the financial help of the old-timers grouped in the American Jewish Committee. In the meantime, older organizations were sharpening their specifically immigrant-oriented operations. B'nai B'rith, regarding itself as the patron of the Romanian Jews who arrived after 1900, was active in settling those Jews in areas in the interior of the country. The order also erected new lodges in the ghettos to service the cultural and social needs of the immigrants and ultimately to weld them with the older stratum into one community. The National Council of Jewish Women assumed new responsibilities particularly with respect to the immigrant Jewish girl. In 1907, in a response to a request from the federal government, the council erected a permanent station for immigrant aid on Ellis Island. The major organization dedicated to immigrant relief, the Baron de Hirsch Fund, expanded, too, and during this decade it enthusiastically boosted projects for removal work and agricultural training.[18]

Organization and experimentation set the tone, and by 1910 it was estimated that American Jews were spending $10 million annually on philanthropy. In light of their tradition, the Germans could take pride in the fact, pointed out by a sympathetic non-Jewish observer, that none of the Jewish immigrants was permitted by coreligionists to become a public charge. Another shred of comfort was purely accidental; with so many destitute Jewish immigrants, anti-Semites would be hard put to bandy about the image "as rich as a Jew."[19]

The multiplication of organizations accompanied suggestions for a scientific approach to philanthropy, consolidation of agencies, and preventive rather than curative charity. Organized charity also meant the replacement of the donor-director by the professional manager and the volunteer by the salaried staff worker. One-man crusades—Nathan Straus's free pasteurized milk stations or Adolph Benjamin's unending battle against the missionaries—became far less common. In 1893 Lillian Wald had taken up residence in the tenements, where she served as social worker, employment agency, psychological counselor, as well as visiting nurse. Her salary, and often food and clothing for her clients, came from Schiff and his mother-in-law. Wald reported directly to them, recounting individual cases which she handled as well as some in which Schiff had taken a personal interest. Within a very short time these modest beginnings led to the erection of the Henry Street Settlement House and the Visiting Nurses Service, agencies with broader programs that serviced non-Jews alongside Jews. Unquestionably more efficient, such faceless agencies perforce watered down the "human touch" in philanthropy. After all, how many scientifically run charities would have taken the money, as Schiff had, to build a fountain at Canal Street and East Broadway solely for the enjoyment of those who occupied the oppressively hot and ill-ventilated tenements of the Lower East Side?[20]

Americanization with Jewish Content

While the emphasis was on organization, specialization, and federation—the latter, a Jewish "first," also influenced general philanthropic trends [21]—a question arose that has continued to plague Jewish organizations. Should Jews maintain separate agencies if they were bereft of specific Jewish content or values? Independent Jewish charities, which since the first half of the nineteenth century had been divorced from synagogal control, steered clear of religious involvement. Hoping to escape the divisiveness and attrition that beset organized religion, philanthropy, particularly when handled by professionals, donned what amounted to nonsectarian garb. When the heavy influx of east Europeans had begun, synagogues in New York and other cities had attempted to carve a more active role in social welfare. Sisterhoods in particular had assumed responsibilities for specific groups of the new immigrants. Before long, however, their work was absorbed by the professional agencies.[22]

The drive for more Jewishness in Jewish philanthropy came from acculturated Jews after the turn of the century. Louis Marshall sounded the note in a paper delivered to the National Conference of Jewish Charities in 1908 calling for religious instruction and observance, and even the teaching of Hebrew, in institutions like settlement houses, orphanages, and reformatories. He hoped that a civil service steeped in the knowledge of Judaism (which was not "apologetic," "mealy-mouthed," or "pasteurized" Judaism) would soon be produced by the Hebrew Union College and the Jewish Theological Seminary. Marshall, and the rabbis who were working at that time for kosher food departments in Jewish hospitals, doubtless believed that institutions with Jewish content would sooner gain the support of the traditional immigrants and allay their suspicions of their Americanized benefactors. It is interesting that the only one to disagree with Marshall at the 1908 conference was Boris

Bogen, a Russian Jew who, as director of Jewish charities in Cincin-nati, was actually an employee of the Germans. According to Bogen, religion could not mix with charity. Besides, he said—and here he laid bare a major area of contention between the German and the ethnic-oriented east European—religion alone did not account for the existence of Judaism.[23]

The gap between Judaism and philanthropy could also be bridged if the modern synagogue moved into the forefront of wel-fare activities. That idea among others propelled Rabbi Stephen S. Wise to found the Free Synagogue in New York in 1907. "Free" meant just that—no dues or pews, not a "rich man's club" or center of wealth and fashion, but a place where Jews of all classes could mix freely. The energetic and charismatic rabbi, who was always an ardent champion of liberal causes, sought to breathe new life into the synagogue by establishing three coordinate departments under its aegis: worship, education, and social services. Through the De-partment of Social Services, he aimed to arouse the social con-science of the synagogue's membership, to fight for social action, and to respond to the needs of the Jewish community. One such need, according to Wise, was to instill greater Jewish content into the philanthropic network and to counter the de-Judaizing as well as depersonalizing aspects of professionalization. In tune with the Social Gospel movement of the day, and along the path charted by Emil Hirsch of Chicago, Wise's plans for the Free Synagogue blended the specific problems of the immigrant with the social-justice crusade of the churches. In a letter to a prominent Chicago minister, the rabbi enumerated the specific questions he hoped to put before his congregation:

The Free Synagogue is planning a series of addresses . . . on the theme "Some Social Problems of Our Age." Among the subjects to be considered under the general title are "Utilization of the Immigrant," "Constructive Charity," "The State and the Wrongdoer," "Child-Saving." . . . I write to ask that you have the kindness to make an address on "The Outreach-ing Church." I trust that you may feel moved to render this important ser-vice. . . . You *must* render this service. . . . It is *your* cause as well as mine. Yours is *the* Outreaching Church. Tell us how you did it, & help us to do likewise.[24]

While the movement was a new one in the twentieth century, it merely turned the American synagogue back to its position of colo-nial and early national days as the prime locus of nonreligious as well as religious communal needs.

The need to instill Jewish content in communal agencies appeared straightforward enough when argued on grounds that it could counteract juvenile crime or the lures of missionaries and their settlement houses for Jewish children.[25] However, when it touched on the issue of Americanization, it raised deeper questions: Were the two aims of Americanization and Jewish commitment compatible or contradictory? Did they share equal importance, or did one take precedence over the other? Could they be made to operate in tandem? The old-timers found no definite answers in their personal experience. True, they or their parents had also been immigrants, but in their case acculturation had been virtually automatic. Now, differences in numbers, density of settlement, American receptivity, and the newcomers' own interpretations of Judaism changed the automatic process into an obstacle course. It was their duty, the established Jews decided, to mediate between the immigrant and his surroundings and to find ways to balance Americanism with Jewishness.

Ever since the 1880s, *Americanization* had been the magic word. To American Jewish leaders it signified a veritable cure-all. Reflecting the environmentalist ideology of the Progressive era, Americanization connoted optimism and the belief in progress. In tune with their Progressive contemporaries, Jews employed terms like *moral uplift* to describe the Americanizing process. By that process the east Europeans would be transformed into clean, healthy, English-speaking, educated, patriotic individuals. Even if the ghetto could not be emptied physically, its psychological stranglehold could be broken. "The ghetto," Rabbi Maurice Harris said, "is a status as well as a place." Morris D. Waldman, rabbi turned social worker, called it "a state of mind." Once free of the ghetto's restraints and its alien way of thinking, the new and now respectable Americans would be readily acceptable to the general society. Simultaneously, while their benefactors would be relieved of a major source of expense and embarrassment, the entire Jewish community would escape the threat of Russianization.[26]

The more acute the ghetto problems and the more intense the oppression in eastern Europe, the more impatient the Germans became. For the benefit of the old and new American Jews and for those still hoping to arrive, the process of Americanization had to be speeded up. The public school, the great equalizer, was central to that process. There, the Russians, like the Germans before them, and, indeed, like all immigrant groups, would learn the country's language and its history. The Jewish school of the east European shtetl, the heder, was worse than useless—it was regressive. A writer in the *Jewish Messenger* had suggested some years back that a family whose children attended heder should be refused charity.[27] The established Jews warmly supported ventures that supplemented the public school's teaching of language and civics—primarily settlement houses as well as special day and evening classes. "We must take [the immigrants] by the hand," Rabbi Abram Hirschberg admonished his colleagues in the Central Conference of American Rabbis, "and we dare not leave them until we have made them at home with our customs and institutions." Neither the Slavs, nor Italians, nor Hungarians, nor any other ethnic group showed the same concern as the Jews for rapid Americanization, a Philadelphia attorney correctly noted at a Jewish Chautauqua meeting in 1905.[28]

In addition to the rudiments of citizenship, the established Jews sought to inculcate values and codes of behavior as part of the Americanization process. The Anglo-Jewish press, for example, purveyed a virtual list of "dos and don'ts" for the benefit of the newcomers.[29] Most of their strictures amounted to a counsel of low visibility: e.g., obey the law; avoid organized Jewish political activity; shun all forms of radical "isms"; guard against self-ghettoization. Implicit in those admonitions were two reminders: (1) Whatever any individual Jew does reflects upon the entire community; (2) we, the Germans, have worked hard to create the image of a law-abiding, loyal, America-oriented group—don't undo it.

The content of the Americanization program of the settlement houses was determined by the Germans with an ever-watchful eye on the non-Jews. The Educational Alliance of New York and similar institutions paid little attention, especially at their inception, to the desires and emotional comfort of the immigrants. The chemist-philanthropist Morris Loeb bluntly stated in 1903:

It is our duty to provide for the Americanization of the Jewish immigrant even more than for his physical welfare. Experience has shown that our Jewish immigrant, if allowed to land and given a fair chance . . . can thrive and prosper without much aid from the outside; but they will *not* be allowed to land, if it becomes apparent that they are willing to eat American bread but not adopt American habits of thought and action. . . . [I]t is our duty toward our fellow-citizens that we shall interpret to these new-comers the traditions of the country to which they have come, we, that is, who are Western by birth and education, who have the American way of thinking and acting, the Jewish way of feeling and sympathizing, both innate.

Condescension was not the issue; to "improve" the immigrant by teaching him English, civics, American history, and American ideals was.[30]

At a conference in 1903, David Blaustein, who served as director of the Educational Alliance at the turn of the century, gave his formula for "The Making of Americans." Most of his recommendations, from the teaching of English and civics to an emphasis on physical education, reflected accepted norms of the Theodore Roosevelt period. When Blaustein underscored the need to break up the ghetto and put the Jew in agriculture, he was echoing the "back to the soil" movement of his day. Since patriotism figured prominently at the time, Blaustein's prescription encompassed that also:

It is part of our work in the making of Americans, to make the immigrant understand and feel what a victory was won for his country at Concord and Lexington, what a deliverance was secured for his children in the Declaration of Independence, that he may feel his share in the glory of America, of which he is a part.[31]

The Americanization program mirrored other opinions current in the Progressive era. Like most Americans, most Jews urged the immigrants to conform to American habits. Few Jews or gentiles crusaded for the preservation of ethnic mores; the retention of separate languages and habits, as President Roosevelt had asserted earlier, was unacceptable. Roosevelt and members of his cabinet watched a performance of Israel Zangwill's play *The Melting Pot*, which portrayed the logical consequences of complete assimilation. In that case, however, even the Germans could not expect the Russians to endorse the playwright's conclusion. To illustrate his idea of the melding of nationalities into the "American symphony," Zangwill had his protagonist, a young Russian Jewish immigrant of Orthodox background, marry a gentile girl whose father had served in the czar's shock troops, the notorious anti-Semitic Black Hundreds.[32]

To some established Jews, Americanization of necessity demanded changes in traditional religious forms, or a degree of de-Judaization. Even defenders of immigrant traditions admitted that society did not view the Jew's desire to preserve his heritage with the same graciousness that greeted similar demands in a Frenchman, a German, or an Englishman. It was his brand of Orthodoxy that kept the Russian Jew alien, Rabbi Louis Grossman contended; if only the "gaberdined Rabbis" would keep their hands off the immigrant children! Those who were bothered by the external trappings of immigrant dress and language—and by the transplanted east European shul and heder—ignored the probable loss of content while concentrating on discarding the objectionable forms. Other acculturated Jews were purposely more extreme. For example, in 1893 the Hebrew Institute was forced to change its name to Educational Alliance. The word *Hebrew* so discomfited certain donors that they threatened to cut off their contributions.[33]

As with relief projects generally, the pendulum in Americanizing institutions began to swing back to greater Jewish content. There was something distasteful about Jewish settlement houses that put up Christmas trees or staged Christmas celebrations before immigrant audiences dressed up in their Sabbath best. The tradition-minded newcomer found a Jewish settlement house bereft of Jewish ideals worse than alien; it posed a real threat to the unity of the home and the religion of the parents.[34]

Orthodox criticism was but one reason for the Germans' change of heart. Under a mounting attack by secularists as well, the Germans were particularly uneasy about the new wave of immigrants who arrived after the pogroms of 1903–1905.[35] The latter appeared more modern, more radical, and more committed to a Yiddishist secular culture than were their predecessors. A contemporary observer described these socialists, anarchists, and atheists as seemingly bent upon destroying all that was Jewish. If, indeed, the radicals had their way, the whole face of the community could be changed. A secularized Jewry of any stripe endangered the continuity of the Jewish religious tradition and reduced Jewishness to an ethnic or racial category. The values of the established Jews, who constantly reiterated that religion was the core, if not the sole meaning, of Judaism, would be swept away. The equally dangerous likelihood was that a secularized community would confirm the racist and prejudiced preachings of anti-Semites. Since Americans benignly accepted religious distinctions, frowned upon ethnic separatism, and hated radicalism, the average American would much prefer the modern religious Jew to the Jewish culturalist or the socialist and atheist of Jewish origins. Therefore, what was un-Jewish in the eyes of the uptowners coincided with what was un-American to their compatriots. The reverse followed logically: the established Jews' brand of Judaism was good Americanism.

The German Jews needed the confidence of the traditionalist in order to withstand the radicals and to retain their influence within the community. By allaying the suspicions of the traditionalist, the old-timers could shore up strength through their kind of institutions, and if those institutions continued to thrive, so would the code of their progenitors. Hegemony might eventually pass to the east Europeans, but the essential shape of the communal structure would remain German. On the other hand, if they alienated all elements of east Europeans, the Germans could look forward to their own eclipse in a hopelessly divided community.

Under pressures of conviction and political expediency, the Germans were prepared to meet at least some of the east Europeans halfway. Representative Germans urged their brethren to understand the spiritual needs of the Russians and cautioned the settlement houses not to overdo Americanization at the expense of Judaism. The Young Men's Hebrew Associations and the Educational Alliance added classes and lectures on religion as well as synagogal services. Yiddish, initially banned from the Educational Alliance, became an accepted medium of instruction, and the celebration of Jewish holidays was urged by director Blaustein. The latter, who often cited the need for religious education to bridge the generation gap among the immigrants, also struck a modern note when he advised that the settlements work to counteract the surprisingly high incidence of intermarriage among the immigrants.[36]

How to reach the newcomers through a Judaism that was both meaningful to them and, at the same time, respectable according to modern standards was yet another problem. To be expected, the Germans denied that the traditional Judaism familiar to the immigrants was the answer. By seeking to perpetuate "semi-religious legends and traditions which the age of civilization rejects as relics of barbarism," east European Orthodoxy obstructed Americanization and acceptance of the newcomers by the American society. In addition, it frequently meant beliefs and practices adhered to out of ignorance, as well as synagogues without proper religious education, "where jargon is cultivated, but the men and women are not." More than likely, the children raised within that framework would reject those habits and turn religiously apathetic or even anti-Jewish.[37] Somewhere between the extremes of secularism and shtetl Orthodoxy a way had to be found to bridge east and west.

The directors of the Jewish Theological Seminary believed that their institution could answer the purpose: The seminary was organized in 1886 largely as a counterthrust to Reform. From the beginning, however, as revealed in a circular letter to established synagogues from Joseph Blumenthal, president of the seminary's lay association, the needs of the east Europeans were at least as important. Blumenthal wrote in 1888:

[W]e have learned much as to the spiritual wants of our poorer brethren. They need ministers who will also be missionaries, to refine their lives, elevate them and maintain that high standard of moral character which has always been the boast of our race. We thus find an increased sphere of action for our Seminary. We have to provide for large congregations ministers who besides being thoroughly trained Hebrew scholars, will be able to attract the young members of their flock by addressing them in the language of the country and by being in sympathy with their religious requirements. But we have also to discharge our duty to our poorer brethren by providing for them ministers *who will be acceptable to them by reason of their religious training,* who will know their spiritual needs and who will be especially trained for their benefit.[38]

The Jewish Theological Seminary assumed the task of Americanizing the immigrant masses by providing them with rabbis and teachers from their own midst whose training under the rubric of "Conservative Judaism" synthesized modernism and traditionalism. In language of instruction and scientific approach to scholarship, the seminary was Western. It required applicants for the rabbinate to hold a B.A. degree and to be well grounded in secular subjects. (Remedial help for the immigrant student in English, mathematics, and Latin was provided by the seminary.) Courses in homiletics, elocution, and pastoral work taught the rabbinical candidates to conduct decorous services, to deliver sermons in English, and, in general, to function as modern ministers. In ideology, however, the seminary represented traditional Judaism. The school demanded that students keep the Sabbath in Orthodox fashion and obey the dietary laws. It also shared the east Europeans' reverence for learning, which it translated into an intensive program of Jewish studies. In sum, board member Jacob Schiff explained, graduates of the seminary were well prepared for their mission to harmonize American life and customs with the "often peculiar" habits of the east Europeans.[39]

Solomon Schechter, second president of the institution, illustrated the seminary's approach by his very background. Romanian-born Schechter had received his scholarly training in Germany and England. A man of wide intellectual interests and world-famous for his contributions to the study of Judaica, he lived like an Orthodox Jew. Schechter heartily endorsed the Americanizing purpose of the seminary and went beyond the hackneyed phrases of immigrant uplift. In 1903 he spoke publicly on how the Jewish Theological Seminary should be guided by American opinions. For example, since Americans displayed intense loyalty to the Bible, the seminary had to pay greater attention to biblical studies than was customary in Europe. Furthermore, a democratic setting like the United States dictated that the seminary place no undue emphasis on distinctions between laity and rabbinate. Judge Mayer Sulzberger of the seminary's board also linked the institution's role with American principles. When he addressed the graduating class of 1906, Sulzberger cautioned them not to overdo Americanization at the expense of Judaism. Although the Americanization of the Russians was "so uniformly and so loudly called for," it was also "profoundly American" to take pride in one's religion.[40]

The seminary had begun a direct outreach program to the east Europeans even before Schechter's arrival. At the turn of the century there existed on the Lower East Side an Auxiliary Society of the Jewish Theological Seminary, an organization of young people committed to aiding the seminary morally and financially. Apparently through its efforts, regular Friday-night services and lectures under the direction of rabbis and senior rabbinical students were instituted at the Educational Alliance. With the reorganization of the seminary, the board, a majority of whom were Reform Jews, intensified their appeal to downtowners. The likelihood was that downtown would not be interested in modern rabbis. "But," one of the seminary's endowers said, "if to the seminary there can be attracted young men from the tremendous colony, who will be educated up town, and then return to the Ghetto, it is believed Russians there will accept them for guidance." The board also looked for a measure of financial aid from the traditionalists. Schiff and Louis Marshall personally canvassed Orthodox congregations in New York City and asked for a $1 tax for the seminary from each member. However, suspicions of an institution directed by Reform Jews where Yiddish was banned as a language of instruction were not easily overcome. Neither the newcomers nor the established Orthodox rallied to the seminary's support.[41]

The idea of training downtowners to serve the immigrant neighborhoods also failed. True, the rabbinical students were largely of Russian origin, but many of the early graduates were called to pulpits in smaller cities without significant ghetto problems. Only after the east Europeans reached their third area of settlement did the then-acculturated masses turn to the seminary for religious leaders. Meantime, the seminary continued to depend on contributions from established German and Reform laymen. That condition in turn necessitated perpetuating the idea of the seminary's Americanizing role. When Louis Marshall appealed in 1913 to philanthropist Julius Rosenwald on behalf of the institution, he wrote:

[The institution] is intended to create a bridge by means of which, while adhering to the principles of Judaism as they have been handed down to us by our forefathers, the foreign-born Jew may nevertheless become imbued with the spirit of American institutions. I am firmly convinced that this institution alone, will save Judaism from irreligion, agnosticism, and even atheism; that it alone will be able to grapple with the serious problems which confront a people violently torn from its ancient moorings, and established in a new and unwonted environment.[42]

Removal from the Ghetto

A wide range of motives—humanitarianism, resentment, frustration, fear—drove the Germans into the vanguard of schemes for removing the ghetto dwellers to less congested areas.[43] From several vantage points, removal promised significant benefits. For the philanthropists, it meant a more equitable sharing of the relief burdens and lower visibility of the Jewish group. The Americanization of the immigrant would be speeded up, and the charge of Jewish clannishness would be refuted. Proof that the United States had room for the east Europeans promised to undercut the appeal of the Zionist movement; the United States was "a good enough Zion," Schiff said when he publicly urged the advantages of distribution.[44] Simultaneously, the immigrant stood to gain. Removal would liberate him from the contaminating ghettos that bred poverty, disease, and immorality. A third beneficiary was the United States, for proper distribution would match up diverse regional needs with available manpower.

The majority of the concerned Germans enthusiastically endorsed the idea of removal *from* the ghetto (even though the immigrants rapidly made their way up the economic ladder and out of the ghetto),[45] but they had no single answer on removal *to* what or where. Farming, a perennial favorite, raised its own side questions. Should the immigrants be settled on the soil individually or in colonies? Other suggestions took heed of the economic habits and proclivities of the majority of east Europeans and recommended moving the immigrant to small towns or to suburbs within easy reach of factories. Some advised first moving the factories out of the ghettos or building model industrial villages; the immigrant workers would follow of necessity. Established Jews on the East Coast did not limit their geographic horizons but usually talked in vague terms about the South and West as the most practical areas for relocation. In 1891 the *Jewish Messenger* combined that perspective with industrial reality and suggested the building of cooperative clothing factories in cities like Duluth.[46]

The various proposals were bandied about within the Jewish and non-Jewish communities after the heavy influx from eastern Europe began. From the turn of the century until World War I, the concept of removal and distribution gained ever-expanding attention and popularity. It was discussed in scores of popular and scholarly journals, by numerous civic and philanthropic organizations, and by state and federal officials and commissions. Presidents Roosevelt and Taft endorsed the idea, and so did groups as diverse as the Salvation Army, the New York Legal Aid Society, and the National Civic Federation. Certain states, eager to build up their industries and populate their land, joined the chorus in support of distribution, and new colonization schemes for Italians as well as for Jews were floated. In 1907 Congress established a Division of Information in the Department of Commerce and Labor "to promote a beneficial distribution of aliens . . . among the several States and Territories desiring immigration."[47]

Within the Jewish community in the first years of the twentieth century the call for geographic distribution was frequently accompanied by an emphasis on economic distribution. That is, Jewish leaders hoped to diversify the occupations of the immigrants at the same time that they resettled them. Special schools or auxiliaries of established organizations provided instruction in mechanical arts and agricultural skills in order to enhance the desirability of the new immigrant. Jewish farmers and skilled mechanics, the established Jews reasoned, would refute the anti-Semitic stereotype of the Jew as parasite and nonproducer. Older laborers, especially in the needle trades, would be less resentful of Jewish economic competition if the Jews were less concentrated and visible in a single industry. Moreover, economic diversification operating in tandem with relocation would facilitate the amalgamation of the newcomers into American life.[48]

The contradiction between what the Germans had practiced for themselves and what they now preached to the east Europeans put them in an awkward position. On the one hand, they who had succeeded in urban commercial pursuits had to defend the Jewish record in merchandising and commerce. Nor could they join the antiurban forces, whose rhetoric, like that of Governor Robert Glenn of North Carolina, indicted New York as "a blot upon the map of our fair country," Chicago as "a disgrace to civilization," and all big cities as moral "plague spots." On the other hand, by adopting non-Jewish criteria for measuring the immigrant's worth, they steered the new arrivals to different paths. Although some denied that they were merely out to satisfy the gentiles, the fear of social disapproval prompted the Germans to repeat the same reservations that the early Sephardim had voiced about the Germans' choice of occupations.[49]

Distribution became primarily a New York crusade. The established Jewish community of that city shouldered the responsibility
of the overwhelming majority of new immigrants. Furthermore, to
non-Jewish observers, the Lower East Side of New York epitomized
not only urban ills and unpalatable aliens, but the growth of Jewish
power as well. In 1905 the *New York Sun* referred to the impending
Jewish domination of New York, and a year later the *Brooklyn Eagle*
described New York as the largest Jewish city in the world whose
inevitable future was "judaization." Such comments, even when
free of malice, upset the old-timers. In a decade when references to
Jewish money power—a potentially volatile component of anti-
Semitism—were well on the rise, prudence dictated that Jewish visibility be lowered. No wonder, then, that the Cincinnati-
based *American Israelite* coupled a non-Jewish story about Jewish affluence with the editorial comment that the "congestion
of the New York Ghetto implies a menace to the standing of every American Jew."[50]

That the Germans were responding primarily to noneconomic
motives in their distribution plans is most apparent in the support
given to "back to the soil" movements. As discussed above, the
virtues of agricultural life had long been touted in American Jewish
circles. Despite the uninterrupted hard times that beset the American farmer from the 1870s on, and despite the numerous failures of
Jewish colonization projects that had been launched in the last
quarter of the nineteenth century, Jews continued to push for the
agricultural settlement of the east Europeans. On Jewish agricultural festivals, rabbis frequently developed that theme in their
sermons. Rabbi Joseph Krauskopf, president of the National Farm
School in Doylestown, Pennsylvania, said hopefully that the pastoral tradition of the ancient Hebrew was pulling the Jews back
to the land. Philanthropist Nathan Bijur insisted that the welfare of
the Jews and, indeed, of all America rested on a strong agricultural class:

[No] matter what is said of the mechanical industries, the development of
fine arts and sciences, it is agriculture which has been, and will ever remain, the backbone of every healthy nation.

Reality forced the champions of Jewish farming in the twentieth
century to abandon colonization schemes in favor of concrete aid to
the individual farmer—e.g., schools to teach farming, agricultural
scholarships for farmers' children, even a farming journal in
Yiddish.[51]

The rhetoric that accompanied the glowing accounts of Jewish farm life in the Anglo-Jewish press and in the speeches of individual spokesmen underscored the characterological and moral regenerative force of agriculture. Agriculture endowed the Jew with self-reliance and self-respect, its proponents asserted. A. R. Levy of Chicago argued further that the structure and discipline inherent in farm living curbed the unrewarding "speculative energy" nourished by the ghetto and changed the immigrant from a dreamer and fantasy spinner into a practical man. In 1910 the *American Israelite* magnified the importance of the second convention of the Federation of American Jewish Farmers. Celebrating "their emancipation from the thraldom [*sic*] of city life," the delegates displayed the salutary effects of country life by their "good color," "firm step," and "independent air."[52] Such opinions echoed earlier physiocratic teachings as well as America's agrarian myth. Jewish protagonists did not admit, however, that they had also absorbed the traditional disdain for the nonproducing Jew that usually accompanied the argument for agriculture. At the risk of being charged with self-hatred, they who had carved their niche in urban life grasped determinedly for ways to ensure the acceptance of the Jew by society.

At the 1902 meeting of the National Conference of Jewish Charities, delegates from New York lashed out at the ignorance and indifference of other Jews to the horrendous situation in that city. All the money in the country, Cyrus Sulzberger said, could not relieve the physical conditions of the tenements, where immigrants were packed in like so many layers of "raisins." Open up that ghetto, he pleaded with the delegates; go back and tell your communities that it was their responsibility to take thousands of newcomers off New York's hands. Nathan Bijur, a New Yorker and vice-president of the conference, concurred: "Are you going to let them rot there, or are you going to help us get them out?" President Leo N. Levi of B'nai B'rith coupled a defense of New York's established Jews with the warning that America's doors would be closed to further Jewish immigration unless other cities helped in the process of removal.[53]

The 1902 conference gave fresh impetus to the work of the Industrial Removal Office (IRO). The seeds of that agency had been sown by B'nai B'rith, which had undertaken the task of distributing through its district lodges the vast numbers of Romanian Jews who arrived in the United States after 1900. In 1901, in order to cope with the congestion problem in a more systematic fashion and to service other east European Jews, the IRO was set up by the Baron de Hirsch Fund. The agency, with headquarters in New York, sought out opportunities for the employment of immigrants through a network of agents and committees in different parts of the country. It would then attempt to fill those requests from the ranks of qualified new arrivals. After the New York office forwarded the immigrants to the specified locations, the outlying committees had the responsibility of aiding them in their adjustment to new jobs and a new environment. Since, at bottom, the system depended on the cooperation and the social-work services of the communities outside New York, the IRO arranged to cover the basic operating costs.[54]

With the IRO's operation a greater realism pervaded removal work. Agriculture was not the answer for those drawn to the cities by economic skills or tastes, or by the lure of the burgeoning urban frontier. It made more sense, Morris Loeb admitted, to send newcomers accustomed to urban life to cities and erstwhile villagers to smaller towns. The *American Hebrew,* a staunch supporter of the IRO, advised that the immigrants be directed to "second-class cities" that could absorb them and not to isolated villages.[55] Indeed, the very fact that Jews outside the metropolises, but still in cities, ferreted out the job openings for the IRO in the first place meant that the employment would be largely in urban areas.

The enthusiasm that the New Yorkers aroused in 1902 and in subsequent trips by leading philanthropists to interior sections of the country could not entirely overcome the objections of other Jewish communities. The latter still regarded their cooperation as a favor to New York. When some of those who were relocated drifted away from their jobs or back to the cities from which they had come, the community's willingness and ability to place new arrivals were further undercut. Southern Jews in particular resented the exploitative possibilities that the Jewish leaders saw in their region. They argued that their climate would be uncomfortable for east Europeans, that few factories or economic opportunities existed in their section, and that Jews could not work alongside free black labor. Why should the South be asked to take more immigrants, than, say, upstate New York or New England, the *Jewish Spectator* of Tennessee asked? Jews also feared that the IRO's role as a labor exchange would evoke the charge of "strike-breaker" and thus harm both the Jewish image and the cause of free immigration.[56]

Another obstacle in the IRO's path was the resistance on the part of the newcomers, who were too bewildered and frightened to face the trauma of a second uprooting. In an attempt to capture immigrant interest before the new arrivals had the opportunity to sink any roots, the IRO posted a Yiddish-speaking rabbi at Ellis

Island who explained the conditions of the city to the immigrants and urged them to continue their journey to the interior. The agency also propagandized at meetings of immigrant societies, and it sent agents into immigrant homes to sell the idea of relocation. Although the panic of 1907 and ensuing depression goaded more immigrants into seeking employment outside New York's garment trade, it simultaneously forced participating outlying communities to cut back on their end of the operation. In 1910 the IRO admitted to having relocated only 50,000 Jews instead of the target figure of 10,000 annually.

The obstacles notwithstanding, the IRO's dedicated sponsors continued to believe in the ability of the agency to eliminate poverty among the immigrants, to hasten their Americanization, and to reduce anti-Jewish prejudice. The *American Hebrew* thought that the IRO influenced large numbers of Jews over and beyond those actually relocated. By making *removal* a word of power, the paper said, the IRO "may . . . take credit for the present mobility of the Jewish mass. It has, by direct and indirect methods, filled many a timid Jew, living in a crowded tenement, with courage to pull up stakes and try his luck in the smaller cities." The IRO also won the approval of prominent non-Jews, and it directly inspired the government's own Division of Information. The effects of removal schemes on the freedom of labor to bargain independently in the capitalist economy troubled men like Samuel Gompers but were not discussed in Jewish circles. The Jews took pride in their innovative philanthropy and kept their sights fixed on the social implications of removal.[57]

A faith in removal and distribution underlay other organizational ventures on the part of the German Jews. In 1900 the Jewish Agricultural and Industrial Aid Society (JAIAS) was created for the purpose of aiding artisans and tradesmen as well as would-be farmers who left the ghetto. At its inception the organization also experimented (unsuccessfully) with the transfer of factories to the suburbs. A more daring scheme of the period was the Galveston project, a plan to land Jewish immigrants at that port and distribute them in areas west of the Mississippi. By avoiding the eastern seaboard entirely, it promised all the benefits of removal plus a solution to the problem of a second uprooting.[58]

A third organization attracting established Jewish leaders was the National Liberal Immigration League. Founded in 1906 by two Jews, Edward Lauterbach and Nissim Behar, this agency adopted a novel tack. It went beyond the Jewish community in mustering support for its twin objectives of free immigration and state-regulated distribution. Prominent Jews joined with Italians, Germans and Slavs, Catholics and Protestants, as well as with American notables—Jane Addams, Andrew Carnegie, and Woodrow Wilson were three of its members—in a carefully orchestrated interethnic and interreligious union unusual for that time. The league staged aggressive publicity campaigns. It organized rallies, drew up petitions, sent delegations to government and party officials, and circulated reams of paper in opposition to restrictionist bills in Congress. In particular it fought efforts to subject immigrants to a literacy test and to a higher head tax. To offset the clamor for restriction, the organization preached that distribution would solve any problems raised by immigration, and it wrote the following objectives into its constitution:

1. To effect the proper regulation of immigration and better distribution of the immigrants.
2. To diminish and prevent the overcrowding of immigrants in large cities, and especially at the ports of entry, by systematically aiding them to go to towns and farming districts in different parts of the country where their services will be most available.

The solution inherent in those objectives, the league asserted, would serve American interests at the same time that it preserved free immigration.[59]

The league's arguments on the benefits of distribution were familiar. On occasion, B'nai B'rith, the Board of Delegates, and the American Jewish Committee cooperated with the new organization, but factors of personality, organizational jealousy, and fear of a negative backlash from high-pressure publicity kept the Jewish establishment to its independent course and its customary tactics. Nevertheless, the league's crusade to gain popular and government sanction for distribution seemed to have rubbed off on the older Jewish agencies, and they, too, edged Jewish removal work into the public arena. In 1910, when congestion on New York's Lower East Side reached a peak, the three older agencies forwarded recommendations on immigration to the federal Immigration Commission. Recounting the Jewish efforts for removal and distribution during the previous ten years, the memorandum asked for increased federal activity along those lines as well as for government aid to the IRO, the JAIAS, and the Galveston project. At a time when Progressive thought was directing the government to a more positive role in public welfare, the Jewish establishment pointed to an area in which private and public sectors could cooperate profitably.[60]

German / Russian Relations

Understandably, the German infatuation with removal and distribution was not shared by the movement's potential beneficiaries. The voluntary ghetto anchored the newly uprooted in a community. It supplied emotional reinforcement—friends, relatives, or at least those who shared similar experiences and modes of living. The immigrant usually found employment within his neighborhood; if he needed relief, the major Jewish philanthropic institutions were on the spot to help out. In the dense Jewish quarter, immigrants heard their own language, read Yiddish newspapers, and bought familiar food. As Henrietta Szold, the tireless worker in communal causes, explained to a convention of the acculturated ladies of the National Council of Jewish Women, the ghetto meant Judaism—synagogues, kosher meat, ritual baths, Hebrew teachers.[61]

The ghetto provided more than security. For those with time to indulge any cultural and social yearnings, what better place to live than in New York? Indeed, David Blaustein reported after a visit to Jewish communities in the South and West on the dissatisfaction of Jews there with the lack of social and intellectual stimulation. Finally, although the masses might not have seen it yet, the ghetto with its concentrated pockets of potential voters held out the prospect of distinct political advantages for the group.[62]

As the immigrants established themselves, their resentment of the popular slurs on them and their neighborhood mounted. In a long and serious petition to President Taft in 1912, the citizens of Orchard, Rivington, and East Houston streets defended themselves against charges by the commissioner of immigration for the port of New York. They outlined in detail the numbers and types of economic and social establishments that residents of their district maintained, and they offered character references from district school principals, librarians, and social workers. The data they compiled attested to a hardworking, moral, intelligent, and civic-minded constituency that was in fact enriching the city.[63]

Outside the Jewish community, views in opposition to distribution ran a broader gamut. Some, like labor leader Samuel Gompers (a Jew only by birth), patrician spokesman Prescott Hall of the Immigration Restriction League, and economist John Commons, thought distribution was merely a subterfuge to deflect popular support of direly needed restrictionist legislation—"a bluff on the part of the Jews and the steamship companies." Others, less vehement, argued that the ghetto showed a vibrant spirit of energy and self-confidence, that the normal upward ladder of mobility would solve the congestion problem, or even that congestion provided the opportunity to structure positive programs for Americanization. When in 1909 Schiff spoke at the Jewish Chautauqua assembly on the desperate need to distribute the immigrants, his comments evoked reactions in the secular press. The *Boston American* responded with an unusual and extensive defense of the Jewish ghetto from a non-Jewish source. The paper listed several objections to Schiff's remarks: (1) Numbers determined political power, and the use of political power could keep down prejudice; (2) living in dense enclaves heightened the survival chances of the group; (3) Jewish neighborhoods worked to keep religion out of public schools and generally for the separation of church and state. With respect to the fear of Jewish power, the newspaper countered: "Some may say that the Jews will become too numerous and too powerful. They won't unless they prove themselves the abler race, and if they prove themselves abler, then they ought to have the power."[64]

More than rational reasons fed the east Europeans' opposition to distribution. They were driven as well by the urge to assert their independence of the "yahudim," as they derisively called their benefactors. The east Europeans sensed, and often with good reason, that many of the Germans regarded them as subhumans who lacked the rudiments of civilized behavior. The Germans never tired of preaching to them through their high-handed philanthropies on how to dress, behave, and even believe. Their own sentiments and sensitivities counted for nothing. Artificial distribution from the ghetto was but another mark of condescension and contempt for their particular way of life.

A flurry of opposition to removal arose in 1903 following a row between downtown (the ghetto) and uptown (the Germans) on the occasion of a new play by Jacob Gordin. The famous Yiddish writer had produced a one-act satire entitled *The Benefactors of the East Side* with all the stereotypic characters—the unctuous and hypocritical Reform rabbi, the cultivated German matron who fears physical contamination from the Lower East Siders, the pompous philanthropist with an Americanized name who entertains an array of ridiculous "sociological" suggestions for training the immigrants in culture and skills. Gordin's play and his concomitant attempts to undercut the Educational Alliance with a rival institution triggered a conciliatory response from some uptowners. Marcus M. Marks, for example, one of the founders of the Educational Alliance, called for volunteers—both workers and directors—from the Lower East

Side to cooperate in building an institution relevant to the immigrants' needs:

The Board of Directors and nearly all the volunteer workers are up-town men and women. . . . But why should not those who have an intimate and thoroughly sympathetic acquaintance with the people who come to the building, step forward to help us in our work? Men and women who live in a different atmosphere and who, even with the best efforts and intentions are not *of* the people, could, I feel sure, master the situation much more successfully with the assistance of earnest and able men who are constantly *in* the life of the East Side.[65]

Downtown representatives of Gordin's stripe were encouraged, however, to challenge publicly the patronage and tutelage of the Germans.

One such challenger and opponent of distribution was Isaac Rubinow, Russian-born physician turned political economist. A few months after the performance of Gordin's play, Rubinow's lengthy attack—written, as one critic said, with "a certain audacity" and "impertinence"—appeared in the columns of the *American Hebrew.* On economic grounds Rubinow blasted the removal projects. Urban concentration and congestion went along with modern industrial growth. The existence in the large cities of better economic opportunities, unmatched by smaller cities or villages, drew not only Jews but other ethnic groups as well as natives and erstwhile farmers. To leave the locus of modern economic activity spelled regression, especially when Jews were best suited physically to city life and light industry. Nor should the Jew be ashamed of industrial labor: "Value produced in the industrial field is just as much value as when brought forth from the soil. . . . Shirts and knee-pants are no less useful, no less important than cotton, corn or wheat." Ghetto life did not preclude mobility, and in economic terms the immigrants were far better off than they had been in Europe.

For social reasons, too, Jews, like other nationalities, were happiest with their own kind. Indeed, the ghetto taught the Jew the basic lesson of American freedom—that in this country he "may look like a Jew, . . . act like one, pray and speak like one, and yet be a respected and free citizen of a republic!" The ghetto quickly inculcated American habits; the immigrants now shaved, wore high collars and Panama hats, drank ice water, and frequented music halls!

Unimpressed by the philanthropists' insistence on rapid Americanization, Rubinow also challenged their fears of increased anti-

Semitism. Jews could not hastily erase prejudice entrenched for hundreds of generations under any circumstances. They had to fight for their rights and for the non-Jew's respect of their rights, and their greatest weapon lay in the political power they wielded as voters in dense urban neighborhoods. The specter of a "Hebrew invasion" or Jewish economic domination was sheer fantasy. If the Jews ever constituted a significant segment of New York's population, it would be a source of strength rather than regret.

Rubinow scored some serious points against the Germans. The latter, he said, endowed removal work with panacealike powers, a "new patent medicine" that promised to cure all ills, and took little account of economic reality or immigrant preferences. The multiple operations on behalf of agricultural settlement or distribution to small cities betrayed an indecisiveness on the part of the established Jews and sapped their resources. To an east European like Rubinow, removal work was as ridiculous as a broom with which to sweep the ocean. Germans latched on to the concept for their own needs and not for the genuine welfare of the rapidly growing community.[66]

In a decade when the east Europeans were becoming more assertive, the tensions between them and the established Jews constituted a significant divisive force within the community. The Germans made no secret of their contempt and resentment. Rabbi Abram Isaacs even tried in an article for a Boston newspaper to dissociate the virtuous old-timers from the admittedly less desirable ghetto dwellers. One of the foremost representatives of the Jewish establishment bluntly summed up the German posture:

The Western Jew treats his co-religionist from Eastern Europe as an inferior. He considers him ignorant, superstitious, bigoted, hypocritical, cunning, ungrateful, quarrelsome, unclean, and in many other ways abominable.

But the other side was equally culpable:

In the eyes of the Eastern Jew, the Western Jew is a cad. His education is superficial and flashy; his philanthropy ostentatious, and insincere; his manners a cheap imitation of the Gentiles upon whom he fawns; his religion a miserable compromise in which appearances count for everything; his assumption of superiority another proof that "every ass thinks himself fit to stand among the king's horses."

Reform in particular was a favorite target of ridicule to "every story-writer and poetaster of the Ghetto," one rabbi commented. Conservative Judaism posed a greater threat to the right-wing Orthodox, who declared a religious ban on the employment of graduates of the Jewish Theological Seminary. No wonder the *American Israelite* complained about the beneficiaries of Jewish philanthropy who turned around and proceeded to excommunicate the philanthropists.[67]

Both sides, however, made conscious efforts in these years to bridge the chasm. Speaking for the downtowners, a leading Yiddish daily in New York circularized a letter on the need for a rapprochement. Representatives of the Germans, for their part, urged a greater appreciation of the ideals and sensitivities of the easterners. A few called to mind how the early Sephardim had scorned the Germans.[68] The established Anglo-Jewish press kept up its criticism of the immigrants' objectionable traits but simultaneously printed articles in praise of the east European's rapid assimilation (immigrant youth built up a fine record in athletics), his admirable thirst for knowledge (crowds lined up at the neighborhood libraries on New York's Lower East Side), and his innate abilities (given half a chance, he would forge beyond the German).[69]

Most bitter about the westerners' attitudes that accompanied relief and Americanization, the newcomer usually failed to see how the established Jews served as a buffer between him and his non-Jewish enemies. German communal leaders and their newspapers attacked the illicit ticket agents who preyed upon the ignorant immigrant, the missionary drives of Protestant churches or individual clerics to ensnare the children, and the hoodlums who (frequently with police connivance) wreaked their malice on the ghetto dwellers. Germans took a prominent role as individuals and through organizations to protect the legal rights of immigrants. Judge Julian Mack, for example, championed the Immigrants' Protective League of Chicago. Attorneys Simon Wolf and Max J. Kohler eloquently spoke for the immigrants in matters relating to exclusion and deportation. Above all, the Germans rose on countless occasions to defend the good name of the Russian when the latter was attacked by anti-Semites or restrictionists for allegedly unpalatable habits or unassimilability. In articles, debates, public statements, and subsidized monographs, they ably assembled statistics and data that refuted popular linkage of the immigrants with crime, insanity, unemployment, poverty, or immorality.[70]

To be sure, defense of the Russians' image redounded to the benefit of the entire community. Nevertheless, the altruistic component cannot be dismissed. Jacob Schiff may have underwritten the Galveston project in order to solve the problem of congestion, but he was equally inspired to find a way for making possible a *larger* immigration from eastern Europe to the United States. "The knowledge that at least somewhere there was a country that opened its arms to the afflicted," the *American Hebrew* wrote, "has enheartened [our coreligionists] in their struggle and chased the wrinkles of gloom from their souls."[71]

Often the pictures the Germans painted for outsiders of their eastern brethren contrasted sharply with their private strictures on the Russians or with the seamier aspects of tenement living that they discussed among themselves. The same Louis Marshall who established a Yiddish newspaper in 1902 in order to provide "everything that the existing Yiddish newspapers are not, namely, clean, wholesome, religious in tone," praised the intelligence of the Yiddish press in testimony before the House of Representatives Committee on Immigration. Cyrus Sulzberger, who talked at Jewish meetings about removal in life-and-death terms, told that same congressional committee that "we must not get hysterical about [congestion], because those men who have gathered [in New York] have made that city great, and are making it greater day by day. . . . If you say to the immigrant population that it must go there no more, but must scatter through various parts of the United States, it would be good for the various parts of the United States, but it would be bad for New York."[72]

The *New York Sun* pointed in 1895 to the steadily growing influence of Jews in the parties and politics of New York City. One reason, the paper said, was the blackballing in 1893 of Theodore Seligman by the Union League Club. As a result, the club's political influence within the Republican party waned, and simultaneously Jews were impelled to come out into local politics as never before. The election of Edward Lauterbach, prominent in Jewish communal affairs, to the chairmanship of the Republican County Committee highlighted that trend. Lauterbach himself ascribed his election in part to the Republican party's "levelling . . . of 'class and racial distinctions.'" At the same time that German Jews were becoming more prominent in both major parties, a second Jewish presence, that of the new immigrant enclave, was making itself felt. The *Sun* reported that for 1894 the Jewish share of the municipal vote was more than 14 percent. It attributed the high figure both to physical reasons (e.g., a higher birthrate among Jews than Christians) and the rapidity with which Jews, more than all other foreign groups, applied for naturalization. Leaders of all parties found among the new citizens those eminently fit to serve their local needs, and, next to the Irish, Jews were ranked as the best politicians. "They are shrewd, diligent, discreet, persistent and judicious. They are practical and businesslike, and easily amenable to political discipline." Equally important, the parties were attracted by the unitary characteristics of the east Europeans. Their family, business, residential, and religious ties indicated a cohesive group whose bloc vote was ripe for the picking.[73]

The German Jews reacted less happily to the politicization of the Russians, for the latter's behavior could well jettison the entire case for invisibility. The socialist and anarchist factions among the immigrants squarely contradicted the moderate conservative posture of the German Jews, identified for the most part with the Republicans after the Civil War. Zionist sympathizers were even worse, imputing that Jews did suffer from political schizophrenia. While it lambasted those deviants, the establishment press reiterated with greater intensity and frequency the rules of the general political game—no Jewish vote, no Jewish political clubs or bosses, no special attraction in Jewish candidates. Consistently the press deprecated the tendencies of the Russians to use or be used by politicians. Its fears no doubt were reinforced when immigration restrictionists like sociologist Edward Ross and economist John Commons blamed the new arrivals—men unsuited for self-government—for any flaws in America's political system.[74]

At the same time, however, the immigrant presence underscored the unreal character of the neutralist political code. The Jewish communal stewards, like the politicians, noted the eagerness of most immigrants to plunge into political waters and the significance of the immigrant vote, concentrated as it was in a few districts. They also acknowledged the group interests of the immigrants—as newcomers seeking to improve their socioeconomic conditions and as Jews still intimately bound to fellow Jews abroad. If the nineteenth-century Germans had been unable to honor the political code consistently, how much more difficult would it be for the Russians.

Growing ambivalence with respect to political activity marked the behavior of the established Jews. They did not repudiate their self-imposed rules, but in the first decade of the twentieth century they increasingly succumbed to the reality of ethnic politics. Mayer Sulzberger, the first president of the American Jewish Committee, called privately for a careful study of the Jewish vote at the same time that the Jewish notables arrayed in the committee publicly continued to deny its existence. While agitating for recognition of Jewish rights in Russia, Jacob Schiff waved the specter of the Jewish-immigrant vote before presidential candidates Roosevelt and Taft. Before World War I, leading Jews approached the platform committees of the two major parties with their grievances against Russia.[75] If American Jewry turned political, the thinking seemed to be, let it be under German direction. Adjustment to the east Europeans thus stiffened the political backbone of the German Jews.

Ghetto conditions accounted for the first public breaks of the Jewish establishment from its political code. In 1899 the *American Hebrew* apologetically announced that the ballot was the only remedy available to the Jewish immigrant victimized by rowdies in different cities. "We are now, as we always have been, utterly opposed to the banding together of Jews as Jews, for what may seem to be political purposes. The only time that such a thing can be in any way excusable, is when it shall become necessary for the Jews, as Jews, to combine, in order to secure their rights. . . . In a small degree, however, we have approached that stage, for there has been so much brutality shown to the poor Jews in Chicago, Brooklyn and other cities, and their appeals to the police have been . . . utterly futile."[76]

More dramatic was the behavior of New York's established Jews in the mayoral election of 1901. That year, the acculturated uptowners actively propagandized among the immigrants of the Lower East Side in support of Seth Low and the Fusion ticket. Some established Jews, like other civic-minded businessmen, had rallied to the side of the good-government forces, which since 1897 had been laboring to break Tammany's scandal-ridden hold on New York. In order to win in a city where 37 percent of the population were immigrants and another 30 percent the children of immigrants, the reformers needed the votes of the ethnic enclaves. Good government also bore upon the interests of the Jewish immigrants. Since the ethnics constituted the core of the needy classes, the anti-Tammany ticket promised neighborhood cleanup drives along with honesty in municipal government. It followed that if the Lower East Side helped the Fusionists to victory, the latter might well take over the mammoth ghetto problems of squalid tenements and inadequate schools that the private Jewish sector could never dream of solving. If reformers effected neighborhood rehabilitation, the visibility of the east European Jews, who like the other new arrivals were blamed for the city's social ills, would be drastically reduced. Immigrant support of Seth Low, ex-president of Columbia University, would also refute the restrictionist charge that bosses, machines, and municipal corruption were the inevitable consequences of free immigration.[77] For those same reasons, the uptown Jews stood to gain. Not only would their philanthropic burdens be eased, but so, too, would their worries about preserving free immigration and an untarnished Jewish image.

One problem particularly irksome to the uptowners concerned prostitution and white slavery among the new arrivals. The fact that vice flourished in the squalor of the Lower East Side, usually under police protection, had long been known. Aired in the press, the subject had been discussed at the turn of the century by the city's Tenement House Commission and by the federal government's Industrial Commission. The exposure had led to demands by public-spirited citizens that the municipal government stamp out the evil. Jews, like members of other ethnic groups in the congested area, suffered the demoralizing consequences of the social evil. In an impassioned outburst that was credited with sparking the reform drive, a young Jewish East Sider had said: "And we—we go with our high resolves . . . to our tenements where evil lurks in the darkness at every step, where innocence is murdered in babyhood, where mothers bemoan the birth of a daughter as the last misfortune, where virtue is sold into a worse slavery than ever our fathers knew, and our sisters betrayed by paid panders; where the name of home is bitter as mockery, for, alas! we have none." Equally abhorrent was the evidence that Jews, too, had their share of pimps and prostitutes. Investigators reported on the seduction of Jewish girls, on Jewish children who openly watched the *nafkes* (Yiddish for prostitutes) at work, and on the incidence of venereal disease among the children. In the eyes of the uptowners, some of whom served on the reform committees, the long-cherished and touted image of Jewish virtue was endangered and the reputation of the entire Jewish group on the line. They resolved that the Lower East Side had to join in cleaning house by supporting the Seth Low ticket. The *American Hebrew,* the weekly periodical representing the established Jewish community, summed it up as follows:

To the shame of our race, it must be confessed, that the vile traffickers in this awful trade are mainly persons of Jewish parents, who have used Jewish young men as their debased agents to debauch Jewish girls. A few years ago Jewish virtue was all pervading. Thank God, it still exists with the great mass of Jewish families. But we may as well face the truth. A miserable, low-minded, conscienceless set of degraded human beings, having Jewish names and of Jewish parentage—for they are not Jews in faith—are dragging down in the mire the fair name of Jew. As Jews, it is a paramount duty to devote our time, our energies, our money in hounding these contemptible wretches out of our community. The opportunity now exists in actively joining the campaign against the Tammany horde, which has corrupted the Police and used its political power for money considerations, in polluting the virtuous Jewish home.[78]

Since over the years its demands for political neutrality had been so loud, the Jewish establishment felt called upon to explain its volte-face. Taking the lead, the *American Hebrew* agreed that the issue of morality demanded that other considerations be put aside:

In the twenty odd years of its existence, *The American Hebrew* has not felt called upon to participate in any political campaign—Municipal, State or National. This year the issue is so unmistakably one of morality, that silence were criminal. Whatever partisanship may exist or may be created, is of no importance by comparison with the overwhelming question of the redemption of the city from the hands of the vicious and corrupt despoilers into which it has fallen. . . . Under such circumstances, the religious newspaper has a clear duty and, with no purpose of influencing any of its readers in any legitimate political controversy, *The American Hebrew* has no hesitancy in saying that on the question before the people of New York on November 5th, there is but one side for honesty, decency and good citizenship.

The *American Hebrew*'s older rival the *Jewish Messenger* refrained from openly supporting the Low ticket. It accepted advertisements from both the Democrats and the Fusionists, and expressed its approval of Low only after the election. In Cincinnati the *American Israelite*, a leading exponent of the neutralist philosophy since the paper's inception in 1854, supported the *American Hebrew*'s views.[79]

It was one thing for the uptowners to urge support of the Fusion ticket and quite another for the Lower East Side to heed their counsel. Jews of the ghetto between 1880 and 1901 had displayed no consistent predictable group behavior in political elections. Personal and Jewish interests divided them among the various parties—Democratic, Republican, Socialist, and reform—and frequently the voters who supported a Democrat in one election switched their allegiance in the next campaign. While many immigrants showed an avid interest in politics, others were apathetic to the political world which, at least in their experience, seemed to be the peculiar domain of the Irish. But although the Democrats could not be entirely sure of the Jewish vote, they still had an edge over their rivals. Political favors, scandals, and traffic in votes notwithstanding, Tammany had the advantage of familiarity. After long years of patiently cultivating the foreign-born, the Democratic machine had become the political way of life of the immigrant neighborhood.[80]

More important, the German-Russian tension threatened to preclude cooperation between the two groups. Isaac Rubinow, who described the contempt of the German Jew for the east European "savage," discussed the "Renaissance of Morals" of 1901. He blamed the exaggerations of uptown for creating the false impression that the Lower East Side ghetto was a nest of immorality and the source of infection for the rest of Manhattan. According to Rubinow, the ghetto dweller, who hated prostitution as much as the affluent Jew, was understandably infuriated by the charge that his standards of morality were lower. "Unfortunately, in our section the workers must occupy the same dwellings as the prostitutes," the Lower East Sider rejoined, "while in your sections decent people can have separate apartments."[81]

Downtowners, however, tempered their resentment of uptown with gratitude, respect, and even awe. Men like Jacob Schiff and Isaac Seligman were successful bankers, members of prestigious civic committees, and powerful enough to command the ear of prominent government officials. Indeed, both uptown and downtown, whatever their differences, would have agreed that Schiff, whose broad philanthropic activities on behalf of Jews and non-Jews ranged from university endowments to agricultural colonization, was the most prominent American Jew of the day. Downtown also took pride in Oscar Straus, a German Jew who had twice served as American minister to Turkey. Of the same circle was Samuel Greenbaum, the Fusionist candidate for the state Supreme Court and a man cherished by downtown for having begun the Aguilar Library. Since such men actively supported municipal reform, that movement became more respectable in the eyes of the Jewish masses and strengthened the appeal of the Citizens' Union, the group behind the Fusionists.[82]

In a campaign pitched primarily to the ethnics, reformers invoked the aid of foreign-language speakers and press, and they printed thousands of circulars in Yiddish, Italian, German, and even Finnish.[83] When addressing themselves to the Jews, the Fusionists concentrated on the theme of protected vice. Since the exposure linking Jews and immorality had struck a raw nerve, the reformers focused their attack on Tammany with Yiddish leaflets calling on voters to save their children and to undo the shame bred in the tenements. The Jewish woman was warned in a special circular that her neighborhood was being inundated by prostitutes and that it was up to the wives and mothers to get their husbands to vote for the Low ticket. Low, the man who stood for the family and for purity in the home, was the man whose election would secure the virtue of New York's girls. A circular in Hebrew entitled *This Matter Depends on You* told its readers to choose whether they wanted family purity or immorality and prostitution, modest daughters or degenerate children.[84]

The most dramatic piece of campaign literature of this genre was a Yiddish pamphlet called *Hilul ha-Shem*—literally, desecration of God's name. Besides including statements in support of Low by Schiff, Seligman, and other prominent Jews, it recounted how the Jewish ghetto had become degraded with its network of prostitutes, cadets (pimps), and gamblers. The chief of police even charged rabbis with lending support to prostitutes. No longer the treasured people, the Jews now bore the name of purveyors of vice on the Lower East Side. But we can undo this desecration of holiness, the pamphlet went on, and we can cleanse ourselves of scandal. The election gives us the opportunity to show that we are not guilty, that the machine that lives off the brothels is to blame. The honor of Jewry hangs on the election. As the biblical verse enjoins: And you shall sweep out the evil from your midst.[85]

Jews of all classes—students, social workers, union members—joined the political activity on behalf of Low's ticket. A representative of the uptowners, Rebekah Kohut, who was the widow of the foremost rabbinic scholar at the Jewish Theological Seminary, traversed alleyways and climbed flights of stairs along with women of the Young Women's Christian Association and Women's Municipal League to address East Side meetings on behalf of reform and Fusion. Cheering on the amateurs and altruists throughout the campaign was the mouthpiece of the established Jews, the *American Hebrew*.[86]

Low's victory generated a genuine, albeit short-lived, enthusiasm in the Jewish quarter. Although uptown and downtown met to congratulate each other and to praise the civic virtue of the Jew, the constructive plans that some advanced for a permanent reform organization in the area, or for an organization that could provide the favors and services with which Tammany had entrenched itself, did not materialize. Uptown almost immediately resumed its habitual posture, at least publicly, of stressing Jewish political neutrality.[87]

The Low administration lasted only two years until Tammany reasserted itself. Within that short term, prostitution and other tenement problems could not be uprooted. Police harassment of peddlers on the Lower East Side seemed to increase; some even said that it indicated calculated revenge against those who had been disloyal to Tammany in the election. In 1902, when the notorious anti-Jewish riot accompanying the funeral of Rabbi Jacob Joseph was investigated, witnesses testified to police terrorism and to police refusal to notice any attackers whose victims happened to be Jews. One Jew said: "Before the Jew became independent in politics . . . there was none of this trouble. But since he has voted against the wishes of the police he must be punished."[88]

For the uptowners the episode had mixed results. On the positive side the campaign demonstrated the influence that the stewards exerted over the newcomers, and it pointed to a way in which the chasm between the two strata of Jews could be bridged. On the other hand, once having unleashed the masses and shown them firsthand the strength that numbers wielded in a democracy, the Germans were contributing to the independence of the east Europeans and making them less amenable to strictures on political behavior.

Prostitution in the Jewish quarter did not end with Low's victory. New York's Committee of Fifteen wrote in its report of 1902: "Almost any child on the East Side . . . will tell you what a 'nafke bias' [Yiddish for brothel] is."[89] Vice was alive and well in the ghetto, and in New York and other cities its presence grew more disturbing to communal spokesmen as the decade wore on. In and of itself a shocking spectacle to the established Jewish leaders, it continued to menace the favorable stereotypes of the law-abiding Jew and the purity of his family life.

Without much public fanfare, Jewish organizations increased their efforts to uproot the evil. They wasted no sympathy on the pimp, but they believed that the women he ensnared were victims of the environment who fell into evil ways only after their arrival in the United States. According to philanthropists, the solitary and lonely Jewish immigrant girl was recruited by the slaver at her place of work (usually a large store), dance halls, cheap lodging places, employment agencies, and matrimonial bureaus. Lured by gestures of friendship, false claims of kinship, or promises of marriage, she was easy prey. To save her, the Educational Alliance distributed Yiddish pamphlets warning of the dangers of dance halls and cadets. The Clara de Hirsch Home, originally endowed by the baroness in 1897 for training immigrant girls in trades, took on the tasks of providing them with proper living accommodations, employment, and even matrimony. Also open to non-Jewish girls, the home was singled out for praise by the Dillingham Immigration Commission

and by the Young Women's Christian Association. The most important of the protective agencies was the National Council of Jewish
Women. At the various ports of entry it stationed female agents
armed with pamphlets printed in English, German, and Yiddish
with warnings to the immigrant girls and addresses in sixty cities
where they could apply in case of need. The names and destinations
of new arrivals were sent to correspondents in more than 250 cities,
and follow-up inquiries were made to ascertain the respectability of
the new arrivals' surroundings.[90] The protection at times may have
been smothering, but the good ladies of the council and the Hirsch
home well understood that the social matrix into which the young
foreigners landed, as well as their recreational needs, were as important as their food and shelter.

Individuals helped, too. Rabbis investigated the evidence of
prostitution in their communities; one, Rabbi Jacob Nieto of San
Francisco, handled cases in his pastoral work. In New York several
prominent Jews underwrote the activities of a lawyer who with the
help of private detectives prepared evidence for use in raiding the
brothels. The *Omaha Bee* reported how Jews pressured a real-estate
operator who rented to a brothel keeper. Clergy and laity joined
numerous antivice civic groups and investigative commissions that
multiplied in the Progressive era. Jews allied with immigrant protective associations, agencies established to guard the rights of the
immigrant, also entered into the antiprostitution crusade. Judge
Julian Mack, first president of the protective association in Chicago,
worried about the vulnerability of the immigrant girl bound for
Chicago or passing through that city on her way farther west. Testifying before the federal Immigration Commission, he pleaded that
the government give special attention to the immigrant who proceeded from Ellis Island to an outlying destination. In Washington,
Secretary of Commerce and Labor Oscar Straus spoke as a Jew as
well as a public official when he pledged his aid to uproot the evil.[91]

Writers in the Anglo-Jewish press roundly encouraged such activities, emphasizing the responsibility of the entire community to
ferret out and punish those Jews involved in the white-slave traffic.[92] "We cannot shirk . . . our duty in this matter," the Board of
Delegates added. "Let . . . each and every Jew, in the United States
and the world, make it his business . . . to show the world conclusively, that we will not permit for a moment, the name of the Jew
to stand as a synonym for such outrageous, villainous and inhuman
conduct."[93]

Meantime, B'nai B'rith and members of the Board of Delegates
grappled with legalities. They fought for stricter state laws punish-

ing prostitution and those who provided the actual housing space for brothels. Jewish cooperation with concerned Christians and with nonsectarian civic groups was especially significant in Chicago. In 1909, as a result of the public outcry, Illinois passed its highly acclaimed "pandering" law, and the Board of Delegates took credit for contributing to the obliteration of the "vile and nefarious traffic."[94]

Just as vice among Jews continued to flourish, so did attacks on Jews for their allegedly disproportionate share in the white-slave traffic. Both vilifiers and defenders of the Jewish community used and misused statistics for their own purposes, but an accurate set of figures was hard to come by. Nevertheless, Jews had their own sources that confirmed the enemy's charges. Louis E. Levy, the president of the Association for the Protection of Jewish Immigrants in Philadelphia, estimated that Jews accounted for 8 percent of the population in that city but for 15 percent of the prostitutes. After a trip to the South, the director of New York's Educational Alliance reported that prostitution was rife in the Jewish communities there. Sadie American of the National Council of Jewish Women had been told privately by a member of the antivice National Vigilance Committee that a large number of the 30,000 prostitutes imported annually into the United States were Jewish. That information also altered the image of the pure Jewish girl led astray by the cruel American environment; she now appeared as the experienced worker whose European-cultivated trade could only contaminate American society. In 1909 the president of the Union of American Hebrew Congregations advised: "There is neither wisdom nor good policy in trying to minimize the responsibility of Jews in the matter by denials or attempts to weaken the testimony against them. I would rather admit that some so-called men and women, unworthy of the name of Jews, were violating every principle of Judaism, Orthodox or Reform, are guilty, and urge that the heaviest punishment that can possibly be inflicted, be meted to them."[95]

That same year, on the eve of New York's mayoral election, the prominent muckraking journal *McClure's* trained its guns on Tammany and its network of protected vice. In an especially lurid piece on prostitution entitled "The Daughters of the Poor," author George Kibbe Turner described the workings of the Jewish prostitution rings and those Jews who grew rich on the sale of human wares. According to Turner, the headquarters for white slavery in the United States was New York, where, with the protection of Tammany, it was controlled by criminals "most of whom were 'Austrian, Russian, and Hungarian Jews.'" Downtown and uptown Jews in New York denounced the article and challenged the accuracy of Turner's facts. Two months later the *American Israelite* of Cincinnati reported that Turner had admitted to a grand jury that he had obtained most of his data from hearsay. His exaggerations aside, Jewish spokesmen tried to explain that although Jews were relatively insignificant in the white-slave traffic, a few inevitably fell victim to their ghetto surroundings. Unlike the situation in 1901, however, when uptowners used the existence of vice to pressure the ghetto to the side of the Fusionists, the downtowners could not be persuaded to an anti-Tammany stand. So enraged were they by the article that for reasons of honor alone they would not join Tammany's opponents, who, like Turner, seemed bent on humiliating the Jews.

For the uptowners, however, Turner's article had introduced a more significant consideration. Nativist and anti-Jewish in tone, it set Jewish prostitution in America within an intricate *international* ring that extended from eastern Europe to New York. Other exposés which also suggested an internationally organized Jewish network followed in rapid succession. One account in 1910 cited a Warsaw newspaper's story of how a counterpart to the New York syndicate was unearthed. The only difference, according to the Polish source, was that Warsaw exported the women while New York imported them. It was an "absolute fact," the American article continued, that "corrupt Jews" were the backbone of the New York traffic. Even the report of the federal Dillingham commission, while finding no evidence for a single monopolistic vice ring, singled out the French and the Jews for importing women of their nationality for immoral purposes.[96]

During a period when specters of Jewish international operation were invoked to frighten proper Americans, it is no wonder that Jewish leaders kept silent on that aspect of the vice problem. Again, their own information had led them even earlier to the same conclusion about a worldwide network of Jewish vice. In November 1902 B'nai B'rith reported that members of its lodge in Germany were working with a German committee against white slavery in Europe. The special function of the German Jews was to watch over their coreligionists in Galicia. A month later the order noted with great discomfiture that the traffic from Europe had surfaced on their American doorstep:

|On| November 21st, in Philadelphia, a number of arrests were made which revealed a network of infamy shocking alike to the Jewish community and

the nation at large. . . . One hundred and thirteen persons were arrested, of which three have been held as men who have been conducting the affairs of a syndicate which has for its purpose the barter and sale of women. The three men bear Jewish names. . . . The men were held under bail pending an investigation and consultation with German officials who have information showing that the traffic had its foreign office in Germany. . . . Many of the women were found to be Jewesses.[97]

After 1902, American Jewish activity on the international aspect was kept under wraps. In 1910 an international conference on white slavery took place in Madrid, and, according to one account, the presence of Sadie American, representative of the National Council of Jewish Women, was important in preventing the conference from erupting into an anti-Semitic session. That same year, a Jewish international conference was held in London. For the Americans there were Miss American and the Haham Gaster of London, official representative of the American B'nai B'rith. Communicating in English, French, and German, the delegates spoke of Jewish participation in a traffic that reached from Europe to Africa, Asia, and the Western Hemisphere. One bit of evidence introduced to prove how deeply involved Jews were was a statement from a rabbi in Oregon on the large number of Jewish prostitutes in the Philippines. According to that statement, if a man came to the islands and identified himself as a Jew, he was immediately asked if he had any nice women to sell! Miss American, who in addition to her numerous civic interests was a loyal feminist, also raised an issue that failed to engage the less enlightened delegates. Since only men served on juries, she maintained, the tendency was to punish the prostitute instead of the real villain, the pimp. Delegates compared notes, exchanged information on what their respective organizations were doing, and passed a host of recommendations urging coordination of efforts. Agreed on the danger that the situation posed to the Jewish group, the conference admitted that their work involved special difficulties so long as the unemancipated Jews of eastern Europe endured abnormal living conditions.[98]

The problem of Jewish vice in all its ramifications was too delicate to publicize, much less to leave to the newly arrived immigrants. With the reputation of the whole community on the line, prudence dictated circumspect and discreet behavior. The principles underlying that behavior had their deep roots in Jewish history and were familiar in the American Jewish experience from earliest times through the better part of the twentieth century: (1) Close ranks and display a united front in the face of attacks from the outside; (2) clean house before the non-Jews learn how filthy the house really is; (3) weed out those responsible for dragging down the image of the entire group.

In their defense of the new arrivals from eastern Europe, as in the antighetto crusade, Jewish leaders were motivated by the fear of immigration restriction. The desperate straits of the Russian Jews under the reign of Nicholas II transcended considerations of comfort among established Jews or even concern about the rise in anti-Semitism. The history of a minority whose misfortunes had led to repeated exiles had seared even those who felt securely rooted in their "new Zion." Although Americans inclined increasingly after 1891 to immigraton restriction, the established Jewish leaders chose the opposite side, a position that their community would continue to hold throughout the twentieth century. In this matter they compromised their usual accommodationist posture in favor of Jewish needs. Critical of the American temper, those like Max J. Kohler defended principles more than Jews. Their work drew them no closer physically or emotionally to the east Europeans. On a deeper level, they needed to assume the responsibilities of kinship for their own psychological well-being as much as for the needs of the refugees.

The older German organizations, B'nai B'rith and the Board of Delegates, had long been involved with immigration matters. The American Jewish Committee, organized in 1906, gave most of its attention before World War I to fighting restriction.[99] Representatives of those elitist organizations resorted to their own tried methods of "backstairs diplomacy"—private meetings with key government officials, discreet pressure on political leaders of both major parties, carefully placed articles in American periodicals, the use of non-Jews as spokesmen to the public. The traditional rule of keeping Jewish interests out of politics and the fear of evoking an anti-Semitic backlash required that the free-immigration cause not be known as Jewish. Accordingly, spokesmen for the agencies, men like Mayer Sulzberger, Simon Wolf, and Max Kohler, preferred to operate as individuals rather than as members of organizational teams. Only in private meetings or correspondence did they reveal carefully orchestrated and coordinated efforts.

Pressure generated by the restrictionist campaign for the adoption of a literacy test forced them to try new tactics. Rival organizations put aside their differences in favor of united action; the American Jewish Committee reluctantly endorsed mass protest meetings and interethnic cooperation; and the conservative Jews welcomed the support they received from the socialists. Again the Jews had to face up to the fact that a minority's influence in a democratic political system rose in proportion to the number of its visible supporters.[100]

Conceivably the cause of free immigration presented an opportunity for cooperation between Germans and east Europeans. The former, however, were still unprepared to admit their coethnics equally to the councils of leadership. Ironically, the same Jews who staunchly defended the tenets of American democracy resisted the democratization of their own community. Leadership brought the communal stewards power within their group and status in the eyes of the non-Jews. They preferred an undemocratic framework that permitted them greater flexibility at the same time that it lowered the visibility of discrete group interests.

In the decade preceding World War I, the era of the elitist stewards began to wane. The system worked best with a homogeneous community of shared values and ways of life. As the east Europeans poured in and changed the face of American Jewry, the leadership no longer flowed naturally from an increasingly amorphous and divided body with many different objectives. Disaffected Jews barred from the upper circle grumbled about stewards and their assumption of power. In 1905, for example, the group who conferred at Portsmouth, New Hampshire, with Count Witte about the Jewish situation in Russian raised a storm of protest from the east Europeans. The few acculturated Jews who identified with the east Europeans joined the opposition. At the organizational meeting of the American Jewish Committee, Rabbi Judah Magnes derided the situation of "Hofjudentum" that obtained in the Jewish community, and called for representative leaders chosen by popular mandate.[101] In the first decade of twentieth-century America, such criticism was consonant with the Progressive temper that preached the extension of representative democracy.

The founders of the American Jewish Committee in 1906 faced the problem of whether leadership should reflect numbers or status. Of the thirty-four who convened to establish a national defense agency, most were young, of German extraction and Reform affiliation, and experienced in the direction of communal agencies. Their debates revealed a fear of the east European immigrants and consequently a reluctance to cast Jewish leadership in a democratic mold. A few, like Louis Marshall, did speak up for a representative body. Jacob Schiff pointed out that a new Jewry had come into being since 1881, and its confidence, so necessary for the success of the new organization, demanded broadening the base of Jewish leadership. Louis Dembitz of Kentucky reassured his colleagues that there was no reason to dread the loss of control to the new immigrants, for the latter would still support the established leaders of the community. The majority, however, opted for an elitist organization, which in its early years continued for the most part the "Hofjude" patterns of which Magnes had complained. But the rumblings of dissatisfaction with the committee's oligarchic structure indicated that the passive masses could not be kept in line much longer.

After two years, the situation in New York took a significant turn. The largest enclave of new immigrants, New York's ghetto, was because of its very size the hardest to amalgamate into older communal patterns. At the same time, its numbers permitted the rapid rise of numerous immigrant associations—philanthropies, *landsmanshaften,* and even labor unions. As Henrietta Szold pointed out, the duplication of secular agencies was downtown's way of asserting its independence. While uptowners encouraged the immigrant organizations that provided self-help, others feared that organizational autonomy would perpetuate separatism and the undesirable traits of both Orthodoxy and radicalism among the newcomers. Downtown was ambivalent, too, relying on the help of the established community even as it demanded recognition of its independence. A compromise was reached with the establishment of the New York Kehillah in 1908. A union of synagogues, fraternal lodges, federations, and professional societies, it put downtown in control of internal affairs—education, philanthropy, religion, social mores. The Kehillah was recognized as the American Jewish Committee's district body for New York City and received the committee's financial support. For its part the committee gained undisputed control in areas of national and international affairs and, more important, the goodwill of New York's Jewish masses. Marshall saw that the committee's support of democracy redounded to its own strength—we have "the democratic function which alone will . . . make the American Jewish Committee the power it should be"—and Schiff heartily endorsed what social scientists would later call aristocratic assimilation:

Here is a desire . . . on the part of the tremendous body of the Jews of New York . . . and these gentlemen who have started this movement come to us and they say "Here we are; we do not want to do anything in excess of good judgment, we do not want to have it thrown in our mouths that we are agitators for power; we want to have the guidance of intelligent men, and we want you to cooperate with us." . . . Shall we repel these men and say . . . we do not want any of them? . . . It is a mighty stream which we have an opportunity to keep in these waters, and the boats are swimming on it, and it is a good opportunity to start them right.

Indeed, the committee had struck a good bargain. It improved its image with the ghetto (Dembitz's prediction about the masses' vote for the established leaders proved correct) and it warded off the possibility of a radical revolt. Control of the purse allowed it to influence the Kehillah's choice of operations. If the Kehillah ventured to step too far out of line—as it did in supporting the idea of an American Jewish congress—it was effectively muzzled by its parent body.[102]

What was done in New York by formal arrangement came about informally in other cities. As the new arrivals grew more numerous and acculturated they set up their own organizational network, which eventually enabled them to escape German tutelage. By the time the war broke out, enough Russians had become sufficiently self-confident to support the formation of a congress—a democratically elected body to present the Jewish position to the peace conference. The committee, which had assumed that it would handle the diplomatic negotiations, was rudely shocked when the Zionist-led congress group bypassed the committee and appealed uccessfully to the Jewish public. The old leadership was caught. The idea of a democratic congress, in a country then experimenting with new political devices to augment the power of the common man, had become a moral and an American issue. The committee faced the choice of remaining outside the congress camp and relinquishing its claim to meaningful leadership or yielding to its opponents and using what influence it retained within the councils of the projected congress. It opted for the latter course, and proceeded in point of fact to eclipse its new colleagues in importance at the Versailles conference.[103]

The year 1914, then, was the watershed in communal leadership. Under the forces of the rapidly maturing east European element and the progressive ideas of the American environment, the monopoly of the Germans had been broken, never to be reinstituted. While the Germans were compelled to make room for the Russians in their synagogues, federations, fraternal orders, and community-wide deliberations, they themselves, now more ethnic-oriented, did not drop out. The sharing of power came about only with reluctance, but it ensured the continuity of those institutions as well as the basic patterns of Jewish behavior formulated by the nineteenth-century Germans.

NOTES

Abbreviations used:
  AH = American Hebrew
  AI = American Israelite
  AJA = American Jewish Archives
  AJHQ = American Jewish Historical Quarterly
  AJYB = American Jewish Year Book
  ASM = Asmonean
  BDAI = Board of Delegates of American Israelites
  CCAR = Central Conference of American Rabbis
  ISR = Israelite
  JM = Jewish Messenger
  JSS = Jewish Social Studies
  LBIYB = Leo Baeck Institute Year Book
  MEN = Menorah
  OCC = Occident
  PAJHS = Publications of the American Jewish Historical Society
  UAHC = Union of American Hebrew Congregations
  WSJHQ = Western States Jewish Historical Quarterly

The location of manuscript material is given in the first reference to such papers. Unless otherwise noted, all Jacob H. Schiff Papers are at the Jewish Theological Seminary of America.

CHAPTER 1
HORIZONS OF FREEDOM

1. *ISR*, 12 Sept. 1856, 3 Oct. 1856; Moshe Rinott, "Gabriel Riesser," *LBIYB* 7 (1962):11–30; Isaac M. Wise, *Reminiscences* (Cincinnati, 1901), pp. 338–39; James G. Heller, *Isaac M. Wise* (New York, 1965), pp. 70–71; Marvin Lowenthal, *The Jews of Germany* (Philadelphia, 1944), pp. 232, 251–52.

2. Jacob Katz, *Out of the Ghetto* (New York, 1978), chaps. 1–8; Adolf Kober, "Jewish Communities in Germany from the Age of the Enlightenment to their Destruction by the Nazis," *JSS* 9 (July 1947):211–12.

3. Katz, *Out of the Ghetto,* chap. 10.

4. Ismar Elbogen, *A Century of Jewish Life* (Philadelphia, 1945), pp. xxxi–xxxii; Lowenthal, *Jews of Germany,* pp. 230–32; Marcus Lee Hansen, *The Atlantic Migration* (New York, 1961), p. 139; Selma Stern-Taeubler, "The Motivation of the German Jewish Emigration to America in the Post-Mendelssohnian Era," in *Essays in American Jewish History* (Cincinnati, 1958), pp. 250–53; Mark Wischnitzer, *To Dwell in Safety* (Philadelphia, 1948), p. 5. One explanation of the cry "Hep! Hep!" is that "Hep" was the acronym of the Crusader chant "Hierosolyma est perdita" ("Jerusalem is destroyed") (Wischnitzer, p. 5).

5. Katz, *Out of the Ghetto,* p. 155.

6. Katz, *Out of the Ghetto,* pp. 193–98; Stern-Taeubler, "Motivation," pp. 253–59; H. G. Reissner, "The German-American Jews (1800–1850)," *LBIYB* 10 (1965):62, 70; H. G. Reissner, "Rebellious Dilemma," *LBIYB* 2 (1957):186–87, 189; Carl Wittke, *Refugees of Revolution* (Philadelphia, 1952), pp. 86–89; Rudolf Glanz, *Studies in Judaica Americana* (New York, 1970), pp. 91–92.

7. H. G. Reissner, "'Ganstown, U.S.A.'— German-Jewish Dream," *AJA* 14 (April 1962):20–31; Guido Kisch, "The Founders of 'Wissenschaft des Judenthums' and America," in *Essays in American Jewish History,* pp. 152–53; Joseph L. Blau and Salo W. Baron, eds., *The Jews of the United States, 1790–1840,* 3 vols. (New York and Philadelphia, 1963), 3:892–93. The *Wissenschaft* movement, conceived of by Zunz, approached the study of Jewish religious and historical development with the tools of critical scholarship. It aimed at showing the relevance and adaptability of the Jewish heritage to the nineteenth-century world.

8. Wittke, *Refugees of Revolution,* pp. 86–89; Adolf Kober, "Jews in the Revolution of 1848 in Germany," *JSS* 10 (April 1948):136, 142–43. Across the Atlantic, American Jews anxiously watched the unfolding of events. Here, too, considerations of the group's image surfaced. The *Occident* loudly defended the patriotism of European Jews and hailed their participation in the revolutionary ranks. With other foreign-language groups, the German Jews of New York memorialized the German heroes who fell on the barricades and, after the collapse of the revolution, urged support of the Committee in Aid of German Political Refugees. Speaking for the refugee cause, Rabbi Max Lilienthal reminded a Jewish audience that its generosity might also serve to counteract anti-Jewish prejudice. Bertram W. Korn, *Eventful Years and Experiences* (Cincinnati, 1954), p. 5; Wittke, *Refugees of Revolution,* p. 33; *OCC* 6 (May 1848, Jan. 1849):61–72, 527; *OCC* 7 (June, Aug. 1849):179, 287; Kisch, "Founders of 'Wissenschaft,'" pp. 153–54.

9. Korn, *Eventful Years,* pp. 1–22. Wittke reported on one Forty-Eighter who, despite his freedom, converted to Christianity and served as a Presbyterian missionary in India (*Refugees of Revolution,* p. 328).

10. Wittke, *Refugees of Revolution,* pp. 2–3; Eric Hirshler, ed., *Jews from Germany in the United States* (New York, 1955), p. 41; Hyman B. Grinstein, *The Rise of the Jewish Community of New York, 1654–1860* (Philadelphia, 1945), p. 24; Max J. Kohler, "The German-Jewish Migration to America," *PAJHS* 9 (1901):102.

11. Wittke, *Refugees of Revolution*, pp. 86, 88; Korn, *Eventful Years*, pp. 2–4, 22; Wischnitzer, *To Dwell in Safety*, p. 25; Nathan Glazer, "Social Characteristics of American Jews," in *The Characteristics of American Jews* (New York, 1965), p. 14.

12. Guido Kisch, "The Revolution of 1848 and the Jewish 'On to America Movement,'" *PAJHS* 38 (March 1949):185–208; Glanz, *Judaica Americana*, p. 28.

13. R. R. Palmer, *The Age of the Democratic Revolution* (Princeton, 1959), chap. 9.

14. Hans Lamm, "The So-called 'Letter of a German Jew to the President of the Congress of the United States of America,' of 1783," *PAJHS* 37 (1947):171–84; Wittke, *Refugees of Revolution*, p. 24; Glanz, *Judaica Americana*, p. 89; Reissner, "'Ganstown, U.S.A.,'" 20; *OCC* 3 (July 1845): 264; Stern-Taeubler, "Motivation," p. 260; *ISR*, 12 Sept. 1856; Jacob R. Marcus, *Studies in American Jewish History* (Cincinnati, 1969), p. 182.

15. Marion T. Bennett, *American Immigration Policies* (Washington, 1963), pp. 333–34; Hirshler, *Jews from Germany*, pp. 22–33. On the conjectural nature of Jewish population statistics see Salo W. Baron, *Steeled by Adversity* (Philadelphia, 1971), pp. 269–80.

16. Cf. C. Bezalel Sherman, *The Jew within American Society* (Detroit, 1965), chaps. 2, 3.

17. Reissner, "German-American Jews," 69–70; Glanz, *Judaica Americana*, p. 19; Hansen, *Atlantic Migration*, pp. 120–26, 139–40; Kober, "Jews in the Revolution of 1848," 137.

18. Sherman, *Jew within American Society*, pp. 68–71; Hirshler, *Jews from Germany*, p. 23.

19. Mack Walker, *Germany and the Emigration, 1816–1885* (Cambridge, 1964), pp. 47–69.

20. See, for example, Stern-Taeubler, "Motivation," pp. 257, 259–61; Gotthard Deutsch, "Dr. Abraham Bettmann, a Pioneer Physician of Cincinnati," *PAJHS* 23 (1915):105–16.

21. James D. Richardson, ed., *A Compilation of the Messages and Papers of the Presidents*, 4 (New York, 1897), 1894.

22. Cushing Strout, *The American Image of the Old World* (New York, 1963), pp. 50–61; John Higham, *Strangers in the Land* (New York, 1973), chap. 1; Maldwyn A. Jones, *American Immigration* (Chicago, 1960), pp. 43, 48, 117, 147–61, 248–49; Lawrence A. Cremin, *American Education: The National Experience* (New York, 1980), p. 8; George M. Stephenson, *A History of American Immigration* (Boston, 1926), p. 242.

23. Glyndon G. Van Deusen, *The Jacksonian Era* (New York, 1963).

24. Jones, *American Immigration*, pp. 89–96, 117, 169–76; Higham, *Strangers in the Land*, chap. 2.

25. Sol Liptzin, *The Jew in American Literature* (New York, 1966), chap. 1, pp. 31–32; Jacob R. Marcus, *Memoirs of American Jews*, 3 vols. (Philadelphia, 1955), 1:203; Jacob R. Marcus, *The Colonial American Jew*, 3 vols. (Detroit, 1970), 2:1096–1103; Lottie Davis and Moshe Davis, *Land of Our Fathers* (New York, 1955); Reissner, "German-American Jews," 63–64; Lorman Ratner, "Conversion of the Jews and Pre–Civil War Reform," *American Quarterly* 13 (Spring 1961):43–53.

26. Marcus, *Colonial American Jew*, 3, chaps. 64–66, pp. 1225–31; Blau and Baron, *Jews of the U.S.*, 3:672, 684–91.

27. Edward Eitches, "Maryland's 'Jew Bill,'" *AJHQ* 60 (March 1971):

269–78; Rudolf Glanz, *The Jew in Old American Folklore* (New York, 1961); Michael N. Dobkowski, *The Tarnished Dream* (Westport, 1979).

28. Hansen, *Atlantic Migration*, chap. 7.

29. Hansen, *Atlantic Migration*, p. 150; Marcus, *Memoirs*, 2:47–48; Reissner, "German-American Jews," 71.

30. Glanz, *Judaica Americana*, pp. 26–27.

31. Glanz, *Judaica Americana*, p. 19; Marcus, *Memoirs*, 3:309; Reissner, "German-American Jews," 72–82; Allan Tarshish, "The Economic Life of the American Jew in the Middle Nineteenth Century," in *Essays in American Jewish History*, pp. 263–93; David Philipson, "Jews and Industries," *MEN* 4 (Feb. 1888):102.

32. Simon Kuznets, "Economic Structure and Life of the Jews," in *The Jews*, ed. Louis Finkelstein, 3d ed., 2 vols. (New York, 1960), 2:1602; Glanz, *Judaica Americana*, p. 21; Rudolf Glanz, "The German-Jewish Mass Emigration: 1820–1880," *AJA* 22 (April 1970):49–66; Stephen Birmingham, *Our Crowd* (New York, 1968), pp. 57–58n; Nathan Glazer, "The American Jew and the Attainment of Middle-Class Rank," in *The Jews*, ed. Marshall Sklare (New York, 1958), pp. 142–43.

33. Barry E. Supple, "Business Elite: German-Jewish Financiers in Nineteenth-Century New York," *Business History Review* 31 (Summer 1957):149–51; Glanz, *Judaica Americana*, p. 51; Robert Ernst, *Immigrant Life in New York City, 1825–1863* (New York, 1949), pp. 84, 253; Joshua Trachtenberg, *Consider the Years* (Easton, 1944), p. 234.

34. U.S. Industrial Commission, *Reports*, 15 (Washington, 1902), 323; Supple, "Business Elite," 151; Birmingham, *Our Crowd*, p. 35; Adolf Kober, "Some Friedmann Family Letters," *PAJHS* 39 (Dec. 1949):175; Marcus, *Memoirs*, 2:7; Harvey O'Connor, *The Guggenheims* (New York, 1937), p. 21.

35. For these and numerous other socioeconomic indicators see George R. Taylor, *The Transportation Revolution, 1815–1860* (New York, 1962).

36. Glanz, *Judaica Americana*, pp. 58, 104–21; Lee M. Friedman, *Pilgrims in a New Land* (Philadelphia, 1948), pp. 434–35; Nathan M. Kaganoff and Melvin I. Urofsky, eds., *Turn to the South* (Charlottesville, 1979), p. 160. At the Winterthur Museum in Wilmington there is a folding peddler's table—multicolored, octagonal, with an attached bench—from the early nineteenth century.

37. Glanz, *Judaica Americana*, p. 105. For a comparison of the Jew and Yankee see pp. 330–57.

38. Glanz, *Judaica Americana*, pp. 61, 106–8, 112–14; Oscar Handlin, *The Uprooted* (New York, 1971), pp. 90–91; Robert E. Levinson, *The Jews in the California Gold Rush* (New York, 1978), pp. 6–8; Floyd S. Fierman, *Some Early Jewish Settlers on the Southwestern Frontier* (El Paso, 1960), pp. 6, 10; Leon Harris, *Merchant Princes* (New York, 1979), pp. 113–15, 123–24, 261; Friedman, *Pilgrims*, p. 435; Lee M. Friedman, "The Problems of the Nineteenth Century American Jewish Peddlers," *PAJHS* 44 (Sept. 1954):2.

39. Eli N. Evans, *The Provincials* (New York, 1973), pp. 40–41; Glanz, *Judaica Americana*, p. 59; Isidor Straus, Autobiographical Notes, typescript (New York, Jewish Theological Seminary), 3–4; Harris, *Merchant Princes*, p. 226.

40. Bertram W. Korn, *The Early Jews of New Orleans* (Waltham, 1969), pp. 212–13, 238–39.

41. Ernst, *Immigrant Life*, pp. 84–86; Tarshish, "Economic Life," pp.

264–65; Friedman, *Pilgrims*, pp. 283, 287; Supple, "Business Elite," 153; Glanz, *Judaica Americana*, pp. 109–11; Lewis E. Atherton, *The Frontier Merchant in Mid-America* (Columbia, 1971), p. 47.

42. Atherton, *The Frontier Merchant in Mid-America*, pp. 13–18, 40, 53; Harris, *Merchant Princes*, pp. xiv–xv, 44, 114. A grocery bill of a Jewish retailer in Rochester (1854) lists the type of supplies purchased from the wholesale grocer—from coffee, tea, and spices to pails, washboards, and twine. David Abeles, grocery list, 1854, American Jewish Archives.

43. Harris, *Merchant Princes*, pp. 3–5; *ASM*, 20 Dec. 1850; Straus, Autobiographical Notes, 7–8, 38–41.

44. James D. Norris, *R. G. Dun & Co., 1841–1900* (Westport, 1978), pp. xvi–xvii; Peter R. Decker, "Jewish Merchants in San Francisco," *American Jewish History* 68 (June 1979):398–99; Clyde Griffen and Sally Griffen, *Natives and Newcomers* (Cambridge, 1978), pp. 122–23; Agnes S. Crume, "A Credit to Old Louisville," *Louisville* 28 (March 1977):40–41, 79–83 (courtesy of Dr. Jeremy Cohen).

45. *OCC* 14 (March 1857):579–80; *JM* 1 March–5 April 1867, 19 April 1867, 3 May 1867; *BDAI Proceedings* (1867), p. 8; Glanz, *Judaica Americana*, p. 145; Morris U. Schappes, ed., *A Documentary History of the Jews in the United States, 1654–1875*, 3d ed. (New York, 1971), pp. 512–13, 716. Discrimination by insurance companies against Jews and "Jew risks" persisted into the twentieth century. *AI*, 11 Sept. 1890, 11 Oct. 1894, 1 July 1909, 10 March 1910.

46. See Harris's lively account, *Merchant Princes*; Supple, "Business Elite," 155.

47. Lee M. Friedman, *Jewish Pioneers and Patriots* (Philadelphia, 1942), chap. 28; Reissner, "German-American Jews," 78; Marcus, *Memoirs*, 1:24, 289, 292–95, 340; Lloyd P. Gartner, *History of the Jews of Cleveland* (Cleveland, 1978), pp. 19–20; Louis J. Swichkow and Lloyd P. Gartner, *The History of the Jews of Milwaukee* (Philadelphia, 1963), p. 14. Government contracts during the war enabled Jacob Elsas of Cincinnati, an owner of a dry-goods and clothing business, to pay for fourteen army volunteers. Jacob Elsas, biography, American Jewish Archives.

48. Friedman, *Pioneers*, p. 337; Glanz, *Judaica Americana*, pp. 110–11; Gartner, *Jews of Cleveland*, p. 18.

49. Friedman, *Pioneers*, p. 326; Ernst, *Immigrant Life*, p. 86; Glanz, *Judaica Americana*, pp. 50, 126–28; Glanz, *Jew in American Folklore*, chap. 16; Judith Greenfield, "The Role of the Jews in the Development of the Clothing Industry in the United States," *YIVO Annual* 2–3 (1948):181.

50. Tarshish, "Economic Life," pp. 279–81; Friedman, *Pioneers*, p. 339; Decker, "Jewish Merchants in San Francisco," 403–4; Marc L. Raphael, "The Early Jews of Columbus, Ohio," in *A Bicentennial Festschrift for Jacob Rader Marcus*, ed. Bertram W. Korn (New York, 1976), p. 438.

51. See, for example, Glanz, *Judaica Americana*, p. 131.

52. William Miller, ed., *Men in Business* (New York, 1962), chaps. 12, 13.

53. Glazer, "American Jew and Middle-Class Rank," p. 141; Glazer, "Social Characteristics," pp. 18–19; John Higham, *Send These to Me* (New York, 1975), p. 144; Tarshish, "Economic Life," p. 271; Glanz, *Judaica Americana*, p. 176; Nathan Goldberg, "Occupational Patterns of American Jews," *Jewish Review* 3 (April 1945):7–8.

54. Stephan Thernstrom, *The Other Bostonians* (Cambridge, 1976), p.

150; Steven Hertzberg, *Strangers within the Gate City* (Philadelphia, 1978), chap. 6; Clyde Griffen, "Social Mobility in Nineteenth Century Pough-keepsie," *New York History* 51 (Oct. 1970):491; Mitchell Gelfand, "Prog-ress and Prosperity: Jewish Social Mobility in Los Angeles," *American Jewish History* 68 (June 1979):408–33; Decker, "Jewish Merchants in San Francisco," 396–407; Raphael, "Early Jews of Columbus," p. 443. Hertzberg (pp. 153–54) singles out other factors to explain mobility in Atlanta.

55. Kuznets, "Economic Structure," p. 1603.

56. Friedman, *Pilgrims*, pp. 434–35; Marcus, *Memoirs*, 2:48; *ISR*, 17 June 1859; Ernst, *Immigrant Life*, p. 85; Glanz, *Judaica Americana*, pp. 22, 52.

57. Hertzberg, *Strangers within the Gate City*, p. 42; Supple, "Business Elite," 168–70; Miller, *Men in Business*, pp. 331, 387.

58. Hertzberg, *Strangers within the Gate City*, pp. 176–77; Peter R. Decker, *Fortunes and Failures* (Cambridge, 1973), pp. 114–17, 238–39; *OCC* 23 (Oct. 1865):319; Higham, *Send These to Me*, chap. 8.

59. Dobkowski, *Tarnished Dream*, chap. 8; Glanz, *Jew in American Folklore*, chap. 5; "Anti-Jewish Sentiment in California—1855," *AJA* 12 (April 1960):19.

60. An article on the subject by Gaster appeared in the *JM*, 23 Sept.–7 Oct 1892.

61. In *ISR*, 25 March 1859.

62. Oscar Handlin's statement that the stereotype was not taken as an offense is contradicted by numerous angry references in the Jewish press. The *JM* suggested (7 May 1897) that Jews not advertise in comic weeklies that printed those caricatures. It also recommended (15 Aug. 1902) that just as the Hibernian Order had advised the Irish, so Jews should boycott plays featuring the stereotypic Jew. Until the organization of the Anti-Defamation League, the CCAR worked to counter the stage Jew image (see reports in *Year Book*, 1910–1914, of the Committee on Church and State). Cf. Handlin's article "American Views of the Jew at the Opening of the Twentieth Century," *PAJHS* 40 (June 1951):323–44.

63. Glanz, *Judaica Americana*, p. 60; *ISR*, 18 Aug. 1854; see also *JM*, 27 July 1860, 13 July 1866, 5 April 1872; *AH*, 27 May 1881, 9 Nov. 1888.

64. Katz, *Out of the Ghetto*, p. 68, chap. 11.

65. Josephine Goldmark, *Pilgrims of '48* (New Haven, 1930), pp. 176, 194, 196–97, 205–8.

66. Janine Perry, "The Idea of Immigrant Distribution in the United States, 1890–1915" (M.A. essay, Hunter College, 1975), 3–7; Jones, *Amer-ican Immigration*, pp. 70, 122–24; Blau and Baron, *Jews of the U.S.*, 3:714–43, 880–84; Grinstein, *Jewish Community of New York*, p. 116; Moses Rischin, ed., *Immigration and the American Tradition* (Indianapolis, 1976), pp. 44–49; Schappes, *Documentary History*, p. 602.

67. Marcus, *Memoirs*, 2:7.

68. Alice Felt Tyler, *Freedom's Ferment* (Minneapolis, 1944), pp. 111–15, 121–32; Glanz, *Judaica Americana*, p. 39.

69. Grinstein, *Jewish Community of New York*, pp. 116–19; Schappes, *Documentary History*, pp. 195–97.

70. *OCC* 15 (Sept. 1857):281–82.

71. *OCC* 4 (Sept. 1846):270–72; *OCC* 15 (Sept. 1857):277–83; Grin-

stein, *Jewish Community of New York*, pp. 123–26; Julius Bien, "History of the International Order B'ne B'rith," *MEN* 4 (June 1887):513–14. See also *ASM*, 20 April 1855.

72. Blau and Baron, *Jews of the U.S.*, 3:879; Grinstein, *Jewish Community of New York*, pp. 117, 126.

73. See, for example, the *Proceedings* of the UAHC for the 1870s. See also below, chap. 7.

74. *JM*, 25 July 1879.

75. Kuznets, "Economic Structure," pp. 1600–1601; Glazer, "American Jew and Middle-Class Rank," p. 146; Naomi W. Cohen, *Not Free to Desist* (Philadelphia, 1972), p. 202.

76. Ira S. Rosenwaike, "The Jewish Population of the United States as Estimated from the Census of 1820," *AJHQ* 53 (Dec. 1963):132; H. S. Linfield, *Statistics of Jews and Jewish Organizations* (New York, 1939), pp. 10–12, 16–17, 23, 30–39; Max J. Kohler, "The Board of Delegates of American Israelites," *PAJHS* 29 (1925):79. The lower figures for Jewish congregations in government censuses stemmed from the government's definition of a "church," which excluded many small congregations. Linfield, *Statistics*, pp. 9–10.

77. Jones, *American Immigration*, pp. 106, 118–20.

78. Linfield, *Statistics*, pp. 35–36, 38; Grinstein, *Jewish Community of New York*, pp. 28, 410; Edwin Wolf and Maxwell Whiteman, *The History of the Jews of Philadelphia* (Philadelphia, 1975), p. 295; Albert B. Faust, *The German Element in the United States*, 2 vols. (New York, 1907), 1:436, 438–39.

79. Tarshish, "Economic Life," pp. 274–76; Hansen, *Atlantic Migration*, p. 140; *ISR*, 1 Aug. 1856, 18 June 1858; *OCC* 7 (April 1849):59; Glanz, *Judaica Americana*, pp. 97–99.

80. Carl Wittke, *We Who Built America*, rev. ed. (Cleveland, 1964), pp. 187, 196–98, 203–4; Faust, *German Element*, 1:436, 575; Linfield, *Statistics*, pp. 32, 37; U.S. Bureau of the Census, *Historical Statistics of the United States* (Washington, 1961), p. 12.

81. Leon A. Jick, *The Americanization of the Synagogue* (Hanover, 1976), pp. 15–16, 25; *OCC* 14 (Dec. 1856):11–25; *OCC* 16 (Sept. 1858):309; Hirshler, *Jews from Germany*, p. 38; Bertram W. Korn, *American Jewry and the Civil War* (Philadelphia, 1951), p. 12; Kohler, "German-Jewish Migration," 98; Joseph L. Blau, *Judaism in America* (Chicago, 1976), pp. 7–20.

82. *OCC* 15 (April 1857):45–46; Kohler, "Board of Delegates," 130.

83. *OCC* 15 (Sept.–Nov. 1857):305, 314–19, 373, 402; *ISR*, 30 Oct. 1857.

84. *OCC* 14 (Dec. 1856):411, 413.

85. Kohler, "German-Jewish Migration," 105; Glanz, *Judaica Americana*, p. 125; Uriah Z. Engelman, "Jewish Statistics in the U.S. Census of Religious Bodies," *JSS* 9 (April 1947):134–39; Sherman, *Jew within American Society*, pp. 132–33. A contemporary sketch of American Jewish life gloried in the "palatial" buildings, proof of the material progress and philanthropic bent of the Jews. *American Jews' Annual* 4 (1888):39–40.

86. Reissner, "German-American Jews," 92; Marcus, *Colonial American Jew*, 2:897; Maurice J. Karpf, *Jewish Community Organization in the United States* (New York, 1938), p. 91.

87. For examples of divisiveness in philanthropy see Grinstein, *Jewish Community of New York*, p. 137; Sherman, *Jew within American Society*, p. 82.

88. Reissner, "German-American Jews," 84; Kohler, "German-Jewish Migration," 103.

89. Cf. Victor Greene, "'Becoming American': The Role of Ethnic Leaders," in *The Ethnic Frontier*, ed. Melvin Holli and Peter Jones (Grand Rapids, 1977), p. 145; John Higham, ed., *Ethnic Leadership in America* (Baltimore, 1978), pp. 19–35.

90. Grinstein, *Jewish Community of New York*, pp. 184–85.

91. Salo W. Baron, *The Jewish Community*, 3 vols. (Philadelphia, 1942), 2:205.

92. Unless otherwise noted, all material on B'nai B'rith is drawn from Julius Bien's history of the order which appeared in installments in *MEN* 1–6 (1886–1889). For a recent account of the formation of B'nai B'rith and its early programs, see Deborah Moore, *B'nai B'rith and the Challenge of Ethnic Leadership* (Albany, 1981), chap. 1.

93. *American Correspondence*, 29 Jan. 1881, 5 Feb. 1881.

94. *MEN* 3 (Nov. 1887):207.

95. See also *MEN* 4 (Feb. 1888):237.

96. Isidor Bush, "The Jewish Orphan Asylum, Cleveland, O.," *MEN* 5 (July 1888):28.

97. Robert J. Greef, "Public Lectures in New York, 1851–1878" (typescript from a Ph.D. diss., University of Chicago, 1945), 6; Grinstein, *Jewish Community of New York*, p. 204; *ISR*, 15 June 1855.

98. Bernard Postal, "B'nai B'rith: A Century of Service," *AJYB* 45 (1943–44):97–116; Lewis Abraham, "Consolidation of Jewish Orders," *MEN* 1 (Dec. 1886):295. For a survey of Jewish orders in the 1880s see *American Jews' Annual* 1 (1884):83–94.

99. Rudolf Glanz, "The Rise of the Jewish Club in America," in *Judaica Americana*, pp. 169–86; Marcus, *Colonial American Jew*, 3:1130, 1150, 1164, 1169–72; Grinstein, *Jewish Community of New York*, p. 205; Isaac M. Wise, "A Sketch of Judaism in America," *American Jews' Annual* 1 (1884):42; *JM*, 12 Jan. 1866, 6 July 1866, 7 March 1873, 5 Aug. 1887, 8 March 1889, 23 Sept. 1892, 7 Oct. 1892.

100. *MEN* 6 (March 1889):184.

101. On the organization and early activities of the YMHA, see Benjamin Rabinowitz, "The Young Men's Hebrew Associations," *PAJHS* 37 (1947):222–32, 234–36, 238–39, 249, 251, 260; *MEN* 3 (July 1887):64; *JM*, 1 April 1874; *AH*, 4 Jan. 1889. For comparative material on the YMCA see C. Howard Hopkins, *History of the Y.M.C.A. in North America* (New York, 1951), chap. 9; Paul Boyar, *Urban Masses and Moral Order in America* (Cambridge, 1978), chap. 7; Aaron I. Abell, *The Urban Impact on American Protestantism* (Hamden, 1962), pp. 8, 43, 45; Winthrop S. Hudson, *American Protestantism* (Chicago, 1961), pp. 111–14.

102. Oscar S. Straus, *Under Four Administrations* (Boston, 1922), pp. 32–33; Rabinowitz, "YMHA," 227; *MEN* 6 (March 1889):184–85; *JM*, 8 May 1874, 9 Oct. 1874.

103. Rabinowitz, "YMHA," 264, 286–93, 299; *MEN* 2 (March 1887):139–41; *MEN* 4 (June 1888):538; *MEN* 6 (April 1889):235.

104. Sherman, *Jew within American Society*, p. 78; Marcus, *Colonial American Jew* 2: chaps. 61–62; *ISR*, 17 Sept. 1858.

105. Malcolm H. Stern, "The Function of Genealogy in American Jew-

ish History," in *Essays in American Jewish History,* pp. 75–76; Kohler, "German-Jewish Migration," 89–91; Kaufmann Kohler, "Three Elements of American Judaism," *MEN* 5 (Nov. 1888):316–18; Bien, in *MEN* 1 (July 1886)·12.

106. Marcus, *Colonial American Jew,* 2:966–67, 1001–6; Bernard D. Weinryb, "Jewish Immigration and Accommodation to America," in Sklare, *The Jews,* pp. 11–13; David de Sola Pool and Tamar de Sola Pool, *An Old Faith in the New World* (New York, 1955), p. 82; Solomon Solis-Cohen, "The Sephardic Jews of America," *MEN* 34 (Jan. 1903):48.

107. Schappes, *Documentary History,* pp. 198–200; Jick, *Americanization of the Synagogue,* pp. 15–16, 25; Grinstein, *Jewish Community of New York,* pp. 5, 49–53, 148–49, 156–58, 168–70, 437–38; Glanz, *Judaica Americana,* p. 123.

108. Glanz, *Judaica Americana,* pp. 11–12, 101, 124, 187–202; Weinryb, "Jewish Immigration," p. 12; K. Kohler, "Three Elements," 318–19; *OCC* 13 (Feb. 1856):542; *OCC* 14 (Dec. 1856):418–19; Sherman, *Jew within American Society,* pp. 65–66; Gelfand, "Progress and Prosperity," 432.

109. Carl Wittke treats the Jews separately in *Refugees of Revolution* and *We Who Built America*; Albert Faust limits his treatment to fleeting mention of Nathan Straus and two Jewish-owned department stores (*German Element*); John A. Hawgood (*The Tragedy of German-America* [New York, 1940]) ignores the Jews entirely.

110. Frederick C. Luebke, *Bonds of Loyalty* (De Kalb, 1974), p. 41.

111. Glanz, *Judaica Americana,* pp. 98–100, 203–55; Hirshler, *Jews from Germany,* pp. 42–45, 51; Reissner, "German-American Jews," 92–94; Carl Wittke, *The German-Language Press in America* (Lexington, 1967), pp. 184–85; *ISR,* 15 Sept. 1854.

112. Luebke, *Bonds of Loyalty,* pp. 47–48; Rinott, "Riesser," 19; Kohler, "German-Jewish Migration," 104; K. Kohler, "Three Elements," 319; *ISR,* 8 Feb. 1856.

113. Glanz, *Judaica Americana,* pp. 12, 245; Hirshler, *Jews from Germany,* p. 50; Bien, in *MEN* 1 (Aug. 1886)·64

114. Glanz, *Judaica Americana,* pp. 206–8, 232–36; Luebke, *Bonds of Loyalty,* pp. 27–28, 42–45, 50; Wittke, *Refugees of Revolution,* pp. 87, 122–23. The interest in a "little Germany" is discussed in Hawgood, *Tragedy of German-America.*

115. Glanz, *Judaica Americana,* pp. 98, 203–55.

116. Glanz, *Judaica Americana,* pp. 226–29; Korn, *Eventful Years,* pp. 15–17; Luebke, *Bonds of Loyalty,* pp. 34–45; Swichkow and Gartner, *Jews of Milwaukee,* pp. 12–60, 121–27; Kohler, "German-Jewish Migration," 102.

117. *OCC* 3 (Nov. 1845):367; *OCC* 4 (Nov. 1846):404; Hirshler, *Jews from Germany,* p. 42; Edith Abbott, *Historical Aspects of the Immigration Problem* (Chicago, 1926), p. 527.

118. See below, chaps. 5, 6. Because of German anti-Semitism the *AI* (13 May 1881) advised against the use of German in Jewish lodges. After 1885 the *JM* (4 June 1886) and the *AH* (29 July 1892) considered the use of German to be unwarranted separatism from the American majority.

119. Luebke, *Bonds of Loyalty,* pp. 292–93, 322; Wittke, *German-Language Press,* p. 238; Cohen, *Not Free to Desist,* pp. 87–88, 90, 98–99, 102–3, 113–14.

120. Emma Felsenthal, *Bernhard Felsenthal* (New York, 1924), p. 19.

CHAPTER 2
"ALIKE WITH ALL OTHER PERSUASIONS"

1. Edwin Wolf and Maxwell Whiteman, *The History of the Jews of Philadelphia* (Philadelphia, 1976), pp. 62–63, 125, 146–50; Morris U. Schappes, ed., *A Documentary History of the Jews in the United States, 1654–1875*, 3d ed. (New York, 1971), pp. 68–69.

2. Charles C. Tansill, ed., *Documents Illustrative of the Formation of the Union of the American States*, 69 Cong., 1st sess., 1907, H. Doc. No. 398, 647.

3. Sidney E. Ahlstrom, *A Religious History of the American People* (New Haven, 1972), pp. 386–87; Martin E. Marty, *Righteous Empire* (New York, 1977), chap. 9; Evarts B. Greene, *Religion and the State* (Ithaca, 1959), pp. 99–101; Winthrop S. Hudson, *American Protestantism* (Chicago, 1961), chap. 2.

4. Oscar Handlin and Mary Handlin, "The Acquisition of Political and Social Rights by the Jews in the United States," *AJYB* 56 (1955):60–61.

5. David M. Eichhorn, *Evangelizing the American Jew* (Middle Village, N.Y., 1978), pp. 37–73, chaps. 7, 8.

6. *A Course of Lectures on Jews by Ministers of the Established Church in Glasgow* (1840; reprint, New York: Arno Press, 1977).

7. Eichhorn, *Evangelizing the American Jew*, pp. 94–95; Isaac M. Wise, *Reminiscences* (Cincinnati, 1901), p. 63.

8. *OCC* 1 (June, Dec. 1843):113–20, 409–14; *OCC* 2 (Sept. 1844):280–81; *OCC* 4 (May 1846):65; *OCC* 15 (June 1857):120–25; Isaac Leeser, *Discourses, Argumentative and Devotional on the Subject of the Jewish Religion* (Philadelphia, 5601 [1841]), pp. 215–33.

9. For examples of religious imagery see Louis Harap, *The Image of the Jew in American Literature* (Philadelphia, 1974), chap. 7; Abraham J. Karp, "The Zionism of Warder Cresson," in *Early History of Zionism in America*, ed. Isidore S. Meyer (New York, 1958), p. 8.

10. *ISR*, 18 Aug. 1854; Eichhorn, *Evangelizing the American Jew*, p. 95.

11. Lee M. Friedman, *Early American Jews* (Cambridge, 1934), pp. 108–9; *OCC* 1 (June, July 1843):146, 188–90; *OCC* 3 (April 1845):41–42.

12. *ISR*, 20 April 1855.

13. *OCC* 4 (June 1846):165–66.

14. Eichhorn, *Evangelizing the American Jew*, pp. 46–47, 52.

15. Isaac Leeser, *The Claims of the Jews to an Equality of Rights* (Philadelphia, 5601 [1841]), pp. 5–18, 51.

16. Naomi W. Cohen, "Pioneers of American Jewish Defense," *AJA* 29 (Nov. 1977):123.

17. The material on Wise is culled from *ISR*, 15 July 1854–25 May 1855, 1 Sept. 1855, 6 Oct. 1855; Eichhorn, *Evangelizing the American Jew*, p. 101.

18. Julia Richman, "The Jewish Sunday School Movement in the United States," *Jewish Quarterly Review* 12 (July 1900):572–73; *OCC* 2 (Jan. 1845):512; *MEN* 5 (July 1888):59.

19. Lawrence A. Cremin, *American Education: The National Experience* (New York, 1980), pp. 61–62, 66; Leeser, *Claims*, p. 86; Leeser, *Discourses*, p. 267; *OCC* 13 (May 1855):87–88; *OCC* 15 (July 1857):201.

20. Eichhorn, *Evangelizing the American Jew*, chaps. 9, 10; *AH*, 3 Jan. 1890, 28 Nov. 1890.

21. *ASM*, 31 Dec. 1852.

22. *PAJHS* 9 (1901):161–62.

23. Hyman B. Grinstein, *The Rise of the Jewish Community of New York, 1654–1860* (Philadelphia, 1945), pp. 269–70.

24. *ASM*, 7 Dec. 1849, 17 Jan. 1851, 2 Nov. 1855, 7 Dec. 1855; *ISR*, 15 Dec. 1854; *OCC* 10 (Dec. 1850):476–78; Grinstein, *Jewish Community of New York*, p. 270; Max J. Kohler, "Phases in the History of Religious Liberty in America with Particular Reference to the Jews, II," *PAJHS* 13 (1905):19–23.

25. Kohler, "Phases in the History of Religious Liberty in America," 30–36; *OCC* 6 (Nov. 1848):404–5.

26. Charles Reznikoff and Uriah Z. Engelman, *The Jews of Charleston* (Philadelphia, 1950), pp. 124–25, 139–40; Abram V. Goodman, *American Overture* (Philadelphia, 1947), chap. 9. In 1824, stimulated in part by the city's liberal views on religion and the close relations they enjoyed with non-Jews, forty-seven Jews of Charleston became the first in the United States to introduce Reform innovations into the synagogue ritual.

27. *OCC* 2 (Jan. 1845):496–510.

28. Abram Simon, "Notes of Jewish Interest in the District of Columbia," *PAJHS* 26 (1918):214–16.

29. Joseph L. Blau and Salo W. Baron, eds., *The Jews of the United States, 1790–1840*, 3 vols. (New York and Philadelphia, 1963), 1:15.

30. Leon Hühner, *Jews in America after the American Revolution* (New York, 1959), pp. 1–35; Ira Rosenwaike, "Further Light on Jacob Henry," *AJA* 22 (Nov. 1970):117; *OCC* 16 (Feb. 1859):532; *JM*, 17 Aug. 1860; BDAI, Minutes 15 July 1866, Archives of the American Jewish Historical Society; BDAI, *First Annual Report of the Executive Committee*, June 1860, pp. 8–10; *BDAI Proceedings* (1867), pp. 7–8.

31. Charles Reznikoff, ed., *Louis Marshall*, 2 vols. (Philadelphia, 1957), 2:967–70.

32. Blau and Baron, *Jews of the U.S.*, 2:443–46; Schappes, *Documentary History*, pp. 26–30; Handlin and Handlin, "Acquisition of Political and Social Rights," 61 ff.

33. *OCC* 2 (Jan. 1845):497–98.

34. Permoli *v.* Municipality, 3 Howard 609; *The Constitution of the United States of America, Analysis and Interpretation*, 88 Cong., 1st sess., 1964, S. Doc. 39, 847.

35. Cohen, "Pioneers," passim.

36. *OCC* 2 (Jan. 1845):497; *OCC* 5 (July 1847, Jan. 1848):205, 500; *OCC* 13 (March 1856):571–72.

37. Joseph L. Blau, ed., *Cornerstones of Religious Freedom in America* (Boston, 1949), pp. 112–13.

38. *OCC* 5 (Jan. 1848):500–504; *ISR*, 19 June 1857.

39. See, for example, *OCC* 7 (Feb. 1850):263–67; *ISR*, 15 Dec. 1854.

40. Marty, *Righteous Empire*, p. 96. For a listing of the cases see Jacob Ben Lightman, "A Study of Reported Judicial Opinions of American Courts Regarding the Status of Jews with Respect to Sunday Laws" (Master's essay, Graduate School for Jewish Social Work, 1933), 267–68.

41. Myron Berman, *Richmond's Jewry* (Charlottesville, 1979), pp. 49–53; *OCC* 2 (Jan. 1845):499; *OCC* 3 (Feb. 1846):561–67; *OCC* 5 (March 1848):585–86; *OCC* 7 (Dec. 1849):468–69.

42. *OCC* 4 (March 1847):615–16.

43. The argument was used in an 1817 case by the lawyer for the defense, Zalegman Phillips, who was the son of Jonas Phillips. A certain Phillips, probably the same one, was Benjamin's lawyer. The identical point was raised and again dismissed in Specht *v.* Commonwealth. Blau and Baron, *Jews of the U.S.*, 1:23–24, 243; Schappes, *Documentary History*, p. 280; *OCC* 6 (Aug. 1848):260–61.

44. *OCC* 4 (March 1847):588–96; *OCC* 5 (March 1848):594–99; *OCC* 6 (April–Dec. 1848):36–39, 186–93, 300–301, 394–99, 447–50; Schappes, *Documentary History*, pp. 279–81.

45. *OCC* 4 (March 1847):568. The religious argument was advanced again in an Ohio case of 1846. A Jew, Jacob Rice, had been fined for trading on Sunday in Cincinnati even though the city ordinance provided exemptions in matters of "common labour" for those who conscientiously observed the seventh day. The Court of Common Pleas found for Rice, but the larger issue of religious freedom and equality was not discussed. However, in *Ex parte* Newman (California, 1858), the Jewish position was vindicated. The court saw religious intent behind the Sunday law and pronounced it unconstitutional. Lightman, "Judicial Opinions," 77, 166–68.

46. *OCC* 6 (Aug.–Sept. 1848):217–24, 256–61, 265–74.

47. *OCC* 4 (March 1847):569; *OCC* 13 (March 1856):574–75. On the issue of calling Jews to court on Saturday, see Lightman, "Judicial Opinions," 75–76.

48. *OCC* 7 (Dec. 1849):468; *OCC* 13 (March 1856):575.

49. *OCC* 16 (Sept. 1858):269–75.

50. *OCC* 5 (July 1847):169–77; *OCC* 13 (March 1856):575; *ASM*, 4 May 1855; *ISR*, 20 Oct. 1854.

51. *OCC* 13 (Feb. 1846):565.

52. Gustavus Myers, *History of Bigotry in the United States* (New York, 1943), pp. 5–6, 11, 81, 184; Greene, *Religion and the State*, pp. 34, 43, 68, 124–26; Goodman, *American Overture*, pp. 135–43.

53. *OCC* 2 (Jan. 1845):504–5; *OCC* 5 (March 1848):594–97.

54. Ray A. Billington, *The Protestant Crusade* (New York, 1938), esp. chap. 5.

55. Bertram W. Korn, *Eventful Years and Experiences* (Cincinnati, 1954), pp. 58–62; Myers, *History of Bigotry*, p. 187; Greene, *Religion and the State*, pp. 110–11.

56. "Anti-Jewish Sentiment in California -1855," *AJA* 12 (April 1960):15–33; *ASM*, 27 April 1855.

57. *ISR*, 22 Sept. 1854; Lawrence H. Fuchs, *The Political Behavior of American Jews* (Glencoe, 1956), p. 32.

58. John A. Forman, "Lewis Charles Levin," *AJA* 12 (Oct. 1960):150–91; Speech of L. C. Levin in the House of Representatives, March 1848, American Jewish Archives.

59. Korn, *Eventful Years*, pp. 65–72; Reznikoff, *Marshall*, 2:957–67; *OCC* 11 (July 1853):225.

60. *AI*, 5 Dec. 1889 (Berkowitz). For examples of the defense of public schools see also David Philipson, *Max Lilienthal* (New York, 1915), pp. 78–80, 89; E. N. Calisch, "Judaism and the Public School System of America," *CCAR, Year Book* 3 (1892):126–29; E. G. Hirsch, "The Aim, Scope, and Method of the Jewish Religious School," *MEN* 34 (March 1903):168-69; *JM*, 28 Feb. 1902.

61. On Riesser see above, chap. 1; Alexander Altmann, *Moses Mendelssohn* (University, Ala., 1973), pp. 518–31; Calisch, "Judaism and the Public School System," 128.

62. See Lloyd Gartner's perceptive article "Temples of Liberty Unpolluted," in *A Bicentennial Festschrift for Jacob Rader Marcus*, ed. Bertram W. Korn (Waltham and New York, 1976), pp. 157–62; Cremin, *American Education*, pp. 181, 498; Grinstein, *Jewish Community of New York*, pp. 235–36.

63. *AI*, 5 Dec. 1889 (Berkowitz); Gartner, "Temples of Liberty," pp. 176–77.

64. Gartner, "Temples of Liberty," pp. 167–73.

65. Gartner, "Temples of Liberty," pp. 165–67; Moshe Davis, *The Emergence of Conservative Judaism* (Philadelphia, 1963), p. 133.

66. *AI*, 5 Dec. 1889 (Berkowitz). On Protestant reaction to Catholic schools, see Billington, *Protestant Crusade*, chap. 6.

67. On the Mortara affair, see below, chap. 5. *JM*, 26 Nov. 1858.

68. Philipson, *Lilienthal*, pp. 105–7, 121, 474–77; *JM*, 19 Jan. 1891.

69. Philipson, *Lilienthal*, p. 122; Gartner, "Temples of Liberty," pp. 174–75.

70. The earlier pattern of defense with respect to the Sunday question persisted after the Civil War While in principle all Sunday laws were symptomatic of a less-than-perfect condition of religious liberty, the primary practical thrust was to secure exemption for Sabbath observers. See, for example, *AH*, 1 July 1887, 13 Feb. 1903; *JM*, 9 Sept. 1870.

71. On the broad range of issues involved in the school question, see Alvin W. Johnson and Frank H. Yost, *Separation of Church and State in the United States* (Minneapolis, 1948), chaps. 2–15. See also *AH*, 28 May 1886, 14 Oct. 1887; *JM*, 12 Nov. 1869.

72. Gartner, "Temples of Liberty," p. 178; *AI*, 15 Sept. 1892; *AH*, 2 March 1888; *JM*, 24 Nov. 1893, 12 June 1896, 13 Dec. 1901.

73. Johnson and Yost, *Separation of Church and State*, pp. 30, 59–60; Loren P. Beth, *The Development of the American Constitution, 1877–1917* (New York, 1971), pp. 231–33.

74. Johnson and Yost, *Separation of Church and State*, chap. 4.; Schappes, *Documentary History*, p. 231; Philipson, *Lilienthal*, pp. 184–86.

75. See Paul A. Carter's suggestive account, *The Spiritual Crisis of the Gilded Age* (De Kalb, 1971), esp. chap. 1.

76. Johnson and Yost, *Separation of Church and State*, p. 62; *AI*, 18 Nov. 1881. On the threat to Protestantism, see Aaron I. Abell, *The Urban Impact on American Protestantism* (Hamden, 1962), pp. 3–10, 61–66.

77. Arthur M. Schlesinger, "A Critical Period in American Religion, 1875–1900," *Massachusetts Historical Society Proceedings* 64 (1930–1932): 523–47; Johnson and Yost, *Separation of Church and State*, p. 31; *Congressional Record*, 50th Cong., 1st sess., 1880, 4455; *Congressional Record*, 51st Cong., 1st sess., 1890, 124; Tobias Schanfarber, "The Problem of Ethical Instruction in the Public Schools," *CCAR Year Book* 21 (1911):241 et seq.

78. *JM*, 17 Feb. 1893; *Proceedings of the National Convention to Secure the Religious Amendment of the Constitution of the United States* (1873), pp. 9–10, 46, 55; Calisch, "Judaism and the Public School System," 126; *UAHC Proceedings* (1909), p. 6186. Cf. Jehuda Reinharz, *Fatherland or Promised Land* (Ann Arbor, 1975), pp. 14–15.

79. Schanfarber, "Problem of Ethical Instruction"; *CCAR Year Book* 21 (1911):108–13; *CCAR Year Book* 24 (1914):136–39.

80. 143 U.S. 457–71.

81. Reznikoff, *Marshall*, 2:936–49.

82. David J. Brewer, *The United States—A Christian Nation* (Philadelphia, 1905), pp. 11–41.

83. *AJYB* 10 (1908–1909):193. The Christian-nation issue was a favorite topic of the *AI* during 1906. See also *CCAR Year Book* 16 (1906):150–71; 17 (1907):90–93; 18 (1908):86–87; 19 (1909):84–87.

84. Sol M. Stroock, "Switzerland and American Jews," reprinted in *The Jewish Experience in America,* ed. Abraham J. Karp, 5 vols. (New York and Waltham, 1969), 3:78–81. For a recent discussion, reworked here, of the Swiss treaty, see Naomi W. Cohen, "American Jews and the Swiss Treaty," *Solomon Goldman Lectures* 3 (Spertus College, Chicago, 1982), pp. 83–100.

85. Selma Stern-Taeubler, "The Motivation of the German Jewish Emigration to America in the Post-Mendelssohnian Era," in *Essays in American Jewish History* (Cincinnati, 1958), pp. 247–61; H. G. Reissner, "The German-American Jews (1800–1850)," *LBIYB* 10 (1965):81, 87; Guido Kisch, "Two American Jewish Pioneers of New Haven," *Historia Judaica* 4 (1942): 16 et seq.

86. *ASM,* 24 and 31 Jan. 1851.

87. *ASM,* 24 Jan.–14 Feb. 1851.

88. *ASM,* 14 Feb. 1851, 14 March 1851; Thomas A. Bailey, *A Diplomatic History of the American People,* 9th ed. (Englewood Cliffs, N.J., 1974), pp. 167, 271; Stroock, "Switzerland and American Jews," 78, 80.

89. Stroock, "Switzerland and American Jews," 83–91; Schappes, *Documentary History,* pp. 319–21; *OCC* 12 (May 1854):95–100; *AI,* 30 June 1904.

90. Cohen, "American Jews and the Swiss Treaty," pp. 91–92; Stroock, "Switzerland and American Jews," 102–15.

91. *OCC* 18 (5 July 1860):93. The Board of Delegates reported incorrectly that the American treaty with Japan also singled out Christians for special protection.

92. Allan Tarshish, "The Board of Delegates of American Israelites (1859–1878)," reprinted in *The Jewish Experience,* 3:134–35; Stroock, "Switzerland and American Jews," 81. The issue of equality again arose when, in the last two decades of the nineteenth century, American Jewish rights were circumscribed by the Ottoman government. In 1887 Turkey attempted to thwart the nascent Jewish nationalist movement among east European Jews by restricting to one month the sojourn in Palestine of all Jews, including Americans. As in the earlier situation in Switzerland, American Jews were not the prime target; the Swiss had objected to all Jews because of the Alsatians, the Turks because of the Russians. But unlike in the Swiss episode, American Jews did not respond with a public campaign. It fell upon Oscar S. Straus, then serving as minister to Constantinople, to keep the State Department mindful of the American Jewish claim to equality. Naomi W. Cohen, *A Dual Heritage* (Philadelphia, 1969), pp. 27–31, 83–87.

CHAPTER 3
THE PROPER AMERICAN JEW

1. Myer S. Isaacs, *The Old Guard and Other Addresses* (New York, 1906), p. 188.
2. *JM*, 29 July 1898.
3. Isaacs, *Old Guard*, pp. 13–38, 118–24. Writing on the death of Sir David Salomons, defender of Jewish rights and first Jewish lord mayor of London, the *JM* extrapolated principles of behavior for its American readers and concluded: "When the Israelites . . . are conspicuous for devotion to the public good, and for consistent lives as Hebrews and Americans, we may anticipate the downfall of the intolerant and bigoted spirit which yet maintains barriers between Jew and Gentile in our republic" (14 Aug. 1873).
4. *JM*, 22 March 1867, 29 July 1875; *OCC* 4 (Aug. 1846):257; *OCC* 10 (Nov. 1852):415.
5. See, for example, *ISR*, 11 Aug. 1854; *JM*, 4 Dec. 1868; *AI*, 15 July 1909.
6. Examples of praise by Christians are found in *OCC* 15 (Aug. 1857): 244–45; James Parton, "Our Israelitish Brethren," *Atlantic Monthly* 26 (Oct. 1870):385–402; *MEN* 6 (Jan. 1889):68–69; *New York Sun* in *AI*, 27 June 1879; *JM*, 2 Aug. 1901; *AH*, 16 Sept. 1881.
7. David A. D'Ancona, "Answer to Anti-Semitism: San Francisco 1883," *WSJHQ* 8 (Oct. 1975):59–64.
8. *OCC* 12 (March 1855):600–601; *Harper's* 17 (Oct. 1858):700–701; *JM*, 30 Aug. 1894; Alice Hyneman Rhine, "Race Prejudice at Summer Resorts," *Forum* 3 (July 1887):525–27; Leo N. Levi, "The Work of the Sons of the Covenant," *MEN* 34 (April 1903):222.
9. Naomi W. Cohen, *A Dual Heritage* (Philadelphia, 1969), pp. 85–87, 155; L. Mayer in *AI*, 4 April 1907; Allan Chase, *The Legacy of Malthus* (New York, 1977), pp. 275–77.
10. David Philipson, *Max Lilienthal* (New York, 1915), pp. 469–72.
11. See, for example, *JM*, 6 July 1877; Emil G. Hirsch in *MEN* 35 (Aug. 1903):95.
12. Leo N. Levi, "The American Hebrews' Work," *MEN* 2 (March 1887):109–10.
13. Robert H. Bremner, *American Philanthropy* (Chicago, 1960), chap. 1; *OCC* 15 (Aug. 1857):247–48; *MEN* 4 (March 1888):317; N. Behar to [N. Leven], 11 Feb. 1901, Alliance Israélite Universelle Papers, American Jewish Archives.
14. *OCC* 5 (April 1847):35; *JM*, 10 Aug. 1860, 1 Aug. 1884, 2 Aug. 1895; *AI*, 17 April 1879; *AH*, 18 Nov. 1881; David Philipson, *The Jew in America* (Cincinnati, 1909), p. 15; Bertram W. Korn, *The Early Jews of New Orleans* (Waltham, 1969), pp. 217–21, 249–58; Rudolf Glanz, *Studies in Judaica Americana* (New York, 1970), pp. 227–28.
15. Eric Hirshler, ed., *Jews from Germany in the United States* (New York, 1955), p. 70; *JM*, 15 Oct. 1878, 3 July 1896; Milton Goldin, *Why They Give* (New York, 1976), pp. 35, 37; Leon Hühner, "Jews in Connection with the Colleges of the Thirteen Original States," *PAJHS* 19 (1910):110, 113–15; *AH*, 10 Nov. 1905.

16. Morris Jastrow, "The Jewish Question in Its Recent Aspects," *International Journal of Ethics* 6 (July 1896):473.

17. Isaac M. Fein, *The Making of an American Jewish Community* (Philadelphia, 1971), p. 75; *MEN* 6 (Jan. 1889):69; *ASM*, 8 June 1855; *AH*, 14 Jan. 1889; Glanz, *Judaica Americana*, pp. 133–34, 227–28; *JM*, 14 Jan. 1887; Goldin, *Why They Give*, p. 37.

18. *AH*, 13 Feb. 1880, 5 March 1880; Alfred D. Low, *Jews in the Eyes of the Germans* (Philadelphia, 1979), pp. 369–77; *MEN* 6 (Jan. 1889):69; Kaufmann Kohler, "Israel's Mission of Light," *MEN* 28 (Jan. 1900):4.

19. *AI*, 4 Jan. 1901.

20. *OCC* 6 (Jan. 1849):469; *JM*, 4 Feb. 1876; *AH*, 16 Feb. 1906; *AI*, 15 Aug. 1907.

21. *OCC* 16 (June 1858):164; Jacob R. Marcus, *The Colonial American Jew*, 3 vols. (Detroit, 1970), 2, chap. 60; *JM*, 21 Dec. 1860, 31 Oct. 1873, 14 May 1875, 28 March 1877, 28 March 1879; *ISR*, 15 Aug. 1856; *AI*, 30 March 1877.

22. Morris U. Schappes, ed., *A Documentary History of the Jews in the United States, 1654–1875*, 3d ed. (New York, 1971), pp. 4–5; *JM*, 15 July 1859; *UAHC Proceedings* (1911), pp. 6634–35; Minutes of the Executive Committee, 7 Nov. 1914, American Jewish Committee Archives.

23. *JM*, 2 Dec. 1887, 17 Oct. 1893, 7 Feb. 1902; John Fiske, *The Dutch and Quaker Colonies in America*, 2 vols. (Boston, 1927), 2:334; Fein, *Making of an American Jewish Community*, p. 75; *OCC* 15 (Aug. 1857):244–45.

24. Bremner, *American Philanthropy*, pp. 43–45; Levi, "American Hebrews' Work," 111; *OCC* 15 (Jan.–March 1858):462–69, 549, 553, 556; *JM*, 30 Dec. 1859, 30 Oct. 1868; *MEN* 4 (March 1888):317.

25. *OCC* 3 (June 1845):168; *OCC* 11 (April 1853, Jan.–Feb. 1854):77, 477 ff., 541 ff.; *OCC* 12 (May, Oct. 1854):90–91, 351 ff.; *OCC* 13 (Feb. 1856):517 ff.

26. *OCC* 13 (May–June 1855):54, 97–107; *JM*, 27 Aug. 1858, 12 and 19 Nov. 1858, 7 Jan. 1870, 14 March 1873; Herman D. Stein, "Jewish Social Work in the United States," in *The Social Characteristics of American Jews* (New York, 1965), pp. 152–53.

27. *JM*, 1 Jan. 1875, 18 May 1883; *OCC* 6 (Jan. 1849):473–75; *OCC* 15 (March 1858):553–61.

28. *OCC* 6 (Jan. 1849):473–75; *OCC* 13 (May 1855):56–57; *JM*, 30 Oct. 1868, 4 Feb. 1876, 28 March 1877, 17 Nov. 1893; Hyman B. Grinstein, *The Rise of the Jewish Community of New York, 1654–1860* (Philadelphia, 1945), pp. 158–59.

29. Bremner, *American Philanthropy*, p. 47; Maurice J. Karpf, *Jewish Community Organization in the United States* (New York, 1938), pp. 85–86; *American Jews' Annual* 4 (1888):39 ff.; *OCC* 6 (Jan. 1849):472; *OCC* 7 (May 1849):71; *OCC* 8 (Aug. 1850):259–61; *OCC* 16 (April 1858):32.

30. Bremner, *American Philanthropy*, chap. 7; Goldin, *Why They Give*, pp. 39–43; Cyrus Adler, *Jacob H. Schiff*, 2 vols. (Garden City, 1929), 1, chap. 11; *AI*, 15 July 1909 (Krauskopf), 1 Sept. 1910; Hirshler, *Jews from Germany*, pp. 70–71; *MEN* 4 (May 1888):465; John F. Sutherland, "Rabbi Joseph Krauskopf: The Urban Reformer Returns to the Land," *AJHQ* 67 (June 1978):342–62.

31. Roy F. Nichols, *The Disruption of American Democracy* (New York, 1962), pp. 139–40; *ASM*, 9, 16, and 30 Oct. 1857; *JM*, 20 Nov. 1857, 10 Sept. 1858; *OCC* 15 (Jan. 1858):462–69; *OCC* 16 (Jan. 1859):464–65.

32. *JM*, 6 and 20 Nov. 1857, 4 Dec. 1857, 1 Jan. 1858; *ASM*, 6 Nov. 1857, 15 and 22 Jan. 1858, 2 April 1858; *OCC* 15 (Feb., March 1858):548, 576; *OCC* 16 (May, Nov., Dec. 1858):115, 405, 447.

33. *ASM*, 6 Nov.–4 Dec. 1857, 18 Dec. 1857–8 Jan. 1858, 5 Feb. 1858, 2 April 1858; *JM*, 20 Nov. 1857, 4 Dec. 1857, 29 Jan. 1858, 12 Feb. 1858; *OCC* 16 (Dec. 1858):445, 449. The Hebrew Benevolent Society's strongest competitor, the German Benevolent Society, also raised impressive sums. Additional monies came from smaller agencies and from balls and soirées run for charity.

34. *OCC* 15 (Jan.–Feb. 1858):500–501, 547–49; *OCC* 16 (April–May 1858):65–66, 112–17.

35. *ASM*, 19 March 1858; *JM*, 26 Feb. 1858, 12 March 1858.

36. *JM*, 8 Oct. 1858; *OCC* 16 (June, Sept.–Dec. 1858):58, 163, 311, 361, 410–11, 457–58.

37. *JM*, 8 Oct. 1858.

38. *AH*, 20 April 1906.

39. *AH*, 20 and 27 April 1906, 4 May 1906; *Chicago Israelite*, 21 April–5 May 1906; Adler, *Schiff*, 1:367–68; Judah L. Magnes and Lee K. Frankel, "Condition of San Francisco Jewry Following the 1906 Earthquake," *WSJHQ* 11 (April 1906):241.

40. Magnes and Frankel, "San Francisco Jewry," 239–42; *AH*, 4, 11, and 25 April 1906; *Chicago Israelite*, 5–19 May 1906, 2 June 1906.

41. *Chicago Israelite*, 2 June 1906; Jacob Nieto, "A 1906 San Francisco Protest and Appeal," *WSJHQ* 9 (April 1977):246–50; Minutes of Meeting of General Committee, 11 Nov. 1906, American Jewish Committee Archives; *AJYB* 10 (1908–1909):243; *AJYB* 11 (1909–1910):244–45, 252–53; *Emanu-El*, 27 March 1908.

42. The political rules were culled principally from readings of the prewar *Occident, Israelite, Asmonean,* and the postwar *American Israelite, Jewish Messenger,* and *American Hebrew.* They are confirmed in biographies and communal histories.

43. Schappes, *Documentary History,* pp. 185–87, 613.

44. *ISR*, 19 Feb. 1858; *OCC* 12 (Feb. 1855):563; *OCC* 15 (May 1857), 93–94.

45. Edith Abbott, *Historical Aspects of the Immigration Problem* (Chicago, 1926), pp. 466, 478 et seq.

46. Lawrence H. Fuchs, *The Political Behavior of American Jews* (Glencoe, 1956), pp. 20–21; Moses Gaster, *History of the Ancient Synagogue of the Spanish and Portuguese Jews* (London, 1901), p. 88 (and cited in Marcus, *Colonial American Jew,* 3:1212).

47. *ASM*, 6 July 1855; *MEN* 39 (Oct. 1905):233–34.

48. *AI*, 16 March 1893. "Political schizophrenia" was a term used by Judge Joseph Proskauer in denying that American Jews were identified politically with Israelis. Louis M. Hacker and Mark D. Hirsch, *Proskauer* (University, Ala., 1978), p. 151.

49. *ISR*, 21 Nov. 1856.

50. *AI*, 3 Aug. 1877, 30 Oct. 1885, 22 July 1909, 6 Oct. 1910 (A. Cohen); *JM*, 3 Aug. 1877.

51. Lawrence H. Fuchs, ed., *American Ethnic Politics* (New York, 1968), pp. 3–4; *OCC* 11 (July 1853):224–25; *JM*, 9 Sept. 1864; *AH*, 20 Aug. 1897.

52. Leon Hühner, "David L. Yulee, Florida's First Senator," in *Jews in the South,* ed. Leonard Dinnerstein and Mary Palsson (Baton Rouge, 1973),

pp. 61–62; Bertram W. Korn, *American Jewry and the Civil War* (Philadelphia, 1951), pp. 158–60, 287; *JM*, 21 March 1862; Schappes, *Documentary History*, p. 396.

53. Morris U. Schappes, "Anti-Semitism and Reaction, 1785–1900," in *The Jewish Experience in America*, ed. Abraham J. Karp, 5 vols. (Waltham and New York, 1969), 1:362–90; Fuchs, *Political Behavior*, pp. 26–29; *ISR*, 21 Aug. 1857. The importance of the Jewish vote had been recognized as early as 1737 in New York. Marcus, *Colonial American Jew*, 1:409–10.

54. *AI*, 21 March 1895; John Hay to Myer S. Isaacs, 1 Nov. 1864, American Jewish Archives; *AH*, 29 Oct. 1886, 11 Nov. 1887, and similar remarks by Stephen Wise in *AI*, 14 Nov. 1907; Minutes of the BDAI, 6 June 1860. The BDAI doubtless recalled how some Jews had argued against the political implications of its very establishment. *ISR*, 18 Nov. 1859, 9 Dec. 1859.

55. Schappes, "Anti-Semitism and Reaction," 1:372–80.

56. American Jewish Archives: *Cincinnati Daily Times*, 2 and 12 Oct. 1858; *Cincinnati Daily Commercial*, 9 Oct. 1858; *Cincinnati Daily Enquirer*, 3 Oct. 1858.

57. Korn, *American Jewry and the Civil War*, pp. 16–18, 21–22, 41–44; Leon A. Jick, *The Americanization of the Synagogue* (Hanover, 1976), p. 136; *JM*, 18 and 25 Jan. 1861. During the war, Sabato Morais's pro-Union sermons led his board to forbid temporarily all sermons in English unless specifically requested by the president (Korn, p. 38).

58. *AH*, 22 Oct. 1880, 20 April 1894; *AI*, 21 Nov. 1889, 23 April 1908; *CCAR Year Book* 1 (1890–1891):78; Stuart E. Rosenberg, "Notes on the Political Attitudes of the *Jewish Tidings*," *JSS* 17 (Oct. 1855):323–24.

59. Peter R. Decker, *Fortunes and Failures* (Cambridge, 1973), p. 116; see also "California's Hebrews," *WSJHQ* 4 (July 1972):200–201; for a similar comment about Cincinnati's Jews see *ISR*, 18 June 1858.

60. *ISR*, 23 May 1856.

61. *JM*, 24 Sept. 1858, 4 Nov. 1859, 1 Nov. 1867, 24 April 1868; *OCC* 11 (June 1853):188; *ASM*, 2 May 1851; *ISR*, 18 Sept. 1857, 17 Sept. 1858, 18 March 1859; *AI*, 25 July 1879, 17 April 1885, 30 Sept. 1887, 28 March 1895; *AH*, 25 April 1884, 19 Sept. 1884. Once, however, the *AI* blamed the lack of Jewish political success on the Jews' disinclination to venture beyond business and the professions (30 Oct. 1885).

62. *JM*, 5 May 1871; *AH*, 25 Oct. 1895; *ISR*, 6 and 21 June 1856, 26 June 1857.

63. *OCC* 12 (Feb. 1855):561–63.

64. *OCC* 2 (June 1844):128–29; *OCC* 4 (Sept. 1846):267–68; *OCC* 6 (Dec. 1848):423–24; *OCC* 7 (April 1849):2–6; *OCC* 15 (Sept. 1857):292–94; *OCC* 16 (Oct. 1858):333; Naomi W. Cohen, "Pioneers of American Jewish Defense," *AJA* 29 (Nov. 1977):128–29.

65. *ASM*, 19 Dec. 1851. In advice to English Jews, Lyon was less restrained: "The Jews must organize a systematic line of operation—they must unite—money and men. Talent they have in plenty. Let a general fund be gathered, and whenever a vacancy occurs in a liberal constituency let it be contested. . . . [I]f men are put up who stand before the world *sans peur* and *sans reproche*, the day will come when a dozen or more Hebrews will be returned—then the vote will be considered of value, and the Ministry of the day, to gain its support will do much to break down the antiquated form which now deprives the British Jew of a valued right." The *Asmonean* was alluding to the right of Jews to sit in Parliament (6 May 1853).

66. *ASM,* 20 and 27 Feb. 1852, 16 July 1852, 10 June 1853, 27 Oct. 1854, 10 and 17 Nov. 1854, 27 April 1855, 4 May 1855, 15 and 22 June 1855, 6 and 27 July 1855, 8 and 15 Aug. 1856, 9 Jan. 1857, 27 March 1857, 14 Aug. 1857, 25 Sept. 1857, 23 Oct. 1857.

67. *Emanu-El,* 16 Oct.–6 Nov. 1908.

68. Fuchs, *Political Behavior,* p. 26; Leon Hühner, "An Early Record of Prominent American Jews," *PAJHS* 12 (1904):163–65; Samuel Oppenheim, "An Early Record of Prominent American Jews," *PAJHS* 18 (1909):209–10.

69. In 1867 an election circular appeared in Hebrew on behalf of Judge Albert Cardozo of New York. The writer obviously disregarded the caveat against appeals for the group's vote. "A New York Election Circular in Hebrew of 1867," *PAJHS* 34 (1937):285–88.

70. Stephen Birmingham, *Our Crowd* (New York, 1968), pp. 76–82; Harvey O'Connor, *The Guggenheims* (New York, 1937), chap. 15. On the east Europeans' political idealism, see, for example, Daniel J. Elazar, "American Political Theory and the Political Notions of American Jews," in *The Ghetto and Beyond,* ed. Peter I. Rose (New York, 1969), p. 215.

71. *JM,* 14 Feb. 1868.

72. Korn, *American Jewry and the Civil War,* pp. 158–59, 165, 167, 177–78; Bertram W. Korn, *Eventful Years and Experiences* (Cincinnati, 1954), pp. 79–97; *ISR,* 17 Sept. 1858, 11 Feb. 1859, 22 and 29 March 1861; *AI,* 16 May 1884, 29 April 1897; *JM,* 25 May 1877. Ex-Senator G. G. Vest of Missouri also drew an analogy between Benjamin and Disraeli in "Judah P. Benjamin: A Senator of Two Republics," *MEN* 35 (Nov. 1903):294–99.

73. Walter Bean, *Boss Ruef's San Francisco* (Berkeley, 1952); *AI,* 13 Feb. 1908, 12 and 26 March 1908, 21 April 1910; *Emanu-El,* April 1908–Nov. 1909.

74. Unless otherwise noted, all references to Straus are from Cohen, *A Dual Heritage,* pp. 21–23, 27–31, 83–90, 152–61, chap. 10.

75. *Outlook,* 21 Sept. 1912, pp. 111–16.

76. *New York Times,* 4 Nov. 1912.

77. A. Lipsky, "The Jewish Vote in the Recent Election," *AH,* 21 Nov. 1913. The four "Jewish" districts in Manhattan and the Bronx that went to Straus were Assembly Districts 3, 6, 26, and 31. In those as well as the three others (10, 21, 29) carried by Straus, the latter ran ahead of Roosevelt, the Progressive candidate for president (New York City Board of Elections, *Annual Report* [1912], pp. 12, 18).

78. Max J. Kohler, "The Jews and the American Anti-Slavery Movement," *PAJHS* 5 (1897):137–55, and 9 (1901):45–56; Fuchs, *Political Behavior,* pp. 35–40; Korn, *Eventful Years,* pp. 11–12; Korn, *American Jewry and the Civil War,* chap. 2. There were attempts both North and South to establish separate Jewish military units, but most opposed segregated service (Korn, *American Jewry and the Civil War,* pp. 116–19).

79. Korn, *American Jewry and the Civil War,* chaps. 2, 3; Schappes, *Documentary History,* pp. 332–33; Maldwyn A. Jones, *American Immigration* (Chicago, 1960), pp. 167–69.

80. Korn, *American Jewry and the Civil War,* chaps. 4, 7; *OCC* 20 (Jan. 1863):460–62; James G. Heller, *Isaac M. Wise* (New York, 1965), pp. 356–57.

81. Korn, *American Jewry and the Civil War,* chap. 6; *AI,* 29 June 1877; Emil G. Hirsch, "The Ancient Anti-Semite and His Modern Successors," in *CCAR, Sermons by American Rabbis* (Chicago, 1896), pp. 122–25; Thomas

County, Georgia, newspaper clipping, Sept. 1862, American Jewish Archives; Max Nordau to Isaac Markens, Karlsbad, 1912, American Jewish Archives.

82. *JM*, 16 Jan. 1863, 28 Oct. 1864, 4 Nov. 1864.

83. Korn, *American Jewry and the Civil War*, pp. 132–38, 277; Joakim Isaacs, "Candidate Grant and the Jews," *AJA* 17 (April 1965):3–16.

84. *JM*, 25 May 1868, 5 and 26 June 1868, 3, 17, and 24 July 1868, 30 Oct. 1868, 4 Dec. 1868, 2 Aug. 1872.

85. *JM*, 26 June 1868; Korn, *American Jewry and the Civil War*, p. 134; *OCC* 26 (Sept. 1868):245–46.

86. *ISR*, 28 Feb. 1868, 27 March 1868, 4 April 1868, 19 and 26 June 1868, 7 Aug. 1868.

87. Works that discuss the Populist role in American anti-Semitism are listed in John Higham, *Send These to Me* (New York, 1975), pp. 118–19, nn. 5, 7.

88. *New York Times*, 15 Sept. 1896; *AH*, 6 Nov. 1896.

89. *AI*, 12 Nov. 1896.

90. *JM*, 3, 17, and 24 July 1896, 7 Aug.–11 Sept. 1896, 25 Sept. 1896, 2 and 16 Oct.–6 Nov. 1896.

91. *AI*, 17 Oct. 1895, 23 Jan. 1896, 25 June 1896, 9, 23, and 30 July 1896, 20 Aug. 1896, 10 and 17 Sept. 1896, 1 and 15 Oct. 1896, 12 Nov. 1896. However, in a decade when talk of Jewish money power increased, Wise defended the Jews against charges that they were economic parasites linked with the oppressive corporations.

92. *AI*, 12 Nov. 1896.

93. M. L. Fox, *Our Coin* [Yiddish] (Chicago [1896]), American Jewish Archives.

94. William J. Bryan to Isaac M. Wise, 30 Nov. 1896, American Jewish Archives; *AI*, 2 Aug. 1894, 15 Oct. 1896, 12 Nov. 1896; *AH*, 6 Nov. 1896.

95. Festus P. Summers, *William L. Wilson and Tariff Reform* (New Brunswick, 1953), p. 200.

96. Cohen, "Pioneers of American Jewish Defense," 129, 138, 146; Adolph M. Radin, "Relief Work among Jewish Inmates of Penal Institutions," *CCAR Year Book* 16 (1906):263–64.

CHAPTER 4
THE AMERICANIZATION OF JUDAISM

1. M. H. Harris, "The Dangers of Emancipation," *CCAR Year Book* 4 (1893):55–63.

2. *OCC* 2 (June, Aug. 1844):128, 237; *OCC* 4 (May 1846):76; *JM*, 13 Oct. 1882; *AH*, 17 Dec. 1897.

3. *OCC* 1 (Jan., Feb. 1844):459–60, 533–35; *OCC* 2 (Jan. 1845):457–66; *OCC* 3 (May 1845):87–91.

4. Bertram W. Korn, *The Early Jews of New Orleans* (Waltham, 1969), p. 214; *OCC* 2 (July 1844):188–89; Moshe Davis, *The Emergence of Conservative Judaism* (Philadelphia, 1963), p. 32.

5. The Fleishmans of Dunn, North Carolina, were among the singular Jews (files of Rabbi Morton Leifman, 1953).

6. Joseph L. Blau and Salo W. Baron, eds., *The Jews of the United States, 1790–1840*, 3 vols. (New York and Philadelphia, 1963), 1:64.

7. For a history of Reform's development, see David Philipson, *The Reform Movement in Judaism*, rev. ed. (New York, 1967).

8. Michael A. Meyer, "Christian Influence on Early German Reform Judaism," in *Studies in Jewish Bibliography, History and Literature in Honor of I. Edward Kiev*, ed. Charles Berlin (New York, 1971), pp. 289–303; *ISR*, 28 July 1854; Leon A. Jick, *The Americanization of the Synagogue* (Hanover, 1976), pp. 82–83, 94; *OCC* 15 (July 1857):200.

9. Blau and Baron, *Jews of the U.S.*, 2:555; Julius Bien, "History of the International Order B'ne B'rith," *MEN* 2 (March 1887):124.

10. Philipson, *Reform Movement*, p. 377; Beryl H. Levy, *Reform Judaism in America* (New York, 1933), p. 79; Nathan Glazer, *American Judaism* (Chicago, 1957), p. 46.

11. Jick, *Americanization of the Synagogue*, chaps. 6, 7.

12. *ISR*, 15 Dec. 1854.

13. *ISR*, 4 July 1856.

14. Bernhard Felsenthal, *The Beginnings of the Chicago Sinai Congregation* (Chicago, 1898); Emma Felsenthal, *Bernhard Felsenthal* (New York, 1924), pp. 20–29.

15. Philipson, *Reform Movement*, chaps. 4, 7.

16. Philipson, *Reform Movement*, pp. 355–57.

17. Davis, *Emergence of Conservative Judaism*, p. 228; Gershon Greenberg, "Samuel Hirsch's American Judaism," *AJHQ* 62 (June 1973):362–82; Gershon Greenberg, "The Significance of America in David Einhorn's Conception of History," *AJHQ* 63 (Dec. 1973):160–84.

18. *ISR*, 13 July 1855, 2 July 1858; Kaufmann Kohler, *Studies, Addresses, and Personal Papers* (New York, 1936), p. 230; David Philipson, *My Life as an American Jew* (Cincinnati, 1941), p. 223; Solomon B. Freehof, "Reform Judaism and Zionism," *Menorah Journal* 32 (April–June 1944):37–38.

19. Oscar Straus, *The Origin of Republican Form of Government in the United States of America* (New York, 1885). See also Naomi W. Cohen, *A Dual Heritage* (Philadelphia, 1969), pp. 6–7, 14–15, chap. 14.

20. *UAHC Proceedings* (1898), p. 4002; *JM*, 9 April 1858, 22 March 1861; David Philipson, *Max Lilienthal* (New York, 1915), pp. 62–64, 66–69; *AI*, 13 April 1877, 3 Oct. 1879.

21. Charles Reznikoff and Uriah Z. Engelman, *The Jews of Charleston* (Philadelphia, 1950), p. 140; *CCAR Year Book* 12 (1902):236; *CCAR Year Book* 17 (1907):182–83; *CCAR Year Book* 22 (1912):281–82; *AI*, 6 Feb. 1919; *OCC* 26 (July, Oct. 1868):199, 333.

22. Isaac M. Wise, *Reminiscences* (Cincinnati, 1901); James G. Heller, *Isaac M. Wise* (New York, 1965); Jacob R. Marcus, *Studies in American Jewish History* (Cincinnati, 1969), pp. 180–94; Davis, *Emergence of Conservative Judaism*, p. 152; *ISR*, 23 Jan. 1857, 12 June 1857.

23. Uriah Z. Engelman, "Jewish Statistics in the U.S. Census of Religious Bodies," *JSS* 9 (April 1947):136.

24. *CCAR Year Book* 5 (1895):11, 85–89; *CCAR Year Book* 6 (1896):85; *CCAR Year Book* 12 (1902):203 ff.; Julia Richman, "The Sunday School Movement in the United States," *Jewish Quarterly Review* 12 (July 1900):580–83.

25. *CCAR Year Book* 4 (1894):73.

26. Maurice Fishberg, "The Jews: A Study of Race and Environment," *Popular Science Monthly* 70 (Jan. 1907):44–47.

27. For a survey of Leeser's background and American career, see Maxine Seller, "Isaac Leeser, Architect of the American Jewish Community" (Ph. D. diss., University of Pennsylvania, 1965), chap. 2.

28. David Philipson, *Centenary Papers and Others* (Cincinnati, 1919), pp. 149–90.

29. *OCC* 1 (Aug. 1843):253–61; *OCC* 2 (June 1844):150–53; *OCC* 12 (June, Nov. 1854):148–53, 405–8; *OCC* 13 (Dec. 1855), 420, 427; Wise, *Reminiscences,* pp. 57, 61, 130, 141–49, 194, 269, 279–81; Leeser's series of anti-Reform editorials appeared in "Judaism and Its Principles" and "Reforming and Deforming," *OCC* 8 (1850–51), and in "Progressive Reforms," *OCC* 12 (1854–55).

30. *OCC* 13 (Dec. 1855):420–30; Davis, *Emergence of Conservative Judaism,* pp. 130–34.

31. *OCC* 13 (1855–56):420–30 and articles by A. Rice, S. Jacobs, B. Illowy; *OCC* 14 (1856–57):185–86, 300–301, 353–55, 378–87, and editorial series "A Survey of the Field"; *ISR,* 2, 16, and 23 May 1856.

32. *ISR,* 5–26 Dec. 1856, 2 Jan. 1857, 20 Feb. 1857.

33. In addition to Leeser's editorial series in *OCC* 8, 12, 14 (see nn. 29 and 31), see *OCC* 14 (July, Sept., Jan., Feb. 1856–57):180–87, 265–85, 475–80, 534–38; *OCC* 15 (June 1857):109–20; *ISR,* 24 April 1857.

34. Alexander Kohut, *The Ethics of the Fathers* (New York, 1920), pp. xxvii–xxviii; see, for example, *CCAR Year Book* 3 (1892):111.

35. Kohut, *Ethics of the Fathers,* pp. ix–xxxvi, xcix–c; Davis, *Emergence of Conservative Judaism,* p. 225.

36. Kohut, *Ethics of the Fathers,* passim.

37. H. G. Enelow, "Kaufmann Kohler," *AJYB* 28 (1926–27):235–50; Kohler, *Studies,* pp. 211, 469–80. Kohler's eulogy of Kohut appears on pp. 539–43.

38. Kohler, *Studies,* pp. 201–35.

39. Davis, *Emergence of Conservative Judaism,* pp. 224, 234–36; Kohut, *Ethics of the Fathers,* pp. civ–cv.

40. Levy, *Reform Judaism in America,* pp. 60–63.

41. S. M. Isaacs, "1847," *OCC* 4 (Feb. 1847):542–43; Davis, *Emergence of Conservative Judaism,* pp. 119–24.

42. Seller, "Isaac Leeser," 87–91.

43. Richman, "Jewish Sunday School Movement," 572–73; Lawrence A. Cremin, *American Education: The National Experience* (New York, 1980), pp. 61–62, 66; Joseph Rosenbloom, "Rebecca Gratz and the Jewish Sunday School Movement in Philadelphia," *PAJHS* 48 (Dec. 1958):71–77; Maxwell Whiteman, "Isaac Leeser and the Jews of Philadelphia," *PAJHS* 48 (June 1959):229n; Joshua Bloch, "Rosa Mordecai's Recollections of the First Hebrew Sunday School," *PAJHS* 42 (June 1953):397–406.

44. Richman, "Jewish Sunday School Movement," 573–75.

45. Jick, *Americanization of the Synagogue,* p. 62; Philipson, *My Life as an American Jew,* p. 115.

46. *UAHC Proceedings* (1899), pp. 4125–26; *UAHC Proceedings* (1904), pp. 4808–10, 4815–17; *UAHC Proceedings* (1905), pp. 5098–5104; *UAHC Proceedings* (1908), p. 6080; *UAHC Proceedings* (1910), p. 6512; *UAHC Proceedings* (1911), p. 6656.

47. Philipson, *Reform Movement,* pp. 373–75; *ISR,* 29 Aug. 1856; *OCC* 15 (June 1857):118–19.

48. Emil G. Hirsch, *Reform Judaism* (n.p., 1885), pp. 11–13; David E.

Hirsch, *Rabbi Emil G. Hirsch* (Chicago, 1968), pp. 10, 108; *Chicago Israelite*, 9 June 1906 (Heller).

49. Stuart E. Rosenberg, "The *Jewish Tidings* and the Sunday Services Question," *PAJHS* 42 (June 1953):371–86; Kaufmann Kohler in *CCAR Year Book* 3 (1892):111–12.

50. Philipson, *Reform Movement*, pp. 375–76; Levy, *Reform Judaism in America*, pp. 92–107.

51. David de Sola Pool and Tamar de Sola Pool, *An Old Faith in the New World* (New York, 1955), pp. 158–74; Jick, *Americanization of the Synagogue*, pp. 70–75, 130; Wise, *Reminiscences*, pp. 23, 45, 223–24; Hyman B. Grinstein, "Communal and Social Aspects of American Jewish History," *PAJHS* 39 (March 1950):271.

52. Wise, *Reminiscences*, pp. 51, 102; Seller, "Isaac Leeser," 20; *OCC* 11 (Jan. 1854):510.

53. Wise, *Reminiscences*, pp. 25, 102, 129, 237; *ISR*, 6 and 27 Oct. 1854, 27 April 1855, 4 May 1855, 5 and 12 Sept. 1856, 31 Oct. 1856, 7 Nov. 1856; Samuel E. Karff, ed., *Hebrew Union College–Jewish Institute of Religion at One Hundred Years* (Cincinnati, 1976), pp. 15–16.

54. Myer S. Isaacs, *The Old Guard and Other Addresses* (New York, 1906), pp. 150–53; E. Hirsch, *Reform Judaism*, p. 5; Philipson, *Centenary Papers*, pp. 229–46.

55. Rabbi I. Leucht characterized the rabbi as a "general utility man," a role adopted, he said, from that of the American minister and vastly different from the sage of the ghetto. *CCAR Year Book* 7 (1897):11–18.

56. M. E[llinger], "From the Old to the New," *MEN* 29 (Nov. 1900):253–69.

57. *CCAR Year Book* 1 (1890):62–79; *CCAR Year Book* 13 (1903):46–55.

58. For the influence of Henry George on the Jewish soap manufacturer Joseph Fels, see Arthur Dudden, "The Single-Tax Zionism of Joseph Fels," *PAJHS* 46 (June 1957):474–91.

59. *JM*, 26 June 1868.

60. Leonard Mervis, "The Social Justice Movement and the American Reform Rabbi," *AJA* 7 (June 1955):172; Charlotte Baum et al., *The Jewish Woman in America* (New York, 1977), pp. 40–41; L. Glen Seretan, "Daniel De Leon, 'Wandering Jew' of American Socialism," *AJHQ* 65 (March 1976):255; Sheila Polishook, "The American Federation of Labor, Zionism, and the First World War," *AJHQ* 65 (March 1976):234.

61. Benny Kraut, *From Reform Judaism to Ethical Culture* (Cincinnati, 1979), esp. pp. 75, 83–85, 107, 124–28, 132; Charles H. Hopkins, *The Rise of the Social Gospel in American Protestantism* (New Haven, 1940), pp. 57–58.

62. Hopkins, *Social Gospel*, passim; Henry F. May, *Protestant Churches and Industrial America* (New York, 1963), pt. 4.

63. May, *Protestant Churches*, p. 194; *CCAR Year Book* 19 (1909):101–2, 432–94; Hopkins, *Social Gospel*, p. 85; Mervis, "Social Justice Movement," 176–79.

64. D. Hirsch, *Emil Hirsch*, pp. 8–9, 107, 183; Mervis, "Social Justice Movement," 197–201. Rabbi Henry Berkowitz wrote in general terms about the inequities of capitalism in 1888, but his answer was primarily a résumé of the relevance of Jewish ethics to the social ills of various ages (*Judaism on the Social Question* [New York, 1888]).

65. D. Hirsch, *Emil Hirsch,* pp. 9, 84; Levy, *Reform Judaism in America,* pp. 62–63; Emil G. Hirsch, "The Doctrine of Jesus," in *Discourses* (New York, n.d.); p. 10, and "Why Am I a Jew, I," in *Discourses,* pp. 16–18.

66. D. Hirsch, *Emil Hirsch,* pp. 16, 23; Mervis, "Social Justice Movement," 173–75, 199; Levy, *Reform Judaism in America,* pp. 63–66.

67. Emil G. Hirsch, "The Inalienable Duties of Man, I–II," in *Discourses.*

68. Hopkins, *Social Gospel,* chaps. 2, 5; D. Hirsch, *Emil Hirsch,* p. 8; Emil G. Hirsch, "Inalienable Duties, II," in *Discourses,* pp. 6–7, and "The Responsibility for the Russian Massacre," in *Discourses,* p. 18.

69. D. Hirsch, *Emil Hirsch,* pp. 8–10, 14, 180–91; Mervis, "Social Justice Movement," 197–99, 202; Joseph L. Blau, ed., *Reform Judaism: A Historical Perspective* (New York, 1973), p. 34.

70. Egal Feldman, "The Social Gospel and the Jews," *AJHQ* 68 (March 1969):302–22.

71. Joseph L. Blau, *Judaism in America* (Chicago, 1976), chap. 1.

72. *AH,* 9 Nov. 1894, 14 Dec. 1894.

73. Abraham A. Neuman, *Cyrus Adler* (New York, 1942), pp. 3–33, 42–47; Jurgen Herbst, *The German Historical School in American Scholarship* (Ithaca, 1965), chap. 2; Cyrus Adler, *Lectures, Selected Papers, Addresses* (Philadelphia, 1933), pp. 162–71; *AH,* 9 Nov. 1894; Louis Finkelstein, "Cyrus Adler: Jew and American," 25 June 1940, Cyrus Adler Papers, Jewish Theological Seminary. For the wide range of Adler's activities see his autobiography *I Have Considered the Days* (Philadelphia, 1945).

74. Cyrus Adler, page proofs of "Address Delivered at the Formal Opening of the Semitic Museum of Harvard University," 5 Feb. 1903, Adler Papers; Cyrus Adler, *Jacob H. Schiff,* 2 vols. (Garden City, 1929), 2:21.

75. Neuman, *Adler,* pp. 45–47, 49, 73–76, 151–56; Joshua Bloch, *Of Making Many Books* (Philadelphia, 1953), pp. 1–45.

76. *MEN* 5 (Sept. 1888):191–93; Neuman, *Adler,* pp. 50–55, 77–80; Adler to R. Gottheil, 26 Feb. 1909, Adler Papers; Adler, *Lectures,* pp. 189–98. On the American Jewish Historical Society, see below, chap. 6.

77. *OCC* 1 (Sept. 1843):301, 303–6; *JM,* 31 May 1895, 7 June 1895, 30 Oct. 1896; *MEN* 18 (June 1895):410–11; *AH,* 6 April 1900; *AI,* 11 July 1907, 26 Dec. 1907, 12 March 1908. For antecedents of Noah's idea and for different attempts in the nineteenth century for a university, see Bertram W. Korn, *Eventful Years and Experiences* (Cincinnati, 1954), chap. 7.

78. CCAR, *Sermons by American Rabbis* (Chicago, 1896), pp. 145–46; cf. William Rosenau's survey of Semitic studies in American colleges, *CCAR Year Book* 6 (1896):99 et seq.

79. Rough draft of letter by Adler to *AH* [1892], Adler Papers.

80. Neuman, *Adler,* pp. 49, 64–65, 84–89, 100–114; Adler, *Lectures,* pp. 43–64; Adler to O. Straus, 10 March 1910, Adler Papers; Adler to R. Gottheil, 26 Feb. 1909, Adler Papers.

81. Adler, *Lectures,* pp. 231–39.

82. Adler, *Lectures,* pp. 60, 237, 294; proposal for a Jewish Theological Quarterly, Adler Papers; Adler to Solomon Schechter, 2 Aug. 1911, Adler Papers.

CHAPTER 5
"ALL ISRAEL ARE RESPONSIBLE FOR ONE ANOTHER"

1. *WSJHQ* 7 (Oct. 1974):43.
2. *OCC* 16 (Nov. 1858):403.
3. *ISR*, 9 Oct. 1857.
4. *OCC* 16 (Oct. 1858):347.
5. See, for example, *JM*, 16 Aug. 1872.
6. Reprinted in Dorothy B. Goebel, ed., *American Foreign Policy* (New York, 1961), p. 25.
7. Thomas A. Bailey, *A Diplomatic History of the American People*, 9th ed. (Englewood Cliffs, N.J., 1974), pp. 167–68, 181, 268–72; Oscar S. Straus, "Humanitarian Diplomacy of the United States," in *The American Spirit* (New York, 1913), pp. 19–38.
8. Jacob R. Marcus, *Memoirs of American Jews*, 3 vols. (Philadelphia, 1955), 1:272–74; Joseph L. Blau and Salo W. Baron, eds., *The Jews of the United States, 1790–1840*, 3 vols. (New York and Philadelphia, 1963), 3: 954–55. Another contemporary commented along similar lines that "then was beautifully proved, that Israelites feel for each other, if even oceans separate and continents intervene between them." *OCC* 10 (June 1852): 166.
9. Blau and Baron, *Jews of the U.S.*, 3:924–52.
10. Cyrus Adler and Aaron M. Margalith, *With Firmness in the Right* (New York, 1946), p. 5; Lawrence H. Fuchs, *The Political Behavior of American Jews* (Glencoe, 1956), p. 30. Referring to prior instances of American humanitarian diplomacy, Aaron Moise of Charleston said: "That as they [the people of Charleston] had cheered the inhabitants of classic Greece, unfortunate, martyred, chivalric Poland in her struggles for freedom, that as they had hailed Texas in her resistance to tyranny, . . . they were now ready to raise their voices in behalf of wounded Israel." Blau and Baron, *Jews of the U.S.*, 3:947.
11. Blau and Baron, *Jews of the U.S.*, 3:934–37.
12. *New York Herald*, 6 April 1850. The paper also informed its readers that the manuscript record of the original trial, exposing the guilt of the Jews, had found its way to New York and was soon to be published. See also *ASM*, 12 April 1850.
13. Bertram W. Korn, *The American Reaction to the Mortara Case* (Cincinnati, 1957), chaps. 1–3.
14. Korn, *Mortara Case*, pp. 33, 36–37; *OCC* 16 (Jan., Feb. 1859):498, 523, 537.
15. Korn, *Mortara Case*, pp. 40, 51–52; *OCC* 16 (Feb. 1859):537–39.
16. Korn, *Mortara Case*, pp. 63, 90–91; Bertram W. Korn, *Eventful Years and Experiences* (Cincinnati, 1954), pp. 11–12; Fuchs, *Political Behavior*, pp. 31–33.
17. Korn, *Mortara Case*, chap. 4, pp. 108–9; *ISR*, 7 Jan. 1859.
18. Morris U. Schappes, ed., *A Documentary History of the Jews in the United States, 1654–1875*, 3d ed. (New York, 1971), pp. 674–75.
19. *OCC* 16 (Feb. 1859):541–42; *ISR*, 4 Feb. 1859; Allan Tarshish, "The Board of Delegates of American Israelites (1859–1878)," reprinted in *The*

Jewish Experience in America, ed. Abraham J. Karp, 5 vols. (Waltham and New York, 1969), 3:125–28.

20. Korn, *Mortara Case,* pp. 37–38.

21. See, for example, *ISR,* 5 Oct. 1858. The *Occident* reported a contrary version. An infant taken from a Jewish orphans' home in New Orleans was given to a Catholic woman who had it baptized. She at first refused to return the baby, but "as New Orleans is not the Roman States," the child was soon restored (16 [Feb. 1859]:552).

22. Korn, *Mortara Case,* pp. 118–20; *ISR,* 25 March 1859.

23. *OCC* 16 (Oct. 1858):346; *ASM,* 19 June 1857.

24. See above, chap. 2; *ASM,* 28 May 1852, 12 and 18 June 1852.

25. Naomi W. Cohen, "American Jews and the Swiss Treaty," in *Solomon Goldman Lectures* 3 (Spertus College, Chicago, 1982), pp. 93–96.

26. Naomi W. Cohen, "The Abrogation of the Russo-American Treaty of 1832," *JSS* 25 (1963):esp. 3–4, 7–8.

27. *JM,* 1 Dec. 1876, 5 Jan. 1877.

28. Adler and Margalith, *With Firmness in the Right,* pp. 29–30. Through the American Roumanian Society, American Jews underwrote the expenses of Benjamin Peixotto, the unsalaried American consul to Bucharest, 1870–1876. Lloyd P. Gartner, "Roumania, America, and World Jewry," *AJHQ* 58 (Sept. 1968):51.

29. *OCC* 1 (Nov. 1843):390–93; Moshe Davis, *The Emergence of Conservative Judaism* (Philadelphia, 1963), pp. 82–83.

30. Max J. Kohler, "The Board of Delegates of American Israelites," *PAJHS* 27 (1925):84–86; Zosa Szajkowski, "The Alliance Israélite Universelle in the United States," *PAJHS* 39 (June 1950):389–443.

31. *OCC* 1 (July 1843):183–87; *OCC* 10 (April 1852, Jan. 1853):37–39, 465–75.

32. *OCC* 10 (April 1852, March 1853):37–39, 582–88; *OCC* 11 (May, June, Aug., Nov. 1853, Jan. 1854):81–89, 180–84, 275–76, 409–13, 510–15. In 1869 the Board of Delegates again explored the prospect of sending missionaries to China, and again Jewish organizations abroad failed to respond. Kohler, "Board of Delegates," 88.

33. Unless otherwise noted, the material for the remainder of the section (through p. 231) is reworked from Naomi W. Cohen, "American Jewish Reactions to Anti-Semitism in Western Europe, 1875–1900," *Proceedings of the American Academy for Jewish Research* 45 (1978): 29–37, 45–48, 62–63. Quotations are documented separately.

34. *AI,* 22 Sept. 1892.

35. *UAHC Proceedings* (1881), p. 1070.

36. Jehuda Reinharz, *Fatherland or Promised Land* (Ann Arbor, 1975), pp. 13–29.

37. Congress became involved only briefly and peripherally. In 1884, shortly after the death of Eduard Lasker, a Jewish member of the Reichstag, the House of Representatives relayed resolutions of sympathy to the German government which Bismarck refused to accept. Congressman S. S. Cox of New York linked the chancellor's rebuff to Germany's anti-Semitism, and said that if Congress swallowed the insult, it would become a partner in German prejudice. Nevertheless, since Bismarck had already explained that he meant no discourtesy to Congress, the matter was not pursued further.

38. Again in 1898 the Board of Delegates explained rather lamely why it hadn't approached the government, this time on behalf of Dreyfus. Since the latter was not an American citizen, the board decided to leave the case to the French. *UAHC Proceedings* (1898), p. 3952.

39. *JM*, 12 March 1880, 12 July 1880.

40. The Unitarian minister was dubbed "Rabbi" Collyer by one orthodox Christian weekly. Emma Felsenthal, *Bernhard Felsenthal* (New York, 1924), p. 44.

41. *New York Times*, 27 Dec. 1880.

42. M. Jastrow, *The Causes of the Revived Disaffection against the Jews* (New York, 1890), pp. 9–10. See also *AH*, 16 Jan. 1885.

43. *The American Israelite* was upset that those who had invited Ahlwardt were Americans (5 Dec. 1895). See also *AH*, 22 Nov. 1895.

44. Cited in Egal Feldman, "American Editorial Reaction to the Dreyfus Case," in *Michael* (Tel Aviv, 1975), 3:122.

45. *JM*, 4 Nov. 1890.

46. Oscar Straus to Andrew Carnegie, 19 Jan. 1904, Andrew Carnegie Papers, Library of Congress.

47. For examples of their activities, see Naomi W. Cohen, *A Dual Heritage* (Philadelphia, 1969), chaps. 4, 7.

48. Adler and Margalith, *With Firmness in the Right*, p. 178; Myer S. Isaacs, *The Persecution of the Jews in Russia* (New York, 1882).

49. Even before the Civil War the *Israelite* had spoken out against czarist despotism and had questioned the favorable press coverage that Russia received in America. *ISR*, 22 June 1855, 17 Aug. 1855, 28 Dec. 1855, 25 April 1856.

50. Cohen, *Dual Heritage*, pp. 57–63; Adler and Margalith, *With Firmness in the Right*, pp. 238–40, 455–68; Oscar Straus to Andrew D. White, 4 Aug. 1892, Andrew D. White Papers, Cornell University; Trustees of Baron de Hirsch Fund to White, 2 Aug. 1892, White Papers.

51. Cohen, "Abrogation," 25–26; Jacob H. Schiff to Herman Bernstein, 17 July 1914, American Jewish Committee (AJC) Archives.

52. Cyrus Adler, *Jacob H. Schiff*, 2 vols. (Garden City, 1929), 1:chaps. 1–2; William Miller, ed., *Men in Business* (New York, 1962), p. 319; *AI*, 5 Jan. 1905; Cohen, *Dual Heritage*, p. 130.

53. Fritz Stern, *Gold and Iron* (New York, 1977), p. 465.

54. Cohen, *Dual Heritage*, pp. 127, 134–36; Jacob H. Schiff to Samuel Jaros, 25 June 1906, Jacob H. Schiff Papers, Jewish Theological Seminary; Schiff to Adolf Kraus, 21 June 1906, Schiff Papers; Schiff to Paul Nathan, 26 July 1906, Schiff Papers; Adler, *Schiff*, 2:121, 136–40; Elting E. Morison, ed., *The Letters of Theodore Roosevelt*, 8 vols. (Cambridge, 1951–54), 5:112–13.

55. Adler, *Schiff*, 2:122–23, 127–28, 142–43; Schiff to Gregory Wilenkin, 10 Dec. 1911, Schiff Papers.

56. Herman Bernstein memorandum, "Some of the Things Ambassador Rockhill Told Me," 23 May 1911, AJC Archives; Gary Dean Best, "Financing a Foreign War," *AJHQ* 61 (June 1972):313–24; Adler, *Schiff*, 1:213–30.

57. Cohen, *Dual Heritage*, p. 132; Adler, *Schiff*, 2:128.

58. Mayer Sulzberger to Cyrus Adler, 11 July 1910, AJC Archives.

59. Adler, *Schiff*, 2:145–46; Cohen, "Abrogation," 7–8.

60. Cohen, "Abrogation," 5; Schiff to William H. Taft, 24 July 1908, 3

Aug. 1908, Schiff Papers; Schiff to Cyrus Adler, 16 Aug. 1910, Schiff Papers; William H. Taft to Schiff, 11 Aug. 1908, AJC Archives; Schiff to Cyrus Adler, 10 June 1910, AJC Archives.

61. Minutes of the Executive Committee, 19 Feb. 1911, AJC Archives; Schiff to Simon Wolf, 24 May 1918, Schiff Papers; Cohen, "Abrogation," 29.

62. "Remarks of Mr. Schiff, Nov. 16, 1911," AJC Archives; Schiff to Simon Wolf, 30 Nov. 1917, Schiff Papers; Cohen, "Abrogation," 33.

63. William H. Taft to P. C. Knox, 11 Sept. 1909, 3 Dec. 1909, 25 Feb. 1910, William H. Taft Papers, Library of Congress; Taft to Jacob Schiff, 23 Feb. 1911, Taft Papers; Taft to Otto Bannard, 17 June 1911, 13 Nov. 1911, Taft Papers; Taft to Hart Lyman [8 April 1911], Taft Papers; Taft to Guild Copeland, 16 Feb. 1911, Taft Papers; Taft to Horace D. Taft, 25 Nov. 1911, Taft Papers.

64. Cohen, "Abrogation," 36–38; Taft to Charles P. Taft, 12 Dec. 1912, Taft Papers.

65. Max J. Kohler, *The Immigration Question* (New York, 1911), p. 1.

66. John Higham, *Strangers in the Land* (New York, 1973), chaps. 4, 5; Samuel Joseph, *Jewish Immigration to the United States from 1881 to 1910* (New York, 1914), p. 174.

67. Esther L. Panitz, "The Polarity of American Jewish Attitudes towards Immigration (1870–1891)," in Karp, *Jewish Experience*, 4:36–50.

68. *JM,* 20 May 1881, 7 and 14 July 1882, 4 July 1884, 10 Dec. 1886, 29 July 1887, 7 Sept. 1888, 12 Oct. 1888, 9 Nov. 1888, 25 April 1890, 5 June 1891, 10 July 1891. The *American Hebrew* agreed (31 Dec. 1897) that the Russians were not the cause of American prejudice.

69. Panitz, "Polarity of American Jewish Attitudes," 51–62.

70. American Jews used the argument of pauper immigration to elicit protests against Russia from the Harrison administration and against Romania from the Roosevelt administration. Cohen, *Dual Heritage,* pp. 60, 124.

71. *JM,* 17 March 1882, 22 Sept. 1882; *Congressional Record,* 47th Cong., 1st sess., 1882, pp. 2183–84; *AH,* 24 March 1882, 21 April 1882, 19 May 1882; Carl E. Schorske, *Fin-de-Siècle Vienna* (New York, 1980), p. 129. The anti-Semite drew justification for his prejudice from America's aversion to the Chinese. See, for example, Joseph Pennell, *The Jew at Home* (New York, 1892), p. 96.

72. Leon Hühner, "Max James Kohler," *PAJHS* 34 (1937):295–301; Irving Lehman, "Max J. Kohler," *AJYB* 37 (1935–36):21–25; Max J. Kohler, *Immigration and Aliens in the United States* (New York, 1936), pp. iii–x. For the broad range of Kohler's immigration work see the bibliography by Edward D. Coleman in *PAJHS* 34 (1937):165–263. On Kohler's use of Jefferson's words, see, for example, his *Immigration Question,* p. 24.

73. Kohler, *Immigration Question; United States Statutes at Large,* 40th Cong., 2d sess., 1868, 15:223.

74. United States *v.* Lee Yen Tai, 185 U.S. 213 (1902); *New York Times,* 24 and 25 Nov. 1901, 7 June 1903; Kohler, *Immigration and Aliens,* p. 253.

75. See numerous references in Coleman's bibliography.

76. *UAHC Proceedings* (1910), p. 6525; *UAHC Proceedings* (1913), pp. 7168–75; Kohler, *Immigration and Aliens,* pp. 1–15, 66–77; Kohler, *Immigration Question,* pp. 1–10; U.S. Immigration Commission, *Reports: Statements and Recommendations Submitted by Societies and Organizations Interested in the Subject of Immigration* 41 (Washington, 1911), 160–76,

238–48; "In Defense of the Immigrant," *AJYB* 12 (1910–11):70–87; *New York Times*, 25 April 1911.

77. Kohler, *Immigration Question*, pp. 5–8; Kohler, *Immigration and Aliens*, pp. 46–65; *AH*, 22 July 1909; U.S. Immigration Commission, *Reports* 41, 160–76; *UAHC Proceedings* (1911), p. 6630.

78. Kohler, *Immigration Question*, pp. 11–22, 24–25; Kohler, *Immigration and Aliens*, pp. 80–82; Kohler in *American Economic Review* 2 (March 1912, Supplement):72–78; *AH*, 25 April 1913; *New York Times*, 14 April 1911.

79. See, for example, Max J. Kohler, "Some Aspects of the Immigration Problem," *American Economic Review* 4 (March 1914):93–108.

80. Kohler, *Immigration Question*, pp. 3, 23–24; *AJYB* 12 (1910–11):73; *New York Times*, 12 Dec. 1914, 16 Dec. 1916, 1 Feb. 1917.

81. *AJYB* 12 (1910–11):73, 76–77; Kohler, *Immigration and Aliens*, pp. 82–84, 200–228; *Survey*, 11 Oct. 1913 (letter by Kohler); *AH*, 10 May 1912; *UAHC Proceedings* (1913), pp. 7165–68, 7171; Morton Rosenstock, *Louis Marshall* (Detroit, 1965), p. 86. Kohler also collected opinions from the press and prominent Americans, and resolutions of mass meetings, which he published under the title *The Injustice of the Literacy Test for Immigrants*.

82. *Congressional Record*, 64th Cong., 1st sess., 1916, pp. 4876–83; Higham, *Strangers in the Land*, chap. 6.

83. Oscar Handlin, *Race and Nationality in American Life* (Garden City, 1957), chap. 5. The *Dictionary* appeared as volume 5 of the U.S. Immigration Commission *Reports* (Washington, 1911).

84. *AI*, 19 Jan. 1911.

85. Barbara M. Solomon, *Ancestors and Immigrants* (New York, 1965), chaps. 5–7.

86. U.S. Immigration Commission, *Reports* 41, 176–81, 276–79; Kohler, *Immigration and Aliens*, p. 85; Kohler, *Immigration Question*, pp. 21–22; Max J. Kohler, "A New Expedient for Restricting Immigration," *Survey*, 14 June 1913; Kohler in *American Economic Review* 2 (March 1912, Supplement):72–78.

CHAPTER 6
THE JEWISH QUESTION AND SOME JEWISH ANSWERS

1. Emma Lazarus, "The Jewish Problem," *Century* 25 (Feb. 1883):602.

2. On the change in Christian attitudes toward the Jews after the Enlightenment, see Léon Poliakov, *The History of Anti-Semitism* 3 (New York, 1975). See also Jacob Katz, *Out of the Ghetto* (New York, 1978), chaps. 6, 12; Carlton J. H. Hayes, *A Generation of Materialism* (New York, 1963), chap. 7. For a penetrating analysis of the new anti-Semitism in Germany, see Fritz Stern, *Gold and Iron* (New York, 1977), chaps. 17, 18.

3. Joseph Jacobs, *The Jewish Question, 1875–1884* (London, 1885).

4. See, for example, Maurice H. Harris in *MEN* 34 (Jan. 1903):39–40.

5. *JM*, 29 June 1883, 6 July 1883.

6. *MEN* 33 (Sept. 1902):195.

7. *New York Times*, 23 and 26 June 1877; Sol Liptzin, *The Jew in American Literature* (New York, 1966), pp. 72–77; Stern, *Gold and Iron*, p. 522n.

8. *AH*, 15 Nov. 1889, 6 June 1890; Louis Marshall in *AH*, 20 June 1913; E. Digby Baltzell, *The Protestant Establishment* (New York, 1966), chap. 5; Richard J. H. Gottheil, *The Life of Gustav Gottheil* (Williamsport, Pa., 1936), p. 182; Rudolf Glanz, *The Jewish Woman in America*, 2 (New York, 1976), 27. A contemporary report on fraternity admissions is in *AI*, 3 Nov. 1904.

9. Max Heller, "Our Salvation," *MEN* 32 (Feb. 1902):95–97.

10. Baltzell, *Protestant Establishment*, chaps. 14–16; Naomi W. Cohen, *Not Free to Desist* (Philadelphia, 1972), pp. 415–28.

11. The portion of this section through p. 265 has been reworked from my article "Anti-Semitism in the Gilded Age: The Jewish View," *JSS* 41 (Summer–Fall 1979):187–210. New material and quotations are footnoted here.

12. *JM*, 14 July 1882.

13. *JM*, 6 July 1877.

14. *AI*, 29 June 1877.

15. Paul A. Carter, *The Spiritual Crisis of the Gilded Age* (De Kalb, 1971).

16. *Proceedings of the National Convention to Secure the Religious Amendment of the Constitution of the United States* (1872), pp. viii–xvi; *Proceedings . . . to Secure the Religious Amendment . . .* (1873), pp. 46, 54–55.

17. *JM*, 27 Feb. 1874.

18. *AI*, 12 May 1876; see also David Einhorn, "America, Whither Are You Going — A Centennial Sermon," *AJA* 28 (April 1976):22.

19. *JM*, 21 Jan. 1876.

20. *JM*, 31 Aug. 1888.

21. Nina Morais, "Jewish Ostracism in America," *North American Review* 133 (Sept. 1881):271–72.

22. *AI*, 22 Oct. 1896.

23. *AH*, 10 Sept. 1896.

24. Gustav Gottheil, "The Position of the Jews in America," *North American Review* 127 (July–Aug. 1878):86.

25. See, for example, Rabbi Henry Berkowitz in *CCAR Year Book* 5 (1895):50; T. Schanfarber in *AI*, 14 July 1910, 8 Aug. 1910.

26. See, for example, E. W. Moise in *JM*, 5 Oct. 1900.

27. Cited in Heywood Broun and George Britt, *Christians Only* (New York, 1931), pp. 290–91.

28. Cohen, "Anti-Semitism in the Gilded Age," 200, 204–5.

29. *JM*, 30 March 1883.

30. Cohen, "Anti-Semitism in the Gilded Age," 200, 204–5.

31. James G. Heller, *Isaac M. Wise* (New York, 1965), pp. 487–88; *Judaism at the World's Parliament of Religions* (Cincinnati, 1894), pp. vii–viii and passim.

32. Cf. the admonitions by the *Jewish Messenger* against attacking Christianity, 4 June 1880, 7 April 1882, 25 March 1887.

33. Heller, *Wise*, pp. 142–44, 624, 629, 633–39, 652–57; *AI*, 1 July 1881; Isaac M. Wise, *A Defense of Judaism versus Proselytizing Christianity* (Cincinnati, 1889); Isaac M. Wise, *Judaism and Christianity, Their Agreements and Disagreements* (Cincinnati, 1883).

34. John B. Weber to Oscar S. Straus, 14 June 1903, Oscar S. Straus Papers, Library of Congress; Mark Twain, "Concerning the Jews," *Harper's* 99 (Sept. 1899):534–35.

35. Charles Reznikoff, ed., *Louis Marshall*, 2 vols. (Philadelphia, 1957), 1:12–14; Louis Marshall to Cyrus Adler, 3 Feb. 1905, Cyrus Adler Papers; *AH*, 20 June 1913; *MEN* 39 (Oct. 1905):233–34; Jeffrey Gurock, "The 1913 New York State Civil Rights Act," *AJS Review* 1 (1976):98–108.

36. John Higham, *Send These to Me* (New York, 1975), p. 153. Some Jews advocated a boycott of the hotels that discriminated. *AI*, 31 July 1890.

37. See above, chap. 1.

38. Cohen, *Not Free to Desist*, pp. 411–15.

39. Probably the earliest American version appeared in 1770, when Congregationalist minister Ezra Stiles heard from a British officer about a secret Jewish intelligence bureau, with international connections, operating out of London. Arthur A. Chiel, "Ezra Stiles and the Jews," in *A Bicentennial Festschrift for Jacob Rader Marcus*, ed. Bertram W. Korn (Waltham and New York, 1976), p. 68.

40. Norman Cohn, *Warrant for Genocide* (New York, 1967), pp. 57–60.

41. See above, chap. 2.

42. Cohen, "Anti-Semitism in the Gilded Age," 196–98; Samuel H. Kellogg, "The Jewish Question in Europe," *New Englander* 160 (May 1881):328–50.

43. Michael N. Dobkowski, *The Tarnished Dream* (Westport, 1979), chap. 6.

44. *AI*, 27 Sept. 1878, 14 Nov. 1879, 16 June 1882, 9 March 1883 (*New Orleans Times-Democrat*), 3 Sept. 1886.

45. Under the caption "Le Juif International" an editorial in the *AH* (15 Feb. 1895) asked for a single voice for world Jewry.

46. On Markens, see *AH*, 14 Sept. 1928; Max J. Kohler, "Isaac Markens," *PAJHS* 32 (1931):129–32.

47. Isaac Markens, *The Hebrews in America* (New York, 1888), esp. pp. 1, 177, chap. 3.

48. Reznikoff, *Marshall*, 2:793–97. At the same time the *New York Tribune* also reported in detail on the wealth of the Jews in New York. Reprinted in *AI*, 4 May 1905.

49. John Higham, *Strangers in the Land* (New York, 1973), pp. 136–54; *Harper's* 59 (Oct. 1879):786–87; *JM*, 28 Oct. 1887; *Nation*, 24 June 1880; *Independent*, 19 July 1906 (reprinted by E. Feldman; see chap. 5 n 44).

50. Naomi W. Cohen, "American Jewish Reactions to Anti-Semitism in Western Europe, 1875–1900," *Proceedings of the American Academy for Jewish Research* 45 (1978):37, 39, 42–43.

51. Cohen, "Reactions to Anti-Semitism in Western Europe," 40.

52. *AH*, 13 March 1884, 9 and 18 April 1884.

53. Emil G. Hirsch, "The Philosophy of the Reform Movement in American Judaism," *CCAR Year Book* 5 (1895):108; *UAHC Proceedings* (1903), pp. 5047–50.

54. Esther Panitz, "In Defense of the Jewish Immigrant," in *The Jewish Experience in America*, ed. Abraham J. Karp, 5 vols. (Waltham and New York, 1969), 5:55–59.

55. [Charles Waldstein], *The Jewish Question and the Mission of the Jews* (New York, 1894).

56. Morris Jastrow, "The Jewish Question in Its Recent Aspects," *International Journal of Ethics* 6 (July 1896):457–79.

57. Benny Kraut, *From Reform Judaism to Ethical Culture* (Cincinnati, 1979), chaps. 1, 4, pp. 190–91; *New York Times*, 3 June 1911, 24 July 1911.

58. M. Jastrow, *The Causes of the Revived Disaffection against the Jews*

(New York, 1890), p. 10; Kraut, *From Reform Judaism to Ethical Culture*, pp. 112 et seq., chaps. 4, 5.

59. Maurice Fishberg, "The Jews: A Study of Race and Environment," *Popular Science Monthly* 70 (Jan. 1907):44–47.

60. A. L. Kroeber, "Franz Boas: The Man," *American Anthropologist* 45 (July–Sept. 1943):5–14.

61. Melville J. Herskovits, *Franz Boas* (New York, 1953); Kroeber, "Boas," 20.

62. William Z. Ripley, *The Races of Europe* (New York, 1899), esp. chap. 14; Franz Boas, *Race, Language and Culture* (New York, 1940), pp. 155–59.

63. Herskovits, *Boas*, p. 4; Franz Boas, *The Mind of Primitive Man*, rev. ed. (New York, 1963), p. 17.

64. Herskovits, *Boas*, pp. 5, 39–40; U.S. Immigration Commission, *Abstracts of Reports*, 2 vols. (Washington, 1911), 2:506, 550–52; Boas, *Race, Language and Culture*, pp. 60–75.

65. Fishberg's articles, which appeared in the *Popular Science Monthly* in 1906–7, were expanded into book form, *The Jews: A Study of Race and Environment* (New York, 1911).

66. Higham, *Strangers in the Land*, pp. 149–57; Barbara M. Solomon, *Pioneers in Service* (Boston, 1956), p. 67.

67. Herskovits, *Boas*, pp. 112, 116–18.

68. *Independent*, 19 July 1906, reprinted by Egal Feldman: see chap. 5 n. 44; Colin Holmes, "Goldwin Smith, a 'Liberal' Antisemite," *Patterns of Prejudice* 6 (Sept.–Oct. 1972):25–30.

69. Goldwin Smith, "Can Jews Be Patriots?", *Nineteenth Century* 3 (May 1878):875–87; Goldwin Smith, "The Jews: A Deferred Rejoinder," *Nineteenth Century* 12 (Nov. 1882):687–709; Goldwin Smith, "The Jewish Question," *Nineteenth Century* 10 (Oct. 1881):494–515; Smith's letter to the editor, *Nation*, 3 March 1881.

70. Cohen, "Reactions to Anti-Semitism in Western Europe," 52–55 and notes.

71. *JM*, 24 July 1891; see articles in *North American Review* aroused by Smith's piece: Sept. 1891, pp. 257–71; Nov. 1891, pp. 513–23; letter in Dec. 1891, pp. 761–62; letter in Feb. 1892, pp. 249–51. Echoes were also heard in *AI*, 17 Dec. 1891, 7 Jan. 1892.

72. Higham, *Strangers in the Land*, pp. 54, 62–67; Edward N. Saveth, *American Historians and European Immigrants* (New York, 1948), pp. 16–31; John J. Appel, "Hansen's Third Generation 'Law' and the Origins of the American Jewish Historical Society," *JSS* 23 (Jan. 1961):15; *AH*, 2 Oct. 1896.

73. Anna L. Dawes, *The Modern Jew*, 2d ed. (Boston, 1886).

74. A term used by Rabbi Jacob Voorsanger of California, *UAHC Proceedings* (1904), pp. 4958–68.

75. Cyrus Adler in *PAJHS* 9 (1902):2.

76. *PAJHS* 1 (1892):iii, 2–3; *PAJHS* 2 (1893):3; *PAJHS* 3 (1894):2–5; *PAJHS* 26 (1918):18; *PAJHS* 41 (June 1952):385–86; minutes of the organization meeting of the American Jewish Historical Society, 7 June 1892, esp. pp. 75, 80, Archives of the American Jewish Historical Society; Naomi W. Cohen, *A Dual Heritage* (Philadelphia, 1969), pp. 14–15, 71–72; Harold J. Jonas, "Writing American Jewish History," *Contemporary Jewish Record* 6 (April 1943): 143–50.

77. Edward Calisch in *JM*, 3 July 1896; Max J. Kohler in *AH*, Dec. 1894–

Jan. 1895. Kohler also prepared the foreword to the 1893 edition of the pioneer work in American Jewish history, Charles Daly's *The Settlement of the Jews in North America* (New York). Mentioning Goldwin Smith by name, Kohler underscored the importance of presenting facts to disprove prejudiced charges (p. vi).

78. Simon Wolf, *The American Jew as Patriot, Soldier and Citizen* (Philadelphia, 1895).

79. Oscar Straus to Theodore Roosevelt, 26 Oct. 1903, Straus Papers; *AJYB* 2 (1900–1901):527–622; Madison C. Peters, *Justice to the Jew* (London and New York, 1899), chap. 5.

80. Cited in David Rudavsky, *Modern Jewish Religious Movements* (New York, 1979), p. 87.

81. Joseph Silverman, "The Renaissance of the Science of Judaism," *MEN* 30 (April 1901):203; *AH*, 16 March 1900.

82. Bernhard Felsenthal, "Jewish Questions," *H.U.C. Journal* 6 (Oct. 1900):23–27.

83. *JM*, 30 March 1883; Emma Felsenthal, *Bernhard Felsenthal* (New York, 1924), esp. pp. 17, 93–94, chap. 3.

84. E. Felsenthal, *Bernhard Felsenthal*, pp. 63–70, 76; Carl Hermann Voss, *Rabbi and Minister* (Cleveland, 1964), p. 41; Norman Bentwich, *For Zion's Sake* (Philadelphia, 1954), pp. 23, 35; Naomi W. Cohen, *American Jews and the Zionist Idea* (New York, 1975), pp. 7–8.

85. R. Gottheil, *Gustav Gottheil*, esp. pp. 182–83, 190–91.

86. R. Gottheil, *Gustav Gottheil*, pp. 147, 182; R. Gottheil's letter in *AH*, 2 Jan. 1903; Richard Gottheil to Theodor Herzl, 5 Oct. 1898, Richard Gottheil Papers, Zionist Archives; Richard Gottheil, *The Aims of Zionism* (New York, 1899), p. 13 and passim; *Jewish Criterion*, 27 Nov. 1903; Marnin Feinstein, *American Zionism, 1884–1904* (New York, 1965), pp. 160–61.

87. *Jewish Chronicle*, 3 July 1896; Richard Gottheil, *Zionism* (Philadelphia, 1914), pp. 20–29, 207–8.

88. R. Gottheil, *Zionism*, pp. 210–12; R. Gottheil, *Aims*, p. 19; R. Gottheil to Theodor Herzl, 30 Nov. 1903, Gottheil Papers; *Jewish Criterion*, 27 Nov. 1903; Judah L. Magnes, *A Republic of Nationalities* (New York, 1909); Cohen, *American Jews and the Zionist Idea*, pp. 16–17.

89. George A. Kohut in *Columbia University Quarterly* 25 (June 1933):139; R. Gottheil to Actions Committee, 12 Jan. 1900, Gottheil Papers; file of R. Gottheil-Herzl correspondence, Gottheil Papers; R. Gottheil in *AH*, 2 Jan. 1903; Feinstein, *American Zionism*, pp. 172, 176.

90. Feinstein, *American Zionism*, pp. 202–3.

91. Feinstein, *American Zionism*, pp. 140, 142, 155, 161, 175, 236; Cohen, *Dual Heritage*, pp. 139–44; Jacob H. Schiff to Oscar Straus, 13 April 1903, Jacob H. Schiff Papers, American Jewish Archives.

92. Cohen, *American Jews and the Zionist Idea*, pp. 6–7. The Zionists among the Orthodox founded a separate organization, the Mizrachi, and those among the socialists the Poale Zion.

93. Melvin I. Urofsky, *American Zionism from Herzl to the Holocaust* (Garden City, 1975), p. 118.

94. The most thorough discussion of Reform's opposition to Zionism remains Naomi R. Wiener, "Reform Judaism in America and Zionism, 1897–1922" (Master's essay, Columbia University, 1949). A more recent treatment of the Reform rabbis' stand on Zionism is David Polish, *Renew Our Days* (Jerusalem, 1976), chap. 2.

95. On the last point, see Carl E. Schorske, *Fin-de-Siècle Vienna* (New York, 1980), pp. 146, 160, 164, 169.

96. *AH*, 16 June 1905.

97. Cohen, *American Jews and the Zionist Idea*, pp. 2, 21–22; Tyler quotation in Isaac M. Fein, *The Making of an American Jewish Community* (Philadelphia, 1971), p. 64.

98. Feinstein, *American Zionism*, pp. 19–20, 60, 66, 70, 72–75; Salo W. Baron, "Changing Patterns of Antisemitism," *JSS* 38 (Winter 1976):15, 31; Dawes, *The Modern Jew*, pp. 42–52; Smith, "Can Jews Be Patriots?", 885; Smith, "The Jews," 709; Telemachus Timayenis, *Judas Iscariot* (New York, 1888), pp. 291–92.

99. "Anti-Jewish Sentiment in California—1855," *AJA* 12 (April 1960):19; *JM*, 4 Aug. 1865; Ernest Samuels, *Henry Adams: The Major Phase* (Cambridge, 1964), p. 356; Dobkowski, *Tarnished Dream*, p. 180; *Judge*, 23 Jan. 1892; *AI*, 16 Feb. 1877; Rudolf Glanz, *Studies in Judaica Americana* (New York, 1970), p. 380. Shortly before the first Zionist Congress a San Francisco newspaper reported that Baron Edmond de Rothschild of Paris was slated to be king of the Jews in a restored Palestine (*AI*, 20 May 1897).

100. Cohen, "Reactions to Anti-Semitism in Western Europe," 59–60.

101. Gotthard Deutsch, "Zionism," *H.U.C. Journal* 4 (Dec. 1899):66; Gotthard Deutsch to Bernhard Felsenthal, 22 July 1898, Bernhard Felsenthal Papers, American Jewish Historical Society; Saveth, *American Historians and European Immigrants*, pp. 47–48.

102. R. Gottheil, *Gustav Gottheil*, p. 192.

103. *CCAR Year Book* 1 (1890):87–88, 103, 109–10, 118, 121; Moshe Davis, *The Emergence of Conservative Judaism* (Philadelphia, 1963), pt. 2; pt. 3, chap. 1.

104. Herbert Rosenbloom, "The Founding of the United Synagogue of America" (Ph.D. diss., Brandeis University, 1970), 69, 71–72, 86–87, 96; Kaufmann Kohler to Jacob H. Schiff, 9 Jan. 1902, American Jewish Archives.

105. Solomon Schechter, *Seminary Addresses and Other Papers* (New York, 1959), pp. 91–104; Kaufmann Kohler, "Zionism or Judaism— Which?", *MEN* 42 (Jan. 1907): 40–41; Herbert Parzen, "Conservative Judaism and Zionism (1896–1922)," *JSS* 23 (Oct. 1961):235–64; Samuel Halperin, *The Political World of American Zionism* (Detroit, 1961), p. 103.

106. Naomi W. Cohen, "The Reaction of Reform Judaism in America to Political Zionism (1897–1922)," *PAJHS* 40 (June 1951):372–82; Samuel E. Karff, ed., *Hebrew Union College–Jewish Institute of Religion at One Hundred Years* (Cincinnati, 1975), pp. 62–67.

107. The texts of Schiff's letters appear in Cyrus Adler, *Jacob H. Schiff*, 2 vols. (Garden City, 1929), 2:164–69. Schechter did not agree to the publication of his letters. See also "Emil Cohn" in *Encyclopaedia Judaica*; Solomon Schechter to Harry Friedenwald, 29 [Aug.] 1907, Harry Friedenwald Papers, Jewish Theological Seminary; Cyrus Adler to Friedenwald, 5 Sept. 1907, Friedenwald Papers; 1907 file: letters and notes on Zionism, Friedenwald Papers; Jacob H. Schiff to Oscar Straus, 26 Sept. 1907, Straus Papers. In a talk delivered seventy-five years later, Dr. Mordecai Kaplan related that Adler had succeeded restraining the board from resigning when Schechter's first statement on Zionism appeared. Rabbinical Assembly, *Proceedings* (1975), p. 350.

108. Jacob H. Schiff to Oscar Straus, 29 Sept. 1907, Straus Papers;

Solomon Schechter to Friedenwald, 29 [Aug.] 1907, Friedenwald Papers; letter from Louis Marshall in *AH*, 20 Sept. 1907.

109. *Jewish Criterion*, 27 Nov. 1903; R. Gottheil, *Aims,* p. 19.

110. Naomi W. Cohen, "The *Maccabaean*'s Message," *JSS* 18 (July 1956):166–68, 171–73; Urofsky, *American Zionism,* chaps. 4–5.

CHAPTER 7
RAZING THE GHETTO WALLS

1. *The Two Hundred and Fiftieth Anniversary of the Settlement of the Jews in the United States, PAJHS* 14 (1906); *AH*, 24 Nov. 1905.

2. Jacob H. Schiff to Oscar S. Straus, 29 Sept. 1907, Oscar S. Straus Papers.

3. *AI*, 12 Sept.–17 Oct. 1901.

4. *MEN* 35 (Aug. 1903):95.

5. *JM*, 29 March 1889.

6. Reprint of *Boston Transcript* article in *AH*, 27 March 1903.

7. An early pamphlet (in American Jewish Archives) describing and criticizing the divisions among European and American Jews was that of Henry Gersoni, *Jew against Jew* (Chicago, 1881).

8. Janine M. Perry, "The Idea of Immigrant Distribution in the United States, 1890–1915" (Master's essay, Hunter College, 1975), 17–23; Esther L. Panitz, "The Polarity of American Jewish Attitudes toward Immigration (1870–1891)," reprinted in *The Jewish Experience in America*, ed. Abraham J. Karp, 5 vols. (Waltham and New York, 1969), 4:52.

9. Leo N. Levi, "The Modern Dispersion," *MEN* 34 (June 1903):335.

10. Cary Goodman, *Choosing Sides* (New York, 1979), pp. 36, 65, 148–49; Will Herberg, "The Jewish Labor Movement in the United States," *AJYB* 53 (1952):18.

11. See, for example, *JM*, 1 March 1901; *AI*, 6 June 1901.

12. Samuel Joseph, *Jewish Immigration to the United States from 1881 to 1910* (New York, 1914), pp. 117, 150–51, 196.

13. References to the contemporary reaction to the Jewish immigrants, much of it in newspapers and periodicals, are too voluminous to cite. One synthetic account is Rudolf Glanz, "Jewish Social Conditions as Seen by the Muckrakers," in *Studies in Judaica Americana* (New York, 1970), pp. 384–407. Two significant government studies are the reports of the U.S. Industrial Commission (1902) and the United States Immigration Commission (1911).

14. Charles S. Bernheimer, ed., *The Russian Jew in the United States* (Philadelphia, 1905), pp. 75, 323; *MEN* 32 (Jan. 1902):64; *Proceedings of the Second National Conference of Jewish Charities* (1902), pp. 214–15; Barbara M. Solomon, *Ancestors and Immigrants* (New York, 1965), p. 35. The problems that New York faced were replicated, albeit in less extreme fashion, in the smaller cities. On Baltimore, see Isaac M. Fein, *The Making of an American Jewish Community* (Philadelphia, 1971), pp. 141–72; on Atlanta, see Steven Hertzberg, *Strangers within the Gate City* (Philadelphia, 1978), chaps. 4, 5.

15. *Proceedings of the Second National Conference . . .* , pp. 209–10.

16. Herman D. Stein, "Jewish Social Work in the United States," in *The Characteristics of American Jews* (New York, 1965), pp. 160–61, 179;

Nissim Behar to [N. Leven], 5 June 1901, Alliance Israélite Universelle Papers, American Jewish Archives; *AI*, 4 Jan. 1901, 24 and 31 July 1902, 9 June 1904, 7 Nov. 1907, 26 Dec. 1907, 2 Jan. 1908, 30 July 1908; Ronald Sanders, *The Downtown Jews* (New York, 1976), p. 182; Lillian Wald to Jacob H. Schiff, 29 Aug. 1893, Lillian Wald Papers, New York Public Library.

17. *JM*, 25 Sept. 1891.

18. An overall survey of various philanthropic enterprises is Boris D. Bogen, *Jewish Philanthropy* (New York, 1917). See also Samuel Joseph, *History of the Baron de Hirsch Fund* (Fairfield, N.J., 1978): Arthur A. Goren, *New York Jews and the Quest for Community* (New York, 1970); Naomi W. Cohen, *Not Free to Desist* (Philadelphia, 1972), pp. 3–24; Monroe Campbell, Jr., and William Wirtz, *The First Fifty Years, a History of the National Council of Jewish Women* (New York, 1943), p. 32; the immigrant-related activities of B'nai B'rith are culled from the *AJYB* and the reports of the order that appeared in *Menorah*.

19. Bogen, *Jewish Philanthropy*, p. 9; Stein, "Jewish Social Work," p. 160; *AI*, 2 April 1908, 23 Dec. 1909.

20. By 1910 Nathan Straus had established seventeen milk stations in New York which were distributing 4 million bottles of pasteurized milk annually. *AI*, 15 July 1909 (Krauskopf), 1 Sept. 1910. On Benjamin, see David M. Eichhorn, *Evangelizing the American Jew* (Middle Village, N.Y., 1978), pp. 113, 137–38, 143, 148, 155, 164–65, 168, 178–80; *AH*, 16 Jan. 1903. In Wald Papers see reports from Lillian Wald to Schiff and Mrs. Loeb, 1893–95; Lillian Wald, *The House on Henry Street* (New York, 1915); Cyrus Adler, *Jacob H. Schiff*, 2 vols. (Garden City, 1929), 1:351–53.

21. Bogen, *Jewish Philanthropy*, p. 44.

22. Sidney E. Goldstein, *The Synagogue and Social Welfare* (New York, 1955), p. 43.

23. *Fifth Biennial Session of the National Conference of Jewish Charities* (1908), pp. 112–21, 143–44; *AJYB* 10 (1908–9):195–96.

24. *MEN* 42 (Jan. 1907):32; Goldstein, *Synagogue and Social Welfare*, pp. 45–48; *Fifth Biennial Session . . .* , pp. 91–108; Carl Hermann Voss, ed., *Stephen S. Wise* (Philadelphia, 1969), pp. 34–35.

25. *Proceedings of the Third National Conference of Jewish Charities* (1904), pp. 117–23; *AH*, 6 March 1903; *AI*, 7 Nov. 1907, 24 Sept. 1908.

26. *Proceedings of the National Council of Jewish Women, Third Triennial Convention* (1902), p. 161; *AI*, 13 June 1901; Morris D. Waldman, *Nor by Power* (New York, 1953), p. 309. The UAHC warned: "If there should grow up in our midst a class of people not imbued with American ideas . . . , all of us will suffer, prejudice and ill judgment will hold us responsible for evils of which we none may be guilty" (*UAHC Proceedings* [1891], p. 2821).

27. *JM*, 28 Aug. 1891.

28. *CCAR Year Book* 14 (1904):183; *AI*, 3 Aug. 1905. Agencies like the Baron de Hirsch Fund (particularly through the Educational Alliance), the National Council of Jewish Women, and the YMHAs took prominent parts in the Americanization program.

29. The editorial pages of the *AH*, *JM*, and *AI*, especially between 1890 and 1910, abound with such directives.

30. *AH*, 20 March 1903; Bogen, *Jewish Philanthropy*, p. 228; *MEN* 39 (July 1905):13.

31. David Blaustein, "The Making of Americans," *MEN* 35 (Dec. 1903):372–73.

32. Roosevelt was cited by the *JM*, 17 Jan 1890; *AI*, 15 Oct 1908, 4 March 1909.

33. *AI*, 13 June 1901, 17 Aug. 1905 (Heller); *Fifth Biennial Session . . .* , p. 127.

34. *Proceedings of the Third National Conference . . .* , pp. 120–23; *Fifth Biennial Session . . .* , p. 126; *AH*, 6 March 1903; *AI*, 16 June 1904 (Heller). On the work of the Educational Alliance of New York, the Americanizing agency par excellence, see Bogen, *Jewish Philanthropy*, chap. 15; a critical view is in Moses Rischin, *The Promised City* (New York, 1964), pp. 101–3.

35. For some contemporary comments on the new wave of immigrants, see *MEN* 42 (Jan. 1907):9; *AI*, 20 Oct. 1910; Bogen, *Jewish Philanthropy*, pp. 234–35.

36. *AI*, 16 June 1904 (Heller), 3, 17 (Heller), and 24 Aug. 1905; *Fifth Biennial Session . . .* , p. 119; Rischin, *Promised City*, p. 240; Blaustein, "Making of Americans," 372–73; *MEN* 39 (July 1905):13.

37. *JM*, 28 Aug. 1891; *AH*, 30 March 1900.

38. Joseph Blumenthal to President of Congregation Beth Jacob, Adar 5648 (1888), Jewish Theological Seminary Files.

39. Moshe Davis, *The Emergence of Conservative Judaism* (Philadelphia, 1963), pt. 3; Herbert Rosenbloom, "The Founding of the United Synagogue of America" (Ph.D. diss., Brandeis University, 1970), 36–38, 51–52, 75; Cyrus Adler, ed., *The Jewish Theological Seminary of America Semi-Centennial Volume* (New York, 1939), pp. 77–81; *AJYB* 4 (1902–3):124; *UAHC Proceedings* (1909), p. 6241.

40. Rosenbloom, "United Synagogue," 56–57; Solomon Schechter, "The Mission of the Seminary," *MEN* 34 (May 1904):302; *MEN* 40 (June 1906):336; *AH*, 12 Jan. 1900. Louis Marshall, who served on the seminary's board, cautioned one young graduate against overdoing Americanization at the expense of Judaism. Charles Reznikoff, ed., *Louis Marshall*, 2 vols. (Philadelphia, 1957), 2:872–73.

41. *AH*, 17 Nov. 1899; *AI*, 9 Jan 1902, 27 June 1907, 11 July 1907, 12 March 1908, 10 Nov. 1910; *MEN* 38 (April 1905):232; *MEN* 40 (March 1906):180; Rosenbloom, "United Synagogue," 100–101.

42. *AI*, 9 April 1908, 29 Oct. 1908; Marshall Sklare, *Conservative Judaism* (Glencoe, 1955), chap. 3; Reznikoff, *Marshall*, 2:873–74.

43. The Jews had also promised Secretary of the Treasury Charles Foster in 1891 that they would relocate the immigrants away from the congested areas. Foster, therefore, more willingly agreed to the Jewish contention that the east Europeans did not fall into the interdicted category of assisted immigrants. Panitz, "Polarity of American Jewish Attitudes," pp. 57–59.

44. Reprint of *New York Tribune* article in *AI*, 12 Aug. 1909.

45. The federal report noted the "surprising rapidity" of economic advancement by the turn of the century. U.S. Industrial Commission, *Reports* 15 (Washington, 1901), 477; see also Thomas Kessner, *The Golden Door* (New York, 1977), chap. 6.

46. Joseph, *Baron de Hirsch Fund*, p. 184; *MEN* 33 (Sept. 1902):179; *AI*, 14 Feb. 1901; *JM*, 1 May 1891, 3 July 1891, 28 Aug. 1891, 16 Oct. 1891.

47. Perry, "Immigrant Distribution," 1–68 passim; Humbert S. Nelli, *Italians in Chicago* (New York, 1970), pp. 15–18.

48. Bogen, *Jewish Philanthropy,* pp. 241–43; Joseph, *Baron de Hirsch Fund,* chap. 6; John F. Sutherland, "Rabbi Joseph Krauskopf: The Urban Reformer Returns to the Land," *AJHQ* 67 (June 1978):345–59; *AI,* 3 July 1902, 28 July 1904, 24 Dec. 1908, 3 Feb. 1910, 13 Oct. 1910.

49. *AI,* 2 Sept. 1909, 3 Feb. 1910; *AH,* 9 June 1905; Julius J. Frank, "The Jews as Commercial Factors," *MEN* 38 (May 1905):285; on the Sephardic attitude, see above, chap. 1.

50. *AI,* 25 May 1905, 3 Aug. 1905, 8 Feb. 1906.

51. Joseph Brandes, *Immigrants to Freedom* (Philadelphia, 1971), chap. 2; *Proceedings of the Third National Conference . . . ,* pp. 147–48; *AH,* 9 June 1905; *AI,* 21 April 1910 (Krauskopf); Joseph, *Baron de Hirsch Fund,* chap. 4.

52. *Proceedings of the Second National Conference . . . ,* pp. 97–107; *AI,* 31 July 1902 (Levy), 8 Dec. 1910.

53. *Proceedings of the Second National Conference . . . ,* pp. 73–82, 214–17, 232–36.

54. Peter Romanofsky, "'To Rid Ourselves of the Burden': New York Jewish Charities and the Origins of the Industrial Removal Office, 1890–1901," *AJHQ* 64 (June 1975):331–43; David M. Bressler, "The Industrial Removal Office" (Paper read at the Jewish Chautauqua, July 1903); Joseph, *Baron de Hirsch Fund,* pp. 187, 191–92.

55. *MEN* 39 (July 1905):16; *AH,* 24 July 1903; *AI,* 2 June 1904, 28 Jan. 1909; Joseph, *Baron de Hirsch Fund,* pp. 142, 185.

56. *Proceedings of the Third National Conference . . . ,* pp. 138–64; *Sixth Biennial Session of the National Conference of Jewish Charities* (1910), pp. 157, 165; *Jewish Spectator,* 30 June 1905; Joseph, *Baron de Hirsch Fund,* pp. 189–91; Marc L. Raphael, "Rabbi Jacob Voorsanger of San Francisco on Jews and Judaism," *AJHQ* 63 (Dec. 1973): 196–97.

57. Bressler, "Industrial Removal Office," 5, 7–8, 11–14; Joseph, *Baron de Hirsch Fund,* pp. 188, 194–96, 200; *AH,* 30 March 1906; *Sixth Biennial Session . . . ,* p. 153; *Proceedings of the National Conference of Charities and Correction* (1909), pp. 227–30; Samuel Gompers, *Schemes to "Distribute" Immigrants,* 63d Cong., 1st sess., S. Doc. No. 21 (Washington, 1913).

58. Joseph, *Baron de Hirsch Fund,* pp. 127–49, 184–85, 205–10; Bernard Marinbach, "The Galveston Movement" (D.H.L. diss., Jewish Theological Seminary, 1976).

59. Perry, "Immigrant Distribution," 72–74; *Constitution and By-Laws of the Liberal Immigration League* (New York, n.d.), pp. 3–4. Much of the material circulated by the league has been bound together by the New York Public Library under National Liberal Immigration League, *Circulars and Copies of Letters, 1907–1912,* and by Columbia University under National Liberal Immigration League, *Literature and Documents.*

60. Cohen, *Not Free to Desist,* pp. 42, 50; Judith Goldstein, "The Politics of Ethnic Pressure" (Ph.D. diss., Columbia University, 1972), 105–7; Rischin, *Promised City,* p. 93; *Recommendations Respecting Revision of the Immigration Laws and Regulations Made by the American Jewish Committee, the Board of Delegates on Civil Rights of the Union of American Hebrew Congregations, the International Order B'nai B'rith to the United States Immigration Commission* (New York, 1910), pp. 23–28; *AI,* 31 Oct. 1907; *UAHC Proceedings* (1907), p. 5989; *UAHC Proceedings* (1910), p. 6408.

61. *Proceedings of the Council of Jewish Women . . . ,* pp. 70–71.

62. David Blaustein, *Memoirs* (New York, 1913), p. 210; *AI,* 23 Feb.

1905, 31 Jan. 1907; *Proceedings of the Third National Conference* . . . , pp. 161–62.

63. *Views on Immigration,* 62d Cong., 2d sess., S. Doc. No. 785 (Washington, 1912).

64. Perry, "Immigrant Distribution," 52, 69–70; *AJYB* 12 (1910–11):33; for reference to Gompers, see n. 57; *AH,* 9 Jan. 1903 (Maxwell); *AI,* 8 and 15 June 1905, 22 July–12 Aug. 1909, 2 Sept. 1909, 11 Aug. 1910.

65. Jacob Gordin, *The Benefactors of the East Side* (Yiddish), printed in Yakov Gordin, *Eyn-akters* (New York, 1917); Isaac Rubinow, "The Jewish Question in New York City," *PAJHS* 49 (Dec. 1959):116–22; *AH,* 6, 20, and 27 March 1903.

66. *AH,* 17 and 24 July 1903, 7 and 21 Aug. 1903, 25 Sept. 1903; see also Rubinow, "Jewish Question," 122–36.

67. *AI,* 26 Dec. 1901 (Isaacs), 11 June 1908; Levi, "Modern Dispersion," 331–32; Schulman in *MEN* 41 (July 1906):21; Rosenbloom, "United Synagogue," 94.

68. *AI,* 11 April 1901 (Philipson), 13 June 1901, 14 May 1908, 10 Nov. 1910; Levi, "Modern Dispersion," 335–36; *MEN* 33 (Dec. 1902):435; *UAHC Proceedings* (1907), p. 5953.

69. *AI,* 20 Oct. 1904, 24 Aug. 1905, 20 Sept. 1906, 19 March 1908; *AH,* 24 Nov. 1905.

70. See, for example, *AI,* 6 June 1901, 12 May 1904, 19 Jan. 1905, 2 May 1907; *AH,* 28 July 1905, 2 March 1906; *MEN* 41 (Nov. 1906):249–50; Henry Barnard, *The Forging of an American Jew* (New York, 1974), p. 88; Naomi W. Cohen, "Responsibilities of Jewish Kinship," in *Jewish Life in America,* ed. Gladys Rosen (New York, 1978), p. 129.

71. Gary Dean Best, "Jacob H. Schiff's Galveston Movement," *AJA* 30 (April 1978):47; *AH,* 24 Nov. 1905.

72. Evyatar Friesel, "The Age of Optimism in American Judaism, 1900–1920," in *A Bicentennial Festschrift for Jacob Rader Marcus,* ed. Bertram W. Korn (Waltham and New York, 1976), p. 135; *AJYB* 12 (1910–11):37, 41.

73. Reprint of *New York Sun* article in *AI,* 7 Feb. 1895.

74. Lawrence H. Fuchs, *The Political Behavior of American Jews* (Glencoe, 1956), pp. 35–37, 41, 44, 275–76; for editorials critical of the immigrants' political leanings, see *JM,* 16 July 1886, 22 April 1887, 10 Jan. 1890; *AH,* 24 Oct. 1884, 27 Aug. 1886, 11 Nov. 1898.

75. *AH,* 14 May 1926; *AI,* 28 June 1903, 2 July 1908; Cohen, *Not Free to Desist,* pp. 30–33, 57; Adler, *Schiff,* 2:146.

76. *AH,* 14 July 1899.

77. Gerald Kurland, *Seth Low* (New York, 1971), pp. 83, 88, 111–21, 369; Naomi W. Cohen, *A Dual Heritage* (Philadelphia, 1969), p. 47; population statistics were culled from the 1900 census by Rubinow, "Jewish Question," 104; for relevant background material, see Melvin G. Holli, "Urban Reform in the Progressive Era," in *The Progressive Era,* ed. Lewis L. Gould (Syracuse, 1974), pp. 136–41.

78. Gustavus Myers, *The History of Tammany Hall* (New York, 1901), pp. 345–46; Jacob A. Riis, "Tammany the People's Enemy," *Outlook,* 26 Oct. 1901, pp. 487 ff.; James B. Reynolds, "Prostitution as a Tenement House Evil," in *The Tenement House Problem,* ed. Robert W. De Forest and Lawrence Veiller, 2 vols. (New York, 1903), 1:10, 19, 50–52, 386; 2:17–23; U.S. Industrial Commission, *Reports* 15, 490; *The City for the People* (Cam-

paign Book of the Citizens' Union, Oct. 1901), pp. 35–36, 105–6; *Facts for New York Parents, Conditions That Are Not to Be Endured* (Pamphlet published for Women's Municipal League by City Club of New York, Oct. 1901), in which six of the eight cases concerning prostitution involved Jews; *AH*, 11 Oct. 1901.

79. *AH*, 25 Oct. 1901; *JM*, 18 Oct.–8 Nov. 1901; *AI*, 17 Oct. 1901, 7 Nov. 1901, 5 Dec. 1901.

80. Irving Howe, *World of Our Fathers* (New York, 1976), pp. 360–70; Bernheimer, *Russian Jew in the U.S.*, pp. 257–59. Those East Side Jews who latched on to Tammany's coattails were considered part of a "lower order," different from the "better class of Hebrews" (Bernheimer, *Russian Jew in the U.S.*; Glanz, *Judaica Americana*, p. 392).

81. Rubinow, "Jewish Question," 110–16.

82. Cf. John Higham, ed., *Ethnic Leadership in America* (Baltimore, 1978), pp. 22–23.

83. Campaign literature in the Citizens' Union scrapbooks, Manuscript Division, Columbia University library, Boxes U 1, W 4, W 25, W 27, and in the New York Public Library, uncatalogued boxes listed under New York (City) Elections, 1901. See also Frank Moss, "National Danger from Police Corruption," *North American Review* 173 (Oct. 1901):478; Everett P. Wheeler, *Sixty Years of American Life* (New York, 1917), pp. 390–91; *JM*, 1 Nov. 1901.

84. Campaign pamphlets in Yiddish: *Save Your Children, Seth Low for Mayor, To the Jewish Woman of the Ghetto, Oak Leaf #10*; in Hebrew: *This Matter Depends on You*, New York Public Library, New York (City) Elections, 1901, nc 13, 14; campaign pamphlet in Yiddish: *Citizens Union! Citizens Union!*, Columbia University, Citizens' Union scrapbooks, W 25.

85. New York (City) Elections, 1901, nc 13, New York Public Library.

86. Bernheimer, *Russian Jew in the U.S.*, p. 258; *AI*, 7 Nov. 1901; Allen F. Davis, *Spearheads for Reform* (New York, 1967), pp. 180–87; *New York Times*, 29 Oct. 1901; Rebekah Kohut, *My Portion* (New York, 1927), pp. 249–50; *AH*, 22 Nov. 1901.

87. *AH*, 22 Nov. 1901, 10 Oct. 1902. The *American Hebrew* had stated even before the election that it hoped never again to become involved in politics. Politics, it said, had to be kept out of Jewish pulpit and press (8 Nov. 1901).

88. Kurland, *Low*, chaps. 7, 8; *AH*, 14 Feb. 1902, 15 Aug. 1902.

89. Committee of Fifteen, *The Social Evil* (New York, 1902), pp. 185–86.

90. *Proceedings of the Third National Conference . . .* , pp. 94–109; *Fourth Biennial Session of the National Conference of Jewish Charities* (1906), pp. 113–16, 120; *Official Report of the Jewish International Conference on the Suppression of the Traffic in Girls and Women* (London, 1910), pp. 64–66, 119, 177, 234–35, 238–41, 252, 254; Bernice Graziani, *Where There's a Woman* (New York, 1967), pp. 28–30; Rudolf Glanz, *The Jewish Woman in America*, 1 (New York, 1976), 189–90; Young Women's Christian Association, *Some Urgent Phases of Immigrant Life* (New York, 1910), p. 18; *Proceedings of the Council of Jewish Women . . .* , p. 14; Egal Feldman, "Prostitution, the Alien Woman and the Progressive Imagination," *American Quarterly* 19 (Summer 1967):201, 204.

91. Clifford G. Roe, *The Great War on White Slavery* (n.p., 1911), pp. 191–93, chap. 16; *AI*, 2 Feb. 1905, 14 Oct. 1909, 10 Feb. 1910 (*Omaha*

Bee); Feldman, "Prostitution," 198; *The Social Evil in Chicago* (Chicago, 1911), p. 7; Willoughby C. Waterman, *Prostitution and Its Repression in New York City* (New York, 1968), pp. 90–91, 95–96; Barnard, *Forging an American Jew,* pp. 88–89; *Reports of the Department of Commerce and Labor* (1908), pp. 19–20.

92. See, for example, *AI,* 7 Oct. 1909, 11 Nov. 1909, 3 Jan. 1910.

93. *UAHC Proceedings* (1910), p. 6400.

94. *UAHC Proceedings* (1910), pp. 6396–400; *UAHC Proceedings* (1911), p. 6532; Roe, *War on White Slavery,* pp. 191–93; *AI,* 31 Oct. 1907, 7 Oct. 1909, 20 Jan. 1910.

95. Goren, *New York Jews and the Quest for Community,* pp. 146–48; *Official Report of the . . . International Conference,* pp. 48, 255; *Jewish Spectator,* 3 March 1905; *UAHC Proceedings* (1910), p. 6399. On the connection between prostitution and nativism see Feldman, "Prostitution."

96. Goren, *New York Jews and the Quest for Community,* pp. 139–44; Feldman, "Prostitution," 195; *AI,* 11 Nov. 1909, 20 Jan. 1910; Ernest A. Bell, *Fighting the Traffic in Young Girls* (Chicago, 1911), pp. 177–81, 188; U.S. Immigration Commission, *Reports* 37, 61st Cong., 3d sess., S. Doc. No. 753 (Washington, 1911), 76–77. The existence of an international ring involving Jews is mentioned in Isaac Bashevis Singer's novel *The Magician of Lublin* (New York, 1960), pp. 115–16.

97. *MEN* 33 (Nov., Dec. 1902):361, 439. B'nai B'rith informed the author (24 June 1979) that its records on the white-slave traffic had been destroyed during the Hanafi Muslim siege of the organization's headquarters in Washington in 1977.

98. Charlotte Baum et al., *The Jewish Woman in America* (New York, 1976), pp. 172–73; *Official Report of the . . . International Conference,* pp. 46–48. The American Jewish Committee denied the existence of an international Jewish network. Henry Berkowitz, "Religion and the Social Evil," *CCAR Year Book* 20 (1910):299–313.

99. Reports of the Board of Delegates appear in the *UAHC Proceedings,* those of B'nai B'rith in *MEN* and *B'nai B'rith News.* On the American Jewish Committee, see Cohen, *Not Free to Desist,* chap. 3.

100. Cohen, *Not Free to Desist,* pp. 40–53.

101. Cohen, *Not Free to Desist,* pp. 6–7; Minutes of conference on organization, 3 and 4 Feb. 1906, American Jewish Committee Archives.

102. Cohen, *Not Free to Desist,* chaps. 1–2; Goren, *New York Jews and the Quest for Community,* chaps. 1–2; Transcript of the annual meeting, 8 Nov. 1908, American Jewish Committee Archives; *Proceedings of the Council of Jewish Women . . . ,* p. 70.

103. Cohen, *Not Free to Desist,* pp. 90–98.

INDEX